Ewa Dąbrowska and Dagmar Divjak (Eds.)
Cognitive Linguistics – Foundations of Language

This volume is part of a three-volume set on Cognitive Linguistics

1   **Cognitive Linguistics** – Foundations of Language
    Ewa Dąbrowska and Dagmar Divjak (Eds.)

2   **Cognitive Linguistics** – A Survey of Linguistic Subfields
    Ewa Dąbrowska and Dagmar Divjak (Eds.)

3   **Cognitive Linguistics** – Key Topics
    Ewa Dąbrowska and Dagmar Divjak (Eds.)

Cognitive Linguistics
Foundations of
Language

Edited by
Ewa Dąbrowska and Dagmar Divjak

ISBN 978-3-11-062297-3
e-ISBN (PDF) 978-3-11-062647-6
e-ISBN (EPUB) 978-3-11-062314-7

Library of Congress Control Number: 2018968024

Bibliographic information published by the Deutsche Nationalbibliothek
The Deutsche Nationalbibliothek lists this publication in the Deutsche Nationalbibliografie;
detailed bibliographic data are available in the Internet at http://dnb.dnb.de.

© 2019 Walter de Gruyter GmbH, Berlin/Boston
Cover image: temmuzcan/iStock/Getty Images Plus
Typsetting: Meta Systems Publishing & Printservices GmbH, Wustermark
Printing and Binding: CPI books GmbH, Leck

www.degruyter.com

Contents

Ewa Dąbrowska and Dagmar Divjak
Introduction —— 1

Benjamin Bergen
Chapter 1: Embodiment —— 11

Russell S. Tomlin and Andriy Myachykov
Chapter 2: Attention and salience —— 36

Dagmar Divjak and Catherine L. Caldwell-Harris
Chapter 3: Frequency and entrenchment —— 61

Michael Ramscar and Robert Port
Chapter 4: Categorization (without categories) —— 87

R. Harald Baayen and Michael Ramscar
Chapter 5: Abstraction, storage and naive discriminative learning —— 115

Ronald W. Langacker
Chapter 6: Construal —— 140

Antonio Barcelona
Chapter 7: Metonymy —— 167

Raymond W. Gibbs
Chapter 8: Metaphor —— 195

Laura J. Speed, David P. Vinson, and Gabriella Vigliocco
Chapter 9: Representing Meaning —— 221

Mark Turner
Chapter 10: Blending in language and communication —— 245

Arie Verhagen
Chapter 11: Grammar and cooperative communication —— 271

Index —— 295

Ewa Dąbrowska and Dagmar Divjak
Introduction

1 What is Cognitive Linguistics?

Cognitive Linguistics is an approach to language study based on the assumptions that our linguistic abilities are firmly rooted in our general cognitive abilities, that meaning is essentially conceptualization, and that grammar is shaped by usage. In the early days, this was quite a bold claim to make, and it was diametrically opposed to the then-dominant generative framework. Nowadays, a growing number of linguists from different backgrounds share these assumptions and unite under the umbrella of Cognitive Linguistics. What draws the various strands of Cognitive Linguistics together is the Cognitive Commitment (Lakoff 1990: 40): all cognitive linguists are, or should be, committed to providing a characterization of the general principles of language that is informed by and accords with what is known about the mind and brain from other disciplines. It is this commitment that makes cognitive linguistics cognitive, and thus an approach which is fundamentally interdisciplinary in nature.

Following from the Cognitive Commitment, there are a number of assumptions that underlie the work of cognitive linguists. First, cognitive linguists share a usage-based view of language: grammar is shaped by usage, so in order to understand how languages are structured, how they have developed historically and how they are acquired by individual learners, we need to study how they are used. Second, cognitive linguists aim to show that speakers can build up language systems from usage by means of general cognitive abilities, such as perception, attention, memory, categorization and abstraction. These core general cognitive abilities are mainly studied outside of the discipline of linguistics, within the Cognitive Sciences. Third, cognitive linguists believe that language exists in order to convey meaning; all elements of language are meaningful, including grammatical constructions (cf. Langacker's conception of "grammar as image", Langacker 1979, 1991). Meaning, for cognitive linguists, involves conceptualization (see Langacker this volume and Speed, Vinson and Vigliocco this volume), is embodied (Bergen 2012 and this volume) and encompasses both dictionary and encyclopaedic information.

Ewa Dąbrowska, University of Birmingham, UK and FAU Erlangen-Nürnberg, DE
Dagmar Divjak, University of Birmingham, UK

https://doi.org/10.1515/9783110626476-001

2 Some history

Cognitive linguistics has its origins in the late 1970s, when a number of linguists became increasingly dissatisfied with the then-prevailing generative paradigm with its focus on an autonomous formal grammar, and began to develop alternative approaches which emphasize function and meaning and the relationship between language and general cognitive processes (see, for example, Langacker 1979; Lakoff 1977; Talmy 1978). These early attempts began to combine into a more coherent and self-conscious movement about ten years later, with the publication in 1987 of George Lakoff's *Women, Fire and Dangerous Things* and Ron Langacker's *Foundations of Cognitive Grammar*, and, in the following year, of *Topics in Cognitive Linguistics*, an influential collection of articles edited by Brygida Rudzka-Ostyn. The next year, 1989, can be regarded as the official birth date of the movement. In the spring of this year, René Dirven organized a symposium in Duisburg at which the International Cognitive Linguistics Association (ICLA) was established. It was also decided to create a new journal, *Cognitive Linguistics*, and a monograph series entitled *Cognitive Linguistics Research*; both are published by De Gruyter Mouton. The Duisburg Symposium was retrospectively renamed the First International Cognitive Linguistics Conference.

Much of the early work in CL focussed on topics that were particularly problematic for generative approaches – prototype effects, radial categories, metaphor and metonymy, and the meaning of grammatical elements which were traditionally regarded as meaningless; but as the approach grew in strength, it expanded into virtually every area of linguistic organization. Several distinct strands emerged, including cognitive grammar, construction grammar, mental space and blending theory, neural theory of language, as well as a large body of more descriptive corpus-based work united under the banner of "usage-based" linguistics.

Today, there are several book series and at least fourteen journals devoted largely or entirely to CL (including *Cognitive Linguistics, Language and Cognition, Review of Cognitive Linguistics, CogniTextes, International Journal of Cognitive Linguistics, Constructions and Frames* and *Voprosy kognitivnoj lingvistiki*). The International Cognitive Linguistics Assocation [http://www.cognitivelinguistics.org/] has over 300 individual members and nearly 500 linguists attend the biennial International Cognitive Linguistics Conference. Sixteen regional and national organizations are affiliated with the ICLA. More and more universities offer courses in CL at undergraduate and postgraduate level; and there is growing interest from related disciplines, in particular, first and second language acquisition, adult psycholinguistics, and clinical linguistics, but also psychology, philosophy, and computer science.

3 About the three-volume set

The aim of this *three-volume* set is to provide state-of-the-art overviews of the numerous subfields of cognitive linguistics written by leading international experts which will be useful for established researchers and novices alike. It is an interdisciplinary project with contributions from linguists, psycholinguists, psychologists, and computational modelling experts and emphasises the most recent developments in the field, in particular, the shift towards more empirically-based research. In this way, it will, we hope, help to shape the field, encouraging interdisciplinary and methodologically rigorous research which incorporates insights from all the cognitive sciences.

The three volumes together contain 34 chapter. Volume 1: The cognitive foundations of language discusses the cognitive processes and abilities which underlie language, including embodiment (Bergen), attention and salience (Tomlin and Myachykov), entrenchment and its relationship to frequency (Divjak and Caldwell-Harris), categorization (Ramscar), analogy, schematization and naïve discriminative learning (Baayen and Ramscar), construal (Langacker), metonymy (Barcelona), metaphor (Gibbs), blending (Turner), conceptualization (Speed, Vinson and Vigliocco) and collaborative communication (Verhagen).

Volume 2: Overviews consists of comprehensive surveys of the major subfields within the discipline. There are chapters on the basic areas of linguistic organization, i.e., phonology (Nathan), lexical semantics (Geeraerts) and construction grammar (Diessel), as well as chapters examining language use in a wider context: language variation and change (Kristiansen and Geeraerts, Hilpert), first and second language acquisition (Matthews and Krajewski, Ellis and Wulff), and discourse, including literary discourse (Hart, Stockwell).

Volume 3: Central topics consists of shorter chapters on specific topics that illustrate the breadth of cognitive linguistic research. Most of these chapters deal with linguistic phenomena that have played a major role in the development of cognitive linguistic research. These include topics such as polysemy (Gries), semantic typology (Koptjevskaja-Tamm), space (Coventry), time (Evans), motion (Filipović and Ibarretxe-Antuñano), fictive motion (Matlock and Bergmann), tense, mood and aspect (Janda), grammaticalization (van der Auwera, Van Olmen and Du Mon), signed languages (Wilcox), argument structure constructions (Casenhiser), and prototype effects in grammar (Taylor). We have also incorporated some additional chapters on themes that are coming to the fore within Cognitive Linguistics: individual differences (Dąbrowska), emergence (MacWhinney), and default non-salient interpretations (Giora).

It becomes clear from this enumeration that the list is not exhaustive: there are many more topics that currently attract a considerable amount of attention, but have not been included for various reasons. Topics that were on our wishlist but did not materialize were, among others, those dealing with spoken language, gesture and multimodality (but see the handbook by Müller et al. 2014), chapters dealing with computational modelling, with case and with linguistic relativity, and chapters focusing on cognition in cognate areas, such as bilingual or translation cognition, to name but a few.

4 The future

The *three-volume set* is intended to be a summary of the most important achievements of contemporary cognitive linguistic research but also a set that looks forward and helps to shape the field in the years to come. For this reason, we conclude this introduction with some comments on what we think the future will bring.

4.1 Hypothesis testing and the use of behavioural and statistical methods

In the early stages (Lakoff 1987; Langacker 1987; Talmy 1978; Goldberg 1995), Cognitive Linguistics was very much an armchair discipline. Practitioners relied on introspection and reflected on linguistic examples, some of which were real and some of which had been constructed. These early analyses of important linguistic phenomena laid the theoretical foundations for much of the discipline. Since then, Cognitive Linguistics has undergone a significant shift towards a more empirical approach. This shift towards empiricism was driven by two main forces.

First, it was recognized from early on (e.g., Langacker 1988) that grammars are shaped by use, and therefore that to understand how grammars develop (in both the historical sense and the sense of individual speakers acquiring their language(s)) we must look at real usage. This lead to linguists working with corpora – large collections of authentic linguistic data. Methods and tools which were already widely used in usage-based lexicography were adopted in cognitive semantics and other areas and new methods were developed. Nowadays, a large body of cognitive linguistic research relies on corpus data; it distinguishes itself from traditional English corpus linguistics in that it considers corpora as tools and corpus linguistics as a methodology, not as a theory or discipline (Renouf 2005).

Secondly, as the body of cognitive-inspired analyses grew, we began to get competing accounts of the same phenomena. For instance, there is an on-going debate about whether it is the main clause or the subordinate clause verb which is the most prominent element in sentences containing a complement clause (such as *I know that she left*). Langacker (1991) adopts the traditional analysis, according to which the main clause verb is the profile determinant, pointing out that the sentence designates "the process of knowing, not of leaving" (436). Other linguists (e.g., Thompson 2002; Verhagen 2005) have argued that the subordinate verb should be regarded as the profile determinant, since (in the vast majority of cases, at least in conversation) it is the subordinate clause which constitutes the speaker's "interactional agenda", while the so-called "main clause" functions merely conveys "the speaker's epistemic, evidential or evaluative stance towards the issue or claim at hand" (Thompson 2002: 134). For instance, in the following excerpt, the main thrust of A's contribution is to indicate that whatever is being discussed is "cool", and B's and C's contributions show that this is how they interpret A's utterance.

A: I think it's cool.
B: It's cool.
C: It's great.
(Thompson 2002: 132)

Langacker (2008: 419) acknowledges this argument, and proposes that we need to distinguish between different kinds of prominence. But how? There is a growing awareness that unless we develop reliable ways of measuring such differences, debates between linguists will be reduced to assertions that one's own intuitions are better than another analyst's. Cognitive linguists need to develop theories that make testable predictions, test these predictions and use the results to revise the theory if necessary, thus completing the empirical cycle.

Some researchers who took this step have adopted experimental methods from psychology (e.g., Ambridge and Goldberg 2008; Bencini and Goldberg 2000; Boyd and Goldberg 2011; Dąbrowska 2008, 2013; Gibbs and Colston 1995; Wheeler and Bergen 2010). While the earlier studies used mostly off-line judgement tasks, cognitive linguists are now increasingly relying on more sophisticated techniques, including on-line reaction time measurements and brain imaging. Many others (e.g., Arppe 2008; Divjak 2010; Geeraerts 1994; Gries 2003; Hilpert 2008; Lemmens 1998) applied sophisticated statistical methods to corpus data. In fact, the increasing reliance on quantitative methods (Geeraerts

2006: 17) has led some to declare that Cognitive Linguistics has taken "a quantitative turn" (Janda 2013: 1). A third line of research aims to combine both approaches and validates corpus-based findings experimentally (for book-length treatments, see Divjak and Gries 2012; Gries and Divjak 2012; Klavan 2012; many more studies have appeared as journal articles).

A question which many cognitive linguists are asking themselves now is: how far do we need to go? Do we all need to become statisticians, psychologists, neurologists? Ideally the answer to this question may be yes, but it seems hardly feasible, and is unlikely to happen in the foreseeable future. Instead, we can collaborate with experts from these fields. This type of interdisciplinarity presupposes a basic knowledge and understanding of cognate disciplines and a convergence in research methodology. It is this type of convergence that we aim to encourage with this set. The empirical trend is clearly on the increase and, it is to be hoped, will continue to gather momentum: human language is just too complex to understand by using traditional introspective methods (cf. Geeraerts 2010).

One way to achieve this goal more quickly would be to get linguists to archive their data and code used for analysis publicly. Some journals, including *Cognitive Linguistics*, already offer their authors the possibility to publish supplementary materials, including data and code, online. Transparency does not guarantee integrity, but it is certainly a step in the right direction as it makes it possible for other researchers to check, re-analyze, or re-intepret existing data and published findings.

A recently launched initiative, TrolLing [opendata.uit.no], takes this example of good practice to the next level by making available an independent platform for publicly archiving data and code, free of charge, to linguists of any theoretical persuasion. Sharing data helps with quality control at the submission and publication stage but also allows researchers to make progress more quickly by making negative results available and by making it possible to pool data, thus saving valuable time and resources.

4.2 Interdisciplinarity

Much of the early theorizing in cognitive linguistics was inspired by research in cognitive psychology, in particular, Eleanor Rosch's work on prototypes and basic level categories (Rosch 1973). While later work continued to draw on these findings, most cognitive linguistic researchers did not engage with more recent developments in psychology. This is evident in many of the chapters in the *Oxford Handbook of Cognitive Linguistics* (Geeraerts and Cuyckens 2007). For instance, Lewandowska-Tomaszczyk's (2007) excellent chapter on polysemy, prototypes, and basic level categories discusses the work of early pioneers like Rosch and Berlin, but not more recent reappraisals (Murphy 2002), work on exemplar theory (Nosofsky 1988, 1992), perceptual symbol systems (Barsalou 1999) or the relevant research in neuroscience (see Ramscar's chapter for a discussion of some of this work). Lewandowska-Tomaszczyk can hardly be blamed for this – the chapter provides a fair summary and assessment of CL work in the last two decades of the twentieth century – but one does feel that this work should be more strongly grounded in psychological research. Likewise, Talmy's chapter on attentional phenomena in the same volume (Talmy 2007), while providing an extremely useful framework for analysing salience in language, does not engage with psychological research on attention at all.

Even at the time the *Oxford Handbook* was published, there was a considerable amount of work which attempted to incorporate insights from more recent research in cognitive psychology and other cognitive science disciplines – work by scholars such as Lakoff, Levinson, Bowerman, Tomasello, Lieven, Bergen, Gibbs, and many others. Some of this work was already discussed in it; and much more has been published since then. Anyone will agree that in order to understand a phenomenon as complex as human language, it is necessary to combine insights from many disciplines, and so interdisciplinary work will continue to gather momentum. We hope that the chapters in these volumes – in particular, the "foundations" chapters – will assist this process.

4.3 The social turn

As explained at the beginning of this introduction, the most important feature uniting the various approaches of cognitive linguistics is a commitment to providing an account of language which is psychologically realistic. Because of this commitment, cognitive linguists have tended to account for linguistic structure by appealing to cognitive factors: languages are the way they are because humans are the way they are. However, properties of language can also be explained by appealing to its main functions, namely, communication and maintaining social cohesion. The two explanations are not, of course, mutually exclusive, but complementary, since human cognition is inherently social (Tomasello 1999). Although cognitive linguists have always recognized this, it is only relatively recently that researchers have begun to integrate the cognitive and social perspective into a single theoretical framework. In fact, in recent years, so many researchers have become interested in this area that we can speak of a genuine "social turn" (see, for example, Croft 2009; Geeraerts 2010; Geeraerts et al. 2010; Geeraerts and Kristinsen Volume 2; Harder 2010; Verhagen 2005, this volume). This development has involved research in three main areas: the role of joint attention and intention reading in language acquisition and use (Matthews and Krajewski Volume 2 and Verhagen this volume), studies investigating how meaning is created by speakers engaged in social interaction (e.g., Du Bois 2014; Du Bois and Giora 2014), and the growing recognition that linguistic knowledge is socially distributed (Cowley 2011; see also Dąbrowska Volume 3). This trend will no doubt continue to flourish: fully integrating the cognitive and social perspective is probably the greatest challenge facing cognitive linguistics today.

5 References

Ambridge, Ben and Adele E. Goldberg (2008): The island status of clausal complements: evidence in favor of an information structure explanation. *Cognitive Linguistics* 19: 357–389.

Arppe, Antti (2008): Univariate, bivariate and multivariate methods in corpus-based lexicography – a study of synonymy. Publications of the Department of General Linguistics, University of Helsinki, No. 44. URN: http://urn.fi/URN:ISBN:978-952-10-5175-3.

Barsalou, Lawrence W. (1999): Perceptual symbol systems. *Behavioral and Brain Sciences* 22: 577–609.

Bencini, Giulia M. L. and Adele E. Goldberg (2000): The contribution of argument structure constructions to sentence meaning. *Journal of Memory and Language* 43: 640–651.

Bergen, Benjamin K. (2012): *Louder than Words: The New Science of How the Mind Makes Meaning.* New York: Basic Books.

Boyd, Jeremy K. and Adele E. Goldberg (2011): Learning what NOT to say: the role of statistical preemption and categorization in a-adjective production. *Language* 87(1): 55–83.

Cowley, Stephen J. (ed.) (2011): *Distributed Language.* Amsterdam: John Benjamins.

Croft, William (2009): Toward a social cognitive linguistics. In: V. Evans and S. Pourcel (eds.), *New Directions in Cognitive Linguistics*, 395–420. Amsterdam: John Benjamins.

Dąbrowska, Ewa (2008): The effects of frequency and neighbourhood density on adult speakers' productivity with Polish case inflections: An empirical test of usage-based approaches to morphology. *Journal of Memory and Language* 58: 931–951.

Dąbrowska, Ewa (2013): Functional constraints, usage, and mental grammars: A study of speakers' intuitions about questions with long-distance dependencies. *Cognitive Linguistics* 24: 633–665.

Divjak, Dagmar (2010): *Structuring the Lexicon: A Clustered Model for Near-Synonymy.* (Cognitive Linguistics Research 43). Berlin: De Gruyter.

Divjak, Dagmar and Stefan Th. Gries (2012): *Frequency Effects in Language Representation.* Volume 2. (Trends in Linguistics. Studies and Monographs. 244.2) Berlin: De Gruyter.

Du Bois, John A. (2014): Towards a dialogic syntax. *Cognitive Linguistics* 25: 359–410.

Du Bois, John A. and Rachel Giora (2014): Towards a dialogic syntax. *Cognitive Linguistics* 25: 351–358.

Geeraerts, Dirk (2006): Introduction. A rough guide to Cognitive Linguistics. In: D. Geeraerts (ed.), *Cognitive Linguistics: Basic Readings*, 1–28. Berlin/New York: Mouton de Gruyter.

Geeraerts, Dirk (2010): Recontextualizing Grammar: Underlying trends in thirty years of Cognitive Linguistics. In: E. Tabakowska, M. Choinski and L. Wiraszka (eds.), *Cognitive Linguistics in Action: From Theory to Application and Back*, 71–102. Berlin: De Gruyter Mouton.
Geeraerts, Dirk (2010): *Theories of Lexical Semantics*. Oxford: Oxford University Press.
Geeraerts, Dirk and Hubert Cuyckens (eds.) (2007): *The Oxford Handbook of Cognitive Linguistics*. Oxford: Oxford University Press.
Geeraerts, Dirk, Stefan Grondelaers, and Peter Bakema (1994): *The Structure of Lexical Variation: Meaning, Naming, and Context*. (Cognitive Linguistics Research 59.) Berlin: Mouton de Gruyter.
Geeraerts, Dirk, Gitte Kristiansen, and Yves Peirsman (eds.) (2010): *Advances in Cognitive Sociolinguistics*. Berlin: Mouton de Gruyter.
Gibbs, Raymond W. and Herbert L. Colston (1995): The cognitive psychological reality of image schemas and their transformations. *Cognitive Linguistics* 6: 347–378.
Goldberg, Adele E. (1995): *Constructions. A Construction Grammar Approach to Argument Structure*. Chicago: University of Chicago Press.
Gries, Stefan Th. (2003): *Multifactorial Analysis in Corpus Linguistics: A Study of Particle Placement*. London and New York: Continuum Press.
Gries, Stefan Th. and Dagmar Divjak (2012): *Frequency Effects in Language Learning and Processing*. Volume 1. (Trends in Linguistics. Studies and Monographs. 244.1) Berlin: De Gruyter Mouton.
Harder, Peter (2010): *Meaning in Mind and Society: A Functional Contribution to the Social Turn in Cognitive Linguistics*. Berlin: Mouton de Gruyter.
Hilpert, Martin (2008): *Germanic Future Constructions A Usage-based Approach to Language Change*. Amsterdam/Philadelphia: John Benjamins.
Janda, Laura A. (ed.) (2013): *Cognitive Linguistics: The Quantitative Turn. The Essential Reader*. Berlin: De Gruyter Mouton.
Klavan, Jane (2012): Evidence in linguistics: corpus-linguistic and experimental methods for studying grammatical synonymy. Dissertationes linguisticae Universitatis Tartuensis 15 (http://hdl.handle.net/10062/27865).
Lakoff, George (1977): Linguistic gestalts. *Chicago Linguistic Society* 13: 236–287.
Lakoff, George (1987): *Women, Fire and Dangerous Things. What Categories Reveal about the Mind*. Chicago: Chicago University Press.
Lakoff, George (1990): The invariance hypothesis. Is abstract reason based on image-schemas? *Cognitive Linguistics* 1: 39–74.
Langacker, Ronald W. (1979): Grammar as image. *Linguistic Notes from La Jolla* 6: 88–126.
Langacker, Ronald W. (1987): *Foundations of Cognitive Grammar*. Volume 1: *Theoretical Prerequisites*. Stanford: Stanford University Press.
Langacker, Ronald W. (1988): A usage-based model. In: B. Rudzka-Ostyn (ed.), *Topics in Cognitive Linguistics*, 127–161. Amsterdam: John Benjamins.
Langacker, Ronald W. (1991): *Concept, Image and Symbol: The Cognitive Basis of Grammar*. Berlin: Mouton de Gruyter.
Langacker, Ronald W. (2008): *Cognitive Grammar: A Basic Introduction*. Oxford: Oxford University Press.
Lemmens, Maarten (1998): *Lexical Perspectives on Transitivity and Ergativity*. (Current Issues in Linguistic Theory 166.) Amsterdam: Benjamins.
Lewandowska-Tomaszczyk, Barbara (2007): Polysemy, prototypes and radial categories. In: D. Geeraerts and H. Cuyckens (eds.), *The Oxford Handbook of Cognitive Linguistics*, 139–169. Oxford: Oxford University Press.

Müller, Cornelia, Alan Cienki, Ellen Fricke, Silva Ladewig, David McNeill, and Sedinha Tessendorf/Jana Bressem (eds.) (2014): *Body – Language – Communication. An International Handbook on Multimodality in Human Interaction*. [Handbücher zur Sprach- und Kommunikationswissenschaft / Handbooks of Linguistics and Communication Science (HSK) 38/1 and 2]. Berlin: De Gruyter Mouton.

Murphy, Gregory L. (2002): *The Big Book of Concepts*. Cambridge: MIT Press.

Nosofsky, Robert M. (1988): Similarity, frequency and category representations. *Journal of Experimental Psychology: Learning, Memory and Cognition* 14: 54–65.

Nosofsky, Robert M. (1992): Exemplars, prototypes and similarity rules. In: A. F. Healy, S. M. Kosslyn and R. M. Shiffrin (eds.), *From Learning Theory to Connectionist Theory: Essays in Honor of W.K. Estes* Vol. 1, 149–168. Hillsdale: Erlbaum.

Renouf, Antoinette (2005): Corpus Linguistics: past and present. In: W. Naixing, L. Wenzhong, and P. Jianzhong (eds.), *Corpora in Use: In Honour of Professor Yang Huizhong*. [English version downloaded from http://rdues.bcu.ac.uk/publ/Past_and_Present.pdf – last accessed 26.1.2015]

Rosch, Eleanor (1973): On the internal structure of perceptual and semantic categories. In: T. E. Moore (Ed.), *Cognitive Development and the Acquisition of Language*, 111–144. New York: Academic Press.

Rudzka-Ostyn, Brygida (ed.) (1988): *Topics in Cognitive Linguistics*. Amsterdam: John Benjamins.

Talmy, Leonard (1978): The relation of grammar to cognition – a synopsis. *Proceedings of TINLAP* 2: 14–24.

Talmy, Leonard (2007): Attention phenomena. In: D. Geeraerts and H. Cuyckens (eds.), *The Oxford Handbook of Cognitive Linguistics*, 264–293. Oxford: Oxford University Press.

Thompson, Sandra (2002): "Object complements and conversation". Towards a realistic account. *Studies in Language* 26: 125–164.

Tomasello, Michael (1999): *The Cultural Origins of Human Cognition*. Cambridge: Harvard University Press.

TroLLing (No date): The Tromsø Repository of Language and Linguistics. [URL: opendata.uit.no]

Verhagen, Arie (2005): *Constructions of Intersubjectivity: Discourse, Syntax and Cognition*. Oxford: Oxford University Press.

Wheeler, Kathryn and Benjamin K. Bergen (2010): Meaning in the palm of your hand. In: S. Rice and J. Newman (eds.), *Empirical and Experimental Methods in Cognitive/Functional Research*, 303–316. Stanford: CSLI.

Benjamin Bergen
Chapter 1: Embodiment

1 Mind and body

There is a long history in philosophy of asking what the relationship is between the mind and the body. This question is as relevant to language as to any cognitive function, since language is at once a mental and a corporeal phenomenon. But perhaps this issue becomes even more relevant for language, a higher cognitive function that arguably distinguishes humans from other animals.

In general, the body appears to matter to the mind in a variety of ways. The concepts we have and the meanings we convey through language are not unrelated to the experiences we have moving our bodies or perceiving the world. But this leaves ample room for uncertainty. Exactly what impact do our bodies have? Are they important for how we learn new language and concepts? Or perhaps we use our bodies in an online fashion to make sense of even conventional language and concepts. Either or both of these may be true not only for things that are transparently related to bodily experiences, like motor actions and visual events, but also for concepts that are abstract in that their relation to the body is more tenuous – things denoted by words like *justice* or *truth*.

Since the 1980s, the idea that the body matters to the mind has been known as *embodiment* (Rosch and Lloyd 1978; Johnson 1987; Varela et al. 1991; Gibbs 2005; for an early precursor, see Merleau-Ponty 1945). This has been a central, orienting concept in cognitive linguistics research since its inception. But as big concepts often do, embodiment means different things to different researchers and its use has changed over time. This chapter begins by outlining the historical conceptions of embodiment in cognitive science. It then describes some of the ways that embodiment has been used in cognitive linguistics, and ends by anticipating the directions that linguistic embodiment research is currently moving in.

2 A brief history of embodiment

2.1 Dualism, monism, and everything in between

In principle, there are different ways the mind could relate to the body, and many of these possibilities have their own champions, arguments, and literatures. The strongest imaginable positions stand in contrast to one another. It could be on the one hand that there is no meaningful relation between the mind and body; the *dualist* position holds that the mind is of qualitatively unique stuff, irreducible to the material realm where the body lives. Or on the other hand, it could be that the mind and body are really one and the same; the strongest *monist* position argues that everything we want to know about the mind can be reduced to physics and explained away in material terms (this proposition therefore sometimes goes under the banner of *eliminative materialism*).

The vast majority of work in cognitive science, and cognitive linguistics as a sub-discipline, resides somewhere between these two extremes. At the time of the writing of this chapter, it's overwhelmingly clear that the body matters in profound ways to how the mind works. In the most banal way, for instance, having an intact, working brain is a pre-requisite to human cognition. Things without brains, like brooms and rocks, do not think, and they do not have language. Somewhat more informatively, the limits and nature of the brain's computational capacity shape what the mind can achieve; human language for instance requires a human brain – an elephant brain will not suffice.

Yet at the same time, it's clear, at least for the purpose of conducting meaningful and useful science, that we would be ill-served to throw out everything we want to know about the mind in an effort to reduce it to other, lower, physical levels of explanation. Even if we believed that in principle everything about human language could be reduced to the biology, chemistry, and ultimately the physics of individuals and the world (and many researchers do hold this non-eliminative materialist position) it currently appears that it is still useful to have a higher level of enquiry that addresses the mind and mental constructs. This is a level at which we can ask questions, formulate theories, and seek answers about how the mind works. For example, even if, ultimately, cognitive-level concepts like CONCEPT or WORD are merely epiphenomenal – even if they can be explained away in terms of underlying biochemistry and physics, it still makes sense for us, at least for the time being, to use the constructs of concepts and words in our science. That's because we're interested in how people learn words, how we figure out what they mean, how their meanings relate to concepts, and so on.

So it's a tacit assumption in most (but not all) of cognitive science that the parts and processes proper to what we think of as the mind need to be explained, and that the brain and body are one possible source of explanation. And because the brain and body seem deeply related to cognition, much of the work in cognitive science asks questions about the extent to which and the ways in which the particularities of the body, including the brain, affect the functioning and properties of the mind, or even, on some accounts constitute the mind themselves. This is the issue of *embodiment*.

2.2 Embodiment in cognitive science

There are roughly as many definitions of *embodiment* as there are people who use the word. I say "roughly" because many people who use the word seem to use it in multiple ways, while others may not have a particularly well formed idea of what they intend it to mean. In general, *embodiment* seems to be used to mean something about how the mind relates to the body. But this relation can come in many guises, and embodiment can signify any of the following things (see Wilson 2002; Ziemke 2003; and Ziemke et al. 2007 for much more thorough reviews):

- There are properties of the mind that can only be explained by reference to the brain or body
- The mind is not just generalized software, but is software than can be run on only one type of hardware, namely the brain
- Individual differences in brain and body produce individual differences in the mind
- For the mind to function, the organism must have a body, including but not limited to a brain (so a brain in a vat wouldn't have the same properties as a brain in a body)
- An individual's experience (presumably in his/her brain and body) are critical to the individual's mind
- The mind is not limited to brain functioning, but also extends to the use of other parts of the body (so that cognition isn't just between the ears)
- The mind is not limited to brain and body functioning, but also extends to the environment in which a person is situated, including other individuals or artifacts.

The version of embodiment that is most prevalent in the cognitive linguistics literature is this particular one:

> the structures used to put together our conceptual systems grow out of bodily experience and make sense in terms of it; moreover, the core of our conceptual systems is directly

> grounded in perception, body movement, and experience of a physical and social nature. (Lakoff 1987: xiv)

There's a lot built into this definition. But there are two key types of embodiment that it hints at. The first argues that the concepts or cognitive machinery we use for various cognitive behaviors, like reasoning, using language, and so on are built, presumably over the course of the development of an individual, from experiences that the individual has, which may be perceptual, motor, or affective in nature. This shapes the properties of those components of the cognitive system. This <u>developmental</u> notion of embodiment is more clearly distinguished in Lakoff and Johnson (1999).

> The claim that the mind is embodied is, therefore, far more than the simple-minded claim that the body is needed if we are to think. [...] Our claim is, rather, that the very properties of concepts are created as a result of the way the brain and body are structured and the way they function in interpersonal relations and in the physical world. (Lakoff and Johnson 1999: 37)

A second possibility is that the links between concepts on the one hand and the perceptual, motor, and affective experiences the individual has had are not lost over the course of development – they continue to play a role in ("grounding" or "making sense of") the use of concepts. This second, <u>online</u> position is described as follows:

> In an embodied mind, it is conceivable that the same neural system engaged in *per*ception (or in bodily movement) plays a central role in *con*ception. That is, the very mechanisms responsible for perception, movements, and object manipulation could be responsible for conceptualization and reasoning. (Lakoff and Johnson 1999: 38)

Although they seem superficially similar, these two possible relations between language and perception or action come with distinct causal and mechanistic claims. Each requires different sorts of evidence and if true has different consequences for what aspects of cognition embodiment is important to, and in what ways. I'll tease some of these differences apart in the next three sections, which cover three major phases of embodiment research in Cognitive Linguistics.

3 The analytical phase

Cognitive Linguistics has used the notion of embodiment to explain facts about language since its inception. There have been three distinct phases in the application of the idea of embodiment to empirical work on language and cognition.

The first, discussed in this section, was *analytical* in that it involved linguists – inspired by work in cognitive psychology – looking for evidence of how the conceptual resources that underlie language use might be embodied through analysis of language. Work in this stage produced results that did not speak much to mechanisms, and as a result were equally compatible with the developmental and online types of embodiment. The second phase, discussed in the next section, is the *process* phase, which involved refinement of the online version of embodiment in a way that has generated a new theoretical framework, and inspired a substantial body of empirical work. And the third phase, which the field is currently moving into, is discussed in section 5. This is the *function* phase, in which researchers are refining their tools in an effort to determine exactly what embodiment does for specific aspects of language use and other cognitive operations.

3.1 Inspiration from cognitive psychology

The earliest self-consciously cognitive linguistic efforts were inspired by neighboring cognitive psychology and cognitive anthropology results suggesting a variety of ways in which language was not independent of the body. For instance, Eleanor Rosch's work on category structure provided evidence that the way we split up the world linguistically depends on the way we interact with it. This is perhaps most obvious in her work on basic level categorization (Rosch et al. 1976). She found that the words people are most likely to use in neutral contexts to describe things (e.g., *tree* for urban North Americans, as opposed to the more specific *pine* or more general *life form*) collect a whole host of properties. Like *tree*, these Basic Level terms tend to be short, learned early, faster to access, among other features. Critically, the taxonomical level that tends to be Basic appears to be dependent on human bodily interactions with the world. The basic level for objects appears to be best explained as the highest level of categorization that shares a common mental image and interactional affordances.

Another line of Rosch's work, on prototypicality, was similarly inspirational to early cognitive linguistics in terms of its contributions to the idea of embodiment (Rosch 1978). Rosch found that not all members of categories are equivalent in terms of people's mental representations. Americans treat robins as better examples of the category bird than they do ostriches, not only when explicitly asked to judge, but also when their reaction time to decide whether each category member is in fact a category member is measured. And there are even asymmetrical effects of prototypicality in reasoning – people are more likely to infer that a property of robins is true of ostriches than the reverse. Again, protoypicality seems to suggest that mental categories are embodied since they depend on our interactions with the world – the prototypical bird varies as a function of exposure, so people with different life histories have different mental categories.

Results like Rosch's inspired cognitive linguists to look, using the tools of analytical linguistics, for places where linguistic distributions appeared to depend on embodied knowledge. There have been five major lines of work to pursue this goal, each of which is addressed in turn below.

3.2 Embodied syntax

One of the central features of human language is that it displays structure at multiple levels (phonological, morphological, syntactic) that goes beyond mere sequence. Humans seem particularly well equipped to learn and use language with all its complexities, and many other animals do not. Consequently, it becomes very interesting to ask what the human capacity for complex linguistic structure is like. Linguistics in the second half of the 20th century was particularly oriented towards syntax, so a great deal of work during this period focused on the nature of the human cognitive capacity for structure at this level.

Beginning in the 1960s, the mainstream Generative (or Chomskian) approach to language posited that syntax is an informationally encapsulated module of the mind to be explained solely on the basis of internal computational principles. This product of a philosophical orientation towards neo-Cartesian dualism led many linguists to reject the possibility that the idiosyncratic and physically constrained working of the brain, the body, or experience could be relevant to the pinnacle capacity of human minds: abstract syntax.

But early cognitive linguists, as well as functionalists, attempted to demonstrate ways in which syntactic knowledge is sensitive to the body and bodily experience – in particular, ways in which meaning actually matters to syntactic form. This was seen as a type of embodiment, since the goals, intentions, knowledge, and beliefs of the individual can't help but be shaped by individual experience, and to the extent that they in turn affect grammar, that would mean that grammar depends on individual world experiences.

A good deal of the argument hinges on what, exactly, constitutes syntactic knowledge per se. At the time, much of the field held up grammaticality judgments as a valid measure of what language users know, and so early Cognitive Linguistics work aimed to determine whether these judgments reflected knowledge that couldn't be syntax-internal, but had to do with the meaning the language user wanted to convey. Consider, for instance, an utterance like *Rupert sneezed me the peanuts*. Determining whether this string of words forms a grammatical sentence or not depends entirely on how plausible the comprehender thinks it is that Rupert could transfer peanuts to someone through sneezing. It might become more plausible if we know that Rupert is not a person but rather an elephant, for example. When meaning intrudes on grammaticality, it is impossible to characterize syntax as a strictly autonomous system (for the full version of this argument, see Goldberg 1995).[1]

Other work in Cognitive Linguistics tried to derive the form of syntactic constructions directly or indirectly from the (embodied) functions people put them to. The idea here was that if the principles that govern syntactic structure can be shown to be syntax-external, then again individual world experiences, as channeled through the body, matter to linguistic knowledge. One well known example is the case of deictic there-constructions, as in *There's the restaurant we were looking for* (Lakoff 1987). Deictic there-constructions behave differently from any other constructions in the language. They start with a deictic demonstrative *there* instead of a subject, have a restricted range of verbs they can use (basically just the copula, and not in the past tense), and the verb is followed by an apparent subject that has a range of restrictions on it. Lakoff (1987) argues that this unique syntactic patterning is due to the unique function it has: linguistically pointing things out in the situated context of use. To the extent that conventional linguistic patterns can be explained as consequences of the functions they're put to, this means that syntax is again not encapsulated from the experiences a language user has had using that expression for embodied communication.

Complementary lines of work on Cognitive Grammar (Langacker 1987, 2002) and Construction Grammar (Goldberg 1995) advance two related ways that embodiment could have an impact on language. The first is the idea that the operations that an individual performs while using language have two facets – one part applies to the form, aggregating and ordering a string, but a second part operates in parallel over its meaning. Researchers in these traditions point to (sometimes subtle) differences in meaning, function, or use across different syntactic forms that may or may not have been previously analyzed as notational or surface variants of one another. For instance, the English double-object construction (as in *The mayor tossed his secretary the keys*) appears to bear a slightly different meaning from the English caused-motion construction (*The mayor tossed the keys to his secretary*), but this is best illuminated by the cases in

---

1 Some linguists deal with this issue by making a distinction between grammaticality (a theory-internal construct) and acceptability (the judgments language users make), and acknowledge that the latter can be influenced by semantic plausibility but reject this possibility for the former (Chomsky 1965).

which only the caused-motion is licit (*The mayor tossed his keys to the floor*) and the double-object version is not (**The mayor tossed the floor his keys*). In its strongest form, the hypothesis that any difference in form entails a corresponding difference in meaning is the Non-Synonymy Principle (Goldberg 1995), and it remains controversial, not in the least because there are different ways to define what synonymy and meaning mean. But to the extent that form and meaning constraints operate in parallel to constrain what is and what is not a licit utterance in a language, it's again impossible to hold syntax apart as a function immune from the body's effects.

The second way in which Cognitive Grammar in particular contributes to embodiment is through the importance placed on individual experience; the idea that language is learned bottom-up, such that individuals interacting with language (presumably in their bodies with their brains in the world) memorize and then schematize over useful and salient linguistic patterns. This is the idea of a usage-based model, which follows in the next section.

3.3 Usage-based models

As indicated by the cognitive psychology work that inspired early embodiment theory in cognitive linguistics, individual world experience might impinge on linguistic knowledge. At the time when Cognitive Linguistics started to coalesce, Linguistics displayed a prevailing research focus (based on the Generative tradition) on universal aspects of linguistic knowledge (both across languages and across speakers of the same language) and on the categorical nature of linguistic knowledge, including categorical and grammatical knowledge (Harris 1995). The idea that individual experience – language use – might affect language knowledge, while not necessarily in opposition to the mainstream, generative view, certainly placed emphasis differently. Indeed, this was very much the argument given by generativists, like Fritz Newmeyer, who in a presidential address to the LSA famously argued that "grammar is grammar and usage is usage" (Newmeyer 2003). Certainly, no-one would argue that people's knowledge is identical to what they say. The fact that I misspell the word *the* as 'teh' 25% of the time when typing quickly doesn't entail that I think that the word is actually spelled 'teh' with probability 0.25. And the same is true of speech errors, disfluencies, and so on. However, the observation that people make and notice errors in production is not tantamount to endorsing a global distinction between knowledge and use, or competence and performance.

This intuition led many Cognitive Linguistics researchers to look to see whether aspects of language use affect undisputedly central representational aspects of language (see Divjak and Caldwell-Harris this volume). Are phonemes expressed in the same way in the same context, or does the frequency of the particular word they occur in affect the degree to which they will be reduced (Bybee and Scheibman 1999; Gahl and Garnsey 2004)? Does the frequency with which verbs occur in certain argument structure patterns predict how language comprehenders process those verbs in those argument structure constructions, and the perceived grammaticality of those verbs in those constructions (Ellis 2002; Gries et al. 2005)? These are questions about how use – typically operationalized in terms of frequency – affects linguistic knowledge.

There isn't much debate any longer about how valid usage-based theories of language are, in large part because the point has been made. Much of the work now done in psycholinguistics takes for granted that knowledge about frequency, both the raw frequency of particular linguistic units or the strength of their tendency to co-occur with others, plays a role in the millisecond-by-millisecond processing of language. That is, it's (nearly) universally accepted in psycholinguistics that people's knowledge of language includes knowledge based on frequency and probability. This has in large part made the debate about use and knowledge irrelevant. People have knowledge of use. And it's clear that if one's theory of language knowledge can only include things that can't be based on use, then this will cause one to define usage-based knowledge as qualitatively different from "core" language knowledge. But this is a debate about labeling and turf, not a real debate about the facts at hand. Use matters. And this means that this particular prong of embodiment work has come back with an answer in the affirmative. Yes, the experiences an individual language user has in the world matter to their linguistic knowledge (Dąbrowska this volume).

One particularly productive dimension of this usage-based approach has been in studies of early language development (Matthews Volume 2). What happens over the course of a child's first several years of life, and how – if at all – does the body matter to what children learn, how, and when? Perhaps the most complete account of how children acquire language from an embodied perspective is provided in Tomasello (2009), who argues that children build language from the ground up, on the basis of their situated experiences with language in use. Critical in this account is an ability that humans have (perhaps uniquely) to read the intentions of others – this is what allows the child to understand what a word refers to or what is intended with a speech act. Intention reading, on Tomasello's account, depends in no small way on bodily interactions, including monitoring, following, and directing attention of others through eye gaze and through bodily gestures.

3.4 Image schemas

A core issue for cognitive linguistics is the nature of the mental representations that underlie meaning. Are they abstract and detached from embodied experiences? A sort of Language of Thought or Mentalese? Or are they fine-grained sensorimotor representations? One idea that has emerged in the cognitive linguistic literature falls between these alternatives, and proposes a kind of mental representation called *image schemas*. The basic notion of an image schema, as articulated by Johnson, is "[...] a recurring dynamic pattern of our perceptual interactions and motor programs that gives coherence and structure to our experience" (1987: xiv).

The idea is that recurring interactional experiences we have in our bodies serve to ground linguistic meaning, as well as conceptualization, reasoning, and so on. As a result, image schemas are thought have certain features (see Hampe and Grady 2005). For one, they are generalized over many similar experiences, and are thus schematic (for instance, there wouldn't be an image schema for a specific container but might be one for a container in general). And although they are schematic, they're still believed to preserve both structural and perceptuomotor aspects of the specific experiences they schematize over. So an image schema for a container, for instance, would specify the schematic relations between the inside, outside, portal, and boundary, all while doing so in a representational modality that preserves the continuous, perception-, action-, or affect-specific content that it derives from – visual details about what a container looks or feels like to interact with. Because image schemas are thought to preserve aspects of the experiences that they're related to, they are characterized as grounded in those experiences. And because they are structured and schematic, they are believed to be usable for the normal sorts of things that concepts are used for, such as interfacing across cognitive systems, combining with one another, and being used in a displaced fashion.

The idea of image schemas has been influential in cognitive linguistics not least because of their perceived potential to explain distributional facts about language. To continue with the container example, there appear to be many words and grammatical structures that impose schematic constraints on how they can compose. For instance, the preposition *in* seems to evoke a schematic notion of containment such that the prepositional object can (at least in the concrete sense of *in*) be anything that can be construed as an instance of a container, from a garbage can to a galaxy. Image schemas are used to account for what *in* specifies its combinatorial affordances to be (it instantiates a container image schema and requires an object that can be a container). But because they're taken as intrinsically grounded (the container schema is bound to the experiences of containers that it's based on), image schemas are also taken as serving the function of grounding the meaning of words and their combinations.

3.5 Polysemy

Embodiment has also had an impact on the Cognitive Linguistic study of polysemy – understanding why words have which multiple meanings (see Gries Volume 3). Why are both the organ at the end of a human leg as well as the end of a bed called *foot*? Why does *hot* refer to both heat and spiciness? Why does the front of a clock share the name *face* with the front of an animal's head?

By the embodiment hypothesis, cases of polysemy like these might be explained by interventions of the human body on word meaning – interventions of different types in the three cases, each of which is merely a representative example of a much larger set of similar cases (Lakoff 1987). For instance, the foot of a bed is systematically co-located with human feet, and a process of metonymy might account for the extension of the word from the body to something body-adjacent (Barcelona this volume). The same process might account for the *head* of a bed. As for the case of *hot*, this word might refer not only to heat but also to spiciness because, given our bodies, the two experiences feel somewhat similar. Other examples of similarity in felt experience as potential mediator for polysemy include *over*, which although it prototypically refers to something that is located above another object in the vertical axis, can also refer to the relation where something merely covers a second object from view, even if they are arranged along a horizontal axis (as a picture can be placed *over* a hole in a wall to conceal it). And finally, we might use the word *face* for either a part of a clock or a part of a body because the former looks like the latter – humans for instance have a roundish thing centered at the top of their bodies, just as do clocks, especially analog ones. Words for body parts might get extended to things that look similar in other cases, like the *eye* of a hurricane or a potato, or the *shoulder* of a mountain.

Early Cognitive Linguistics was populated by many studies, exploring exactly these types of polysemy, trying to come to terms with the range and frequency of patterns like these within and across languages (Brugman 1981; Lindner 1983; Lakoff 1987; Tyler and Evans 2001; Bergen and Plauché 2005; among others). The upshot of this work is that there appear to be systematic relations among word senses, many of which plausibly relate to the body, including those exemplified above. As Gibbs and Colston (1995) point out however, without confirmation from other types of evidence, like psycholinguistic experimentation, this work presents only part of the story.

3.6 Metaphor

But likely the most widely recognized and influential place where embodiment has played a role in Cognitive Linguistics is metaphor (Gibbs this volume). It's not hard to believe that the body should matter to language about perception and action is structured. But it would be more surprising and revealing if we were to find that the body also matters to how language used to talk about abstract concepts like morality and transfinite numbers. That is what an embodied theory of metaphor would claim.

If the ability for abstract thought in general is grounded in our experiences in our bodies, then this would have important consequences. For one, in practical terms, it would be impossible to study any human cognitive endeavor without taking into consideration its bodily grounding, whether it be economic or political decision making or logical or mathematical inference. (Indeed, this has been a large part of George Lakoff and his colleagues' research program, applying embodied cognitive science to philosophy [Lakoff and Johnson 1999], math [Lakoff and Núñez 2000], and politics [Lakoff 1996]). Second, in terms of the question of the relation of the mind to the body, it would suggest that the body matters even to the least likely of mental capacities – if any human capacity is immune to embodied influence, then certainly it would be abstract thought. And third, in terms of the organization of the mind, embodiment of abstract concepts would suggest massive reuse of and interconnection among the various brain systems we have evolved, and would argue against any sort of strict modularity. At its core, the embodied metaphor story is a story about how we come to think and talk about abstract concepts, basing our understanding on concrete perceptual, motor, and affective experiences.

Certain parts of the literature on metaphor highlight aspects of embodiment. For one, it has often been observed that the body and bodily experiences are frequently taken as source domains, sometimes systematically across languages, and sometimes not (Kövecses 2002). Moreover, the preferred explanation for why bodily experiences come to act as sources for abstract targets is that the two systematically co-occur in early experience – perhaps because we co-experience affection and warmth, warmth, which can be concretely felt by the body, comes to relate to and subsequently structure and stand for affection. If this is true, then the body would play an integral role in the formation of metaphor.

But as noted by Grady (1997) there are exceptions. We have metaphors like THEORIES ARE BUILDINGS or SOCIETY IS A FABRIC, in which the source, though assuredly more concrete than the target, is nevertheless not particularly related to early bodily experience, and certainly not systematically co-occurring with the target. Perhaps, Grady has suggested, there are different sorts of metaphor. Some, so-called *primary metaphors*, are embodied in the way suggested above for AFFECTION IS WARMTH. Others, like THEORIES ARE BUILDINGS, are grounded indirectly through the combination of multiple primary metaphors.

How can we tell exactly how embodied metaphorical language and thought is? Work on polysemy, including ways in which the body has been hypothesized to matter through metaphor, metonymy, and so on, has been extremely influential in the growth of prominence of Cognitive Linguistics research. At the same time however, there are limits to what it can reveal about embodiment, perhaps best articulated through an example. The word *see* describes both vision and comprehension, and there are systematicities in which words have which pairs of such meanings. But how and when does the body matter to these patterns? That is, in exactly what way is embodiment intervening? It's possible that in the minds of contemporary adult English users, there is a functional connection between understanding and vision such that when they use the word *see* in the understanding sense, they are also activating knowledge about vision. But distributional linguistic evidence by itself is not compatible uniquely with this possibility. Gibbs et al. (1997) nicely articulate a range of possible degrees of metaphorical embodiment (see also Boroditsky 2000). Perhaps adult language users access vision only when reflecting consciously on polysemy patterns, as linguists do, but not when normally using language. Perhaps embodiment plays a role in the development of adult language and concepts, but fades away once a system is learned. This is the idea that metaphor helps people learn about abstract concepts by bootstrapping them off of more concrete ones, but that these connections are severed once developing minds have learned that seeing is not in fact understanding. And a more extreme version is also possible – perhaps embodiment only matters as a force in language change; on this account metaphors are cognitively "dead" and embodiment that might have mattered at the time of creation or adoption of novel senses for words is no longer relevant in either developing or adult language users once those changes have been propagated throughout a language community.

And to complicate things even more the same degree of embodiment need not necessarily apply to all users of a language or to all units within a language. So it could be that dead metaphors exist alongside ones that are fully alive, cognitively. And linguistic analysis by itself can't discriminate which language is embodied in which way for which people.

To deal with this limitation, different sorts of evidence have brought to bear on how active a role embodiment plays in what functions.
- Some evidence comes from novel uses of metaphor or metonymy to produce new uses for words that aren't already polysemous. For instance, if meta-

phorical mappings are still active in the minds of language users, then this should manifest in systematic interpretations of extensions of source domain language to target domains. A metaphor like UNDERSTANDING IS SEEING has a large number of lexical items with a foot in each domain, like *see, clear, cloudy,* and so on. But researchers have pointed out at times that completely novel extensions, while unconventional, are readily interpretable (Lakoff 1993). For instance, the intended meaning of *I'd need a scanning electron microscope to see your point* is probably not lost on many English speakers. Novel extensions like this naturally follow the same structural patterns of existing conventional polysemy patterns (understanding is still seeing, things that are hard to understand are hard to see, and so on). And they are interpreted exactly in these terms. So this might constitute evidence that the bodily systems for visual perception matter to our ability to understand language about comprehension.
- Studies of cognitive development have asked whether embodiment plays a role in the acquisition of concepts. For instance, it could be that learning about understanding involves passing through knowledge about vision. Corpus work shows that, for this case in particular, children begin producing the word *see* in situations that involve both sight and comprehension before they begin to also use the word for cases of comprehension in which sight is not relevant (Johnson 1999). This evidence is consistent with the idea that embodiment operates in the development of concepts and acquisition of language.
- Studies of semantic change have shown that words change meanings over time in directions predicted by synchronic metaphor, in the direction from more concrete to more abstract. For instance, words for vision gain additional meanings over time to denote knowledge as well (like the English word *see* has) (Sweetser 1991).

Again, however, although analysis of language patterns is revealing, it is ultimately unable to ascertain whether embodiment has an online function in language use. And because this is a particularly appealing version of embodiment, this has been one major direction of recent theory and investigation, one that has required more contact with experimental psychology and psycholinguistics.

4 Process

Lakoff and Johnson's proposal for online embodiment is that "the same neural system engaged in *per*ception (or in bodily movement) plays a central role in *conception*" (1999: 38). Clearly this has been an influential idea. But stated in these broad terms, it's hard to derive specific claims about what mechanisms of the brain and mind are used to what end during the performance of exactly what cognitive tasks, and exactly with what timecourse. To become useful in explaining how people use language, this idea needs to be fleshed out in a theory of exactly how, when, and why which systems would be used during what linguistic and other cognitive functions. In the late 1990s, several research groups converged on a shared idea about how language use might be embodied, online, using systems that perform primary functions for perception, action, or affect. The idea was a simple one: perhaps the language user constructs denotational meaning in his or her mind by activating perceptual, motor, and affective systems to create or recreate the experience of the described scene. This is the *embodied simulation hypothesis* (Bergen 2012; see also Speed et al. this volume).

The embodied simulation hypothesis has been fleshed out in different ways (Barsalou 1999; Narayanan 1997; Glenberg and Kaschak 2002; Zwaan 2004; Feldman and Narayanan 2004; Gallese and Lakoff 2005; Feldman 2006; Bergen and Chang 2005, 2013; Bergen 2012). Some models are implemented computationally, making claims about exactly what processes lead what embodied mechanisms to be brought online at what time (like Embodied Construction Grammar [Bergen and Chang 2005, 2013; Feldman 2006]). Others describe hypothesized mechanisms in verbal terms, but in terms detailed enough to draw out predictions about timecourse of use of mechanisms and degree of detail (Kaschak and Glenberg 2000; Zwaan 2004; Barsalou et al. 2008)

Because these models make nuanced claims about cognitive processes, the appropriate tools for testing them are more properly drawn from the experimental methods of cognitive psychology and psycholinguistics, tools that afford measurements of cognitive operations over time in the online production or processing of language. Much of the work starting in the early 2000s asked people to perform both a linguistic task and a perceptual or motor task, in some order. The premise was that if perceiving some stimulus or performing some action used brain systems that were also recruited by language about similar percepts or actions, then the two tasks should interact. Typically, these studies measure reaction times. For instance, Glenberg and Kaschak (2002) had people read sentences describing motion towards or away from the body (like *You are closing/opening the drawer*) and then press a button to indicate whether they made sense or not, which was placed either close to or farther away from the experiment participants' own bodies. They found that people were faster to initiate their movement when the direction they had to move their hand in was the same as the direction of motion implied by the sentence. In another study focusing on vision, Zwaan et al. (2002) had people read sentences about objects that implied them to have a particular shape, like an egg in a pan versus a fridge. The participants then saw an image that depicted the object in the same implied shape or a different one, and had to judge whether it had been mentioned in the previous sentence or not. Though the answer to these critical sentences was always 'yes', reactions times differed – again, people were faster when the shape implied by the sentence and depicted by the image matched.

Another early line of work exploited brain imaging, mostly functional Magnetic Resonance Imaging (fMRI). The basic idea was that if understanding language about actions or perceivable events uses brain systems for action or perception in an online fashion, then known motor or perceptual regions should become differentially active when people were processing relevant language. A number of studies found precisely this. For instance, Tettamanti et al. (2005) presented people with sentences about hand, foot, or mouth actions while they laid in an fMRI scanner. They found that parts of the motor strip – the part of the brain that sends electrical signals to skeletal muscles – lit up in a body-part-specific way. The part of the motor strip that controls leg actions was more active when people were processing leg action sentences, and so on.

And these findings extend, albeit in a somewhat more complicated way, to language not about perceivable eventualities and performable actions, but also to language about abstract concepts that are only metaphorically related to perception and action. For instance, Glenberg and Kaschak's original work on action-sentence compatibility effects showed the same strength of effect when people were processing language not only about concrete motion, but also about abstract transfers (for instance, *You dedicated the song to Dan* versus *Dan dedicated the song to you* [Glenberg and Kaschak 2002]). What's more, Wilson and Gibbs (2007) found that performing a source-domain action primes comprehension of metaphorical language using that source domain. For instance, making a fist leads to faster subsequent comprehension of *grasp a concept*, and swallowing leads to faster comprehension of *swallow an idea*. There is also brain imaging work showing that even when processing metaphorical language, the perceptual and motor systems in comprehenders' brains light up in ways corresponding to language about the source domain. For instance, Boulenger et al. (2009) found that foot-controlling parts of the motor system become active when people are processing metaphorical language using foot actions as a source domain (like *Pablo kicked the habit*), while hand-controlling parts light up during processing of metaphorical language using hand actions as source domain concepts (like *John grasped the concept*).

Consequently, as a first-order issue, there is now a sizeable stable of experimental findings showing that language interacts with perception and action in an online fashion. This is especially true of language about perceptual or motor content, but extends at least in a number of studies to metaphorical language or language about abstract concepts.

However, fleshing out predictions of online embodiment to make concrete experimental predictions has also resulted in a great deal of nuance in the actual findings.

Some experiments find facilitation effects between language on the one hand and perception or action on the other (Zwaan et al. 2002; Glenberg and Kaschak 2002). Others find interference (Richardson et al. 2003; Bergen et al. 2007). And this has spawned a good deal of thought about exactly what factors lead effects to occur in what direction and what this all says about how systems for perception and action are in fact used during language production and processing (Kaschak et al. 2005; Bergen 2007).

Other work has shown that embodiment effects sometimes are and sometimes are not detected. This is especially true with metaphorical language, where for instance, some brain imaging studies have found perceptual or motor areas lighting up during processing of metaphorical language using perception or motor control as source domains (Boulenger et al. 2009) while others have not (Aziz-Zadeh and Damasio 2008). The situation is similar with literal language about perceivable or performance events, where the detectability of an embodiment signature appears to depend on subtle features of the linguistic signal, including grammatical aspect (Bergen and Wheeler 2010) and person (Sato and Bergen 2013). Moreover, it's known people can process meaning more or less deeply, and it's possible that while deep processing is associated with embodiment effects, superficial processing uses different strategies (as suggested by Barsalou et al. 2008).

It's important to note that not just motor systems of the brain but also bodily effectors might be engaged in real time processes of meaning-making. The most obvious uses are in iconic gesture (Hostetter and Alibali 2008) and signs (Taub 2001; Wilcox Volume 3). When a gesture or sign iconically models or represents an action or the shape, orientation, or motion of an object, it may be serving as an embodied analogue representation. A topic of current discussion is whether and to what extent these uses of the body play a role in meaning-making, beyond other linguistic signs and gestures.

5 Functional role

There's now little doubt that hearing or reading language about perceptible entities and events can result in measurable activity in the brain systems responsible for perception, and the same goes for language about action and the brain's motor systems. But these findings don't answer a more important question: what exactly is the use of perceptual and motor systems good for? What does it do? This is the question of the functional role of online embodiment. And it remains unanswered.

When we move, as the field has, from viewing language statically and analytically to considering language use as an online process, we're confronted with the question of mechanism. What is the best characterization we can come to of how language users produce or process language in real time? What are the component parts of that system? What exactly do they contribute to the outcome – the behavioral results we can measure and the subjective consequences, for example, experiences of successful comprehension?

There are many proposed possible functions that the online use of perception and actions systems could play in language use. The jury is still out, but some proposals include:

- Lexical access: In language comprehension, figuring out what word was intended might be facilitated by performing embodied simulation of the hypothesized sense, or by simulation of the described content preceding that word. In language production, selecting the right word representation might be mediated by accessing perceptual and motor knowledge about the referent of that word.
- Representational substrate: Denotational meaning might be represented in perceptual/motor terms. That is, what we think of as a message to be formulated in language production or to be decoded in comprehension in fact is a perceptual or motor simulation. To the extent that simulations performed by speaker and hearer are similar, they can be said to have similar representational content.
- Inference: An unquantified but surely important portion of language comprehension is performing inferences to flesh out unstated properties. Some of this inference-drawing may use perceptual or motor simulation – perhaps when you read that *Tristan spent all night at the pub and has a headache this morning*, you fill your preferred causal explanation (drinking alcohol? too loud in the pub?) through a process of simulating what the scene would be like, based on but not limited to the explicitly articulated details.
- Contextual specification: Words have varied and underspecified denotational ranges. Perhaps embodiment plays an online role in fleshing out the details in a given context – perhaps a given utterance has fundamentally the same denotational meaning regardless of context of use, but varies in its context-specific interpretation by dint of how comprehenders bring their perceptual/motor systems to bear in any given instance (Mahon and Caramazza 2008).

For example, perhaps when presented with *The chicken is sick*, people activate different perceptual and motor knowledge about chickens than they do when presented with *The chicken is delicious*.

- None. Perhaps what appears in experiments to be signatures of embodiment is in fact nothing more than the product of spreading activation based on associative learning that doesn't actually play a functional role in language use. It's possible that people have come to associate words like *jump* with perceptual and motor experiences that tend to co-occur with producing or perceiving that word. Just as a dinner bell might lead automatically to salivation, so *jump* might lead automatically to motor or perceptual traces of jumping. But this does not mean that the motor or perceptual systems play any functional role in language use. It could well be that comprehension and production proceed perfectly well without these associations.

This, then, is the current state of the house that embodiment built. We know that perceptual, motor, and affective systems are activated in a content-specific way during language use. But we don't know what that activation does, mechanistically, for language users. And this is where the attention of embodiment researchers is beginning to turn.

One promising way to investigate function is through knock-out effects. If some cognitive function, say some aspect of language use, relies in a functional way on a piece of brain circuitry, then when that piece of brain is unavailable, either permanently or temporarily, then the cognitive function should be impaired. That's basically the logic of dissociation studies, where damage to a particular brain region knocks out certain cognitive capacities but not others. Applied to embodiment, this logic goes like this: if certain aspects of language use, like those listed above, are in fact functionally dependent on the use of systems for perception or action, then the loss of these brain systems should make it harder, or even impossible, for people to perform these specific language functions.

There are different ways to knock out a piece of brain tissue in general. The most decisive method is what neuroscientists working with animal models often do – to excise tissue in a careful and localized way. The problem is that only humans have human language and removing brain tissue is not possible with human subjects. So other, less invasive but necessarily coarser means are necessary. One is to take naturally occurring cases of brain damage, and triangulate a particular region that happens to be an overlapping region damaged across patients. The challenges of this neuropsychological approach to dissociations are well known – it's rare to find patients with localized damage to a region of interest, in addition to the fact that the brain's plasticity after trauma means that the patient's brain will have been reorganizing itself since the insult. Another approach is to use transcranial magnetic stimulation (TMS), which induces a transient magnetic field from the outside of the skull that interrupts activity in a narrow, local part of cortex for a brief moment. But there remain concerns about TMS, both in terms of unknown long-term effects on subjects exposed to it, as well as uncertainty about its underlying physical mechanism. And finally, there are behavioral measures, like adaptation. Neurons can be fatigued by continuous presentation of some stimulus, which leads them to respond less strongly after adaptation than before.

Each of these approaches has seen some use in the function-of-embodiment literature. For instance, Damasio and Tranel (1993) found that patients who suffer damage to the left temporal cortex, where the shapes and other visual properties of objects are represented, often also lose access to nouns. At the same time patients who suffer from lesions to the left frontal cortex, an area dedicated to motor control, tend to have difficulties with verbs. Work using TMS has shown similar results. Shapiro and colleagues (2001) applied TMS to motor areas, and found that this impaired performance on verb production but not on noun production. And finally, there has been some work using behavioral manipulations to fatigue certain brain circuitry. Glenberg et al. (2008) fatigued people's motor systems controlling hand motion in a particular direction, away or towards the body by having them move hundreds of beans in one direction or the other. Then they had them make judgments about sentences describing motion in the same direction or a different direction. They found that when the motor system had been fatigued with action in a particular direction, it took people longer to make judgments about sentences describing motion in the same direction. In sum, a variety of techniques are now being brought to bear on the question of whether embodiment plays a role in online language use, and if so, what role (Speed et al. this volume). But with only a handful of studies pursuing this question so far, the field remains wide open.

6 The future of embodiment in cognitive linguistics

Embodiment as a blanket approach seems to have less substance now than perhaps it had thirty years ago. In part this is because it has been a victim of its own success. The ideas expressed under the banner of embodiment have caught on, so that, in a way only sociologists of science can explain, embodiment has become a hot topic. Everything, it seems, is embodied. Which means that calling research or findings embodied has become less specific and less informative. In addition, the battles that were waged under the banner of embodiment have for the most part been won. It's now inconceivable to most cognitive scientists that language, including syntax, could be informationally encapsulated, or that language wouldn't use other systems, including of the brain and body, or that individual experience wouldn't matter. These are, for the most part, taken as proven hypotheses. So there would appear to be little work left for embodiment as a general concept to do.

But the future of embodiment depends on what we consider it to be. Is it a single answer to a single question? (Is the mind embodied? Yes.) Or is it a class of questions about how the mind might relate to the body? If the latter, then we have barely scratched the surface. And to the extent that we're still asking questions about how language is shaped by the body, we're asking questions about the embodiment of mind. Here are some examples of embodiment-related questions that have persisting potential impact:
- When and how are abstract concepts (including those pertaining to math, time, and so on) embodied? To what extent does embodiment of abstract concepts change through development and depend on the use to which they're being put?
- What are the limits of online perceptual/motor embodiment and what's happening in those cases that seem to indicate disembodied processing?
- What's the functional role of these systems?
- What's the developmental role?

Moving forward, two trends that have already struck elsewhere in the embodiment literature will likely find purchase in Cognitive Linguistics as well (aside from an orientation towards function, as discussed in the last section, which appears to be leading in current embodiment work on language). The first is the situated component of embodiment. It's not merely the case that we have bodies that might be relevant to the functioning of the mind, but that those bodies are embedded in environments, which they interact with continuously. Situatedness can be relevant to language in a variety of ways. The way we use language is not independent of the situations of use; deixis, reference, gesture, and so on, which are already topics under cognitive linguistic scrutiny, might be well served by a careful look at how the situated nature of linguistic cognition affects the form and processing of language.

The second relevant trend is one that's somewhat more philosophically radical; the idea that it's not merely the brain that performs cognitive operations, but that other parts of the body are also, at times, organs of cognition (Clark and Chalmers 1998; Menary 2006). When people use their fingers to count out days of the week, for instance, external parts of their bodies are part of the physical structure that is performing cognitive operations. To the extent that people's bodies are engaged to perform cognitive functions during the production, comprehension, or learning of language, aren't parts of the organism other than the brain also the material substrate of the mind? And what's more, to the extent that parts of the material world, like writing for instance, serve similar functions, can they also constitute part of the substructure of cognition. To the extent that they are, then it's not merely that language is embodied in the brain; it's embodied in bodies and the material world around them, which, in concert, enact cognition (Hutchins 1995).

There's no longer any question that the body matters to the mind. The continuing question of embodiment is exactly how.

7 References

Aziz-Zadeh, Lisa and Antonio Damasio (2008): Embodied semantics for actions: Findings from functional brain imaging. *Journal of Physiology (Paris)* 102: 35–39.

Barcelona, Antonio (this volume): Metonomy. Berlin/Boston: De Gruyter Mouton.

Barsalou, Lawrence W. (1999): Perceptual symbol systems. *Behavioral and Brain Sciences* 22: 577–609.

Barsalou, Lawrence W., Ava Santos, W. Kyle Simmons, and Christine Wilson (2008): Language and simulation in conceptual processing. In: M. De Vega, A.M. Glenberg, and A. Graesser (eds.), *Symbols, Embodiment, and Meaning*, 245–283. Oxford: Oxford University Press.

Bergen, Benjamin (2007): Experimental methods for simulation semantics. In: M. Gonzalez-Marquez, I. Mittelberg, S. Coulson, and M. J. Spivey (eds.), *Methods in Cognitive Linguistics*, 277–301. Amsterdam: John Benjamins.

Bergen, Benjamin (2012): *Louder Than Words: The New Science of How the Mind Makes Meaning*. New York: Basic Books.

Bergen, Benjamin and Nancy Chang (2005): Embodied construction grammar in simulation-based language understanding. In: J.-O. Östman and M. Fried (eds.), *Construction Grammars: Cognitive Grounding and Theoretical Extensions*, 147–190. Amsterdam: Benjamins.

Bergen, Benjamin and Nancy Chang (2013): Embodied construction grammar. In: T. Hoffmann and G. Trousdale (eds.), *Oxford Handbook of Construction Grammar*. Oxford: Oxford University Press.

Bergen, Benjamin, Shane Lindsay, Teenie Matlock, and Srinivas Narayanan (2007): Spatial and linguistic aspects of visual imagery in sentence comprehension. *Cognitive Science* 31: 733–764.

Bergen, Benjamin and Madelaine C. Plauché (2005): The convergent evolution of radial constructions: French and English deictics and existentials. *Cognitive Linguistics* 16(1): 1–42.

Bergen, Benjamin and Kathryn Wheeler (2010): Grammatical aspect and mental simulation. *Brain and Language*, 112: 150–158.

Boroditsky, Lera (2000): Metaphoric structuring: Understanding time through spatial metaphors. *Cognition* 75: 1–28.
Boulenger, Véronique, Olaf Hauk, and Friedemann Pulvermueller (2009): Grasping ideas with the motor system: Semantic somatotopy in idiom comprehension. *Cerebral Cortex* 19: 1905–1914.
Brugman, Claudia (1981): *The Story of Over: Polysemy, Semantics, and the Structure of the Lexicon*. New York: Garland.
Bybee, Joan and Joanne Scheibman (1999): The effect of usage on degrees of constituency: the reduction of don't in English. *Linguistics* 37(4): 575–596.
Chomsky, Noam (1965): *Aspects of the Theory of Syntax*. Cambridge: MIT Press.
Clark, Andy and David Chalmers (1998): The extended mind. *Analysis* 58(1): 7–19.
Damasio, Antonio and Daniel Tranel (1993): Nouns and verbs are retrieved with differently distributed neural systems. *Proceedings of the National Academy of Sciences (USA)* 90: 4957–4960.
Dąbrowska, Ewa (volume 3): Individual differences. Berlin/Boston: De Gruyter Mouton.
Divjak, Dagmar and Catherine Caldwell-Harris (this volume): Frequency and entrenchment. Berlin/Boston: De Gruyter Mouton.
Ellis, Nick (2002): Frequency effects in language processing. *Studies in Second Language Acquisition*, 24(2), 143–188.
Feldman, Jerome (2006): *From Molecule to Metaphor: A Neural Theory of Language*. Cambridge: MIT Press.
Feldman, Jerome and Srinivas Narayanan (2004): Embodied meaning in a neural theory of language. *Brain and Language* 89: 385–392.
Gahl, Susanne and Susan Garnsey (2004): Knowledge of grammar, knowledge of usage: Syntactic probabilities affect pronunciation variation. *Language* 80: 748–775.
Gallese, Vittorio and George Lakoff (2005): The brain's concepts: The role of the sensory-motor system in conceptual knowledge. *Cognitive Neuropsychology* 22: 455–479.
Gibbs Jr., Raymond W. (2005): *Embodiment and Cognitive Science*. Cambridge: Cambridge University Press.
Gibbs Jr., Raymond W. (this volume): Metaphor. Berlin/Boston: De Gruyter Mouton.
Gibbs Jr., Raymond. W., Josephine Bogdanovich, Jeffrey Sykes, and Dale Barr (1997): Metaphor in idiom comprehension. *Journal of Memory and Language* 37(2): 141–154.
Gibbs Jr., Raymond W. and Herbert Colston (1995): The cognitive psychological reality of image schemas and their transformations. *Cognitive Linguistics* 6: 347–378.
Glenberg, Arthur M. and Michael P. Kaschak (2002): Grounding language in action. *Psychonomic Bulletin and Review* 9(3): 558–565.
Glenberg, Arthur. M., Marc Sato, and Luigi Cattaneo (2008): Use-induced motor plasticity affects the processing of abstract and concrete language. *Current Biology* 18: R290–R291.
Goldberg, Adele E. (1995): *Constructions: A Construction Grammar Approach to Argument Structure*. Chicago: Chicago University Press.
Grady, Joseph E. (1997): Theories are buildings revisited. *Cognitive Linguistics* 8: 267–290.
Gries, Stefan Th. (volume 3): Polysemy. Berlin/Boston: De Gruyter Mouton.
Gries, Stefan, Beate Hampe, and Doris Schonefeld (2005): Converging evidence: Bringing together experimental and corpus data on the association of verbs and constructions. *Cognitive Linguistics* 16(4): 635.
Hampe, Beate and Joseph Grady (eds.) (2005): *From Perception to Meaning: Image Schemas in Cognitive Linguistics*. Berlin: Mouton de Gruyter.

Harris, Randy (1995): *The Linguistics Wars*. New York: Oxford University Press, USA.
Hostetter, Autumn B., and Martha W. Alibali (2008): Visible embodiment: Gestures as simulated action. *Psychonomic Bulletin and Review* 15(3): 495–514.
Hutchins, Edwin (1995): *Cognition in the Wild*. Cambridge: MIT Press.
Johnson, Christopher (1999): Metaphor vs. conflation in the acquisition of polysemy: The case of *see*. In: M. K. Hiraga, C. Sinha and S. Wilcox (eds.), *Amsterdam Studies in the Theory and History of Linguistic Science* Series 4, 155–170. Amsterdam/Philadelphia: John Benjamins.
Johnson, Mark (1987): *The Body in the Mind: The Bodily Basis of Meaning, Imagination, and Reason*. Chicago: University of Chicago Press.
Kaschak, Michael P. and Arthur M. Glenberg (2000): Constructing meaning: The role of affordances and grammatical constructions in sentence comprehension. *Journal of Memory and Language* 43: 508–529.
Kaschak, Michael P., Carol J. Madden, David J. Therriault, Richard H. Yaxley, Mark E. Aveyard, Adrienne A. Blanchard, and Rolf A. Zwaan (2005): Perception of motion affects language processing. *Cognition* 94: B79–B89.
Kövecses, Zoltán (2002): *Metaphor: A Practical Introduction*. Oxford: Oxford University Press.
Lakoff, George (1987): *Women, Fire, and Dangerous Things*. Chicago: University of Chicago Press.
Lakoff, George (1993): The contemporary theory of metaphor. *Metaphor and Thought* 2: 202–251.
Lakoff, George (1996): *Moral Politics: What Conservatives Know that Liberals Don't*. Chicago: University of Chicago Press.
Lakoff, George and Mark Johnson (1999): *Philosophy in the Flesh*. New York: Basic Books.
Lakoff, George and Rafael Núñez (2000): *Where Mathematics Comes From: How the Embodied Mind Brings Mathematics into Being*. New York: Basic Books.
Langacker, Ronald (1987): *The Foundations of Cognitive Grammar: Volume I: Theoretical Prerequisites* Stanford: Stanford University Press.
Langacker, Ronald (2002): *Concept, Image, and Symbol*. Berlin: Mouton de Gruyter.
Lindner, Susan. J. (1983): *A Lexico-semantic Analysis of English Verb Particle Constructions with "out" and "up"*. Bloomington: Indiana University Linguistics Club.
Mahon, Bradford Z. and Alfonso Caramazza (2008): A critical look at the embodied cognition hypothesis and a new proposal for grounding conceptual content. *Journal of Physiology-Paris* 102: 59–70.
Matthews, Danielle and Grzegorz Krajewski (volume 2): First language acquisition. Berlin/Boston: De Gruyter Mouton.
Merleau-Ponty, Maurice (1945): *Phénoménologie de la Perception*. Paris: Éditions Gallimard.
Menary, Richard (2006): Attacking The Bounds of Cognition. *Philosophical Psychology* 19(3): 329–344.
Narayanan, Srinivas (1997): *KARMA: Knowledge-based active representations for metaphor and aspect*. University of California, Berkeley Doctoral dissertation.
Newmeyer, Frederick (2003): Grammar is grammar and usage is usage. *Language* 79(4): 682–707.
Richardson, Daniel C., Michael J. Spivey, Lawrence W. Barsalou, and Ken McRae (2003): Spatial representations activated during real-time comprehension of verbs. *Cognitive Science* 27: 767–780.
Rosch, Eleanor (1978): Principles of categorization. In: E. Rosch and B. B. Lloyd (eds.), *Cognition and Categorization*, 27–48. Hillsdale: Erlbaum.

Rosch, Eleanor and Barbara B. Lloyd (eds.) (1978): *Cognition and Categorization*. Hillsdale: Erlbaum.

Rosch, Eleanor, Carolyn B. Mervis, Wayne Gray, David Johnson, and Penny Boyes-Braem (1976): Basic objects in natural categories. *Cognitive Psychology* 8: 382–439.

Sato, Manami and Benjamin Bergen (2013): The case of the missing pronouns: Does mentally simulated perspective play a functional role in the comprehension of person? *Cognition* 127(3): 361–374.

Shapiro, Kevin A., Alvaro Pascual-Leone, Felix M. Mottaghy, Massimo Gangitano, and Alfonoso Caramazza (2001): Grammatical distinctions in the left frontal cortex. *Journal of Cognitive Neuroscience* 13(6): 713–720.

Speed, Laura, David P. Vinson, and Gabriella Vigliocco (this volume): Representing meaning. Berlin/Boston: De Gruyter Mouton.

Sweetser, Eve (1991): *From Etymology to Pragmatics: Metaphorical and Cultural Aspects of Semantic Structure*. Cambridge: Cambridge University Press.

Taub, Sarah F. (2001): *Language from the Body: Iconicity and Metaphor in American Sign Language*. Cambridge: Cambridge University Press.

Tettamanti, Marco, Giovanni Buccino, Maria Cristina Saccuman, Vittorio Gallese, Massimo Danna, Paola Scifo, Ferruccio Fazio, Giacomo Rizzolatti, Stefano F. Cappa, and Daniela Perani (2005): Listening to action-related sentences activates fronto-parietal motor circuits. *Journal of Cognitive Neuroscience* 17: 273–281.

Tomasello, Michael (2009): *Constructing a Language: A Usage-based Theory of Language Acquisition*. Cambridge: Harvard University Press.

Tyler, Andrea and Vyvyan Evans (2001): Reconsidering prepositional polysemy networks: The case of over. *Language* 77(4): 724–765.

Varela, Francisco J., Eleanor Rosch, and Evan Thompson (1991): *The Embodied Mind: Cognitive Science and Human Experience*. Cambridge: MIT Press.

Wilcox, Sherman (volume 3): Signed language. Berlin/Boston: De Gruyter Mouton.

Wilson, Margaret (2002): Six views of embodied cognition. *Psychonomic Bulletin and Review* 9: 625–636.

Wilson, Nicole L. and Raymond W. Gibbs, Jr. (2007): Real and imagined body movement primes metaphor comprehension. *Cognitive Science* 31: 721–731.

Ziemke, Tom (2003): What's that thing called embodiment? *Proceedings of the 25th Annual Meeting of the Cognitive Science Society*. 1305–1310. Hillsdale: Lawrence Erlbaum.

Ziemke, Tom, Jordan Zlatev, and Roslyn Frank (eds.) (2007): *Embodiment* (Vol. 1). Berlin/New York: Mouton de Gruyter.

Zwaan, Rolf A. (2004): The immersed experiencer: Toward an embodied theory of language comprehension. In: B. H. Ross (ed.), *The Psychology of Learning and Motivatio* Volume 43, 35–62. New York: Academic Press.

Zwaan, Rolf A., Robert A. Stanfield, and Richard H. Yaxley (2002): Language comprehenders mentally represent the shapes of objects. *Psychological Science* 13: 168–171.

Russell S. Tomlin and Andriy Myachykov
Chapter 2: Attention and salience

1 Introduction

Our sentences about the world are organized to properly convey the constantly changing visual environment. This skill develops early in life. When fully developed, it entails constant, regular, and automatic mappings from elements of a visual scene onto sentence constituents and the grammatical relations between them. The visual system contributes initially to this process by providing perceptual information for conceptual and linguistic analysis but the perceptual information that enters the language production system is not organized indiscriminately. The attentional system filters information for processing based on its noticeability, importance, or relevance. This process allows representing salience parameters in linguistic output. Individual languages' grammars have specific devices responsible for this representation.

Consider, for example, an event in which a cowboy is punching a boxer. This event can be described in multiple ways including the following:
a) *The cowboy is punching the boxer.*
b) *The boxer is/gets punched by the cowboy.*
c) *It's the boxer that the cowboy is punching.*

Although these do not exhaust the structural alternatives in English that can be used to describe the event, they portray three distinct structural possibilities:
a) An active clause with *the cowboy* as syntactic subject in initial position[1] with *the boxer* as object in final position.
b) A passive clause with *the boxer* as syntactic subject in initial position and *the cowboy* part of an adverbial in final position.
c) A cleft sentence with *the boxer* the pre-posed object of the complement clause with *the cowboy* as subject.

There are important theoretical questions to consider for these cases and their relation to the conceptualizations of the event described above.

---

[1] Please note that subject and initial position are not the same structural category, nor is one defined by the other. There is no such thing in the grammar of English as "subject position".

Russell S. Tomlin, Eugene, USA
Andriy Myachykov, Northumbria University, UK

https://doi.org/10.1515/9783110626476-003

1. How do speakers select among the alternative structures when describing the event? Are the resulting choices holistic (e.g., active or passive) or incremental (e.g., assign a referent to subject or initial position with corresponding cascading resolution of other grammatical matters)?
2. What relationship holds between event perception and the way speaker describes it?
3. Are the mapping principles universal; that is, do different languages map the perceived event onto comparable linguistic categories?

We assume that selecting among the structural alternatives is biased by how the event is perceived and conceptualized. From that viewpoint, the examples (a) and (b) highlight the relative importance or salience of one referent over the other. Theoretically, this difference can be operationalized via pragmatic categories like *topic*, *theme*, or *focus* (Tomlin et al. 2010), or Figure-Ground relations (Talmy 2000a, 2000b, 2007; Langacker 1987, 1991), or a degree of perceptual salience of the event itself (Prentice 1967; Tannenbaum and Williams 1968; Turner and Rommetveit 1968; Osgood and Bock 1977; Flores d'Arcais 1987; Sridhar 1988).

Many theorists subscribe to the idea that *attentional processes* bias the initial event conceptualization and that the resulting conceptual map is then translated into linguistic output as the event is described. However, linguistic and psychological traditions tend to focus somewhat differently on the interplay between attention and language. These differences, often inadequately articulated, have drawn the foci of investigation in somewhat distinct directions. The psychological literature tends to focus primarily on the role of attention in changing the information flow during language production (e.g., the role of priming) while the linguistic literature puts focus on the factors that lead to the selection of *particular* linguistic forms and on typological or cross-linguistic comparisons.

In the next section, we discuss the processes underlying event conceptualization; the interplay between conceptual and linguistic representations in language production, with the specific focus on the grammar organization within utterance formulation; and a set of more detailed questions about the role of attention in sentence generation. This is followed by a review and discussion of the principal research in attention and language with an emphasis on sentence production.

2 Theoretical considerations

The over-arching question driving research on attention and language is deceptively simple: How are attentional processes implicated in the language faculty, including production and comprehension? The question is, in fact, rather complex with at least three fundamental questions making distinctive contributions to advancing the over-arching question of the role of attention in language production and comprehension. The pursuit of these questions motivates our understanding of the grammatical operations involved during visually situated sentence production.

1. How is attention deployed during events conceptualization?
2. Do speakers and hearers exploit attentional processes in their communicative efforts? For example, do speakers organize their utterances to reflect allocation of attentional resources to components of conceptual representations? Similarly, do speakers seek to manipulate the listeners' attentional state in response to their linguistic input?
3. How do languages grammaticalize hypothetical correspondences between the aspects of attentional performance and the corresponding linguistic categories?

In a way, the first question motivates the other two, and there is a widespread and deep literature addressing this first question. A full review of this question falls outside the scope of this chapter; however, we see work on event perception and representation as an essential prerequisite for our understanding of the interface between attention and language faculty, beginning as early as Yarbus (1967) and running through a number of important scholars including Newtson (Newtson 1973; Newtson and Engquist 1976; Newtson et al. 1977) and the Gibsonian tradition (Shaw and Pittinger 1978). Within linguistics the numerous contributions of Talmy (1988a, 1988b, 2000a, 2000b, 2007) and others (Langacker 1987, 1991) seek to reverse engineer aspects of conceptual representation and the possible deployment of attention within them.

The second question has been the province of a great deal of psychological research. These efforts embrace, mostly implicitly, the long-held distinction between the grammar, the knowledge of the language itself, and the parser, the operating system that is employed when the grammar is utilized. One of the important questions is how does the order of encountering components of a conceptual representation affect the order of their mention in language?

The third question evolved with an extended tradition of discourse studies stretching from Weil's (1887) comparative study of ancient Greek and Latin with their modern counterparts, through the Prague School (Dahl 1974; Daneš 1974,

1987; Firbas 1974, 1987a, 1987b; Hăjicová 1984), and on to contemporary work by Halliday (Halliday 1976), Chafe (Chafe 1974, 1979, 1980, 1994, 1998), Givón (Givón 1983, 1988), Lambrecht (Lambrecht 1994), Gundel (Gundel 1988a, 188b), Prince (Prince 1981, 1985), Vallduvi (Vallduvi 1992), Bates and MacWhinney (MacWhinney 1977; MacWhinney and Bates 1978) and many others (see Tomlin et al. 2010 for a review). The role of attentional processes in language processing is interesting primarily to the extent it plays a role in the coding relations of the functional grammar. Further, when linguists address a comparative question, they do not presume that each language must do what English does. Generalizations about language arise from empirical study of typologically diverse languages, and no amount of success with English alone permits generalizations about language overall.

A good deal of psycholinguistic research on attention and grammar is directed at understanding of how perceptual salience and the distribution of attention among competing referents biases the ordering of elements and the assignment of corresponding grammatical roles in a visually situated spoken sentence. Not surprisingly, this tradition provides most of the empirical evidence about the interplay between attention and grammar during language processing. The next section provides a comprehensive summary of these empirical findings and a discussion of their theoretical importance.

However, before we discuss this empirical evidence we need to outline the theoretical framework for a grammar and language processing. One of the most popular models of sentence production (Levelt 1989) includes a conceptualizer dedicated to mapping a conceptual representation onto a pre-verbal message, where the pre-verbal message is semantically complete and annotated for pragmatic roles like *topic*, *focus*, and *given information*. The pre-verbal message serves as input to an utterance formulator, which includes operation of the lexicon and the structural grammar, leading to a grammatical representation fully detailed for lexical, grammatical, and phonological information. Finally, the articulator operates on this input resulting in spoken (or written) linguistic output. Levelt's model serves well for our purposes with two modifications. Although the formulation of the preverbal message is quite detailed in terms of macro- and micro-planning, we believe it is useful to think of the pre-verbal message simply as the conceptual representation of the currently perceived event with no need for a supervening layer of semantic representation. Also, we see the grammar of Levelt's model as a *functional* grammar in which structure-independent semantic and pragmatic relations are mapped onto syntactic relations and structures. While there are certainly generalizable characteristics to these inventories, it is nonetheless an empirical question what constitutes for any given language its particular inventory of semantic and pragmatic relations, its particular inventory of syntactic relations and structures, and the particular details of how the former is mapped into the latter (Tomlin 1985, 1994).

There are four mapping possibilities. It is possible that there *is no relationship* between a given syntactic form and semantic or pragmatic function. This is the null hypothesis for other kinds of interaction. It is possible that the linguistic form does interact with semantic or pragmatic function, either to *syntactically code* the function or *pragmatically signal* it. A syntactic form syntactically codes a given function if, and only if, the presence of the function in the message requires the speaker automatically and invariably to use the specific syntactic form, and the hearer, upon hearing the specific linguistic form, automatically and invariably recovers the associated function. A syntactic form pragmatically signals a function if the presence of the form permits the hearer to infer a particular function in a given context, but there is no automatic production requirement on the speaker. Finally, it is possible that the syntactic form correlates highly with some semantic or pragmatic function but still does not interact with it systematically. Such an *afunctional correlation* occurs when an additional semantic or pragmatic function intervenes between the examined form and function, unnoticed or not analyzed by the linguist.

The principal difficulties facing functional analysis center on determining whether linguistic data reveal a significant correlation between form and function and, if there is one, whether the correlation is one exploited by speaker and hearer during discourse interactions. It is best to think of syntactic coding and pragmatic signalling as stronger and weaker kinds of rule-like behavior, where the degree of such a behavior is tied to automaticity of mapping and derived from the frequency of use. A good example of syntactic coding is found in English subject-verb agreement, with the conventional mapping in American English of grammatical plural onto plural verb agreement (*The legislature convenes again in August* vs. *The legislatures convene again in August*). A clear case of pragmatic signalling is seen in the use of the English conjunction *and*, which gets used to convey both temporal sequence and causality, though neither can be said to constitute a definitive rule for its use. It is common to describe these rule-like behaviors in terms of *grammaticalization*, the extent to which a language deploys concrete structural forms to manifest some semantic or pragmatic function.

It should not be assumed that the details of mappings between semantics/pragmatics and syntactic relations and syntactic structures are universal or that the analysis of English and similar European languages is adequate to formulate generalizations about the interplay of attention with grammar. There is in fact considerable variability in how languages manage semantic and pragmatic functions, and this problem cannot be set aside for long in the pursuit of understanding how attention interacts with grammar. The logic of cross-linguistic issues is better approached outside of a discussion of attention. The cross-linguistic or typological variability that languages display in possible functional mappings can be succinctly demonstrated by considering TIME. A given event is located in time with respect to the moment the speaker describes it either in the past, the present or the future. The grammar of English maps just two of these onto linguistic form (tenses): past tense (*-ed*) and present tense (*-s*) or zero. English deals with future time through an extensive inventory of periphrastic future constructions (*be about to* V, *be going to* V, *will* V) or adverbials (Quirk et al. 1985). The semantics of present and past time are grammaticalized in English onto two tenses; the semantics of future time is *not* grammaticalized in English but is managed through periphrastic means only. Many languages – Bahasa Indonesia or Mandarin for example – have no syntactic codings of time whatever but rely exclusively on adverbials of time or on context to manage events in time for purposes of discourse. Further, while it is common in linguistics and psycholinguistics to do so, there is no *a priori* reason to suppose that time must be divided universally into just three parts.

3 Empirical research

The psychological literature provides (1) structural (2) developmental and (3) behavioral reasons to conclude that linguistic performance may rely upon allocation of attentional resources. The structural argument includes evidence that the human brain is flexibly organized so that the same cortical region often supports a variety of mental operations. For example, neuroimaging studies in reading identify brain areas involved in chunking visual letters into words, associating letters with sounds, and providing entry into a distributed lexicon of semantics. Chunking visual letters into words takes place in a posterior visually specific area of the left fusiform gyrus (McCandliss et al. 2003). In the right hemisphere similar areas are involved in the perception and individuation of faces (Kanwisher et al. 1997). While these areas were first thought to be word and face specific, more recent conceptualizations argue that they are related more to process of chunking of visual elements or individuation of complex forms which can be performed on other inputs (Gauthier et al. 1999). This same principle of localized mental operations over domain specific representations may explain why Broca's area seems important for forms of non-speech motor activity (e.g., Pulvermuller and Fadiga 2010). For example, structural ERP research has shown a large area of activation in the anterior cingulate gyrus during lexical search (Abdulaev and Posner 1998; Raichle et al. 1994). The same area is known to be involved in conflict resolution and executive attention (Fan et al. 2002; Posner and Petersen 1990; Petersen and Posner 2012). An fMRI study (Newman et al. 2001) revealed that syntactic violations elicit significantly greater activation in superior frontal cortex – the area largely involved in attentional control. ERP studies of syntactic violations confirm existence of two electrophysiological brain signatures of syntactic processing: an early left anterior negativity (LAN) and/or a late positive wave with a peak at 600 ms (P600) (Hagoort et al. 1993). Hahne and Friederici (1999) hypothesized that the LAN is a highly automated process whereas the P600 involves more attention. They tested this hypothesis in a study manipulating the proportion of correct sentences and sentences with structural violations in them. Syntactically incorrect sentences appeared in a low (20 % violation) or a high (80 % violation) proportion conditions. Both conditions led to the elicitation of the LAN effect while only low proportion of incorrect sentences resulted in P600. These results support the idea that LAN is an automated first-pass sentence parsing mechanism accompanying syntactic processing while the P600 component is a second-pass parsing that requires a deliberate deployment of executive attention. Together these findings demonstrate that the brain localizes *processes* or mental operations not particular *representations* (either linguistic or non-linguistic). Sharing processing regions may lead to sharing resources between domain-specific and domain-general operations computed in the same area.

Developmental research provides more reasons to hypothesize that attention and language are intimately linked (Matthews and Krajewski volume 2). A number of studies suggest that attentional amplification of visual input is actively used by caretakers during the early stages of language development. Consistent pairing of attentional focus to real-world objects and events with the corresponding names and structures helps the infant build firm associations between the perceived world and the language about it. Experiments show for example that both individual and joint gazes of infants and caretakers can serve as indicators of current learning processes such as matching names to their referent objects (Baldwin 1995; Carpenter et al. 1998; Dominey and Dodane 2004; Estigarribia and Clark 2007). The establishment of the attention-language interface is a starting point in the development of a more complex linking system, one mapping event semantics onto sentence structure. Surprisingly, the rudiments of this system are in place already by 2–3 years of age. Research has shown that children regularly scan visual referents of transient events following the way they are described in auditorily perceived sentences (Arunachalam and Waxman 2010; Yuan and Fisher 2009). In this learning process the associations between event semantics and syntax are regulated by directing the child's attention to the structurally relevant elements of the described scene. The ability to successfully represent the perceptual details in the syntactic structure has been recently reported for children as young as 3–4 years old (Ibbotson et al. 2013). Some theorists (e.g., Mandler 1992) proposed that after initial visual analysis perceptual information in the child's mind becomes represented in a form of image schemas that support development of more abstract conceptual representations and derived thematic and structural relationships. Overall, the role of attentional control in language development suggests an early and a potentially strong coupling between the distribution of attention in the environment and the organization of the language about this environment.

The link between attending to objects and acting on them remains strong in adults. People tend to look at objects in their actions regardless of whether they linguistically describe their actions on these objects or not (Ballard et al. 1997). Understanding of linguistic processing as a subsystem of other behavioral tasks suggests that a similar link can be expected between attending to objects and naming them in a sentence. Indeed, some theoretical proposals claim that perceptual regularities are represented in the syntactic system. For example, Landau and Jackendoff (1993; also Jackendoff 1996) suggested that representing objects in the human mind (*what*) and locations (*where*) maps directly onto the distinction between nouns and prepositions.

3.1 Attention and syntactic choice

One aspect of visual attention important for linguistic research is its selective nature (Langacker this volume; Bock and Ferreira 2014). The surrounding world contains excessive perceptual information available for processing; attention facilitates selection of the information most relevant to making behavioral decisions (e.g., Chun and Wolfe 2001). This selectivity is central to many definitions of attention. For example, Corbetta (1998: 831) notes that "Attention defines the mental ability to select stimuli, responses, memories, or thoughts that are behaviorally relevant among the many others that are behaviorally irrelevant". Selection among stimuli leads to selection between competing responses (Fan et al. 2002). From this point of view linguistic behavior is not an exception as speakers often need to select between different names in order to refer to the same entity and they need to select among different syntactic alternatives when describing the same event.

The control of visual attention in experimental tasks is often achieved through a cueing paradigm (Posner, 1980). A cue here is something that determines a stimulus's salience. It can be an independent marker "pointing" to the stimulus (e.g., an arrow) or it can be a feature of the stimulus itself (e.g., a stimulus' size or luminance). Cues can be exogenous or endogenous, and they can be explicit or implicit; their presence can result in either overt or covert deployment of attention (Posner and Raichle 1994). Exogenous cues are external to the perceiver's mind. Endogenous cues originate from within the perceiver's mind and are guided by internally generated plans and/or intentions. An explicit cue is a clearly noticeable and, therefore, consciously processed marker (e.g., an arrow pointing toward a location on the screen presented long enough to be noticed and looked at. An implicit cue directs attention in a more subtle manner; it is usually presented for duration shorter than would be necessary for conscious processing (e.g., 50 msec.). An implicit cue is typically unnoticed but its display is sufficient for attracting attention and directing the gaze toward a cued location. Eye-movements do not necessarily accompany attentional shifts although they typically follow the allocation of attention (Fischer 1998). This property underlies the difference between overt and covert deployment of attention. An overt attentional shift occurs when the eyes move to align the visual focus with the attended object. A covert shift directs the focus of attention outside of the visual focus making the two foci dissociable (Posner 1980).

3.1.1 Referential priming

The potential of salient referents to occupy prominent sentential roles was reported in the early research that used variants of a *referential priming* paradigm. A participant previews a visual referent for some time before the target event involving this referent appears on the screen. The experimental instruction may differ from sentence verification to sentence description but the general prediction remains the same: The information about the referent extracted during the preview will facilitate its accommodation in the produced sentence. Thus, this *primed* referent may be more likely to become the starting point or (in English at least) the subject of a sentence describing the target event. Similarly, the perceiver in a sentence verification study may be faster to verify the target sentence as correctly describing the target event when this sentence starts with the primed referent or places it as its subject.

One of the earliest studies (Prentice 1967) investigated how attentional focus on the referent established by referent preview affects elicitation of active and passive voice English sentences. Participants described pictures of simple transitive events involving two characters – Agent and Patient (e.g., *a fireman kicking a cat*) – after previewing one of them. In half of the trials participants previewed eventual Agents and in the other half eventual Patients. Target sentences were analysed for the Agent-Patient ordering. When the previewed referent was the Agent, participants were more likely to produce active voice sentences (e.g., *The fireman is kicking a cat*); when the previewed referent was the Patient they were more likely to produce passive voice sentences (e.g., *The cat is being kicked by the fireman*). Hence, the speakers were primed to place the previewed referent first and make it the sentential subject. The cueing effect was not equally strong in the Agent-preview and the Patient-preview trials: while Agent-cued trials resulted in almost 100 % active-voice sentences the Patient-cued trials elicited about 40–50 % passive-voice sentences. This shows how canonicality (i.e., preference for active voice in English) can act as a factual constraint on the degree to which perceptual processes may affect linguistic choices.

A recent study (Myachykov et al. 2012) investigated how informative (referent preview) and uninformative (pointer to referent's location) visual cues affect syntactic choice in English transitive sentence production. Two types of cues were used: (1) a pointer to the subsequent referent's location or (2) a picture of the corresponding referent (i.e., referent preview) in the same location. Crucially, while the first cue simply directs the speaker's attention to the referent's location, the second cue additionally reveals the referent's identity. Cueing the Agent or the Patient prior to presenting the target event reliably predicted the likelihood of selecting this referent as the sentential subject and triggered the associated choice between active and passive voice. However there was no difference in the magnitude of the general cueing effect between the informative (preview) and uninformative cueing conditions (location pointer). This suggests that attentionally driven syntactic choice relies on a direct and automatic mapping from attention to sentence and that this mechanism is independent of the degree of the referent's conceptual accessibility provided by referent preview.

3.1.2 Perceptual priming

Results of the referential priming studies prompted the development of theoretical accounts which related attentional processing to sentence organization. For example, Osgood and Bock (1977) suggested that the referent's salience (or *vividness*) may predict its positioning in a sentence with the most prominent referents assuming the most prominent positions. But what is the most prominent position in a sentence? The importance of sentential starting points was pointed out by MacWhinney (1977) who suggested that the salient referent tends to occupy the initial position in a sentence thus triggering structural organization of the sentence. The *starting point* however does not always have to correspond to the most prominent grammatical role (subject) in the sentence although in English this is almost always the case.

Contrasting with this positional view, Tomlin (1995, 1997) suggested that salient referents tend to occupy the most prominent syntactic role, e.g., syntactic subject, thus offering *the grammatical-role* hypothesis for perceptually driven syntactic choice. Initially this idea was tested in a study using a very strong variant of a *perceptual priming* paradigm known as the "FishFilm" (Tomlin, 1995). In a typical perceptual priming experiment speakers describe visually perceived events while their attention is directed to one of the event's referents by a cue unrelated to (and uninformative about) the cued referent. In its essence, therefore, the perceptual priming paradigm is a psycholinguistic adaptation of a visual cueing paradigm (Posner, 1980). In Tomlin's study, participants observed and described an animated interaction between two fish in which one fish always ended up eating the other. In half of the trials an explicit visual cue (arrow pointer) was presented above the Agent fish and in the other half of trials above the Patient fish. The results demonstrated that in virtually 100 % of the Agent-cued trials participants produced an active voice sentence (e.g., *The red fish ate the blue fish*). When the cue was on the Patient participants nearly always produced a passive voice sentence (e.g., *The blue fish was eaten by the red fish*). Tomlin concluded that attentional cueing promotes the assignment of the Subject-role (to either the Agent or the Patient) in an English transitive sentence thereby triggering the choice between active and passive voice.

Although Tomlin's results were very persuasive the FishFilm paradigm itself received significant methodological criticism (e.g., Bock et al. 2004). The most critical points were (1) the repetitive use of the same event without filler materials (2) the explicit nature of the visual cue (and related experimental instructions) and (3) the joint presentation of the cue and its target. Obviously in real life visual salience is more subtle; hence a more tacit manipulation of the attentional focus may be necessary to further substantiate the role of perceptual priming on syntactic choice. Gleitman and colleagues (Gleitman et al. 2007) conducted a study that avoided the methodological problems of the FishFilm paradigm. In this study participants observed and described interactions between two referents portrayed in still pictures. Speakers' attention was directed to the location of one of the referents by means a visual cue (a black square). The cue appeared on the screen *before* the target picture in the place of one of the subsequently presented referents. The cue was presented for only 65 msec. and participants remained largely unaware of its presence. This *implicit* cueing procedure was nevertheless successful in directing attention to the cued area of the screen (as revealed by eye-movement data) and subsequently to one of the referents (e.g., Agent or Patient). The use of filler materials minimized the probability of using event-specific linguistic strategies. In addition to the active/passive alternation the experiment included picture materials for a variety of other syntactic choices including symmetrical predicates (e.g., *X meets Y / Y meets X / X and Y meet*), verbs of perspective (e.g., *X chases Y / Y flees X*), and conjoined noun-phrases (e.g., *X and Y ... / Y and X ...*). Gleitman et al's syntactic alternation results largely confirmed Tomlin's findings yet their effects were much weaker due to the far more subtle perceptual cueing manipulation: Speakers were 10 % more likely to produce passive voice sentences when the cue attracted their attention to the Patient location. In the remaining 90 % of the Patient-cued trials speakers still produced the canonical active voice structure.

Indeed this result (as well as Tomlin's original findings) does not differentiate between a *positional* versus a *grammatical-role* account of perceptual cueing effects mainly because in English transitive sentences the syntactic subject is virtually always confounded with the sentential starting point. However, the symmetrical predicate data in Gleitman et al. (2007) provide some interesting new insights in this respect. When describing a symmetrical event speakers may choose among various canonical active voice options e.g.: (1) *The man kissed the woman* (2) *The woman kissed the man* (3) *The man and woman kissed* and (4) *The woman and the man kissed*. Structural variants (1) and (2) rely on a canonical SVO-frame and the choice between them may reflect both positional (starting point) and grammatical-role (Subject) preferences for the most salient referent. The choice between structures (3) and (4) involves only positional mappings as the two referents are part of the same conjoined noun phrase (CNP) in Subject position. The participants in Gleitman et al. (2007) produced all four possible alternatives. Moreover they tended to assign the visually cued referent to an early position in the sentence i.e., to the Subject-position when choosing an SVO-frame (1 or 2) and to the first element when choosing a CNP-frame (3 or 4). Most interestingly the perceptual cueing effect was stronger when participants used an SVO-frame (31 %) than when they used a CNP-frame (23 %). This could suggest a *hybrid* system of attention-driven syntactic choice either with a stronger bias toward the grammatical-role assignment component or with additive effects of perceptual cueing on both linear positioning and grammatical-role assignment.

Perceptual priming studies using other structures came to similar conclusions. For example Forrest (1996) explored the visually cued production of locative sentences in English. As in Gleitman et al. (2007) speakers' attentional focus was attracted not to the cued referent itself but to its location prior to the target event presentation. The experimental materials were simple line drawings of locative events, for example a picture of *A star left of a heart*. Prior to target display presentation an explicit visual cue appeared in the location of either the star or the heart. As a result speakers tended to produce sentences like *A star is left of a heart* when the star's location was cued and *A heart is right of a star* when the heart's location was cued.

Together these results provide important evidence about the extent of the perceptual priming effect on syntactic choice in English. First, they demonstrate that the referent's salience alone can successfully predict syntactic choice in a variety of syntactic structures. Second, they suggest that the strength of the perceptual priming effect depends on the power of the cue (e.g., its explicitness) and the strength of the association between the cue and the referent. However, distinct features of English grammar, namely the tendency to confound the Subject role with the sentential starting point, make it difficult to distinguish between positional and the grammatical-role accounts of perceptually driven syntactic choice. The data from Gleitman et al. (2007) hint at the existence of a hybrid system of perceptually driven syntactic choice in which perceptual cueing affects both grammatical-role assignment *and* positioning of a constituent in a sentence. Research on languages with flexible word order may help to address this question more directly.

The studies reviewed thus far used English as the target language – an SVO language with a highly constrained word order. For example, in describing a transitive event the speaker of English primarily selects between the active voice and the passive-voice SV(O) options.[2] Hence the grammatical subject in English usually coincides with the sentential starting point. This feature makes it difficult to distinguish between assignment of the grammatical roles and linear ordering of constituents. Other languages allow for a more flexible organization of sentences. Three recent studies analyzed perceptually primed syntactic choice in Russian (Myachykov and Tomlin 2008), Finnish (Myachykov et al. 2011), and Korean (Hwang and Kaiser 2009) sentence production. Unlike English these three languages permit flexible word ordering making at least some permutations of Subject, Verb, and Object grammatical. Russian and Finnish, like English, are SVO languages but, unlike English, they permit both Object-initial and Verb-initial constructions and thus allow a wider range of topicalization constructions. Korean is an SOV language that permits placement of subject and object before the verb (which always follows its arguments). Although topicalization is possible in these languages it is not freely licensed. For example, factors related to discourse context (e.g., contrast of given/new information) were shown to predict ordering of sentential constituents in Russian (Comrie 1987, 1989; Yokoyama 1986), Finnish (Kaiser and Trueswell 2004; Vilkuna 1989), and Korean (Choi 1999; Jackson 2008). The same, however, is true for English (e.g., Chafe 1976; Downing and Noonan 1995; Givón 1992; Halliday 1967; *inter alia*). More importantly, the role of discourse-level factors does not pre-

---

[2] There is an order-only alternative possible, so-called topicalization, but this is not used for these descriptions.

clude the possibility that speakers of these other languages also accommodate referential salience in syntactic choice. The lack of corresponding evidence makes perceptual priming research in flexible word order languages very useful. Importantly, voice-based alternations are also possible in these three languages but they are greatly dispreferred and less frequent (e.g., Siewierska 1988; Vilkuna 1989; Zemskaja 1979) than in English (e.g., Svartvik 1966). In a perceptual priming task, speakers of flexible word order languages could map the salient referent either onto the subject or onto the sentential starting point without subject-role assignment. Such languages provide an optimal test-bed for independent predictions from the linear ordering and the grammatical-role accounts of perceptually driven syntactic choice.

Myachykov and Tomlin (2008) analyzed Russian transitive sentence production using the FishFilm paradigm (see Tomlin 1995). They hypothesized that if the visually cued referent becomes the sentential subject Russian speakers, like their English speaking counterparts, should be more likely to alternate between active and passive voice when describing FishFilm events. Alternatively, they may choose to use topicalization which in the Patient-cued condition would result in an increased percentage of Object-initial active voice structures. This would support a linear-ordering account of perceptual priming effect on syntactic choice. The results supported the latter view: Russian speakers produced 20 % more Object-initial (OVS or OSV) active voice structures (plus ca. 2 % passive voice sentences) when the perceptual cue was on the Patient. This perceptual priming effect is noticeably smaller than in Tomlin's (1995) study with English speakers who produced passive voice sentences in nearly 100 % of the Patient-cued trials. This is especially noteworthy given the fact that Myachykov and Tomlin (2008) employed exactly the same manipulations as Tomlin (1995).

Myachykov et al. (2011) compared perceptual priming effects between English and Finnish. Similarly to Gleitman et al. (2007) participants described pictures of transitive events after their attention was directed to the location of either the Agent or the Patient by an implicit (70 ms) visual cue. The data from the English participants replicated earlier findings (Gleitman et al. 2007): there was a reliable main effect of Cue Location with participants producing 94 % active voice sentences in the Agent-cued trials and 74 % active voice sentences in the Patient-cued trials. One difference between the form of the passive voice in Russian and in Finnish is that the passive voice in Finnish is not only infrequent but also always realized without a by-phrase (Kaiser and Vihman 2006). Hence it may be difficult to induce passivization in a study using events that always involved two protagonists. Topicalization however is equally possible in Finnish and in Russian. Therefore, one could expect a reduced yet noticeable effect of perceptual priming in Finnish through topicalization similar to Russian. However, there was no reliable word order alternation in Finnish although the cueing manipulation was equally effective (as revealed in saccades to the cued locations). Virtually the same result was observed in Hwang and Kaiser (2009) who used an implicit cueing paradigm in a study with Korean: participants described transitive events (e.g., dog biting policeman) after their attention was directed to either the Agent or the Patient via the presentation of an implicit visual cue. Similar to the results of Myachykov et al. (2009) the cueing manipulation was successful (in terms of attracting initial fixations); however this did not lead to any perceptual priming effect affecting syntactic choice.

Together these results suggest the existence of language-specific differences in how visual cueing affects syntactic choice. The exact nature of these differences is not yet clear. It is possible that the largely dispreferred status of the passive voice in languages like Russian and Finnish makes mapping of a salient Patient referent onto the Subject role problematic. The same explanation is offered by Hwang and Kaiser who proposed that Korean has a strong bias toward actives with canonical word-order (SOV) and that passives in Korean are more marked than in English. However, it is important to remember that the decrease in the cue power was responsible for the decrease of the overall perceptual priming effect observed in Gleitman et al. (2007) as compared to Tomlin (1995). At the same time a FishFilm experiment with Russian (Myachykov and Tomlin 2008) also revealed a reliable yet greatly decreased perceptual priming effect compared to Tomlin (1995). Put together these studies suggest that in flexible word-order languages the extent of perceptual priming is consistently weaker than in the fixed word-order languages. An important question is why is this so? We propose that the grammatical-role assignment mechanism operates as the primary syntactic device responsible for representing the speaker's attentional focus while linear ordering of the constituents is only employed when the grammatical-role assignment mechanism is not easily available. In English transitive sentence production, the two routes coincide making the overall perceptual priming effect stronger. In languages like Russian and Finnish only the linear-ordering route is available (because of the unavailability of the passive); hence there is a much weaker effect in Russian (Myachykov and Tomlin 2008) and respectively null effects in Finnish (Myachykov et al. 2009) and Korean (Hwang and Kaiser 2009). Supporting the grammatical-role assignment view a recent FishFilm study using a VOS-language (Malagasy) demonstrated that speakers of Malagasy consistently assign the cued referent to the final Subject role (Rasolofo 2006). This provides further support for the dominance of the grammatical-role mechanism over the linear-ordering one: availability of structures that allow for direct mapping between the salient referent and the Subject makes the importance of linear ordering for the accommodation of referential salience in syntactic choice irrelevant.

The assignment of the grammatical roles in a spoken sentence and the resulting syntactic choice do not depend solely on the salience characteristics of the described event. Other factors such as prior activation of lexical and syntactic units affect the likelihood of selecting one structure over another too. One could naturally assume that the final choice of structure is a product of many interacting forces and little is known about how perceptual priming interacts with other priming parameters known to influence the speaker's choice of syntax, including both *lexical* (Bock and Irwin 1980) and *syntactic* priming (Bock 1986).

Similarly to perceptual priming, lexical priming (e.g., recent exposure to the word designating the referent) has been shown to increase the likelihood of the primed referent becoming the sentential starting point and/or its subject. This can be achieved by priming referent-related nouns (Bates and Devescovi 1989; Bock and Irwin 1980; Ferreira and Yoshita 2003; Flores D'Arcais 1975; Osgood and Bock 1977; Prat-Sala and Branigan 2000) or verbs related to the event portrayed in the target trial (Melinger and Dobel 2005). In addition, syntactic priming refers to a tendency to repeat the whole syntactic configurations of structures that the speaker has previously encountered or produced (for recent reviews cf. Branigan 2007; Ferreira and Bock 2006; Pickering and Ferreira 2008). Some accounts of syntactic priming claim that the tendency to repeat syntax from sentence to sentence has a strong lexical component (e.g., Pickering and Branigan 1998); other accounts claim that syntax is reproduced without necessary reference to either conceptual or lexical information (e.g., Bock and Loebell 1990; Bock et al. 1992; Desmet and Declercq 2006; Scheepers 2003).

Independent of these theoretical differences any interactive properties of the distinct priming effects established at different production stages remain largely unknown. This has motivated the experiments reported in Myachykov, Garrod, and Scheepers (2012). These experiments investigated syntactic choice in English transitive sentence production by combining priming manipulations at both linguistic and non-linguistic levels. In each of the three reported experiments, participants described visual events after receiving combinations of the following priming manipulations: (1) perceptual priming, (2) lexical (verb match), and (3) syntactic priming. Across all three experiments there were clear and robust perceptual priming effects even in the presence of concurrent linguistic manipulations (syntactic priming and verb match) (Bock et al. 2004; Kuchinsky and Bock 2010). These findings provide further evidence that perceptual information about the referents (e.g., referential salience) plays an integral and distinct role during the assignment of syntactic roles alongside available lexical and syntactic information. Importantly, the simultaneously observed syntactic priming effect *did not* interact with the perceptual priming effect suggesting that interactions between priming effects are constrained by a *neighborhood* principle, according to which only immediately *neighboring* processing stages (e.g., message and lemma; lemma and syntax) can interact with one another in determining syntactic choice while non-neighboring stages (message and syntax) cannot. The ubiquitous presence and comparable magnitude of the perceptual and the syntactic priming effects hint at the existence of a dual-path mapping mechanism akin to Chang (2002). According to dual-path mapping non-linguistic effects (such as perceptual salience) and linguistic effects (such as syntactic and lexical accessibility) can affect subject assignment independently and in parallel, each producing its individual biases.

One important additional finding was that the perceptual priming effect interacted with the verb-match effect. The visual cueing effect (the increase in the proportion of passive-voice responses in the Patient-cued condition) remained relatively unaffected by the verb match manipulation. This may indicate that speakers have a general tendency to use salient patients as subjects of their sentences (and correspondingly select a passive-voice frame) regardless of the co-presence of linguistic cues competing for the same choice. The verb match effect in this scenario would result from a relatively higher activation of the otherwise dispreferred passive voice frame when the prime verb matches the target event (cf. Melinger and Dobel 2005 who found that isolated verbs can indeed prime syntactic frames). Importantly this passive promoting verb match effect was only observed when the visual cue was on the agent or in the situation when the visual cue did not simultaneously compete for the choice of passive. One possibility is that matching prime verbs can only make the passive voice alternative to the canonical active more available in absence of a visual cue competing for the same choice: In the Agent-cued condition (supporting active voice) the verb cue is informative as it provides a cue toward the alternative (passive voice); in the Patient-cued condition (supporting passive voice) the verb cue is uninformative as it supports the same response as the Patient-cue itself. If this interpretation is correct then it follows that lexical information (whether the prime verb matches the target event or not) is considered only after perceptual information (visual cueing) has already been integrated into the grammatical encoding process. Thus perceptual information would take priority over lexical information (at least in the current experimental setup where the visual cue was always delivered most recently i.e., immediately before the target event). This theoretical scenario entails an interesting prediction, namely that it should be possible to register an independent transitive verb-match effect (more passive voice target descriptions after presenting a matching prime verb) in the absence of any visual cues to either Agent or Patient.

Still, the exact mechanism of the integration of non-linguistic and linguistic information during sentence production is not totally clear. We assume, as Bock and Levelt (1994) argue, that sentence production begins with the creation of a message – a conceptual representation of the event to be encoded linguistically. Accessibility of non-linguistic information about the referents extracted at this stage can vary (Bock and Warren 1985). As a result the speaker may be biased to process the more salient referents ahead of the less salient ones. If such preferential processing continues all the way to grammatical encoding and overt articulation, it is likely that the salient referent is encoded in a sentence before other referents. In English this may lead to the salient referent mapping onto the subject. Our data confirmed this hypothesis. Participants were more likely to assign the subject role to the Agent and choose the corresponding active-voice frame when the Agent was cued, and they were likewise more likely to assign the subject to the Patient and select the corresponding passive-voice frame when the cue was on the Patient. Importantly, the visual cueing used in these experiments did not provide participants with any information that might reveal the referent's identity or its semantic properties. Hence, simply directing visual attention to the location of the referent is enough to affect speakers' likelihood of producing an active or a passive voice sentence (cf. Gleitman et al. 2007; Myachykov et al. 2012; Tomlin 1995, 1997).

4 Conclusions

This chapter reviewed evidence for a regular link between visual attention and syntactic organization in discourse. A number of reviewed studies demonstrate how speakers regularly alternate between structural alternatives as a function of their attentional focus on one of the referents of the described events. The persistence of such an attentionally driven assignment of syntactic roles confirms that in English the attentionally detected referent tends to map onto the prominent syntactic relation (i.e., subject) in a produced sentence. However, the exact mapping from attention to syntax in different languages is far from certain. One possibility is that different languages' grammars provide speakers with *different* means of grammatically encoding perceptual properties of the described world. Another possibility is that the link between attentional focus and the choice of syntax via the assignment of subject *is* more or less universal in that speakers always *try* to map the salient referent onto subject. However, the accessibility of alternatives (e.g., active vs. passive) is not always equal across languages. When a direct mapping is much less accessible (e.g., passive in Russian), the attempt to map the visually focused referent onto subject needs to be discontinued. In this case, a "second-best" mapping may be used – one that *is not* syntactically coded in the language's grammar. One example is Russian speakers' tendency to resort to topicalization instead of activating the theoretically available passive when they attempt to preferentially position the salient patient in their transitive sentences. This assignment through topicalization, however, is secondary to a more preferred and automated direct mapping mechanism; hence, its use is associated with slower sentence production rates and inflated eye movement measurements, such as eye-voice spans (see Myachykov 2007). We propose that the grammatical role assignment mechanism and the positional assignment mechanism form a hierarchical dual-path system that allows grammatical representation of the perceptually salient referent in a sentence. This system is hierarchical in two ways. First, while the grammatical role mapping mechanism is a common but language-specific mapping based on syntactic coding, the positional mapping is, in principle, available regardless of the existence of the corresponding grammatical role mapping mechanism. It is undoubtedly easier to freely arrange the constituents in a language that licenses topicalization grammatically, e.g., via case marking, but it is still quite impossible to use "semi-legal" positioning devices like dislocations in languages that do not normally permit topicalization. Second, these two mapping mechanisms are hierarchically related in that in languages like English grammatical role assignment dominates over positional assignment. For example, speakers try to activate structural alternatives that permit direct mapping from attentional focus to subject before they (1) abandon this attempt in favour of a more dominant structure that requires remapping (e.g., the use of active voice in Patient-salient situations) or (2) using topicalization as the second-best mapping alternative.

All this does not generally mean that *subjecthood* only reflects attentional focus on a referent. What it means is that when attentional focus needs to be represented, the speaker tries to do it by assigning the subject role to the most salient referent in the scene. The problem is that the corresponding structural contrast may not always be available, as in languages like Russian and Finnish, because passives are rare or largely dispreferred. When the grammatical role assignment mechanism is not easily available the speaker looks for an alternative. In flexible word-order languages this alternative is topicalization. As a result a linear-ordering mechanism is used to accommodate referential salience in terms of word order but with detrimental effects on the speed of processing and the strength of the overall perceptual priming effect.

5 References

Abdullaev, Yalchin and Michael Posner (1998): Event-related brain potential imaging of semantic encoding during processing single words. *Neuroimage* 7: 1–13.

Arunachalam, Sudha and Sandra Waxman (2010): Meaning from syntax: evidence from 2-year-olds. *Cognition* 14(3): 442–446.

Baldwin, Dare (1995): Understanding the link between joint attention and language. In: C. Moore and P. Dunham (eds.), *Joint Attention: Its Origins and Role in Development*, 131–158. Hillsdale: Lawrence Erlbaum Associates.

Ballard, Dana, Mary Hayhoe, and Polly Pook (1997): Deictic codes for the embodiment of cognition, *Behavioral and Brain Sciences* 20: 723–742.

Bates, Elizabeth and Antonella Devescovi (1989): Crosslinguistic studies of sentence production. In: B. MacWhinney and E. Bates (eds.), *The Crosslinguistic Study of Sentence Processing*, 225–256. Cambridge: Cambridge University Press.

Bock, Kathryn (1986): Syntactic persistence in language production. *Cognitive Psychology* 18: 355–387.

Bock, Kathryn and Victor Ferreira (2014): Syntactically speaking. In: M. Goldrick, V. Ferreira, and M. Miozzo, (eds.), *The Oxford Handbook of Sentence Production*, 21–46. New York: Oxford University Press.

Bock, Kathryn and David Irwin (1980): Syntactic effects of information availability in sentence production. *Journal of Verbal Learning and Verbal Behavior* 19: 467–484.

Bock, Kathryn, David Irwin, and Douglas Davidson (2004): Putting first things first. In: J. Henderson and F. Ferreira, (eds.), *The Integration of Language, Vision, And Action: Eye Movements And the Visual World*, 249–278. New York: Psychology Press.

Bock, Kathryn and Willem J. M. Levelt (1994): Language production: grammatical encoding. In: M. Gernsbacher (ed.), *Handbook of Psycholinguistics*, 945–984. New York: Academic Press.

Bock, Kathryn and Helga Loebell (1990): Framing sentences. *Cognition* 35: 1–39.

Bock, Kathryn, Helga Loebell, and Randel Morey (1992): From conceptual roles to structural relations: bridging the syntactic cleft. *Psychological Review* 99: 150–171.

Bock, Kathryn and Richard Warren (1985): Conceptual accessibility and structural structure in sentence formulation *Cognition* 21: 47–67.

Branigan, Holly (2007): Syntactic priming. *Language and Linguistics Compass* 1(1/2): 1–16.

Carpenter, Malinda, Katherine Nagell, and Michael Tomasello (1998): Social cognition, joint attention, and communicative competence from 9 to 15 months of age. *Monographs of the Society of Research in Child Development* 63(4): 1–143.

Chafe, Wallace (1974): Language and consciousness. *Language* 50: 111–133.

Chafe, Wallace (1976): Givenness, contrastiveness, definiteness, subjects, topics, and points of view. In: C. Li (ed.), *Subject and Topic*, 25–56. New York: Academic Press.

Chafe, Wallace (1979): The flow of thought and the flow of language. In: T. Givón (ed.), *Discourse and Syntax*, 159–181. New York: Academic Press.

Chafe, Wallace (1980): The deployment of consciousness in the production of narrative. In: W. Chafe (ed.), *The Pear Stories: Cognitive, Cultural, and Linguistic Aspects of Narrative Production*, 9–50. Norwood: Ablex.

Chafe, Wallace (1994): *Discourse, Consciousness, and Time: The Flow and Displacement of Conscious Experience in Speaking and Writing*. Chicago: University of Chicago Press.

Chafe, Wallace (1998): Language and the flow of thought. In: M. Tomasello (ed.), *The New Psychology of Language: Cognitive and Functional Approaches to Language Structure*, 93–111. Mahwah: Lawrence Erlbaum.
Chang, Franklin (2002): Symbolically speaking: a connectionist model of sentence production. *Cognitive Science* 26: 609–651.
Choi, Hye-Won (1999): *Optimizing Structure in Context*. Stanford: CSLI.
Chun, Marvin and Jeremy Wolfe (2001): Visual attention. In: E. B. Goldstein (ed.), *Blackwell Handbook of Perception*, 272–310. Oxford: Blackwell.
Comrie, Bernard (1987): *The World's Major Languages*. London: Croom Helm.
Comrie, Bernard (1989): *Language Universals and Linguistic Typology*. Chicago: University of Chicago Press.
Corbetta, Maurizio (1998): Frontoparietal cortical networks for directing attention and the eye to visual locations: Identical, independent, or overlapping neural systems? *Proceedings of the National Academy of Sciences* 95(3): 831–838.
Dahl, Östen (1974): Topic-comment structure in a generative grammar with a semantic base. In: F. Daneš (ed.), *Papers on Functional Sentence Perspective*, 75–80. The Hague: Mouton.
Daneš, František (1974): Functional sentence perspective and the organization of the text. In: F. Daneš (ed.), *Papers on Functional Sentence Perspective*, 106–28. The Hague: Mouton.
Daneš, František (1987): On Prague school functionalism in linguistics. In: R. Dirven and V. Fried (eds.), *Functionalism in Linguistics*, 3–37. Amsterdam: John Benjamins.
Desmet, Timothy and Mieke Declercq (2006): Cross-linguistic priming of syntactic hierarchical configuration information. *Journal of Memory and Language* 54: 610–632.
Dominey, Peter and Christelle Dodane (2004): Indeterminacy in language acquisition: the role of child-directed speech and joint attention. *Journal of Neurolinguistics* 17: 121–145.
Downing, Pamela and Michael Noonan (1995): *Word Order in Discourse*. Vol. 30 of Typological Studies in Language. Amsterdam/Philadelphia: John Benjamins.
Estigarribia, Bruno and Eve Clark (2007): Getting and maintaining attention in talk to young children. *Journal of Child Language* 34: 799–814.
Fan, Jin, Bruce McCandliss, Tobias Sommer, Amir Raz, and Michael Posner (2002): Testing the efficiency and independence of attentional network. *Journal of Cognitive Neuroscience* 3(14): 340–347.
Ferreira, Victor and Kathryn Bock (2006): The functions of syntactic priming. *Language and Cognitive Processes* 21(7/8): 1011–1029.
Ferreira, Victor and Hiromi Yoshita (2003): Given-new ordering effects on the production of scrambled sentences in Japanese. *Journal of Psycholinguistic Research* 32(6): 669–692.
Firbas, Jan (1974): Some aspects of the Czechoslovak approach to problems of functional sentence perspective. In: F. Daneš (ed.), *Papers on Functional Sentence Perspective*, 11–37. The Hague: Mouton.
Firbas, Jan (1987a): On the delimitation of theme in functional sentence perspective. In: R. Dirven and V. Fried (eds.), *Functionalism in Linguistics*, 137–156. Amsterdam: John Benjamins.
Firbas, Jan (1987b): On two starting points of communication. In: R. Steele and T. Threadgold (eds.), *Language Topics: Essays in Honour of Michael Halliday*, volume 1, 23–46. Amsterdam: John Benjamins.
Fischer, Burkhart (1998): Attention in saccades. In: R. D. Wright (ed.), *Visual Attention*, 289–305. New York: Oxford University Press.

Flores d'Arcais, Giovanni B. (1975): Some perceptual determinants of sentence construction. In: G. B. Flores d'Arcais (ed.), *Studies in Perception: Festschrift for Fabio Metelli*: 344–373. Aldo Martello-Giunti.

Flores d'Arcais, Giovanni B. (1987): Perceptual factors and word order in event descriptions. In: G. Kempen (ed.), *Natural Language Generation: New Results in Artificial Intelligence, Psychology, and Linguistics*, 441–451. Dordrecht: Martinus Nijhoff.

Forrest, Linda (1996): Discourse goals and attentional processes in sentence production: the dynamic construal of events. In: A. Goldberg (ed.), *Conceptual Structure, Discourse, and Language*, 149–162. Stanford: CSLI Publications.

Gauthier, Isabel, Michael Tarr, Adam Anderson, Pawel Skudlarski, and John Gore (1999): Activation of the middle fusiform 'face area' increases with expertise in recognizing novel objects. *Nature Neuroscience* 2: 568–573.

Givón, T. (1983): *Topic Continuity in Discourse A Quantitative Cross-Language Study.* Amsterdam/Philadelphia: John Benjamins.

Givón, T. (1988): The pragmatics of word order: predictability, importance, and attention. In: M. Hammond, E. A. Moravcsik and J. Wirth (eds.), *Studies in Syntactic Typology*, 243–284. Amsterdam: John Benjamins.

Givón, T. (1992): The grammar of referential coherence as mental processing instructions. *Linguistics* 30: 5–55.

Gleitman, Lila, David January, Rebecca Nappa, and John Trueswell (2007): On the give-and-take between event apprehension and utterance formulation. *Journal of Memory and Language* 57: 544–569.

Gundel, Jeanette (1988a): Universals of topic-comment structure. In: M. Hammond, E. Moravcsik and J. Wirth (eds.), *Studies in Syntactic Typology*, 209–239. Amsterdam: John Benjamins.

Gundel, Jeanette. (1988b): *The Role of Topic and Comment in Linguistic Theory.* New York: Garland.

Hagoort, Peter Colin Brown, and Jolanda Groothusen (1993): The syntactic positive shift as an ERP measure of syntactic processing. *Language and Cognitive Processes* 8: 439–484.

Hahne, Anja and Angela Friederici (1999): Electrophysiological evidence for two steps in syntactic analysis: early automatic and late controlled processes. *Journal of Cognitive Neuroscience* 11(2): 194–205.

Hăjicová, Eva (1984): Topic and focus. In: P. Sgall (ed.), *Contributions to Functional Syntax, Semantics, and Language Comprehension*, 189–202. Amsterdam: John Benjamins.

Halliday, M.A.K. (1967): Notes on transitivity and theme in English (part 2) *Journal of Linguistics* 3: 199–244.

Halliday, M.A.K. (1976): Theme and information in the English clause. In: G. Kress (ed.), *Halliday: System and Function in Language*, 174–188. London: Oxford University Press.

Hwang, Heeju and Elsi Kaiser (2009): The effects of lexical vs. perceptual primes on sentence production in Korean: An on-line investigation of event apprehension and sentence formulation. 22nd CUNY conference on sentence processing. Davis, CA.

Ibbotson, Paul, Elena Lieven, and Michael Tomasello (2013): The attention-grammar interface: Eye-gaze cues structural choice in children and adults. *Cognitive Linguistics* 24(3): 457–481.

Jackendoff, Ray (1996): The architecture of the linguistic-spatial interface. In: P. Bloom, M. Peterson, L. Nadel, and M. Garrett (eds.), *Language and Space*, 1–30. Cambridge: MIT Press.

Jackson, Kyuseek Hwang (2008): The effect of information structure on Korean scrambling. Ph.D. dissertation. Department of Linguistics, University of Hawaii.

Kaiser, Elsi and John Trueswell (2004): The role of discourse context in the processing of a flexible word-order language. *Cognition* 94: 113–147.

Kaiser, Elsi and Virve-Anneli Vihman (2006): Invisible arguments: Effects of demotion in Estonian and Finnish. In: T. Solstad and B. Lyngfelt (eds.), *Demoting the Agent: Passive and Other Voice-Related Phenomena*, 111–141. Amsterdam: John Benjamins.

Kanwisher, Nancy, Josh McDermott, and Marvin Chun (1997): The fusiform face area: A module in extrastriate visual cortex specialized for face perception. *Journal of Neuroscience* 17: 4302–4311.

Kuchinsky, Stephanie and Kathryn Bock (2010): From seeing to saying: Perceiving, planning, producing. 23rd CUNY Sentence Processing Conference. New York.

Lambrecht, Knud (1994): *Information Structure and Sentence Form*. Cambridge: Cambridge University Press.

Landau, Barbara and Ray Jackendoff (1993): "What" and "where" in spatial language and spatial cognition. *Behavioral and Brain Sciences* 16: 217–265.

Langacker, Ronald W. (1987): *Foundations of Cognitive Grammar*, vol. 1: *Theoretical Perspectives*. Stanford: Stanford University Press.

Langacker, Ronald W. (1991): *Foundations of Cognitive Grammar*, vol. 2: *Descriptive Application*. Stanford: Stanford University Press.

Langacker, Ronald W. (this volume): Construal. Berlin/Boston: De Gruyter Mouton.

Levelt, Willem J.M. (1989): *Speaking*. Cambridge: MIT Press.

MacWhinney, Brian (1977): Starting points. *Language* 53(1): 152–168.

MacWhinney, Brian and Elizabeth Bates (1978): Sentential devices for conveying givenness and newness: A cross-cultural developmental study. *Journal of Verbal Learning and Verbal Behavior* 17: 539–558.

Mandler, Jean (1992): How to build a baby: II. Conceptual primitives. *Psychological Review* 99(4): 587–604.

Matthews, Danielle and Grzegorz Krajewski (volume 2): First language acquisition. Berlin/Boston: De Gruyter Mouton.

McCandliss, Bruce, Lauren Cohen, and Stanislas Dehaene (2003): The visual word form area: Expertise for reading in the fusiform gyrus. *Trends in Cognitive Sciences* 7: 293–299.

Melinger, Alissa and Christian Dobel (2005): Lexically-driven syntactic priming. *Cognition* 98: B11–B20.

Myachykov, Andriy (2007): Integrating perceptual, semantic, and syntactic information in sentence production. Ph.D. dissertation, University of Glasgow.

Myachykov, Andriy, Simon Garrod, and Christoph Scheepers (2010): Perceptual priming of syntactic choice during English and Finnish sentence production. In: R. K. Mishra and N. Srinivasan (eds.), *Language and Cognition: State of the Art*, 53–71. Munich: Lincom Europa.

Myachykov, Andriy, Simon Garrod, and Christoph Scheepers (2012): Determinants of syntactic choice in visually-situated sentence production. *Acta Psychologica* 141(3): 304–315.

Myachykov, Andriy, Dominic Thompson, Simon Garrod, and Christoph Scheepers (2012): Referential and visual cues to syntactic choice in sentence production. *Frontiers in Psychology* 2: 396.

Myachykov, Andriy and Russell Tomlin (2008): Perceptual priming and syntactic choice in Russian sentence production. *Journal of Cognitive Science* 9(1): 31–48.

Newman, Aaron, Roumyana Pancheva, Kaori Ozawa, Helen Neville, and Michael Ullman (2001): An event-related fMRI study of syntactic and semantic violations. *Journal of Psycholinguistic Research* 30(3): 339–364.

Newtson, Darren (1973): Attribution and the unit of perception of ongoing behavior. *Journal of Personality and Social Psychology* 28: 28–38.

Newtson, Darren and Gretchen Engquist (1976): The perceptual organization of ongoing behavior. *Journal of Experimental Social Psychology* 12: 436–450.

Newtson, Darren Gretchen Engquist, and Joyce Bois (1977): The objective basis of behavior units. *Journal of Personality and Social Psychology* 35: 847–862.

Osgood, Charles and Kathryn Bock (1977): Salience and sentencing: Some production principles. In: S. Rosenberg (ed.), *Sentence Production: Developments in Research and Theory*, 89–140. Hillsdale: Erlbaum.

Petersen, Steven and Michael Posner (2012): The attention system of the human brain: 20 years after. *Annual Review of Neuroscience* 35: 73–89.

Pickering, Martin and Holly Branigan (1998): The representation of verbs: Evidence from syntactic persistence in language production. *Journal of Memory and Language* 39: 633–651.

Pickering, Martin and Victor Ferreira (2008): Syntactic priming: A critical review. *Psychological Bulletin* 134(3): 427–459.

Posner, Michael (1980): Orienting of attention. *Quarterly Journal of Experimental Psychology* 32: 3–25.

Posner, Michael and Steven Petersen (1990): The attention system of the human brain. *Annual Review of Neuroscience* 13: 25–42.

Posner, Michael and Marcus Raichle (1994): *Images of Mind*. New York: Scientific American Library.

Prat-Sala, Merce and Holly Branigan (2000): Discourse constraints on syntactic processing in language production: A cross-linguistic study in English and Spanish. *Journal of Memory and Language* 42: 168–182.

Prentice, Joan (1967): Effects of cuing actor vs. cuing object on word order in sentence production. *Psychonomic Science* 8: 163–164.

Prince, Ellen (1981): Towards a taxonomy of given-new information. In: P. Cole (ed.), *Radical Pragmatics*, 223–256. New York: Academic Press.

Prince, Ellen (1985): Topicalization and left-dislocation. *Annals of the New York Academy of Sciences* 433: 213–225.

Pulvermüller, Friedemann and Luciano Fadiga (2010): Active perception: sensorimotor circuits as a cortical basis for language. *Nature Reviews Neuroscience* 11(5): 351–360.

Quirk, Randolph, Stanley Greenbaum, Geoffrey Leech, and Jan Svartvik (1985): *A Comprehensive Grammar of the English Language*. London: Longman.

Raichle, Marcus, Julie Fiez, Tom Videen, Ann-Mary McCleod, Jose Pardo, Peter Fox, and Steven Petersen (1994): Practice-related changes in the human brain: functional anatomy during non-motor learning. *Cerebral Cortex* 4: 8–26.

Rasolofo, Andoveloniaina (2006): Malagasy transitive clause types and their functions. Ph.D. dissertation. Department of Linguistics, University of Oregon.

Scheepers, Christoph (2003): Syntactic priming of relative clause attachments: persistence of structural configuration in sentence production. *Cognition* 89: 179–205.

Shaw, Robert E. and John Pittenger (1978): Perceiving change. In: H. Pick, Jr. and E. Saltzman (eds.), *Modes of Perceiving and Processing Information*, 187–204. Hillsdale: Erlbaum.

Siewierska, Anna (1988): The passive in Slavic. In: M. Shibatani (ed.), *Passive and Voice*, 243–289. Amsterdam: John Benjamins.
Sridhar, Shikaripur N. (1988): *Cognition and Sentence Production: A Cross-Linguistic Study*. New York: Springer-Verlag.
Svartvik, Jan (1966): *On Voice in the English Verb*. The Hague/Paris: Mouton and Co.
Talmy, Leonard (1988a): Force dynamics in language and cognition. *Cognitive Science* 12: 49–100.
Talmy, Leonard (1988b): The relation of grammar to cognition. In: B. Rudzka-Ostyn (ed.), *Topics in Cognitive Linguistics*, 165–205. Amsterdam: Benjamins.
Talmy, Leonard (2000a): *Toward a Cognitive Semantics*, Volume 1: *Concept Structuring Systems*. Cambridge: MIT Press.
Talmy, Leonard (2000b): *Toward a Cognitive Semantics*, Volume 2: *Typology and Process in Concept Structuring*. Cambridge: MIT Press.
Talmy, Leonard (2007): Attention phenomena. In: D. Geeraerts and H. Cuyckens (eds.), *The Oxford Handbook of Cognitive Linguistics*, 264–293. London: Oxford University Press.
Tannenbaum, Percy and Frederic Williams (1968): Generation of active and passive sentences as a function of subject and object focus. *Journal of Verbal Learning and Verbal Behavior* 7: 246–250.
Tomlin, Russell (1985): Foreground-background information and the syntax of subordination. *Text* 5: 85–122.
Tomlin, Russell (1994): Functional grammars, pedagogical grammars, and communicative language teaching. In: T. Odlin (ed.), *Perspectives on Pedagogical Grammar*, 140–178. London: Cambridge University Press.
Tomlin, Russell (1995): Focal attention, voice, and word order. In: P. Downing and M. Noonan (eds.) *Word Order in Discourse*, 517–552. Amsterdam: John Benjamins.
Tomlin, Russell (1997): Mapping conceptual representations into linguistic representations: The role of attention in grammar. In: J. Nuyts and E. Pederson (eds.), *Language and Conceptualization*, 162–189. Cambridge: Cambridge University Press.
Tomlin, Russell, Linda Forrest, Ming Ming Pu, and Myung Hee Kim (1997): Discourse semantics. In: T. van Dijk (ed.), *Discourse as Structure and Process*, 63–111. London: Sage.
Tomlin, Russell, Linda Forrest, Ming Ming Pu, and Myung Hee Kim (2010): Discourse semantics. In: T. A. van Dijk (ed.), *Discourse Studies: A Multidisciplinary Introduction*, 78–137. London: Sage.
Turner, Elizabeth Ann and Ragnar Rommetveit (1968): Focus of attention in recall of active and passive sentences. *Journal of Verbal Learning and Verbal Behavior* 7: 543–548.
Vallduvi, Enric (1992): *The Informational Component*. New York: Garland.
Vilkuna, Maria (1989): *Free Word Order in Finnish*. Helsinki: Suomalaisen Kirjallisuuden Seura.
Weil, Henri (1887): *The Order of Words in the Ancient Languages Compared with That of the Modern Languages*. Trans. C. W. Super. Boston: Ginn.
Yarbus, A. L. (1967): *Eye Movements and Vision*. NY: Plenum Press.
Yokoyama, Olga (1986): *Discourse and Word Order*. Amsterdam/Philadelphia: Benjamins.
Yuan, Sylvia and Fisher, Cynthia (2009): "Really? She Blicked the Baby?": Two-year-olds learn combinatorial facts about verbs by listening. *Psychological Science* 20: 619–626.
Zemskaja, Elena (1979): *Russkaja razgovornaja rečʼ: lingvističeskij analiz i problemy obučenija* [Russian colloquial speech: A linguistic analysis and teaching difficulties]. Moskva: Russkij Jazyk.

Dagmar Divjak and Catherine L. Caldwell-Harris
Chapter 3: Frequency and entrenchment

After half a century of self-imposed exile from the cognitive scene, cognitive linguists are putting language back on stage: language is no longer considered a highly specialized and largely autonomous cognitive module, needing special treatment. Instead, cognitive linguists endorse a sophisticated view of learning and memory-based processing. Key to this is the assumption that frequency-sensitive learning results in mental representations optimized for a particular environment. Human beings appear to extract frequency information automatically from their environment (see review in Ellis 2002). Both infants and adults use statistical properties of linguistic input to discover structure, including sound patterns, words and the beginnings of grammar (Saffran et al. 1996). This allows children to learn and adults to refine a probabilistic grammar grounded in our language experience (Diessel 2007; MacWhinney 1998; Saffran 2003).

Whether frequency-sensitive learning really constrains theories of the language faculty remains controversial, however (for an overview of the debate to date, see Lieven 2010; Ambridge and Lieven 2011; Evans 2014; Matthews and Krajewski volume 2), and there is a lack of understanding as far as the mechanics are concerned. As recently as 2010, Schmid (2010: 125) concluded his chapter on the relation between frequency in the text and entrenchment in the mind by saying that "so far we have understood neither the nature of frequency itself nor its relation to entrenchment, let alone come up with a convincing way of capturing either one of them or the relation between them in quantitative terms".

We are less pessimistic. In the current chapter we survey new perspectives on frequency and show how and when frequency-sensitive learning may result in mental representations or memories that vary in robustness and efficiency.[1]

---

[1] In order to present a coherent narrative in the space available, we have had to omit many relevant papers in the corpus- psycho- and neuro-linguistic traditions. We hope that readers with backgrounds in these areas will understand that these omissions are consequences of the space limitations imposed, and that readers who are new to these approaches can use the references that we have supplied to find the many interesting studies that we could not cover here. We thank Hans-Jörg Schmid and two further anonymous reviewers of our chapter for their thoughtful comments and suggestions for improvement.

Dagmar Divjak, University of Birmingham, UK
Catherine L. Caldwell-Harris, Boston University, USA

https://doi.org/10.1515/9783110626476-004

Perspectives from both experimental psychology and cognitive linguistics are integrated, with the aim of providing a review that will facilitate future research. We start with the origins of the interest in frequency in cognitive psychology and its interpretation and application in linguistics (section 1). We then present how the concept of entrenchment has been interpreted in theoretical linguistics, and review the cognitive and neural mechanisms supporting language structures that vary in entrenchment (section 2). In section 3 we discuss new directions, controversial issues and open questions.

1 What is frequency?

In experimental psychology, frequency is a practical term that was, and still is, used to capture how frequently a stimulus (such as a word or a phrase) is encountered and processed in the environment.[2] Within psycholinguistics and cognitive linguistics, frequency most often refers to the number of times a particular chunk of language (such as a phoneme, word, or phrase) occurs in a specified environment. Frequency is typically used in a relative sense, to categorize some stimuli as being more or less prevalent in the environment than other stimuli.

Frequencies can be obtained in a variety of ways. Some approaches yield subjective results, e.g., asking speakers to estimate frequency of use for a range of language stimuli on a Likert scale from, for example, never encountered to encountered several times a day (Balota et al. 2001). Other approaches yield objective results and rely on counting occurrence of types of stimuli using computer-readable databases or corpora (see also section 1.4). Historically, most corpora have been drawn from printed text, given the difficulty of transcribing spoken conversations (e.g., Francis and Kucera 1982; Davies 2010), yet many written and spoken corpora now exist in diverse languages (see http://tiny.cc/corpora for an overview).[3]

---

[2] Because frequency is known to exert a strong influence on processing speed, psycholinguists need to avoid the "confound of frequency" and thus routinely match their experimental items for frequency when comparing reaction times to different categories of words or other language structures.

[3] A creative approach to obtaining a large corpus based on spoken language is SUBTL, a large database of frequency norms based on a corpus of subtitles from TV and films (Brysbaert and New 2009). Subjective frequency measures are known to correlate moderately to highly with counts from corpora (Balota et al. 2001; Caldwell-Harris et al. 2012). Using frequency counts based on a large database of subtitles from TV and films results in higher correlations with processing times than do frequencies from texts (Brysbaert and New 2009). This substantiates

We first describe the standard ways in which frequency is measured in linguistics. We then provide an overview of frequency effects, i.e., how human beings react differently to higher frequency stimuli compared to lower frequency stimuli. Finally, we draw attention to a range of measures that can help shed light on how frequency effects are rooted in basic brain mechanisms; these measures have been developed within corpus-based and computational approaches but have not (yet) made it into mainstream Cognitive Linguistics.

1.1 Type versus token frequency

Research on frequency in linguistics was given an impetus by the pioneering work of Joan Bybee and collaborators who distinguished between type and token frequencies. The distinction between type and token frequency is important because these two types of frequencies play different roles in the productivity of linguistic structures (Bybee and Thompson 2000).

Token frequency refers to how often a particular form appears in the input, e.g., all instances of the past tense form of *read*, but excluding the present tense form (even though it is spelled identically). Type frequency refers to the number of distinct items that are used in or within the structure of interest "whether it is a word-level construction for inflection or a syntactic construction specifying the relation among words" (Ellis 2002: 166). An example is the number of verbs that create their past-tense by changing an *-ow* form to *-ew*, as in *throw → threw, blow → blew, grow → grew*.

Token frequency facilitates learning via repetition. The more often a particular token is experienced, the easier it becomes to access and use (Bybee and Hopper 2001). Because it comes with ease of access and use, token frequency can be a conservative force that protects high-frequency structures from analogical leveling.

In contrast to the effects of high type frequency, high token frequency promotes the entrenchment or conservation of irregular forms and idioms; the irregular forms survive because they are high in frequency, which means they are encountered and processed more often (although an irregular form can also survive because it is highly similar to a high frequency item, e.g., *behold, forsake*). Type frequency can also guide learners to create a category out of a type (Bybee 1995; Bybee and Hopper 2001). According to Bybee and Thompson (2000), there are three reasons for this:

---

the intuition that how words occur in dialogue is a more representative measure of their entrenchment than is their frequency of occurrence in written text.

a) the more lexical items that are heard in a certain position in a construction, the less likely it is that the construction is associated with a particular lexical item and the more likely it is that a general category is formed over the items that occur in that position
b) the more items the category must cover, the more general are its criterial features and the more likely it is to extend to new items
c) high type frequency ensures that a construction is used frequently, thus strengthening its representational schema and making it more accessible for further use with new items.

1.2 How can frequency influence processing?

The study of frequency effects has its origin in the seminal psychological research of Cattell (1886). Cattell was the first to demonstrate the word frequency effect, i.e., that higher frequency words are recognized more quickly than lower frequency words. Since the development of the information processing paradigm in psychology in the 1960s–1980s, it has become accepted that frequency is among the most robust predictors of human performance in general (Hasher and Zacks 1984; Howes and Solomon 1951). Human beings are also surprisingly good at providing frequency estimates for a range of language stimuli, suggesting that accumulating frequency information occurs automatically (Hasher and Zacks 1984; Jurafsky 1996; Saffran 2003).

Frequency effects have been found in virtually every subdomain of language that has been studied. Comprehensive reviews of frequency and its effects on first and second language learning, representation and change now exist (Sedlmeier and Betsch 2002; Ellis 2002; Diessel 2007; Blumenthal-Drame 2012; Gries and Divjak 2012; Divjak and Gries 2012; Hilpert volume 2). Given these reviews, we will focus on providing a taxonomy of types of frequency effects, to set the stage for explaining these effects as the result of frequency-sensitive learning.

1.2.1 Types of frequency effects

It has been most common to study frequency effects using single isolated words, and indeed, the (single) word frequency effect is one of the most robust findings in experimental psychology (Monsell 1991). Frequency effects have also been found for phonemes, morphemes and multi-word expressions, and have been attested for items across the low to high frequency range although less research exists on the former (but see Bannard and Matthews 2008; Caldwell-Harris et al. 2012; Snider and Arnon 2012; Divjak 2017 for recent work on these effects in low frequency structures). Although most of our citations below concern the (single) word frequency effect, note that usage-based linguists propose single-system models and predict frequency effects for all linguistic units: simple and complex, lexical and grammatical.

Frequency effects have been demonstrated for at least four types of behavior:

Faster and easier processing. Using the paradigm of perceptual identification, high frequency words are identified more quickly than low frequency words (Whaley 1978; Monsell 1991). In natural reading using eye-tracking, readers' eye fixations are usually shorter for more frequent words, suggesting greater ease at obtaining the meaning and integrating it with sentence context (Rayner and Duffy 1986).

More accurate processing. Retrieving high frequency items is less subject to error than retrieving low frequency items (Balota et al. 2012; Howes and Solomon 1951; MacKay 1982). When participants are asked to name visually displayed words, a common error is to produce the high-frequency orthographic neighbor of a low frequency target word, as in the case of uttering '*blue*' for the target '*blur*' (Grainger 1990). Analogous errors are made in spoken word tasks.

Resistance to noise. In visual displays containing ink blots or obscured letters, high frequency words are more accurately detected (McClelland and Rumelhart 1981). In the spoken domain, high frequency words are recognized more accurately when embedded in noise (Pollack et al. 1959).

Resilience to brain damage and aging. As semantic dementia progresses from mild to severe, patients have increasing difficulty naming low frequency objects, such as rare animals and items of furniture (Rogers and McClelland 2004). Naming of specific attributes of objects is impaired before naming of more general attributes.

In addition to the behavioral effects of frequency listed above, the neural signatures that accompany language processing vary for high and low frequency stimuli. Event-related potentials (ERPs) measure brain electrical activity that is time-locked to presentation of a word or other linguistic stimulus. A great deal is now known about how wave forms vary for lexical attributes such as word concreteness, word class, semantic ambiguity, and word frequency (Van Petten 1993). Bigram/trigram frequencies appear to influence the ERP wave form as early as 90 ms after the word is displayed (using single word presentations; Hauk et al. 2006). Lexical (word) frequency has its effect slightly later, at 110 ms post-stimulus onset (Lee and Federmeier 2012). Lexical status, operationalized in these studies as the word/pseudo word distinction, does not influence wave forms until 160 ms, simultaneously with the effects of semantic coherence of a word's morphological family. Researchers have inferred that words that are high in frequency also tend to be orthographically regular and contain frequent sub-lexical units. The word frequency effect at 110 ms is thus best understood as reflecting sensitivity to orthographic and possibly morphological regularities. In addition, different types of information are believed to be organized in cascades with interactive feedback (Hauk et al. 2006; Rogers and McClelland 2004). We will return to ERP findings later when discussing the role of context in frequency and entrenchment.

1.2.2 Are frequency effects causal?

The frequency with which words occur is strongly correlated with other characteristics (Cutler 1981). Highly frequent words tend to be short in length, concrete rather than abstract, easily imaginable, and have early age-of-acquisition (Whaley 1978). Word frequency also correlates positively with many lexical attributes that have been quantified from corpora, such as orthographic neighborhood density, syntactic family size, noun-verb ratio and number of meanings (Balota et al. 2012; Baayen 2010; Cutler 1981).

Researchers have long suspected that these correlated factors, rather than the extent to which people have been exposed to words, may contribute to the processing advantage found. To determine how increased usage itself may be responsible for frequency effects, researchers have tried to identify people who could reasonably be expected to have different usage histories. One method has been to compare the lexical processing by persons from different occupations or social groups. In a lexical decision study using nurses, law students and engineers, each group responded more quickly to words relevant to their area of expertise (Gardner et al. 1987). This finding at the word-level was replicated for phrases. Religious Jews have faster processing of religious phrases than secular Jews (Caldwell-Harris et al. 2012). These findings establish that at least part of the frequency effect is due to language users' actual experience with those words and phrases.

1.3 Is it contextual diversity that causes "frequency" effects?

The standard meaning of frequency, and the one we assumed above, is the frequency with which a stimulus is repeated in the environment. This can be called frequency$_{rep}$. Over the last decade, evidence has accumulated that factors which are highly correlated with frequency$_{rep}$ are more strongly correlated with behavioral outcomes than frequency$_{rep}$ itself. One of these factors is the typical context of occurrence of words (Adelman et al. 2006; Brysbaert and New 2009; McDonald and Shillcock 2001).

The discovery of the powerful effect of "contextual diversity" (CD) emerged from data-mining large corpora to extract frequency counts and other values associated with words. Because many words are part of multi-word utterances, researchers sought to understand how much of lexical learning is contextual in nature. McDonald and Shillcock (2001) used principle component analysis over vectors to measure target words' contexts, while Adelman et al. (2006) simply used the number of passages or documents in which words occurred. Even when using this very crude way to operationalize "context", contextual diversity (CD) predicted more variance in lexical decision and naming latencies than did frequency$_{rep}$, suggesting that CD is the psychologically more relevant variable.

Research on explanations for frequency effects turned another corner with Jones et al. (2012) claim that what really facilitates lexical processing is semantic diversity. Like Adelman et al. (2006), they counted the number of distinct documents in which a word occurred but defined the similarity of any pair of documents as a function of the proportion of overlapping words in those two documents. A word's semantic distinctiveness was defined as the mean dissimilarity over all of the documents in which it occurred. When used to predict lexical decision and naming times from the Balota et al. (2007) English lexicon database, semantic distinctiveness predicted more variance in response times than word frequency and contextual distinctiveness.

1.4 Contextualized frequency measures

As discussed, psycholinguists have spent decades focusing on word form (token) frequency, and only in the last years have explored alternatives to frequency$_{rep}$ such as contextual diversity. In contrast, among corpus linguists, context has always been a salient issue, and linguists have worked on capturing context in more sophisticated ways. In the section below, we discuss measuring phrase frequency, conditional probabilities, and relational measures from the perspective of corpus linguistics.

Work on lexicography rarely used counts of the occurrence of an individual word form in isolation. This is because words may express different meanings depending on the context. Classical concordances return a list of usage examples of the item of interest and count its number of occurrences. Words are thus typically examined in their phrasal or sentential context. Indeed, collocations, i.e., words that are regularly used together giving rise to an association, and colligations, where a lexical item is linked to a grammatical one, are important concepts in corpus linguistics (McEnery and Hardie 2012: 122–123). Raw frequencies do not provide a reliable way of distinguishing collocates objectively from frequent non-collocates. The combination of *the* and *review* will be rather frequent due to the frequency of *the*, but *the review* is not a collocation; *peer review*, on the other hand, is. To address this issue collocation scores were calculated that compare expected to observed frequencies to establish whether the observed frequency of co-occurrence is greater than what one would expect to find by chance given the frequencies with which each of the words that form the pair occur. Readers familiar with corpus linguistics will have encountered the terms Mutual Information (MI), T-score (Church and Hanks 1990) and Log-likelihood ratio score (or G2, developed by Dunning 1993). The number of association measures available within computational corpus linguistics has grown rapidly over the last decades and we refer to Evert (2005) and Pecina (2009) for exhaustive inventories.

Within linguistics, these mathematically complex measures that capture the strength of association between two items have been perceived to be "so technical that even linguists who had applied them with some success admitted they were not able to see behind the formulas and to interpret the actual linguistic significance" (Schmid 2010: 107). This led Schmid to create conceptually simpler collostructional measures, attraction and reliance (Schmid 2000: 54). Schmid's measures were designed to capture the interaction between nouns and constructions (rather than the association between two words). They take into consideration the linguistic relation between a so-called node and its collocate, be it another word or a construction, but do not compare observed with expected frequencies. Attraction and reliance were therefore soon supplemented by a set of collostruction techniques (Stefanowitsch and Gries 2003) that pair respect for the relation between a node and its collocate(s) with significance testing. Whether or not statistical significance testing is a desirable property of association measures remains a topic of debate (Schmid and Kuchenhoff 2013; Gries 2013; Divjak under review; Levshina under review).

Corpus linguists have also developed measures of contextual diversity, using the label "dispersion". Dispersion quantifies the homogeneity of the distribution of a word in a corpus (Lyne 1985). Gries (2008, 2010) provides an overview of dispersion measures, including those that penalize words for not occurring uniformly across a corpus. Behavioral data in this area is scarce, but Baayen (2010) shows that dispersion (defined as number of texts in which a word appears) is the second best single predictor of response latencies, after frequency-as-repetition but before contextual diversity (defined as percentage of films containing the word). Although frequency emerges as the best single predictor, frequency of occurrence, in the sense of pure repetition, is not a particularly important predictor in itself, but is instead highly correlated with a number of other factors. It is also interesting to note that dispersion appears to be highly correlated with word frequency ($r = 0.82$ reported by McDonald and Shillcock 2001; see also Baayen 2010).

Computational psycholinguists have argued that conditional probabilities (defined as the likelihood to encounter a word given it context, for example)[4] are more appropriate than frequencies for explaining language processing in general. Jurafsky (1996) showed that a probabilistic model differs in its predictions from the frequency-based models traditional in psycholinguistics, with true probabilities essential for a cognitive model of sentence processing (cf. Saffran et al. 1996 who showed that infants use transitional probabilities to segment speech and detect word boundaries). The usefulness of probabilities has been well-known within information-theory, where measures such as entropy and surprisal have been developed. Entropy is a measure of the unpredictability of information content: something that is predictable has low entropy, whereas something that is unpredictably has high entropy. In a similar vein, the surprise ratio, also called "suprisal" (Barlow 1990), measures how unexpected a sequence is, given the probabilities of its components.[5] Suprisal has been used in psycholinguistic models (Hale 2001; Levy 2008; Jaeger 2010; Fernandez Monsalve et al. 2012) and in computational emergentist models (e.g., ADIOS, see Solan et al. 2005).

Contextualized frequency yields better predictions than isolated frequencies, even for low frequency words, and this can be expected: the brain makes use of learned contextual regularities. Seminal studies from the 1970s, such as Biederman et al. (1973), demonstrated already that objects are recognized faster and more accurately when accompanied by contextual information. Although for most research purposes, frequency$_{rep}$ should still be adequate for statistically equating stimuli, it is useful to be aware of alternative measures, since they help address the question of how frequency effects are obtained and are rooted in basic brain mechanisms, a topic addressed later in this chapter.

2 What is entrenchment?

Entrenchment was introduced to Cognitive Linguistics as a theoretical construct by Langacker (1987). Langacker used the term entrenchment to explain how

---

[4] Relative frequencies are conditional probabilities calculated on the basis of one sample only and can be treated as conditional probabilities given a sufficient level of faith in the representativeness of the sample.
[5] Hale (2001) showed that the difficulty of a word is proportional to its surprisal (its negative log-probability) in the context within which it appears.

linguistic structures are created and shaped through use. A key objective of cognitive linguistics is to determine whether and how the structure of language can result from patterns of usage. It was thus an important step in the foundational writings by cognitive linguists to discuss how linguistic patterns are mentally encoded, and how these representations vary with usage. In this section, we review what cognitive linguists mean by entrenchment and connect their theoretical ideas with contemporary views of learning and memory.

2.1 Cognitive linguists' characterizations of entrenchment

In his seminal book, *Foundations of Cognitive Grammar*, Langacker (1987: 59) made the case for a

> continuous scale of entrenchment in cognitive organization. Every use of a structure has a positive impact on its degree of entrenchment, whereas extended periods of disuse have a negative impact. With repeated use, a novel structure becomes progressively entrenched, to the point of becoming a unit; moreover, units are variably entrenched depending on the frequency of their occurrence.

Langacker's definition of entrenchment focuses on the role of entrenchment for representation, looking at the storage and organization of structures in our mental inventory. Langacker's characterization of entrenchment is noteworthy on two accounts: it states explicitly that 1) increasing frequency of occurrence deepens entrenchment and that 2) increasing entrenchment can lead to qualitative differences in representation, as when a frequently co-occurring sequence becomes a unit in memory. In other words, it suggests that an increase in frequency deepens entrenchment, and that at a certain point entrenchment may lead to unitization.

Bybee's (2007: 324; cf. also 2007: 10, 279) characterization also emphasizes how repeated use leads to unitization, but she additionally refers to the processing characteristics of automatization and increased fluency or fluidity: "Each token of use of a word or sequence of words strengthens its representation and makes it more easily accessed. In addition, each instance of use further automates and increases the fluency of the sequence, leading to fusion of the units". Important in this second definition is the addition that a number of separate entities can fuse into one larger unit, a phenomenon known as fusion or chunking. Chunk status implies that the unit can be retrieved from mental storage as a whole rather than by accessing the individual component parts and parsing them on the basis of rules or schemas (see also De Smet and Cuyckens 2007: 188).

Blumenthal-Drame (2012: 68 f.) developed a working definition of entrenchment for her neuroimaging study of multimorphemic words. For this, she drew on concepts of gradedness, fluency, and unitization:[6]

> [h]igher token frequencies in usage will correlate with a gradual increase in ease of processing, more precisely enhanced fluidity in composition or parsing. At some point, this process will lead to a new, holistic representation. After this point, facilitation – more precisely, ease of retrieval ... – will still continue to increase as a function of frequency.

Blumenthal-Drame (2012) argued that, crucially, these continuous properties seem to be related to processing, that is to changes in the use of stored entities, rather than the inventory of stored entities, as they imply that the process of fusing separate entities becomes easier and more fluid. She concluded that "entrenchment must be seen as a multi-layered phenomenon which is modulated by several stimulus variables and which affects different inter-related yet relatively independent processing dimensions at the same time" (Blumenthal-Drame 2012: 193).

Croft and Cruse (2004: 292) had already stressed the idea that with increasing use, structures continue to accrue representational strength and increase in automaticity, stating that "entrenchment comes in degrees, even beyond the minimum threshold required for independent storage".

From this brief survey, the family resemblance structure among the various characterizations of entrenchment becomes apparent. What these characterizations have in common is the belief that entrenchment refers to a process of strengthening memory representations. This may result in a general reduction in processing effort (automatization), gestalt formation ("unitization" à la Langacker) and/or chunking accompanied by formal reduction ("fusion" à la Bybee).[7]

Trying to define entrenchment in theory alone does not seem useful, however, and we now turn to some empirical work on the topic. Within usage-based linguistics proper, most empirical work on entrenchment has been carried out by acquisitionists. A classic question in language acquisition is how children construct grammatical categories and rules when adults rarely correct childrens' grammatical errors, an issue related to poverty of the stimulus arguments

---

[6] There is some terminological proliferation in the entrenchment literature, with several terms pointing in the same direction, i.e., fluency, processing ease, automatization and routinization. We have opted for the term "fluency" to capture both ease in producing and comprehending speech.

[7] There are also linguists who see entrenchment as a cognitive process to be distinguished from the societal process of conventionalization (Schmid 2010; Mukherjee 2005).

(Pullum and Scholz 2002). According to Braine and Brooks (1995), attending to frequently occurring constructions can mitigate the lack of negative evidence. They propose the "entrenchment hypothesis": repeated presentations of a verb in particular constructions (e.g., *The rabbit disappeared*) cause the child to probabilistically infer that the verb cannot be used in non-attested constructions (e.g., **The magician disappeared the rabbit*). Learning from positive evidence will create verb-argument structures which have a strength proportional to how often a verb has been heard with that argument structure (this line of inquiry is taken further by work on statistical pre-emption, see Goldberg 2011; Boyd and Goldberg 2011; Casenhiser and Bencini volume 3; see Ambridge et al. (2013: 49–55) for a comparison of entrenchment with pre-emption).

An implication of this view is that when an argument structure has been learned to a stable level of entrenchment, it will pre-empt alternatives, unless they have been independently witnessed. A second implication is that overgeneralizations will be less common, and will subjectively feel less acceptable for high frequency verbs than for semantically-matched lower frequency verbs. For example, **The magician vanished the rabbit* feels slightly more acceptable than **The magician disappeared the rabbit*, since this inference from absence is stronger for the higher-frequency verb *disappeared*. Ambridge (2013) confirmed that children were more accepting of low frequency verbs being used in novel high frequency constructions, than of high frequency verbs being used in alternative constructions. For alternating ones, such as the dative and locative constructions, the effects were less pervasive (see Ambridge and Lieven 2011: 252–254). This leaves open the question of how speakers deal with newly witnessed or rarely attested alternatives: since they have been independently witnessed they should no longer be pre-empted on a strict entrenchment account.

Like other researchers, Braine and Brooks (1995: 368) did not take a stance on the precise quantitative relation between representational strength and frequency of usage. They merely note that with age there appears to be an increase in flexibility in switching between sentence constructions to meet conversational demands (e.g., to have particular arguments as subject or as object). Our contribution here will therefore be to draw insights about learning and memory from cognitive psychology, so that cognitive psychology can underpin Cognitive Linguistics.

2.2 Entrenchment: what learning does to the brain

To be maximally helpful to linguists who want to draw on insights from cognitive science and learning, we suggest a working definition of the relation between frequency and entrenchment. Frequency facilitates language processing because the available mental representations have been shaped by frequency-sensitive learning. As such, they are prepared to process stimuli that vary widely in their probability of occurrence in the environment (Elman 1993; Saffran et al. 1996). From a cognitive science perspective, mental representations can be considered stable attractors in the brain's dynamic neural networks (MacWhinney 1998). These dynamic patterns vary along a continuum of strength of representation.

2.2.1 The neurocognitive basis of entrenchment

How are "strong" representations (or "deep attractors") mentally represented differently from weaker representations? There are several ways to conceive of representational strength, as has been done via modeling in artificial neural networks (Rogers and McClelland 2004). Strength of representations can correspond to heavily weighted connections from some input features to processing units inside the networks' architecture. There can also be large numbers of connections, and more redundant connections. Weighted connections between processing units are functionally akin to neurons' dendrites and axons. Specific links between processing units that frequently match inputs to their expected outputs are strengthened, inspired by the Hebbian learning principle (Hebb 1949) in neuroscience that "neurons that fire together wire together".

It may seem odd to equate entrenched linguistic forms with something as prosaic as "memory". But entrenched forms must be memories (Bar 2011; Daelemans and Van den Bosch 2005). Memories capture information that has been encoded and can influence future processing; there is no requirement for memories to be conscious or to be recallable. This is clear from the classic distinction between declarative and procedural memories, also termed explicit and implicit memory. Declarative memories are those for which we have conscious recognition, including episodic memories. For language stimuli, we may be able to consciously recall autobiographical episodes when a specific word or phrase was used. Or we can have recognition memory – and be able to reliably confirm that a phrase such as "about which" is familiar and we have likely used it thousands of times. We can also confirm that the phrase "which about" is not familiar and indeed we may never have used it; it is highly unlikely to exist as an entrenched unit (Caldwell-Harris et al. 2012).

2.2.2 Is there a threshold number of occurrences required for entrenchment?

The cognitive science perspective provides a framework for thinking about some of the outstanding questions in the relationship between frequency and entrenchment. It is commonly assumed that a stimulus sequence needs to be encountered a certain number of times before it becomes unitized (i.e., encoded as such in memory). According to this view, once complex stimuli are encoded as units, their mental representations grow in strength as a function of experience. This common view lacks empirical support (Gurevich et al. 2010). Researchers have not been able to find evidence of what might be a frequency threshold for multimorphemic or multiword utterances. Alegre and Gordon (1999) have proposed a threshold of 6 occurrences per million words for inflected forms, but frequency effects have been observed well below that threshold (Baayen et al. 1997; Baayen et al. 2007; Blumenthal-Drame 2012; Arnon and Snider 2010; Caldwell-Harris et al. 2012, Divjak 2017), and are found for all frequency ranges for morphologically simple controls (Alegre and Gordon 1999).

A second counterargument is logical. If a single exposure is below the threshold where a counter begins accruing evidence, then the counter of exposures remains set to 0, and logically no experience can accrue (Gurevich et al. 2010). It may be more fruitful to assume that evidence accrues from the first exposure, but that speakers cannot formulate reliable hypotheses until sufficient evidence has accumulated: Divjak (2017) finds frequency effects for rare lexico-syntactic combinations in Polish (< .66 pmw) but shows that these effects are driven by words that themselves occur at least 6 times pmw. Erker and Guy (2012) propose to think of frequency as a gate-keeper or potentiator: some constraints on subject personal pronoun use in Spanish are activated or amplified by high frequency. This is expected on a probabilistic approach to language, and can also be explained by what we know from memory research, in particular from research on how information is transferred from immediate working memory to long term memory.

2.2.3 The role of procedural and declarative memory systems

Memory for specific episodes is believed to be part of the declarative memory system, mediated by the hippocampus and medial temporal structures (Cohen and Squire 1980). The declarative memory system performs one-trial learning, but such information is subject to rapid decay. Recurring events are learned via the procedural system, mediated by neocortical structures (Gupta 2012). Here, slow learning allows information to be incrementally integrated into long term memory structures, where they have rich associations with many patterns, facilitating generalization and abstraction.

Connectionist models have been used to describe how human languages draw on both the procedural and declarative systems for learning (Gupta 2012; Rogers and McClelland 2004). The procedural system is most efficient at encoding systematic mappings using distributed representations. In distributed representations, multiple patterns are stored across the same set of processing units, allowing for extraction of regularities. Novel patterns can be rapidly learned via minor changes to the weighted connections in the network, but these minor changes will typically be overwritten again as soon as new patterns come in.

Learning unique arbitrary mappings, such as the link between word forms and meanings, can be done if sparse or localist representations are used, since the patterns won't interfere with each other. It has been proposed that hippocampal structures use sparse representational structures to implement arbitrary associations, including episodic and short-term memories (Rogers and McClelland 2004). Arbitrary associations can be permanently learned only with considerable exposure/training. Theorists propose that with continued rehearsal and learning, these associations are gradually displaced from the fast-learning hippocampal system and integrated into the neocortical procedural system.

Learning lexical items, morphological patterns and syntactic constructions is complex and relies on the integration of these two brain systems (see Gupta 2012 for a review). Learning a new morphological variant can usually be handled by the procedural system because it involves minor adjustments to established sound-to-motor patterns. Novel mappings, such as learning to pronounce a foreign word or learning someone's name, require creating new pathways between inputs and outputs, and thus may be initially stored as part of episodic memory. If that novel information is never encountered again, the weighted connections that represent it will be overwritten as new patterns are encountered. But if that stimulus is repeatedly encountered, each exposure provides another training trial in which it can be integrated into long-term memory structures in the neocortex.

2.2.4 Encoding in context

Appreciation is growing that language processing has more in common with memory retrieval than has previously been assumed (Adelman et al. 2006; see also the computational linguistic project called memory based learning [MBL], Daelemans and Bosch 2005).

The brain mechanisms that underlie entrenchment specify a major role for repeated experience, whether it is overt experience in the environment, or mental rehearsal during silent rumination. The best recall is for material that has been encountered at varying times and locations (i.e., in separated contexts).[8]

---

[8] This is the same finding as from the educational literature, where cramming for a test yields less enduring learning than do spaced study periods (Carpenter et al. 2012).

To explain why words with high contextual diversity are recognized more quickly, Adelman et al. (2006) turned to research on the advantage of spaced exposures for long-lasting learning (Anderson and Schooler 1991). Exposures that are widely spaced in time and occur in different contexts have the strongest impact on learning. The reason is that repeated stimuli that re-occur immediately may be processed as if they were a single episode, because of the phenomenon of repetition suppression (Grill-Spector et al. 2006). When a word (or other stimulus) is presented twice in rapid succession, the second occurrence is considered "primed" – it is more easily processed compared to following an unrelated stimulus (Lee and Federmeir 2012). But this ease-of-recognition brings with it reduced neural activation. This repetition suppression plausibly results in less opportunity for strengthening connections, meaning that less learning (and less entrenchment) occurs for items that are encountered repeatedly in a short period of time. Not surprisingly, people have the poorest recall for "massed practice", meaning training on items that are encountered within a defined time period, or in a single, predictable context, as is typical of classroom academic learning. High frequency$_{rep}$ thus does not in and of itself ensure integration into long term memory structures.

Another relevant line of thought comes from the perspective of "rational analysis of memory", which posits that it is adaptive from an evolutionary perspective to only encode items which are likely to reoccur in the future (Anderson and Schooler 1991). Indeed, a view from evolutionary and cognitive psychology is that the purpose of memory is not to remember past events, but to have mental resources to guide future action (Bar 2011). The greater the diversity of environments in which something has occurred in the past, the more probable is it to reoccur in the future. Simple frequency$_{rep}$ therefore strengthens an item's representation less than if the item was experienced in a different context.

Effects of contextual diversity appear to arise naturally in a learning model that includes context. Baayen (2010) found that contextual diversity is an emergent property of a computational model originally developed to explain morphological processing, the naive discriminative reader (NDR; see also Baayen this volume). In the NDR model lexical meanings are learned from contextually rich input.[9] These are letter bigrams and trigrams drawn from a window of four

---

[9] The NDR model shares some features with connectionist models, using an error-driving learning algorithm to map from inputs (representations of letters) to outputs (representations of meanings). It differs from connectionist models by using straightforward symbolic representations for letters, letter pairs and meanings. It only uses one forward pass of activation, with weights set on links computed from corpus-derived co-occurrence matrices.

words rather than from words in isolation. The activation of a meaning on a given trial is obtained by summing the weights from the active letters and letter pairs to that meaning. The NDR model correctly predicted a range of morphological phenomena and showed contextual diversity effects. The contextual diversity accounted for substantially more variance in word recognition efficiency than did word frequency. Another success of the model was that it also predicted phrase frequency effects (Baayen and Hendrix 2011), which are known to be quite robust (Arnon and Snider 2010). Other computational models, such as the memory based learning approach (Daelemans and Bosch 2005) have likewise reported that token frequencies of linguistic patterns do not enhance classification accuracy.

3 Continuing controversies and open questions

In this final section, we highlight a few of the controversies and open questions concerning frequency and entrenchment within Cognitive Linguists. In our view, entrenchment is best thought of as the procedure that gives rise to mental representations through frequency sensitive learning. These mental representations are effectively memories, and thus concepts from current work on memory apply. Taking a broader cognitive science perspective also has the advantage of offering new points of view for two commonly asked questions about the relationship between frequency and entrenchment.

3.1 What can be entrenched?

A frequently asked question is: what can be entrenched? Single words, complex phrases, lexical items, abstract schemas? If entrenched expressions are mental representations of language forms which are either implicit or explicit memories, then, yes, all of these can be entrenched. The more difficult question is whether entrenchment necessarily implies chunking and chunk storage

It has been common practice to view frequency effects as proof of the existence of mental representations. If frequency effects were found for a specific morpheme sequence, then researchers felt justified in viewing that morpheme sequence to be mentally represented as a discrete unit. For example, Blumenthal-Drame concluded from her study of the processing of multimorphemic words that "[...] the effects of token frequency at different levels of language description attest to the necessity of positing full storage of tokens, irrespective of whether they are complex or simple" (2012: 193; cf. also Bannard and Matthews 2008; Arnon and Snider 2010).

Recent computational modeling casts doubts on the wisdom of these assumptions. Baayen's (2010; 2011) naive discriminative learner model contained no representations corresponding to whole words or phrases, only letter unigrams and bigrams (see also Baayen this volume). The model nevertheless showed frequency effects for multi-word units. Based on this demonstration, Baayen (2011) argued that specific morpheme sequences (including multiword expressions) show frequency effects: the model develops its own representations that are frequency sensitive, as a by-product of learning form-to-meaning mappings that vary in frequency.

3.2 Can we resolve the tension between storage and computation?

Another take on this problem comes from the discussion about the relationship between storage and computation. It continues to be debated whether frequency effects are observed because a frequent multimorphemic word or multiword expression is stored as a unit or whether its pieces are more rapidly assembled.

Blumenthal-Drame argued that "[...] highly independent representations will be holistically retrieved rather than analytically processed" (2012: 187). Tremblay et al. (2011: 595) provided evidence for holistic storage but noted at the same time that behavioral research may not be able to distinguish between holistic retrieval and speeded online computation. Other researchers have suggested that the tension between storage and computation is unnecessary. Shaoul proposed that "this graded effect of probability [...] is a side-effect of the emergent nature of n-gram processing" (2012: 171).

In other words, the neural patterns which mediate language processing contain expectations of how patterns will be completed. Any given syllable encountered in a speech stream activates expectations for a subset of all possible syllables based on prior processing (Elman 1993; Baayen and Hendrix 2011). Expectations are activated quickly and effortlessly, as if the predicted sequence was stored separately as a ready-made unit (see Baayen this volume). This view of expectation generation and processing rather than chunk storage is consistent with the workings of a probabilistic grammar. Given this, and the fact that frequency effects have been observed where they were not expected (section 3.1), we would not subscribe to the view that frequency effects are evidence of or reliable diagnostics of unit storage.

3.3 Which frequency measure is ideal for predicting entrenchment?

A key question that has received attention only recently (Divjak 2008; Wiechmann 2008; Gries 2013; Schmid and Kuchenhoff 2013; Divjak 2017; Levshina 2015) is which frequency measure or family of measures is best suited to predict entrenchment? Do different frequency measures correlate with different incarnations of entrenchment (as summarized in section 2.1)? Issues that are currently debated in assessments of the usefulness of existing frequency measures include the uni- or bi-directionality of the measure, and the inclusion of contingency information and the relevance of statistical null-hypothesis testing.

Although earlier experimental work supports association measures (Gries et al. 2005; Ellis and Ferreira-Junior 2009; Ellis and Simpson-Vlach 2009; Colleman and Bernolet 2012), research contrasting association measures and conditional probabilities (Divjak 2008, 2017; Levshina 2015; Wiechmann 2008; Blumenthal-Drame 2012; Shaoul 2012) shows that conditional probabilities are the favored predictors for a range of linguistic behaviors. Wiechmann (2008), for example, surveyed a wide range of association measures and tested their predictivity using data from eye-tracking during sentence comprehension. The best measure at predicting reading behavior was minimum sensitivity. This measure selects the best of the two available conditional probabilities, i.e., P(verb|construction) and P(construction|verb).

Recent studies have compared uni-directional probability measures to bi-directional measures; while the former calculate, for example, P(verb|construction) or how likely the verb is given the construction; the latter would supplement this information with a calculation of how likely the construction is given the verb and compute both P(verb|construction) and P(construction|verb). Divjak (2008, under revision) obtained sentence acceptability ratings on dispreferred and often low frequency Polish combinations of verbs and constructions. Levshina (under review) used gap filling and sentence production tasks on the Russian ditransitive. Both these studies surveyed a number of association measures, including conditional probabilities, and found that uni-directional probability measures explained behavioral performance at least as well as bi-directional measures. In a similar vain, Blumenthal-Drame (2012) studied the processing of complex word forms in English, using a variety of tasks and both reaction time as well as fMRI measurements. Her conclusion was that (log) relative frequencies (the ratio between surface ([root + affix] and base [root] frequencies) predict entrenchment best. Moreover, none of the probability-based measures that outperformed the others on the tasks described above related observed to expected frequencies in order to perform null-hypothesis statistical significance testing. The information gained from relating observed to expected frequencies the way this is done in statistics may have low psychological relevance to speakers.

3.4 The importance of context

Seminal studies from the 1970s, such as Biederman et al. (1973), demonstrated that objects are recognized faster and more accurately when accompanied by contextual information. This translates straightforwardly to language, and linguists have indeed focused on frequency effects in language units varying in size from phonological to morphological and syntactic contexts. Even disciplines that have been preoccupied with frequency counts, such as corpus linguistics, have borne this principle in mind. Indeed, core concepts in corpus linguistics are collocations, i.e., words that are regularly used together giving rise to an association, and colligations, where a lexical item is linked to a grammatical one. It therefore comes as a surprise to linguists that psychologists interested in language have long focused on words in isolation. Yet behavioral evidence is accumulating that supports linguists' intuitions. One example comes from ERP studies of word processing in sentence context. The magnitude of the N400 component (meaning a negative voltage occurring 400 ms after presentation of a word) indicates difficulty integrating a word with its sentence context. Very large N400s occur for words that are anomalous in their sentence context. N400 wave forms are influenced by word frequency, being largest for very low frequency words. This suggests that contextual integration is most difficult for rare words. However, this frequency effect is strongest at the beginning of a sentence and diminishes for successive words in a semantically congruent sentence (but not a scrambled sentence; van Petten 1993). In van Petten's (1993) study, by the 5th word of a sentence, the N400 frequency effect had disappeared. This suggests that when sufficient context has been encountered, low frequency words are no more difficult to integrate into their context than are high frequency words.

3.5 Is frequency the most important factor for creating entrenched representations?

Following work in the cognitive sciences, we suggest that the answer to this question be "no". Frequency is an important contributor, but the relevance of a stimulus for learners' goals may be more important than frequency per se. Entrenchment can occur without repetition frequency, since robust memories can be formed with single-trial learning. A language example is fast mapping, whereby children and adults infer the meaning of a word from context (Carey and Bartlett 1978). But a strong mental representation will be formed from a single instance only in special cases, such as those associated with intense emotions. Future work on frequency that draws on insights from research on learning, memory and attention and contrasts frequency with salience will no doubt shed light on this question.

4 References

Adelman, James S., Gordan D. A. Brown, and Jose F. Quesada (2006): Contextual diversity, not word frequency, determines word-naming and lexical decision times. *Psychological Science* 17: 814–823.

Alegre, Maria and Peter Gordon (1999): Frequency effects and the representational status of regular inflections. *Journal of Memory and Language* 40: 41–61.

Ambridge, Ben (2013): How do children restrict their linguistic generalizations: An un-grammaticality judgment study. *Cognition* 125: 49–63.

Ambridge, Ben and E. Lieven (2011): *Child Language Acquisition. Contrasting Theoretical Approaches.* Cambridge: Cambridge University Press.

Ambridge, Ben, Julian M. Pine, Caroline F. Rowland, Franklin Chang, and Amy Bidgood (2013): The retreat from overgeneralization in child language acquisition: Word learning, morphology and verb argument structure. *Wiley Interdisciplinary Reviews: Cognitive Science* 4: 47–62.

Anderson, John R. and Lael J. Schooler (1991): Reflections of the environment in memory. *Psychological Science* 2: 396–408.

Arnon, Inbal and Neal Snider (2010): More than words: Frequency effects for multi-word phrases. *Journal of Memory and Language* 62: 67–82.

Baayen, R. Harald (2010): Demythologizing the word frequency effect: A discriminative learning perspective. *The Mental Lexicon* 5: 436–461.

Baayen, R. Harald (2011): Corpus linguistics and naive discriminative learning. *Brazilian Journal of Applied Linguistics* 11: 295–328.

Baayen, R. Harald, Ton Dijkstra, and Robert Schreuder (1997): Singulars and plurals in Dutch: Evidence for a parallel dual-route model. *Journal of Memory and Language* 37: 94–117.

Baayen, R. Harald and Peter Hendrix (2011): Sidestepping the combinatorial explosion: Towards a processing model based on discriminative learning. In LSA workshop *Empirically examining parsimony and redundancy in usage-based models.*

Baayen, R. Harald (this volume): Analogy and schematization. Berlin/Boston: De Gruyter Mouton.

Baayen, R. Harald, Lee H. Wurm, and Joanna Aycock (2007): Lexical dynamics for low-frequency complex words. A regression study across tasks and modalities. *The Mental Lexicon* 2(3): 419–463.

Balota, David A., Maura Pilotti, and Michael J. Cortese (2001): Subjective frequency estimates for 2,938 monosyllabic words. *Memory and Cognition* 29: 639–647.

Balota, David A., Melvin J. Yap, Michael J. Cortese and Keith A. Hutchison, Michael J. Cortese, Brett Kessler, Bjorn Loftis, James H. Neely, Douglas L. Nelson, Greg B. Simpson, and Rebecca Treiman (2007): The English lexicon project. *Behavior Research Methods* 39: 445–459.

Balota, David A., Melvin J. Yap, Keith A. Hutchison, and Michael J. Cortese (2012): Megastudies: Large scale analysis of lexical processes. In: J. S. Adelman (ed.), *Visual Word Recognition* Vol 1. London: Psychology Press.

Bannard, Colin and Danielle Matthews (2008): Stored word sequences in language learning the effect of familiarity on children's repetition of four-word combinations. *Psychological Science* 19(3): 241–248.

Bar, Moshe (ed.) (2011): *Predictions in the Brain. Using our Past to Generate a Future.* Oxford: Oxford University Press.

Barlow, Horace B. (1990): Conditions for versatile learning, Helmholtz's unconscious inference and the task of perception. *Vision Research* 30: 1561–1571.

Biederman, Irving, Arnold L. Glass, and E. Webb Stacy (1973): Searching for objects in real-world scenes. *Journal of Experimental Psychology* 97: 22–27.

Blumenthal-Drame, Alice (2012): *Entrenchment in Usage-Based Theories. What Corpus Data Do and Do Not Reveal About The Mind.* Berlin: De Gruyter.

Boyd Jeremy K. and Adele E. Goldberg (2011): Learning what not to say: the role of statistical preemption and categorization in "a"-adjective production. *Language* 81 (1): 1–29.

Braine, M. D. S. and Brooks, P. J. (1995): Verb argument structure and the problem of avoiding an overgeneral grammar. In M. Tomasello and W. E. Merriman (eds.), *Beyond Names for Things: Young Children's Acquisition of Verbs*, 353–376. Hillsdale: Erlbaum.

Brysbaert, Marc and Boris New (2009): Moving beyond Kučera and Francis: A critical evaluation of current word frequency norms and the introduction of a new and improved word frequency measure for American English. *Behavior Research Methods* 41: 977–990.

Bybee, Joan (1995): Regular morphology and the lexicon. *Language and Cognitive Processes* 10: 425–455.

Bybee, Joan (2007): *Frequency of Use and the Organization of Language.* Oxford: Oxford University Press.

Bybee, Joan and Paul Hopper (eds.) (2001): *Frequency and the Emergence of Linguistic Structure.* Amsterdam: John Benjamins.

Bybee, Joan and Sandra Thompson (2000): Three frequency effects in syntax. *Berkeley Linguistics Society* 23: 378–388.

Caldwell-Harris, Catherine L., Jonathan Berant, and Edelman Shimon (2012): Entrenchment of phrases with perceptual identification, familiarity ratings and corpus frequency statistics. In: D. Divjak and S. T. Gries (eds.), *Frequency Effects in Language Representation*. Volume 2, 165–194. Berlin: Mouton de Gruyter.

Carey, Susan and Elsa Bartlett (1978): Acquiring a single new word. *Papers and Reports on Child Language Development* 15: 17–29.

Carpenter, Shana K., Nicholas J. Cepeda, Dough Rohrer, Sean H. K. Kang, and Harold Pashler (2012): Using spacing to enhance diverse forms of learning: Review of recent research and implications for instruction. *Educational Researcher* 24: 369–378.

Casenhiser, Devin and Giulia Bencini (volume 3): Argument structure constructions. Berlin/Boston: De Gruyter Mouton.

Cattell, James M. (1886): The time it takes to see and name objects. *Mind* 41: 63–65.

Church, Kenneth W. and Patrick Hanks (1990): Word association norms, mutual information and lexicography. *Computational Linguistics* 16: 22–29.

Cohen, Neal J. and Larry R. Squire (1980): Preserved learning and retention of pattern analyzing skill in amnesia: Dissociation of knowing how and knowing that. *Science* 210: 207–210.

Colleman, Timothy and Bernolet, Sarah (2012): Alternation biases in corpora vs. picture description experiments: DO-biased and PD-biased verbs in the Dutch dative

alternation. In: D. Divjak and S. T. Gries (eds.), *Frequency Effects in Language Representation*. Volume 2, 87–125. Berlin: Mouton de Gruyter.
Croft, William and Cruse, Alan (2004): *Cognitive Linguistics*. Cambridge: Cambridge University Press.
Cutler, Anne (1981): Making up materials is a confounded nuisance, or: Will we be able to run any psycholinguistic experiments at all in 1990? *Cognition* 10: 65–70.
Daelemans, Walter and Antal Van den Bosch (2005): *Memory-Based Language Processing*. Cambridge: Cambridge University Press.
Davies, Mark (2010): Corpus of Contemporary American English. Available from http://www.americancorpus.org/.
De Smet, Hendrik and Hubert Cuyckens (2007): Diachronic aspects of complementation: Constructions, entrenchment and the matching-problem. In: C. M. Cain and G. Russom (eds.), *Studies in the History of the English Language III: Managing Chaos: Strategies for Identifying Change in English*, 1–37. Berlin: Mouton de Gruyter.
Diessel, Holger (2007): Frequency effects in language acquisition, language use, and diachronic change. *New Ideas in Psychology* 25: 108–127.
Divjak, Dagmar (2008): On (in)frequency and (un)acceptability. In: B. Lewandowska-Tomaszczyk (ed.), *Corpus Linguistics, Computer Tools and Applications – State of the Art*, 1–21. Frankfurt: Peter Lang.
Divjak, Dagmar (2017): The role of lexical frequency in the acceptability of syntactic variants: evidence from that-clauses in Polish. Cognitive Science 41(2): 354–382.
Divjak, Dagmar and Stefan Th. Gries (eds.) (2012): *Frequency Effects in Language Representation* Volume 2. Berlin: De Gruyter.
Dunning, Ted (1993): Accurate methods for the statistics of surprise and coincidence. *Computational Linguistics* 19(1): 61–74.
Ellis, Nick C. (2002): Frequency effects in language processing: a review with implications for theories of implicit and explicit language acquisition. *Studies in Second Language Acquisition* 24: 143–188.
Ellis, Nick C. and Fernando Ferreira-Junior (2009): Constructions and their acquisition: Islands and the distinctiveness of their occupancy. *Annual Review of Cognitive Linguistics* 7: 188–221.
Ellis, Nick C. and Rita Simpson-Vlach (2009): Formulaic language in native speakers: Triangulating psycholinguistics, corpus linguistics, and education. *Corpus Linguistics and Linguistic Theory* 5: 61–78.
Elman, Jeffrey L. (1993): Learning and development in neural networks: The importance of starting small. *Cognition* 48(1): 71–99.
Erker Daniel and Gregory R. Guy (2012): The role of lexical frequency in syntactic variability: Variable subject personal pronoun expression in Spanish. Language 88(3): 526–557.
Evans, Vyvyan (2014): *The Language Myth: Why language is not an instinct*. Cambridge: Cambridge University Press.
Evert, Stefan (2005): The statistics of word co-occurrences: Word pairs and collocations. Ph.D. Dissertation, Institut für maschinelle Sprachverarbeitung, University of Stuttgart. Retrieved from http://www.stefan-evert.de/PUB/Evert2004phd.pdf.
Fernandez Monsalve, Irene, Stefan L. Frank, and Gabriella Vigliocco (2012): Lexical surprisal as a general predictor of reading time. *Proceedings of the 13th Conference of the European Chapter of the Association for Computational Linguistics*, 398–408. Avignon: Association for Computational Linguistics.

Francis, W. Nelson, and Henry Kucera (1982): *Frequency Analysis of English Usage: Lexicon and Grammar*. Boston: Houghton-Mifflin.

Gardner, Michael K., E. Z. Rothkopf, Richard Lapan, and Toby Lafferty (1987): The word frequency effect in lexical decision: Finding a frequency-based component. *Memory and Cognition* 151: 24–28.

Goldberg, Adele E. (2011): Corpus evidence of the viability of statistical preemption. *Cognitive Linguistics* 22(1): 131–154.

Grainger, Jonathan (1990): Word frequency and neighborhood frequency effects in lexical decision and naming. *Journal of Memory and Language* 29: 228–244.

Gries, Stefan Th. (2008): Dispersions and adjusted frequencies in corpora. *International Journal of Corpus Linguistics* 13: 403–437.

Gries, Stefan Th. (2010): Dispersions and adjusted frequencies in corpora: further explorations. In: S. Th. Gries, S. Wulff and M. Davies (eds.), *Corpus Linguistic Applications: Current Studies, New Directions*, 197–212. Amsterdam: Rodopi.

Gries, Stefan Th. (2013): 50-something years of work on collocations: what is or should be next. *International Journal of Corpus Linguistics* 18(1) 137–165.

Gries, Stefan Th. and Dagmar Divjak (eds.) (2012): *Frequency Effects in Language Learning and Processing* Volume 1. Berlin: De Gruyter.

Gries, Stefan Th., Beate Hampe, and Doris Schönefeld (2005): Converging evidence: Bringing together experimental and corpus data on the association of verbs and constructions. *Cognitive Linguistics* 16(4): 635–676.

Grill-Spector, Kalanit, Richard Henson, and Alex Martin (2006): Repetition and the brain: neural models of stimulus-specific effects. *Trends in Cognitive Sciences* 10: 14–23.

Gupta, Prahlad (2012): Word learning as the confluence of memory mechanisms: Computational and neural evidence. In: M. Faust (Ed.), *Handbook of the Neuropsychology of Language*, Volume 1, 146–163. Oxford: Wiley.

Gurevich, Olya, Matt Johnson, and Adele E. Goldberg (2010): Incidental verbatim memory for language. *Language and Cognition* 2(1): 45–78.

Hale, John (2001): A probabilistic early parser as a psycholinguistic model. In *Proceedings of the second meeting of the North American Chapter of the Association for Computational Linguistics on Language technologies*, 1–8. Stroudsburg: Association for Computational Linguistics.

Hasher, Lynn and Rose T. Zacks (1984): Automatic processing of fundamental information: The case of frequency of occurrence. *American Psychologist* 39: 1372.

Hauk, Olaf, Matthew H. Davis, M. Ford, Friedemann Pulvermüller, and William D. Marslen-Wilson (2006): The time course of visual word recognition as revealed by linear regression analysis of ERP data. *Neuroimage* 30: 1383–1400.

Hebb, Donald O. (1949): *The Organization of Behavior*. New York: Wiley and Sons.

Hills, Thomas T., Michael N. Jones and Peter M. Todd (2012): Optimal foraging in semantic memory. *Psychological Review* 119: 431–440.

Hilpert, Martin (volume 2): Historical linguistics. Berlin/Boston: De Gruyter Mouton.

Howes, Davis H. and Richard L. Solomon (1951): Visual duration threshold as a function of word-probability. *Journal of Experimental Psychology* 416: 401–410.

Jaeger, T. Florian (2010): Redundancy and Reduction: Speakers Manage Information Density. *Cognitive Psychology* 61(1): 23–62.

Jones, Michael N., Johns, Brendan T., and Gabriel Recchia (2012): The role of semantic diversity in lexical organization. *Canadian Journal of Experimental Psychology* 66: 115–124.

Jurafsky, Dan (1996): A probabilistic model of lexical and syntactic access and disambiguation. *Cognitive Science* 20: 137–194.

Langacker, Ronald W. (1987): *Foundations of Cognitive Grammar*, Volume I, *Theoretical Prerequisites*. Stanford: Stanford University Press.

Lee, Chia-Lin and Federmeier, Kara D. (2012): In a word: ERPs reveal important lexical variables for visual word processing. In: M. Faust (Ed.), *The Handbook of the Neuropsychology of Language*, Volume 1, 184–208. Oxford: Wiley-Blackwell.

Levshina, Natalia (2015): How to do Linguistics with R. Data exploration and statistical analysis, 223–239. Amsterdam: John Benjamins.

Levy, Roger (2008): Expectation-based syntactic comprehension. *Cognition* 106: 1126–1177.

Lieven, Elena (2010): Input and first language acquisition: Evaluating the role of frequency. *Lingua* 120: 2546–2556.

Lyne, Anthony A. (1985): Dispersion. In: *The Vocabulary of French Business Correspondence*, 101–124. Geneva/Paris: Slatkine-Champion.

MacKay, Donald G. (1982): The problems of flexibility, fluency, and speed accuracy trade-off in skilled behavior. *Psychological Review* 89: 483–506.

MacWhinney, Brian (1998): Models of the emergence of language. *Annual Review of Psychology* 49: 199–227.

Matthews, Danielle and Grzegorz Krajewski (volume 2): First language acquisition. Berlin/Boston: De Gruyter Mouton.

McClelland, James L. and David E. Rumelhart (1981): An interactive activation model of context effects in letter perception: Part 1. An account of basic findings. *Psychological Review* 88: 375–407.

McDonald, Scott A. and Richard Shillcock (2001): Rethinking the word frequency effect. The neglected role of distributional information in lexical processing. *Language and Speech* 44(3): 295–323.

McEnery, Tony and Andrew Hardie (2012): *Corpus Linguistics: Method, Theory and Practice.* Cambridge: Cambridge University Press.

Monsell, Stephen (1991): The nature and locus of word frequency effects in reading. In: D. Besner and G. W. Humphreys (eds.), *Basic Processes in Reading: Visual Word Recognition*, 148–197. Hillsdale: Lawrence Erlbaum.

Mukherjee, Joybrato (2005): *English Ditransitive Verbs: Aspects of Theory, Description and a Usage-Based Model* (Language and Computers 53). Amsterdam/New York: Rodopi.

Pecina, Pavel (2009): Lexical association measures: Collocation extraction. *Studies in Computational and Theoretical Linguistics* 44(1/2): 137–158.

Pollack, Irwin, Herbert Rubenstein, and Louis Decker (1959): Intelligibility of known and unknown message sets. *The Journal of the Acoustical Society of America* 31: 273–279.

Pullum, Geoffrey K. and Barbara C. Scholz (2002): Empirical assessment of stimulus poverty arguments. *The Linguistic Review* 18: 9–50.

Rayner, Keith and Susan A. Duffy (1986): Lexical complexity and fixation times in reading: Effects of word frequency, verb complexity and lexical ambiguity. *Memory and Cognition* 14: 191–201.

Rogers, Timothy T. and James L. McClelland (2004): *Semantic Cognition: A Parallel Distributed Processing Approach.* Cambridge: MIT Press.

Saffran, Jenny R. (2003): Statistical language learning: Mechanisms and constraints. *Current Directions in Psychological Science* 12: 110–114.

Saffran, Jenny R., Richard N. Aslin, and Elissa L. Newport (1996): Statistical learning by 8-month-old infants. *Science* 274: 1926–1928.

Schmid, Hans-Jörg (2000): *English Abstract Nouns as Conceptual Shells. From Corpus to Cognition.* Berlin/New York: Mouton de Gruyter.

Schmid, Hans-Jörg (2010): Does frequency in text really instantiate entrenchment in the cognitive system? In: D. Glynn and K. Fischer (eds.), *Quantitative Methods in Cognitive Semantics: Corpus-Driven Approaches*, 101–133. Berlin: Walter de Gruyter.

Schmid, Hans-Jörg and Helmut Küchenhoff (2013): Collostructional analysis and other ways of measuring lexicogrammatical attraction: Theoretical premises, practical problems and cognitive underpinnings. *Cognitive Linguistics* 24(3): 531–577.

Sedlmeier, Peter and Tilmann Betsch (eds.) (2002): *Frequency Processing and Cognition.* London: Oxford University Press.

Shaoul, Cyrus (2012): The processing of lexical sequences. PhD Dissertation. University of Alberta, Edmonton. http://hdl.handle.net/10402/era.26026

Snider, Neal and Inbar Arnon (2012): A unified lexicon and grammar? Compositional and non-compositional phrases in the lexicon. In: D. Divjak and S. Gries (eds.), *Frequency Effects in Language Representation* Volume 2, 127–164. Berlin: Mouton de Gruyter.

Solan, Zach, David Horn, Eytan Ruppin, and Shimon Edelman (2005): Unsupervised learning of natural languages. *Proceedings of the National Academy of Sciences* 102: 11629–11634.

Stefanowitsch, Anatol and Stefan Th. Gries (2003): Collostructions: Investigating the interaction of words and constructions. *International Journal of Corpus Linguistics* 82: 209–243.

Tremblay, Antoine, Bruce Derwing, Gary Libben, and Chris Westbury (2011): Processing advantages of lexical bundles: Evidence from self-paced reading and sentence recall tasks. *Language Learning* 61: 569–613.

Van Petten, Cyma (1993): A comparison of lexical and sentence-level context effects and their temporal parameters. *Language and Cognitive Processes* 8: 485–532.

Whaley, C. P. (1978): Word-nonword classification time. *Journal of Verbal Learning and Verbal Behavior* 17: 143–154.

Wiechmann, Daniel (2008): On the computation of collostruction strength. *Corpus Linguistics and Linguistic Theory* 42: 253–290.

Michael Ramscar and Robert Port
Chapter 4: Categorization (without categories)

1 Introduction

Cognitive linguists view language as a social artifact shaped by learning and cultural transmission, and emphasize the role of *categorization* in shaping our linguistic capacities (Lakoff 1987; Taylor 2003). This has resulted in something of a division of labor, as linguists seek to explain the role of categorization in shaping the functional properties of language, while psychologists seek to uncover the cognitive bases of categorization itself.

These endeavors share many assumptions and questions: how do people decide that an aspect of a scene should be labeled (in English) *a mountain* or *tree*? How do they determine that an instance of speech contains the sound [ɒ] that distinguishes *water* from *waiter*? And both approaches assume that the fact that people use words like *water* and *waiter* indicates they have access to the *concepts waiter, water,* and *[ɒ]*. These concepts are discrete mental units that (somehow) specify their content, and can be combined with other concepts to create thoughts, utterances and sentences.

Although this assumption makes some intuitive sense, it not clear that English speakers' use of the word *tree* does warrant the assumption that each speaker possesses a coherent, unified representation of the concept *tree*, or that trees form a coherent class of natural objects (Wittgenstein 1953; Quine 1960). Moreover, the struggles that are evident when categorization researchers seek to define the object of their study suggest that these assumptions may be unwarranted:

> The concept of concepts is difficult to define, but no one doubts that concepts are fundamental to mental life and human communication. Cognitive scientists generally agree that a concept is a mental representation that picks out a set of entities, or a category. That is, concepts refer, and what they refer to are categories. (Rips et al. 2013: 177)

However, because *reference* and *representation* are as ill defined as *concept*, describing concepts as mental representations that refer to classes of entities in the world simply exchanges one poorly defined term for another. This problem

---
Michael Ramscar, Tübingen, DE
Robert Port, Bloomington, USA

led Wittgenstein (1953) and Quine (1960) to reject the idea of concepts as discrete constructs, and emphasize instead the way that words function in systems, and the way that meanings result from the way words are *used* in these systems.

This distinction – between concepts as discrete mental tokens, and concepts as emergent aspects of systems – is usually glossed over in the literature, but its implications for language, both for semantics and for linguistic categories themselves, are far-reaching. To establish which characterization better describes the results of many years of empirical study, this chapter reviews the results of this work, along with the many computational models that have been developed to account for them, and recent work seeking to match these models to neural structures in the brain.

The findings of these lines of work make it clear that our minds do not learn inventories of discrete, stand-alone concepts. Instead, human conceptual capabilities are systematic: they are the product of a rich capacity to discriminate and learn *systems* of alternative responses (behaviors, affordances, words, etc.) and to use them in context. From this perspective English speakers do not acquire discrete concepts of *tree* or *friend*, but rather they learn a system of linguistic contrasts, and they learn how to discriminate when to use the words *tree* (rather than *bush*, *oak* or *shrub*) or *friend* (rather than *buddy* or *pal*) in order to satisfy their communicative goals. We conclude this review by briefly describing what this implies for future directions of research in cognitive linguistics.

2 Concepts, categories and categorization

2.1 Concepts and labels

It seems clear that the existence of individual nouns need not entail the existence of corresponding individuated cognitive representational entities yet speakers tend to talk about *concepts* as if they are discrete, countable things. Thus dictionaries characterize *concepts* as "directly intuited objects of thought" or "ideas of things formed by mentally combining their characteristics" (passing the buck of defining *concept* onto *idea* and *object of thought*). This practice extends to the categorization literature, which focuses on either discrete, artificially defined concepts, or the nature of frequent linguistic items like *tree*.

From this circumscribed perspective, researchers seek to explain how cognitive representations of concepts can be described in terms of relations between *features* (and where a *category* is the set of instances that exemplify a *concept*). To work, this approach requires clear definitions of what concepts and features are, and this, as noted above, is problematical: if the only thing that unifies the category of *games* is the fact that we call them games – i.e., they share the feature of being called *game* in English – then a definition of the concept *game* will add no more to our understanding of concepts than saying that *games* are whatever English speakers call *games*. Further, as Wittgenstein (1953) observed, if we take the common English word *game*, then *baseball* is a game, whether played by children for fun or by professionals for their livelihood; *polo* and *hopscotch* are games, as are *scrabble*, *solitaire*, and *monopoly*; yet *stockbroking* is not usually called a game, nor are *proofreading* nor *cavalry-charges* (military *maneuvers* are called games in peacetime but not wartime). And although many local similarities can be seen between different games, there are equally many local similarities between games and non-games (Goodman 1972), such that it appears that the only things that joins *games* together while ruling out *non-games* is the fact that some things are conventionally called *games* while others are not (Ramscar and Hahn 1998).

The circular relationship between labels and concepts is not restricted to abstract words like *game*: the English word *tree* does not correspond to a coherent class of objects, even leaving aside uses like *tree diagram*. Biologically, pine trees are *gymnosperms* (conifers), whereas oak trees are *angiosperms* (flowering plants). Oaks share an evolutionary lineage with cacti, daisies and roses; pines belong to a more primitive genus (Lusk 2011). *Vegetable* is a similar pseudo-natural kind: English *tomatoes* are vegetables, but most other edible fruits are not (Malt et al. 2010). And while even natural concepts (in the colloquial sense of the word concept) seem arbitrary because they lack defining features, defining features in turn raises problems that are disturbingly similar to those posed by concepts: What are they? Do features themselves merely reflect labels, etc. (Ramscar et al. 2010b; Port 2010; Port and Leary 2005)?

To illustrate the subtle problems these issues pose when it comes to forming a clear understanding of the role of concepts in categorization, consider a rare attempt to clearly define the terms concept and category from the literature: Goldstone and Kersten (2009) describe concepts as mental representation of individuals or classes that specify *what* is being represented and how to categorize it. They then note that if a concept is a mental representation of a class, and a category a set of entities that are appropriately categorized together by that concept, this leaves the question of whether concepts determine categories or categories determine concepts open:

> If one assumes the primacy of external categories of entities, then one will tend to view concept learning as the enterprise of inductively creating mental structures that predict these categories. [...] If one assumes the primacy of internal mental concepts, then one tends to view external categories as the end product of applying these internal concepts

> to observed entities. An extreme version of this approach is to argue that the external world does not inherently consist of rocks, dogs, and tables; these are mental concepts that organize an otherwise unstructured external world. (Goldstone and Kersten 2003: 600)

However, the basis for these distinctions is dubious: It is demonstrably the case that the world does *not* inherently consist of rocks, dogs, and tables. *Dog* and *table* are English words (i.e., culturally defined labels), and there is little evidence to support the idea that natural partitions in the universe are constrained by the vocabulary of English. Indeed, as *tree* and *vegetable* illustrate, there is little reason to believe the English lexicon maps onto reality in a privileged way at all; *trees* are simply what English speakers call trees.

So what is a concept, and how do categories relate to concepts? The answer is that in practical terms, regardless of what researchers take the relationship between words and reality to be, concepts are determined by the ways things are labeled. A rock is an instance of *rock* if English speakers would call it a rock, and when researchers talk about two items as instances of a concept they simply mean that the items can be spoken about using the same linguistic symbol (and, as Gahl 2008 shows, even apparent homophones are symbolically distinct).

This point even extends to the artificially defined concepts used in experiments, because the features used in their definitions are themselves linguistic concepts like red, square, etc. Indeed, even where concepts are only implicitly labeled in a study's procedure – for example in pigeon experiments, or in abstract discrimination tasks – the relevant stimulus dimensions will have been explicitly labeled at some point in its design (e.g., Zentall et al. 2014; Billman and Knutson 1996).

In other words, irrespective of whether researchers believe in the primacy of the word or the primacy of the world, in practice they study concepts that are determined by labels. For clarity, in the rest of this review the word *concept* will be used to describe a specific relationship between a group of items: that they share a label, typically a word (or phrase, discriminable symbol, etc.).[1] We will use *concept learning* to describe the way the relationship between a set of items and a label is learned: That is, the process by which people learn whatever it is that enables them to respond to new items in a manner appropriate to a label. *Category* will be used to describe a set of items with a common label

---

[1] This does not means that people only learn in reference to labels, or that they only acquire "conceptual knowledge" that can be labeled. Rather, for obvious reasons, there is little discussion of completely non-verbalizable content in the categorization literature.

(including new items that could be considered to be members of that category in an appropriate context), and *categorization* will be used to describe the various things people are asked to do with category members, i.e., sort them, label them, make inferences about them, etc.

2.2 One label; Two ideas

Many of the confusions that abound in discussions of categorization research arise out of the fact that it comprises two distinct lines of study:
1. *Concept learning* experiments originating in the associative paradigms that dominated early psychology, and which focus on classification and response discrimination tasks, usually employing artificial concepts;
2. Studies of *the structure of natural language concepts* that measure people's behavior as they respond to uses of words and phrases.

Because these two approaches employ the same terminology, but embody very different methodological approaches, potential for confusion abounds in the literature, especially when, as is common, results from studies of artificial concepts are discussed in the same breath as natural concepts.

2.3 Concept learning: from rules and definitions to prototypes and exemplars

Studies of *concept learning* typically examine people's ability to discriminate the appropriate dimensions of stimuli and learn to match them to discrete responses (Hull 1920; Smoke 1932). Researchers examine questions such as whether associations increase gradually or are better characterized in all-or-none terms (Trabasso and Bower 1968) and whether learning conjunctive dimensions (e.g., *blue* AND *triangular*) is easier than disjunctive dimensions (e.g., *blue* OR *triangular*; Bruner et al. 1956; Shepard et al. 1961).

Because artificial concepts are defined by feature-combinations, researchers often equate concept learning with acquiring a rule defining some kind of membership criterion (e.g., *"rule-based" concepts*; Smoke 1932): concepts are descriptions of the appropriate dimension(s) for class inclusion and categorization is a process in which item features are matched to rules across an inventory of concepts. Rule-based concept learning thus resembles early speculations about word meanings, e.g., Frege's (1892) distinction between the *intensions* and *extensions* of concepts (which is still widely used in linguistic analyses today): A concept's intension is the set of attributes defining its members, while its extension comprises its actual members.

Thus the intension of *bachelor* might include characteristics such as male, unmarried and adult, making its extension the set of male, unmarried adults in the world, which would mean that both the Pope and an unmarried man cohabiting with the same partner for 25 years are bachelors. One can, of course, amend the intension of bachelor to exclude Popes and cohabitees to fix this, but what is important to note here is a critical *difference* between natural language and artificial concepts: the latter are whatever a researcher defines them to be, whereas definitions for natural language concepts can only be imputed.

It follows that, theoretically, the question of **whether** there is an appropriate conceptual definition for bachelor at all is equally as valid as **what** the conceptual definition of bachelor is. Or, to put it another way, although the definitional status of artificial concepts can be taken for granted, valid definitions for natural concepts might not actually exist (Wittgenstein 1953). Intriguingly, this latter notion is supported by the results of artificial concept learning studies themselves: Findings from numerous experiments indicate that people don't actually learn to represent rules or feature specifications for carefully defined concepts even when they encounter them (Sakamoto and Love 2004).[2]

For example, Posner and Keele (1970) showed that people are better at classifying previously unseen *typical* artificial category exemplars than less typical exemplars they have actually seen in training. Along with numerous other similar findings, this result suggests that people learn *prototypical* information about item-categories, such that even well defined concepts are not learned as definitions.

Other findings muddy the waters still further. When typicality differences are controlled for, participants *are* better at categorizing items seen in training than new items (Nosofsky 1992; Smith and Minda 2000). Similarly, less typical new items similar to items seen in training are categorized more accurately and quickly than typical new items that are not (Medin and Schaffer 1978). These results suggest that participants learn details about the specific items they are exposed to (i.e., exemplars) rather than abstracting rule-based representation or pure prototypes.

On the other hand, concept learning does result in some abstraction: Posner and Keele (1967) showed that although participants retain information about the letters *a* and *A* for a couple seconds, these initial encodings give way to representations in which *a* and *A* are stored as exemplars of a more abstract

---

[2] Since "features" in artificial concepts are natural concepts at another level of abstraction, these findings are not entirely surprising.

(case-invariant) letter name. Similarly although participants adjusting the length of a reference line to that of a Müller-Lyer stimulus which is either in view or in memory exhibit a pattern of bias consistent with the Müller-Lyer effect in both cases, the adjustments made from memory are further biased towards the average line length presented in the experiment (Crawford et al. 2000).

What people learn about concepts is further influenced by the tasks they perform in experiments (Love 2002). Learning in inference tasks (answering questions like, "This is a mammal. Does it have fur?") highlights dimensions that are typical rather than diagnostic of concepts (which in this case would involve milk-producing glands). By contrast, classification tasks ("This has milk-producing glands. Is it a mammal?") promote learning of the diagnostic information that discriminates between categories (Yamauchi et al. 2002).

Finally, Brooks et al. (1991) have shown how specific exemplars play a role in experts' use of well-defined concepts. For example, doctors often base diagnoses on recent cases, rather than more general abstractions, suggesting that expertise involves the acquisition of knowledge about relevant exemplars, as well as rules.

This body of results is incompatible with the idea that concepts are defined in memory by stable feature sets, or that such things are even plausible as theoretical postulates (Ramscar et al. 2013d, 2014). Even where people learn clearly specified concepts, they learn both more and less than a definitional account might imply, and what they learn is influenced by the tasks they perform during learning, by context, and by the process of learning itself (Arnon and Ramscar 2012; Ramscar et al. 2013d).

2.4 The structure of natural language concepts and the basic level

The other line of categorization research examines the knowledge associated with the words used in languages (Rosch and Mervis 1975; Rosch et al. 1976). Rosch and colleagues argued that everyday concepts are not structured in ways that reduce to definitions based on necessary and sufficient features. Although a given feature might be common to many items corresponding to a word's usage (e.g., *birds fly*), it might not be common to all (*penguins*) and it might also be common to items labeled using other words (*insects*). Rosch et al. proposed that natural concepts have a *family resemblance* structure, and that category membership (labeling) depends on similarities between members of a category.

An idea that naturally follows from this suggestion is that there are better and worse examples of a concept: Category members that share more properties with other members should better exemplify a concept than those sharing fewer properties. And studies confirm that people believe canaries are better examples of *birds* than *penguins* (Rosch and Mervis 1975), and that these goodness judgments correlate with the number of features that a given example shares with other examples.

Rosch et al. (1976) argue that the distribution of features among concepts results in natural clusters that maximize within-category similarity and minimize between-category similarity. They termed these basic-level concepts. Examples would be *dog* (as opposed to *dachshund*, or *pet*) and *house* (as opposed to *duplex*, or *mansion*). Rosch et al. suggest that basic-level categories are (a) preferred by adults in naming objects in tasks that contrast various levels of abstraction (b) used more in child directed speech, (c) learned first by children, and (d) are associated with the fastest categorization reaction times.

Although Rosch et al. repeatedly show that people are more likely to use basic level words than those at other levels in their abstraction hierarchy, they paradoxically maintain this is *not* because basic level words are more frequent (presenting evidence from small written corpora in support of this idea). However, it is worth noting first that Rosch et al. acknowledge that "basic level" categories can be influenced by culture and expertise (thus, for a real-estate agent, *colonial* may be a basic-level concept), and second, that word frequency effects are ultimately conditioned on an individual's experience, not corpus statistics (Ramscar et al. 2014). Further, the basic level labels studied by Rosch et al. are high frequency English nouns. Because of this, it is unclear whether basic level categories should be seen as offering insight into the structure of the world, personal and cultural structures, or interactions between the two (Malt et al. 2010).

Work in this tradition poses another problem for discrete theories of concepts because it provides evidence that some – if not all – natural language categories lack clear boundaries. Labov (1973) showed that there is a great deal of variability in the way people use terms such as *cup*, *bowl*, etc., with different labels being assigned to the same containers both between speakers and within speakers depending upon the linguistic context. If people are asked to look at a picture of an object whose shape is half way between a (tea) *cup* and a (soup) *bowl* and told that it contains mashed potatoes, they tend to consider the object to be a *bowl*. But if the ambiguous object contains hot coffee, it tends to be considered a *cup*. Similarly, in a study of exemplar-category pairs (e.g., *apple-fruit* or *chair-furniture*) McCloskey and Glucksberg (1978) found not only substantial between- and within-participant disagreement on category membership (measured over successive test-sessions) but also that levels of disagreement correlate with independently derived typicality ratings: McCloskey and Glucksberg's participants were certain that *chair* belonged to the category *furniture*, and that *cucumber* did not. However, there was much disagreement as to whether a *bookend* belonged to the category *furniture*, with many participants differing in their judgments from one session to the next.

Categorization in one domain can also be influenced by information from another. For example, thinking about space can influence subsequent temporal categorization judgments: the question *Next Wednesday's meeting has been moved forward two days: what day is the meeting on now?* is more likely to be answered with Friday than Monday by people who have been encouraged to think about moving towards a physical destination rather than staying in one place (Boroditsky and Ramscar 2002; Evans volume 3). Rating the sensibility of fictive motion sentences (e.g., *Seven trees ran along the driveway* vs. *There were seven trees along the driveway*) also produces a similar, predictable influence on temporal categorization (Ramscar et al. 2010a). However, although time and space seem to be systematically linked, the basis of this linkage ultimately appears be lexical: the patterns of priming observed in these experiments are highly consistent with patterns of lexical co-occurrence in English (Ramscar et al. 2010a).

Finally, we should note that Rosch (1978) argued that it would be a mistake to assume that the discovery of prototype effects indicated that word meanings are themselves represented by prototypes. Yet the idea that concepts *can* be assumed to have prototypical representations has since been proposed in various guises: as *frames* (e.g., Fillmore 1982); as *Idealized Cognitive Models* (ICMs, Lakoff 1987); as *image schemas* (Johnson 1987); and *domains* (Lakoff 1993). It is thus worth stressing that none of these suggestions make it clear what is or is not part of a specific frame, ICM, or domain, or indeed how concepts are actually represented in terms of these constructs. Thus despite the fact that these suggestions are often referred to as theories of representation, they are more akin to the phenomenological descriptions that Rosch suggested prototypes actually are than theories of conceptual representation (Cienki 2007; these points also apply to *ad hoc categories*, Barsalou 1983).

2.5 Two traditions – one conclusion

Results from both lines of categorization research support the conclusion that words are *not* associated with invariant context-independent definitions. Even the learning of well-defined concepts appears to be sensitive to a range of contextual factors, such that people learn context-sensitive representations of even rule-based artificial concepts. It appears that natural language concepts do not have stable structures within or between individual speakers in a community

(Ramscar et al. 2013d), and that people's use of words (and phrases) reflects conventions that probabilistically govern language use in context. That is, while it is clear that people learn and use conceptual knowledge in systematic ways, the results reviewed here offer little support for the idea that this behavior relies on or reflects their possession of discrete representations of concepts.

3 Computational models of categorization

Numerous computational models have been proposed to account for the empirical results discussed above, allowing theoretical proposals about conceptual representations to be evaluated by formal simulations of behavior. The development of categorization models has been a particular feature of the artificial concept learning literature, in part because the controlled nature of artificial stimuli is more amenable to formalization than the study of everyday concepts based on social convention. However, one of the earliest and most influential computational models of categorization (Collins and Quillian 1969) is an outlier in that it sought to formally characterize everyday semantic knowledge.

3.1 Hierarchical semantic networks

The Collins and Quillian model proposes that word use reflects a hierarchical network in which stimulus properties are stored in memory according to their generality or specificity in relation to a set of related concepts. This postulates, for example, a taxonomic representation of animal knowledge where properties general to all animals such as *breathing* are stored at the top of the hierarchy with the concept *animal*. Properties generally true of fish are stored at the *fish* node, and general bird properties are stored at the *bird* node. Properties distinctive to individual sub-kinds (e.g., *robin*) are stored with the specific concept nodes they characterize (e.g., the property *red-breasted*). In this model, category membership can then be defined in terms of the positions of nodes in the hierarchical network. Many properties of each category can be read off from its position. Thus the node for *salmon* does not directly store the information that salmon are *animals*, since that fact is specified by the hierarchical connection between the *salmon*, *fish* and *animal* nodes.

However the Collins and Quillian model is not a straightforward inheritance model as these are commonly understood in computer science: this is because sub-kinds on lower nodes do not always inherit all the properties of higher nodes. For example, *can fly* is associated with the *bird* node – because flying is usually a distinctive property of birds – and exceptions to this feature (i.e., *penguin*) are stored at a sub-kind node for *does not fly*. Thus while it is often reported that increases in network distance between concepts and properties successfully predict the time it takes people take to verify that concepts have a given property (e.g., people verify that a *canary* is *yellow* faster than that it *has feathers*), given the lack of any principles specifying exactly *where* in the hierarchy a given feature is represented positively or negatively, it is more accurate to say that Collins and Quillian's intuitions about the relationship between the various words used for nodes and features correlated well with the behavior of their participants. (Nb. to some extent this criticism applies to *all* models that describe formal relationships between sets of arbitrary conceptual features defined by modelers.)

3.2 Prototype models

Prototype models are characterized as seeking to formalize concept representations in which degree of fit to the category is evaluated for the purposes of categorization. A *prototype* represents information about all relevant dimensions of the items in a stimulus set with the information represented as some kind of average value across all exemplars. In a prototype model, a novel item is classified as a member of the category whose prototype it is most similar to (e.g., Hampton 1995). The values used to define the prototype for each category are updated when new examples are encountered. These models thus seek to capture the critical structure of a category, without having to encode every detail of every item that a participant has seen.

Prototype models were developed to try to create accounts of discrete concepts that could nevertheless explain people's sensitivity to the degree to which features correlate across the exemplars of a concept. In a prototype model, similarity can be viewed in geometric terms – the closer together items are in feature-space, the more similar they are. Thus more typical category members will be closer in space to the prototype, and less typical category members will more distant. Prototype models account well for findings relating to graded typicality, and offer a formal account of why new exemplars that are very prototypical are likely to be judged as being the better examples of a given category than items farther from the prototype.

However, these models fail to account for other findings in the literature. For example, prototype models do not store information about the frequency of specific exemplars, yet it is clear that people are sensitive to this information (Kruschke 1996). Moreover, the averaging process at the heart of prototype representations can yield anomalous results: If the members of a disjunctive category comprise either large black vertical lines or small white horizontal lines, then averaging across both dimensions produces a medium-sized grey diagonal line. This would fail to represent any of the relevant dimensions of the items associated with the concept appropriately, and measurements of similarity between this prototype and the actual set of members would not provide a good estimate of category membership.

Neither of these problems immediately falsify prototype models: there is no in-principle reason why exemplar frequency could not be incorporated into a prototype representation. Nor is there any reason why multiple prototypes could not be used to represent categories that are not linearly separable (although this might be hard to implement in a principled way). However, a more serious problem for prototype models is that they do not easily accommodate people's ability to recognize specific exemplars of concepts. For example, people asked to listen for the recurrence of a word in a lengthy, spoken wordlist do better when repeated words are presented by the same voice rather than a different one (Palmeri et al. 1993), suggesting that people store more auditory speech detail than linguists often suppose, and that models that store category summaries discard too much information about the speech signal to provide an adequate account of people's behavior.

3.3 Exemplar models

In an *exemplar model* (e.g, Nosofsky 1991, 1992) every example of a concept is stored in memory in all its detail. Novel items are classified by their similarity to previously learned exemplars, and category membership is determined by a weighted voting system in which a new item is assigned to the category for which the summed pairwise similarities are greatest (Kruschke 1992).

Interestingly, because of the way this voting process works, exemplar models are able to account for the typicality effects that led to the development of prototype models. This is because more typical exemplars, which, of course, lie near the center of the feature space of a category (the prototype), share more similarities with other exemplars than less typical items. Because the number of votes an item receives is a function of these similarities, a typical new item receives greater support than a less typical item.

Exemplar models have been tremendously influential, and yet what is perhaps their most important feature is usually least remarked upon in the literature: exemplar models do not contain, or even attempt to define, unitary representations for concepts. Instead, they typically contain a system of exemplars that is related to a system of labels, and a methodology for incorporating new items into this system and for dynamically generating labels for unlabeled items.

3.4 Systems models

Prototype models are often criticized for throwing away too much information, whereas exemplar models challenge our intuitions through the promiscuity of their assumptions about storage and processing. What is clear is that depending upon the context in which a concept is learned, or the goal of the learner, more or less information is discarded in learning. Moreover, the processes that appear to be involved in learning and storage inevitably result in encodings in which some stimulus dimensions are ignored in order to increase the discriminability of encoded items (Kruschke 2001; Ramscar et al. 2010b).

However, while it is unclear that a "pure" exemplar model even makes theoretical sense, simply because identifying exemplar is itself an act of classification at a different level of abstraction (Ramscar et al. 2010b), what is interesting about exemplar models is that they seek to capture people's behavior in tasks rather than seeking to define concepts: They treat categorization as in inherently systematic process relying on multiple exemplar representations, and yet they successfully account for many empirical phenomena (Nosofsky 1990).

The shift towards trying to model systematic behaviors rather than defining representations has led to models that employ multiple representations to find the middle ground between maximal abstraction (with minimal storage, e.g., prototypes) and minimal abstraction (with maximal storage, e.g., "pure" exemplar models). For example, the RATIONAL model of categorization (Anderson 1991) neither stores every exemplar nor does it rely entirely on prototypes. Instead, the model creates hybrid representations in which a new item may either be used to update an existing cluster of similar examples (as in a prototype model) or, if unique enough, may initiate a new cluster. Which choice is made is a function of the probability that the new item belongs to an existing cluster. When this probability is below a given threshold, a new cluster is created. If above the threshold, the existing cluster that it is most similar is updated to reflect the new exemplar. RATIONAL is thus capable of acquiring clusters that function like rules, or sets of clusters that function like exemplars, depending on the categories being learned.

Other systems apply explicitly different mechanisms (rules initially; exemplars later) at different stages of concept learning (Johansen and Palmeri 2002), while in others (e.g., ATRIUM: Erickson and Kruschke 1998; COVIS: Ashby et al. 1998), the contributions of rule-based and exemplar learning are flexible, and depend more on the learning context, or the context in which categorization decisions are made.

Whereas most models seek to learn the representational system that best segregates a training set, a more recent clustering model, SUSTAIN (Love et al.

2004) was developed to account for the fact that people learn different information about items according to their context and goals. In unsupervised learning, when a learner has no specific goal in mind, SUSTAIN adds clusters much as RATIONAL would, in order to minimize classification error. However, if a learner is, say, inferring the properties of an item as part of a task, this goal can influence what is learned about the items. SUSTAIN is thus able to capture the differences in learning that occur in different task environments.

Depending on the conceptual structure being learned, and whether a goal is present or not, the structure of the clusters SUSTAIN learns for any given label can functionally resemble either rule-based, prototype or exemplar models. What is important to note is that the internal structure of these representations are highly sensitive to the context provided by the presence (or absence) of goals. Depending on context, different information will be represented in the clusters and different information discarded in learning or used in categorization. The success of the SUSTAIN model when it comes to fitting a wide range of behavioral phenomena suggests that people may learn different representations when learning concepts in inference and classification tasks and thus contributes further evidence that human category learning involves multiple processes, and that what is learned depends on a learners' goals and prior experience (Mack et al. 2013).

4 The neural bases of categorization

Results from cognitive neuroscience research support the findings reviewed so far in that they indicate there is no single neural circuit for concept learning (Seger and Miller 2010; Davis et al. 2014), and suggest that categorization is best understood in relation to the overall architecture of the brain's perceptual- and motor- learning and memory systems. (Understanding the relevant neural architecture also requires an understanding of brain anatomy and physiology that few linguists currently have, so while this section may be challenging, we hope readers will appreciate its relevance to our understanding of concepts.)

4.1 Perceptual concepts

Numerous neural structures are involved in the discrimination of classes of visual stimuli, and even systems usually considered to be primarily engaged in perceptual processing exhibit evidence of tuning in response to categorization tasks: Different neuronal assemblies in the inferior temporal cortex (ITC) respond selectively to different category types, such as complex shapes (Logothetis and Scheinberg 1996) or faces (Kanwisher et al. 1997). Studies of trained monkeys have shown that individual neurons in the ITC show selectivity for, say, trees or fish, and these neurons are relatively insensitive to variance within these categories (Vogels 2008).

Human patients with impaired higher order memory systems (e.g., medial temporal lobe lesions) or Parkinson's disease (which impairs corticostriatal learning) retain their ability to implicitly learn prototype patterns presented in a series of random dot displays in a classification task (each pattern is labeled either "A" or "not A"; Bozoki et al. 2006). In contrast, imaging studies show that neuronal assemblies in the extrastriate visual cortex (roughly, Brodmann Area 18/19 or visual area V2) deactivate selectively when dot patterns that conform to a previously learned prototype are presented (Koenig et al. 2008), and patient studies have found that performance on this task is impaired in Alzheimer's disease, which often damages this area (Zaki et al. 2003).

However, although extrastriate assemblies appear to learn perceptual prototypes (whether this represents long-term potentiation or short-term adaptation is an open issue), learning and representing the range of discriminations manifest in visual categorization clearly involves a range of functional systems, with different brain regions involved in learning in different contexts (Seger and Miller 2010).

4.2 Higher-level concept learning

The prefrontal cortex (PFC) plays a key role in rule-based learning (Monchi et al. 2001), however, its contribution to the learning *process* is best described as supervising input to other learning systems in the striatum and MTL (Ramscar and Gitcho 2007; Thompson-Schill et al. 2009) both by maintaining representations of explicit goals and by allocating attentional resources (Miller and Cohen 2001).

This characterization is supported by imaging studies of rule-based learning (Konishi et al. 1999; Monchi et al. 2001; Smith et al. 1998) and behavioral experiments showing that tasks that disrupt working memory or attention (known PFC functions) drastically impair performance on rule-based learning tasks (Waldron and Ashby 2001; Zeithamova and Maddox 2006). It is worth noting in this context that rule-based concept learning is very different from linguistic convention learning, where there is evidence that limiting PFC involvement actually benefits learning (Ramscar and Yarlett 2007; Ramscar et al. 2013a).

The actual learning systems most connected with the PFC, and which serve to discriminate the stimulus dimensions that encode concepts for long-term retention are located in the corticostriatal and medial temporal lobe regions (Seger and Miller 2010). The striatum (comprising the caudate, putamen, and nucleus accumbens, *Nacc*) implements an error-sensitive learning system that discriminatively strengthens and weakens associations between stimulus dimensions and behavioral responses and predicted outcomes in learning (Schultz 2006). In contrast to the perceptual regions described earlier, this system appears to learn the predictive, discriminatory codes that support future categorization behavior. However, the exact level at which striatal learning serves to encode concepts is open to question.

One reason why the role of striatal learning in categorization is hard to pin down is that the medial temporal lobe (MTL) also supports learning that is sensitive to prediction error (Davis et al. 2012a, 2012b; see Ramscar et al. 2010b for a tutorial), and also serves an encoding function. As with the striatal system, it is not clear *exactly* what part the MTL plays in concept learning or at what level of abstraction it encodes (indeed, it is not even clear whether this question is appropriate without reference to a learner's prior experience and goals). Some theories have proposed that the MTL learning system approximates an exemplar-model (Ashby and Maddox 2005); however evidence has been presented to suggest that the MTL stores representations of both rules (Nomura et al. 2007) and prototypes (Reber et al. 1998).[3]

It is of course possible that the striatal system might learn one form of conceptual representation, and the MTL another (Bornstein and Daw 2012). However, in reality it is unlikely that the function of *either* system corresponds exactly to any of the models reviewed above. As Kruschke (2008: 269) observes in this regard, "[a] representational assumption for a model does not necessarily imply that the mind makes a formal representation [...] Only a formal model requires a formal description." The brain's actual representational formats should not be expected to correspond to the ones researchers use to model behavior. Similarly, it is unlikely that the functions of brain regions map neatly to functions posited by researchers, such that perception is a function of one system, and learning and categorization others. Indeed, Bussey and Saksida (2007) propose that local brain functions are based on a hierarchy determined by the

---

[3] To confuse matters further, some researchers deny the MTL plays any role in category learning (Ashby et al. 1998). However, this claim also conflicts with any broad definition of categorization, simply because perirhinal cortex – part of the MTL – appears critical to object recognition, and in particular, the discrimination of objects into old and new sets (Winters et al. 2004). Since old/new discrimination is thought of as an important categorization behavior, this debate helps illustrate how categorization is often poorly defined and circumscribed in the literature.

levels of stimulus representations that systems process, rather than traditional cognitive functions like language or memory.

From this perspective, regional functions are differentiated by the levels of stimulus complexity they process (Cowell et al. 2010a, 2010b), and the striatum and MTL are not qualitatively different learning systems, but rather they learn and encode stimulus representations at different levels of abstraction (e.g., features, objects, contexts, etc.). Depending on the experience of the speaker and the context, learning might be focused in the MTL *or* in the striatum, and the degree each region is engaged in specific categorization behavior will depend on the experience of the individual and the behavioral context (Davis et al. 2012a, 2012b).

4.3 Categorization in the brain

Many neural systems contribute to the behaviors we call categorization: There is no categorization area, but rather, consistent with the predictions of systems models such as SUSTAIN, the degree to which brain regions engage in categorization depends on a task, its context and prior learning.

5 Concepts, contrasts and communication

From a linguistic perspective, the general lesson to be drawn from this review is that despite theorists' intuitions about concepts as abstract mental tokens suitable for binding to phrase, word, or morpheme-sized phonetic patterns, this conception of concepts is not supported by research results. Rather, the literature shows:

1. Category assignments vary with context. An item can be an exemplar of one category in one context, and another category in another context.
2. Even when people learn concepts with clear and consistent definitions, the representations they acquire diverge from these definitions.
3. When people list the properties of natural concepts, they may produce convergent sets of features that characterize these concepts, but these generally do not adequately define or discriminate between concepts.
4. The tasks people perform when learning to categorize has a strong effect on the representations they acquire.
5. Depending on the task and context in which people perform categorization tasks it appears that a variety of brain regions are differentially engaged in the behaviors we call categorization.

It seems clear that in the course of learning the relationships between a set of items and a label, people do not abstract a discrete concept that specifies these relationships. Instead, categorization can engage almost any aspect of a person's knowledge, depending on their experience, the context and the task. These conclusions are supported by modeling efforts which show how conceptual behaviors are best accounted for by systems in which behavioral outcomes do not imply explicit knowledge representations (Baayen et al. 2013) and in which consistent conceptual behavior emerges without the use of the discrete representations our intuitive understanding of the word concept implies (Love et al. 2004). These conclusions are further supported by neuroscience findings revealing the equally varied and complex relationship between categorization behaviors and neural processes.

5.1 Learning, discrimination and language

If, as seems clear, concepts are not mental tokens, then explaining the role of words in communication is likely to depend on our understanding the processes governing word use. Providing a detailed account of the processes that support the learning and use of language is beyond the scope of this review (indeed, we do not pretend that we have a comprehensive account). However, one implication of these results is easy to state and is clearly important to understanding of language: it is clear to us that concept learning is a *discriminative process*. In explaining what this means, and why it is important, we will try to sketch out some of its implications for our understanding of human communication.

We noted above that the brain regions that support learning about lexical "concepts" implement *error-driven learning processes* (Schultz 2006). Most psychologists and linguists labor under the erroneous belief that learning is a combinatorial process in which correlations lead to simple associations forming between stimuli (Rescorla 1988). However, the error-driven learning processes that have been shown to govern what we call associative learning are *discriminative* (Ramscar et al. 2013c). That is, they reapportion attentional and representational resources to minimize future *predictive* uncertainty (Rescorla and Wagner 1972; Sutton and Barto 1998).

Importantly, although linguistic meaning is rarely couched in these terms, it is clear that that uncertainty reduction lies at the heart of communication: Virtually every linguistic act – even saying, "Hello!" – is intended to reduce a listener's uncertainty, whether about the world, about the thoughts and feelings of a speaker, or a speaker's sincerity, etc. Error-driven learning tunes the representation of relevant features of the environment by incrementally discriminating against uninformative cues (those that do not improve predictions) and reinforcing informative cues (those that do tend to support successful predictions) in response to events as they unfold (Ramscar et al. 2010b). It generates predictive representations that serve to minimize uncertainty in discriminating between sets of possible outcomes (i.e., about what a speaker might mean in a given context, or what verbal gesture might be uttered next).

These representations are formed by a process of learning to *ignore* – i.e., discriminate against cues that are not informative for the discrimination being learned. If learners learn the relationships between utterances in context and specific words by this process, it implies that they will learn about the contexts in which a word can be expected to occur or be appropriately used. This learning will occur as a result of speakers' attempts to predict the next segment, syllable or word that an interlocutor uses.

This in turn suggests that the relationship between categories (a domain with a huge array of dimensions) and labels (a domain with a relatively small number of phonetic dimensions) is subject to an important constraint. A naïve view of labels is that they serve to encode or otherwise map onto meanings, such that that they support the retrieval of underlying semantic categories. For example, it is usually supposed that a phonological pattern like *dog* serves as a pointer or a link to the concept of dog. However, the evidence we have reviewed indicates that learners acquire a variety of representations comprising information at numerous of levels of abstraction relating to a word like *dog*, and mapping a low-dimensional space of labels onto this set of high-dimensional representations in a determinate way is not possible (Ramscar et al. 2010b).

Linguists have assumed since Saussure that the relationship between words and meanings is bidirectional (suggested by the up and down arrows in Saussure's model for a *linguistic sign* connecting a graphic image of a tree – the meaning – with the orthographic Latin word *arbor*). The array of evidence indicating that conceptual learning processes are error-driven makes clear that this relationship must actually be unidirectional. Error-driven learning processes encourage the acquisition of representations in which word meanings – and other words in the context – are part of a high-dimensional predictive code that allows word identities to be discriminated and uncertainty about communicative intentions to be reduced. They are completely unsuited to acquiring representations in which words directly encode meanings such that Meanings predict Signals *and* Signals predict Meanings (Ramscar et al. 2010b).

It is interesting to consider representational proposals such as *frames*, *ICMs*, *image schemas*, and *domains* in this light. When these proposals are conceived of as theories of representation, it is assumed that at some level, something that resembles a frame (or ICM, image schema or domain) *corresponds* to a similar level of linguistic construction (or feature), such that at an appropriate level of granularity, the frame (ICM, image schema or domain) *represents* the meaning of a construction or feature (i.e., these structures are thought to facilitate the process of going from the signal to the meaning). We noted above that none of these proposals has been described with the specificity required to explain how this actually works, and it is likely that the problems of mapping spaces of different dimensionalities this would entail means that it is impossible to do so (Ramscar et al. 2010b). (Although these proposals fail to meet the criteria for theories of representation, they may still be useful phenomenological descriptions of some aspects of the knowledge encoded in discriminative linguistic and conceptual systems; Rosch 1978.)

5.2 The concept of information

The predictive, discriminative codes that error-driven learning processes generate share many properties with the codes that *information theory* specifies for artificial communication systems (Shannon 1948). It is thus worth highlighting that artificial information systems are not merely digital in the commonly understood sense that they make use of binary codes of ones and zeros, but also in the more interesting sense that in information theory, the "information" communicated in systems is broken down into a system of discrete, discriminable states that can be encoded by various combinations of ones and zeros.

Shannon (1948: 379) defines artificial communication as the process of:

> reproducing at one point either exactly or approximately a message selected at another point. Frequently the messages have meaning; that is they refer to or are correlated according to some system with certain physical or conceptual entities. *These semantic aspects of communication are irrelevant to the engineering problem.* [Our emphasis]

Artificial communication systems encode discriminable messages in a common *source code* (which defines a system for contrasting between messages) and a receiver makes use of this code in order to discriminate (select) the actual message that has been sent in a signal from other possible signals. There is no meaning in this signal itself, but rather in the context of the source code, the zeros and ones that each message comprises serve to incrementally reduce uncertainty about the actual message being received.

Although it may seem counterintuitive, the findings we have reviewed indicate that the way in which we learn new conceptual distinctions is best characterized as a process that increases either the number of words and phrases that our minds are able to discriminate or the range of contexts across which known words and phrases can be discriminated (Ramscar et al. 2010b). Thus, for example, Ramscar et al. (2013d) show that changes in people's ability to learn the paired association of arbitrary words across the lifespan can be accurately predicted if the process is modeled discriminatively. People's ability to learn frequently co-occurring pairs, like *lock* and *door* differs little with age, whereas word pairs like *jury* and *eagle* become increasingly difficult to learn. Because the latter co-occur extremely rarely, discriminative learning causes them to become *negatively* associated in a system predicting lexical events. However, since both words are relatively infrequent, it takes many years of language experience for speakers to learn to this relationship well enough to exploit the negative expectation of *eagle* given *jury* in everyday language use. Negative associations not only help explain why learning pairs like *jury* and *eagle* gets more difficult the older a speaker as compared to pairs like *lock* and *door*, they allow discriminative learning models (Rescorla and Wagner 1972) to quantitatively predict the changes in their learnability across the lifespan with remarkable accuracy (Ramscar et al. 2013d).

From a discriminative perspective, language learning can be characterized as acquiring and mastering a predictive code for a system of lexical and phrasal contrasts. Language production can then be seen as the process of using this system to construct a message that best represents a speaker's intended meaning. A linguistic *signal* can be thought of as all of the conventional audible and visible behaviors of a speaking person (or, in written language, orthographic and other visual cues). Because the listener possesses a system of conventionalized knowledge relating semantic cues to signals that is similar to the one the speaker uses to construct her *message*, he is able to anticipate (that is, at least partially predict) the speaker's intended meaning by reconstructing the message from the signal itself. Other aspects of the message will be contained in the differences between what the speaker says and the learner predicts, and these differences will result in learning; an essential aspect of linguistic communication.

There is much consensus among cognitive linguists that intention reading – social prediction – is an important component of word learning (Tomasello 2003, 2008). The perspective we describe – which is a function of the way people learn to relate words to the world (Ramscar et al. 2013b) – simply extends intention reading to language processing more generally. Comprehension arises out of what listeners know – which enables them to predict a speaker – and what listeners *learn* from the speaker: identifying the words and constructions that a speaker actually says leads to learning about why a speaker made the choices they did.

Just as the source code lies at the heart of artificial communication systems, *linguistic codes* are the heart of language. The linguistic code is the entire conventionalized inventory of phones, words, idioms, expressions, collocations and constructions shared by a community of speakers and listeners that enable them to communicate. Importantly, rather than something that is explicitly encoded in the words of a message, meaning is merely implicit in the common linguistic code. The conventionalized, *systematic* relations that hold probabilistically between all the linguistic signals as well as between the signals and the world enable listeners to incrementally reduce uncertainty about the messages speakers send in context (Ramscar et al. 2010b; 2013c). In a linguistic signal – that is, in an utterance or piece of text – the occurrence of a word does not serve as a pointer to a concept, but rather in the context of the signal and the message, the word serves to reduce the listener's uncertainty about the speaker's intent. As is the case with an artificial communication system, the meaning is never "in" the signal. Instead the signal serves to reduce uncertainty in the listener's head about the actual intended meaning in the speaker's message (Ramscar and Baayen 2013).

5.3 Meaning and learning

Characterizing human communication in this way highlights a very obvious difference between human and artificial communication systems: Human communicators learn as they go, whereas most artificial systems don't. Thus whereas the goal of an artificial communication system is to send a signal that is predictable with $p = 1$, messages in human communication are rarely, if ever, intended to be perfectly predictable simply because they are *intended* to evoke or even highlight a listener's uncertainty about some aspect of what a speaker intends.

A number of researchers working on language have concluded that language understanding includes a process of making moment-to-moment predictions about what is coming next when listening to speech (Altmann and Mirkovic 2009; Kutas and Federmeier 2007). However this kind of moment-to-moment prediction has usually been seen as *assisting* the comprehension of linguistic signals that encode meanings in the traditional concept-by-concept ways that categorization research was expected to illuminate. Our review suggests this research can offer no such illumination simply because words do not *encode* meanings. Rather, because prediction drives learning, and because the function of learning is uncertainty reduction, prediction lies at the heart of linguistic communication. Seen from this perspective, moment-to-moment prediction in language does not merely help in the processing of language, but rather, because prediction drives learning, it is a critical part of the process that makes linguistic communication meaningful (Ramscar and Baayen 2013).

We end by acknowledging that although the view of communication we have sketched out manages to avoid many of the problems involved in appealing to illusory mechanisms like concepts, it paints a picture of language that is very different from traditional ideas, and that likely clashes with many researchers' beliefs about what language is. On the other hand, this perspective is still consistent with the impetus behind much work in cognitive linguistics in that its assumptions are shared with theories of learning and cognitive processing on multiple levels. And it is highly compatible with the findings of the research reviewed here.

6 Summary

Despite the way categorization researchers often describe their object of study, the detailed results of their work show that the representation of conceptual knowledge does not involve a neat story about inventories of individuated conceptual tokens. Rather, these results show that conceptual knowledge is as bound by context as language is itself (Malt 2013). Looking beyond naïve, intuitive conceptions of concepts, it is clear that cognitive linguists have much to learn from researchers' increasing understanding of the processes that give rise to systematic categorization behavior. We have sketched one way in which the insights that have arisen out of research into concepts and categories is likely to have an impact on our understanding of language. It will be fascinating to see what develops out of a richer synthesis of these lines of enquiry in the future.

7 References

Altmann, Gerry and Jelena Mirković (2009): Incrementality and prediction in human sentence processing. *Cognitive Science* 33: 1–27.
Anderson, John R. (1991): The adaptive nature of human categorization. *Psychological Review* 98: 409–429.
Arnon, Inbal and Michael Ramscar (2012): Granularity and the acquisition of grammatical gender: How order of acquisition affects what gets learned. *Cognition* 122(3): 292–305.
Ashby, Gregory, Leola Alfonso-Reese, And Turken, and Elliott Waldron (1998): A neuropsychological theory of multiple systems in category learning. *Psychological Review* 105(3): 442–481.
Ashby, Gregory and Todd Maddox (2005): Human category learning. *Annual Review of Psychology* 56: 149–178.

Baayen, Harald, Peter Hendrix, and Michael Ramscar (2013): Sidestepping the combinatorial explosion: Towards a processing model based on discriminative learning. *Language and Speech* 56(3): 329–347.

Barsalou, Lawrence (1983): Ad hoc categories. *Memory and Cognition* 11(3): 211–227.

Billman, Dorrit and James Knutson (1996): Unsupervised concept learning and value systematicity: A complex whole aids learning the parts. *Journal of Experimental Psychology: Learning, Memory, and Cognition* 22: 458–475.

Bornstein, Aaron and Nathaniel D. Daw (2012): Dissociating hippocampal and striatal contributions to sequential prediction learning. *European Journal of Neuroscience* 35(7): 1011–1023.

Boroditsky, Lera and Michael Ramscar (2002): The roles of body and mind in abstract thought. *Psychological Science* 13(2): 185–189.

Bozokia, Andrea, Murray Grossman, and Edward Smith (2006): Can patients with Alzheimer's disease learn a category implicitly? *Neuropsychologia* 44(5): 816–827.

Brooks, Lee, Geoffrey Norman and Scott Allen (1991): Role of specific similarity in a medical diagnostic task. *Journal of Experimental Psychology: General* 120(3): 278.

Bruner, Jerome, Jacqueline Goodnow, and George Austin (1956): *A Study of Thinking*. New York: John Wiley and Sons, Inc.

Bussey, Tim and Lisa Saksida (2007): Memory, perception, and the ventral visual-perirhinal-hippocampal stream: Thinking outside of the boxes. *Hippocampus* 17: 898–908.

Cienki, Alan (2007): Frames, Idealized Cognitive Models and domains. *The Oxford Handbook of Cognitive Linguistics*, 170–187. Oxford: Oxford University Press.

Collins, Allan and Ross Quillian (1969): Retrieval time from semantic memory. *Journal of Verbal Learning and Verbal Behavior* 8(2): 240–247.

Cowell, Rosemary, Tim Bussey, and Lisa Saksida (2010a): Components of recognition memory: Dissociable cognitive processes or just differences in representational complexity? *Hippocampus* 20(11): 1245–262.

Cowell, Rosemary, Tim Bussey, and Lisa Saksida (2010b): Functional dissociations within the ventral object processing pathway: Cognitive modules or a hierarchical continuum? *Journal of Cognitive Neuroscience* 22: 2460–2479.

Crawford, Elizabeth, Janellen Huttenlocher, and Peder Hans Engebretson (2000): Category effects on estimates of stimuli: Perception or reconstruction? *Psychological Science* 11(4): 280–284.

Davis, Tyler, Bradley Love, and Alison Preston (2012a): Learning the exception to the rule: Model-based fMRI reveals specialized representations for surprising category members. *Cerebral Cortex* 22(2): 260–273.

Davis, Tyler, Bradley Love, and Alison Preston (2012b): Striatal and hippocampal entropy and recognition signals in category learning: Simultaneous processes revealed by model-based fMRI. *Journal of Experimental Psychology: Learning, Memory, and Cognition* 38: 821–839.

Davis, Tyler, Gui Xue, Bradley Love, Alison Preston, and Russell Poldrack (2014): Global neural pattern similarity as a common basis for categorization and recognition memory. *Journal of Neuroscience* 34(22): 7472–7484.

Erickson, Michael and John Kruschke (1998): Rules and exemplars in category learning. *Journal of Experimental Psychology: General* 127(2): 107–140.

Evans, Vyvyan (volume 3): Time. Berlin/Boston: De Gruyter Mouton.

Fillmore Charles (1982): Frame semantics. In: Linguistic Society of Korea (ed.), *Linguistics in the Morning Calm*, 111–137. Seoul: Hanshin.

Frege, Gottlob (1892): Über Sinn und Bedeutung. *Zeitschrift für Philosophie und philosophische Kritik* 100: 25–50.
Gahl, Suzanne (2008): "Thyme" and "Time" are not homophones. The effect of lemma frequency on word durations in spontaneous speech. *Language* 84: 474–496.
Goldstone, Robert and Alan Kersten (2003): Concepts and categories. In: A. F. Healy and R. W. Proctor (eds.), *Comprehensive Handbook of Psychology*, Volume 4:00 *Experimental Psychology*, 591–621. New York: Wiley.
Goodman, Nelson (1972): Seven strictures on similarity. In: N. Goodman (ed.), *Problems and Projects*. New York: The Bobbs-Merrill Co.
Hampton, James (1995): Testing the prototype theory of concepts. *Journal of Memory and Language* 34(5): 686–708.
Hull, Clarke (1920): Quantitative aspects of the evolution of concepts. *Psychological Monographs* XXVIII(1.123): 1–86.
Johansen, Mark and Thomas Palmeri (2002): Are there representational shifts during category learning? *Cognitive Psychology* 45(4): 482–553.
Johnson, Mark (1987): *The Body in the Mind: The Bodily Basis of Meaning, Imagination, and Reason*. Chicago: University of Chicago Press.
Kanwisher, Nancy, Josh McDermott, and Marvin Chun (1997): The fusiform face area: a module in human extrastriate cortex specialized for face perception. *The Journal of Neuroscience* 17(11): 4302–4311.
Koenig, Phyllis, Edward Smith, Vanessa Troiani, Chivon Anderson, Peachie Moore, and Murray Grossman (2008): Medial temporal lobe involvement in an implicit memory task: Evidence of collaborating implicit and explicit memory systems from and Alzheimer's disease. *Cerebral Cortex* 18: 2831–2843.
Konishi, S., M. Kawazu, I. Uchida, H. Kikyo, I. Asakura, and Y. Miyashita (1999): Contribution of working memory to transient activation in human inferior prefrontal cortex during performance of the Wisconsin Card Sorting Test. *Cerebral Cortex* 9(7): 745–753.
Kruschke, John (1992): ALCOVE: An exemplar-based connectionist model of category learning. *Psychological Review* 99: 22–44.
Kruschke, John (1996): Base rates in category learning. *Journal of Experimental Psychology: Learning, Memory and Cognition* 22: 3–26.
Kruschke, John (2001): Toward a unified model of attention in associative learning. *Journal of Mathematical Psychology* 45(6): 812–863.
Kruschke, John (2008): Models of categorization. *The Cambridge Handbook of Computational Psychology*, 267–301. Cambridge: Cambridge University Press.
Kutas, Martha and Kara Federmeier (2007): Event-related brain potential (ERP) studies of sentence processing. In: G. Gaskell (ed.), *Oxford Handbook of Psycholinguistics*, 385–406. Oxford: Oxford University Press.
Labov, William (1973): The boundaries of words and their meanings. In: C.-J. N. Bailey and R. W. Shuy (eds.), *New Ways of Analyzing Variation in English*, 340–373. Washington, DC: Georgetown University Press.
Lakoff, George (1987): *Women, Fire, and Dangerous Things: What Categories Reveal About the Mind*. Chicago: University of Chicago Press.
Lakoff, George (1993): The contemporary theory of metaphor. *Metaphor and Thought* 2: 202–251.
Logothetis, Nikos and David Sheinberg (1996): Visual object recognition. *Annual Review of Neuroscience* 19(1): 577–621.

Love, Bradley (2002): Comparing supervised and unsupervised category learning. *Psychonomic Bulletin and Review* 9: 829–835.

Love, Bradley, Douglas Medin, and Todd Gureckis (2004): SUSTAIN: A network model of category learning. *Psychological Review* 111(2): 309–332.

Lusk, Christopher (2011): Conifer–angiosperm interactions: Physiological ecology and life history. *Smithsonian Contributions to Botany* 95: 158–164.

McCloskey, Michael and Sam Glucksberg (1978): Natural categories: Well defined or fuzzy sets? *Memory and Cognition* 6(4): 462–472.

Mack, Michael, Alison Preston, and Bradley Love (2013): Decoding the brain's algorithm for categorization from its neural implementation. *Current Biology* 23: 2023–2027.

Malt, Barbara (2013): Context sensitivity and insensitivity in object naming. *Language and Cognition* 5: 81–97.

Malt, Barbara, Silvia Gennari, and Mutsumi Imai (2010): Lexicalization patterns and the world-to-words mapping. In: B. Malt and P. Wolff (eds.), *Words and the Mind: How Words Encode Human Experience*, 29–57. Oxford: Oxford University Press.

Medin, Douglas and Marguerite Schaffer (1978): Context theory of classification learning. *Psychological Review* 85(3): 207–238.

Miller, Earl and Jonathan Cohen (2001): An integrative theory of prefrontal cortex function. *Annual Review of Neuroscience* 24(1): 167–202.

Monchi, Oury, Michael Petrides, Valentina Petre, Keith Worsley, and Alain Dagher (2001): Wisconsin card sorting revisited: Distinct neural circuits participating in different stages of the task identified by event-related functional magnetic resonance imaging. *Journal of Neuroscience* 21: 7733–7741.

Nomura, Emi, Todd Maddox, Vincent Filoteo, David Ing, Darren Gitelman, Todd Parrish, Marchsel Mesulam, and Paul Reber (2007): Neural correlates of rule-based and information-integration visual category learning. *Cerebral Cortex* 17(1): 37–43.

Nosofsky, Robert (1991): Tests of an exemplar model for relating perceptual classification and recognition memory. *Journal of Experimental Psychology: Human Perception and Performance* 17: 3–27.

Nosofsky, Robert (1992): Similarity scaling and cognitive process models. *Annual Review of Psychology* 43(1): 25–53.

Palmeri, Thomas, Stephen Goldinger, and David Pisoni (1993): Episodic encoding of voice attributes and recognition memory for spoken words. *Journal of Experimental Psychology: Learning, Memory, and Cognition* 19(2): 309–328.

Port, Robert (2010): Language is a social institution: Why phonemes and words do not have explicit psychological form. *Ecological Psychology* 22: 304–326.

Port, Robert and Adam Leary (2005): Against formal phonology. *Language* 81: 927–964.

Posner, Michael and Steven Keele (1967): Decay of visual information from a single letter. *Science* 158: 137–139.

Posner, Michael and Steven Keele (1970): Retention of abstract ideas. *Journal of Experimental Psychology* 83(2): 304–308.

Quine, Willard Van Orman (1960): *Word and Object*. Cambridge: MIT Press.

Ramscar, Michael and Harald Baayen (2013): Production, comprehension and synthesis: A communicative perspective on language. *Frontiers in Language Sciences* 4: 233.

Ramscar, Michael, Melody Dye, Jessica Gustafson, and Joseph Klein (2013a): Dual routes to cognitive flexibility: Learning and response conflict resolution in the dimensional change card sort task. *Child Development* 84(4): 1308–1323.

Ramscar, Michael, Melody Dye, and Joseph Klein (2013b): Children value informativity over logic in word learning. *Psychological Science* 24(6): 1017–1023.
Ramscar, Michael, Melody Dye and Stewart McCauley (2013c): Error and expectation in language learning: The curious absence of 'mouses' in adult speech. *Language* 89(4): 760–793.
Ramscar, Michael and Nichole Gitcho (2007): Developmental change and the nature of learning in childhood. *Trends In Cognitive Science* 11(7): 274–279.
Ramscar, Michael and Ulrike Hahn (1998): What family resemblances are not: The continuing relevance of Wittgenstein to the study of concepts and categories. *Proceedings of the 20th Annual Conference of the Cognitive Science Society,* University of Wisconsin – Madison.
Ramscar, Michael, Peter Hendrix, Bradley Love, and Harald Baayen (2013d): Learning is not decline: The mental lexicon as a window into cognition across the lifespan. *The Mental Lexicon* 8(3): 450–481.
Ramscar, Michael, Peter Hendrix, Cyrus Shaoul, Petar Milin, and Harald Baayen (2014): The myth of cognitive decline: Non-linear dynamics of lifelong learning. *Topics in Cognitive Science* 6: 5–42.
Ramscar, Michael, Teenie Matlock, and Melody Dye (2010a): Running down the clock: The role of expectation in our understanding of time and motion. *Language and Cognitive Processes* 25(5): 589–615.
Ramscar, Michael and Daniel Yarlett (2007): Linguistic self-correction in the absence of feedback: A new approach to the logical problem of language acquisition. *Cognitive Science* 31: 927–960.
Ramscar, Michael, Daniel Yarlett, Melody Dye, Katie Denny, and Kirsten Thorpe (2010b): The effects of feature-label-order and their implications for symbolic learning. *Cognitive Science* 34(6): 909–957.
Reber, Paul, Craig Stark, and Larry Squire (1998): Contrasting cortical activity associated with category memory and recognition memory. *Learning and Memory* 5(6): 420–428.
Rescorla, Robert (1988): Pavlovian conditioning: It's not what you think it is. *American Psychologist* 43: 151–160.
Rescorla, Robert and Allan Wagner (1972): A theory of Pavlovian conditioning: Variations in the effectiveness of reinforcement and nonreinforcement. In: A. H. Black and W. F. Prokasy (eds.), *Classical Conditioning II: Current Research and Theory,* 64–99. New York: Crofts.
Rips, Lance, Edward Smith, and Douglas Medin (2013): Concepts and categories: Memory, meaning, and metaphysics. In: K. J. Holyoak and R. G. Morrison (eds.), *The Oxford Handbook of Thinking and Reasoning,* 177–209. Oxford: Oxford University Press.
Rosch, Eleanor (1978): Principles of categorization. In: E. Rosch and B. B. Lloyd (eds.), *Cognition and Categorization,* 27–48. Hillsdale: Erlbaum.
Rosch, Eleanor, and Carolyn Mervis (1975): Family resemblances: Studies in the internal structure of categories. *Cognitive Psychology* 7(4): 573–605.
Rosch, Eleanor, Carolyn Mervis, Wayne Gray, David Johnson and Penny Boyes-Braem (1976): Basic objects in natural categories. *Cognitive Psychology* 8(3): 382–439.
Sakamoto, Yasuaki and Bradley Love (2004): Schematic influences on category learning and recognition memory. *Journal of Experimental Psychology: General* 33: 534–553.
Schultz, Wolfram (2006): Behavioral theories and the neurophysiology of reward. *Annual Review of Psychology* 57: 87–115.

Seger, Carol and Earl Miller (2010): Category learning in the brain. *Annual Review of Neuroscience* 33: 203–219.

Shannon, Claude (1948): A mathematical theory of communication. *Bell Systems Technical Journal* 27(3): 379–423.

Shepard, Roger, Carl Hovland, and Herbert Jenkins (1961): Learning and memorization of classifications. *Psychological Monographs* 75: 13.

Smith, David and Paul Minda (2000): 30 categorization results in search of a model. *Journal of Experimental Psychology: Learning, Memory, and Cognition* 26(1): 3–27.

Smith, Edward E., Andrea L. Patalano, and John Jonides (1998): Alternative strategies of categorization. *Cognition* 65(2): 167–196.

Smoke, Kenneth (1932): An objective study of concepts formation. *Psychological Monographs* XLII(191): 1–46.

Sutton, Richard and Andrew Barto (1998): *Reinforcement Learning*. Cambridge: MIT Press.

Taylor, John (2003): *Linguistic Categorization*. Oxford: Oxford University Press.

Tomasello, Michael (2003): *Constructing a Language: A Usage-Based Theory of Language Acquisition*. Cambridge: Harvard University Press.

Tomasello, Michael (2008): *Origins of Human Communication*. Cambridge: MIT Press.

Thompson-Schill, Sharon, Michael Ramscar, and Evangelia Chrysikou (2009): Cognition without control: when a little frontal lobe goes a long way. *Current Directions in Psychological Science* 8(5): 259–263.

Vogels, Rufin (2008): Categorization of complex visual images by rhesus monkeys. Part 2:00 single-cell study. *European Journal of Neuroscience* 11(4): 1239–1255.

Waldron, Elliott and Gregory Ashby (2001): The effects of concurrent task interference on category learning: Evidence for multiple category learning systems. *Psychonomic Bulletin and Review* 8(1): 168–176.

Winters Boyer, Suzanne Forwood, Rosemary Cowell, Lisa Saksida, and Tim Bussey (2004): Double dissociation between the effects of peri-postrhinal cortex and hippocampal lesions on tests of object recognition and spatial memory: Heterogeneity of function within the temporal lobe. *Journal of Neuroscience* 24: 5901–5908.

Wittgenstein, Ludwig (1953): *Philosophical Investigations*. London: Blackwell.

Yamauchi, Takashi, Bradley Love, and Arthur Markman (2002): Learning non-linearly separable categories by inference and classification. *Journal of Experimental Psychology: Learning, Memory, and Cognition* 28: 585–593.

Zaki, Safa, Robert Nosofsky, Nenette Jessup, and Frederick Unverzagt (2003): Categorization and recognition performance of a memory-impaired group. *Journal of the International Neuropsychological Society* 9(3): 394–406.

Zeithamova, Dagmar and Todd Maddox (2006): Dual-task interference in perceptual category learning. *Memory and Cognition* 34(2): 387–398.

Zentall, Thomas, Edward Wasserman, and Peter Urcuioli (2014): Associative concept learning in animals. *Journal of the Experimental Analysis of Behavior* 101(1): 130–151.

R. Harald Baayen and Michael Ramscar
Chapter 5: Abstraction, storage and naive discriminative learning

1 Introduction

The English sentence *you want milk* can be uttered in a variety of circumstances, such as a mother about to feed her baby (answer: *bweeeh*), a father asking a toddler whether she would like a glass of milk (answer: *yes please*), or an air hostess serving black tea in economy class (answer: *sure*). Furthermore, similar sentences (*you want coffee, you want water, would you like coffee, would you like a cup of coffee*) can also be produced and understood appropriately across a wide variety of contexts. What are the cognitive principles that allow us to produce and understand these and a great many other different sentences across an even greater kaleidoscope of contexts and situations?

In this chapter, we discuss three very different approaches that have sought to answer this fundamental question about the workings of language. We begin with the oldest one, the structuralist tradition and its formalist offshoots, which posits that rules obtained by a process of abstraction are essential to understanding language. The second approach argues that generalizations are achieved not through abstraction, but by analogical reasoning over large numbers of instances of language use stored in memory. Finally, the third takes the perspective that to understand language and linguistic productivity, it is essential to take into account well-established basic principles of discrimination learning.

2 Abstraction

In traditional abstractionist approaches to language, it is assumed that the contexts in which a question such as *you want milk* can be uttered are so varied that the properties characterizing these contexts must be powerless as predictors of a given utterance. Accordingly, a child learning language is thought to face the problem of abstracting away from all the irrelevant contextual information in

---

R. Harald Baayen, Tübingen, DE
Michael Ramscar, Tübingen, DE

order to identify a level of elemental representations that capture abstract commonalities in instances of usage.

The common core of the set of utterances of *you want milk* is thus identified as roughly an abstract tri-partite knowledge structure comprising the phonological elements ($[(ju)_w(wɒnt)_w(mɪlk)_s]$) a syntactic structure comprising the elements ($[_{NP}$ you$[_{VP}$ want $[_{NP}$ milk]]]) and a semantic structure comprising the elements DESIRE(YOU, MILK).

It is then assumed that rules link the volitional agent element in the semantic structure to the subject element of the syntactic structure, while other rules specify that the pronoun element *you* is the string of phonemic elements [ju]. Typically, in order to keep the knowledge base as lean as possible, only the most elementary units (phonemes, morphemes, semantic primitives) and the rules for combining these units into well-formed sequences are stored in memory. Thus, the semantic structure DESIRE(YOU, MILK) would not be available in memory as such. Instead, only a more abstract structure, DESIRE(X, Y) would be stored, where X is a symbolic placeholder for any volitional agent able or imagined to be able to have desires, and Y any object, person, state, or event that is desired, or can be imagined to be desirable.

To further cut down memory requirements, and to make the relationships between words and utterances as transparent as possible, inheritance hierarchies (a formalism developed in the context of object-oriented programming languages) have been adopted in this context (see, e.g., Steels and De Beule 2006, for fluid construction grammar). Thus, instead of having to store different kinds of milk (*cow milk, goat's milk, sheep milk, mother milk, camel milk, coffee milk, coconut milk, ...*) and all their properties as separate lexical entries, one can set up one entry for the most typical kind of milk (e.g., the cow milk as bought in the supermarket),

MILK: [type: thing;
properties: concrete, inanimate, imageable, fluid, ...;
function: to be consumed by drinking;
color: white;
source: cows],

and keep the entries for the other kinds of milk lean by having them inherit all the properties defined in the entry for milk except for where otherwise specified:

CAMEL MILK:
MILK [source: female camels].

When a mother offers milk to her child, while uttering *you want milk*, the semantic structure of the utterance may thus be characterized by lexical conceptual structures (Jackendoff 1990) such as

OFFER(MOTHER, CHILD, MILK)
ASK(MOTHER, CHILD, IS-TRUE(CHILD(DESIRE, MILK))).

These structures are, however, themselves the outcome of the application of more abstract semantic structures

OFFER(X, Y, Z)
ASK(X,Y, IS-TRUE(DESIRE, Y, Z)))

which also cover utterances such as *you want to play* and *you want to sleep*.

Several proposals have been made as to how such abstract structures (and the elements that they combine) might be identified or acquired. One class of theories holds that the language learner is genetically endowed with a set of abstract rules, constraints or primitives. This innate knowledge of an underlying universal abstract grammar relieves the learner of having to figure out the basic principles of human grammars, since these basics can be assumed to already be in place. Accordingly, the learner's task is reduced to solving simpler problems such as figuring out the proper word order in English for three-argument verbs in the light of innate knowledge such as verbs can have three arguments, word order can be fixed, etc.

However, innate rules and constraints by themselves have no explanatory value. Moreover, a half a century of research has not lead to any solid, generally accepted results that confirm that the basic principles of formal (computer) languages developed in the second half of the twentieth century are part of the human race's genetic endowment.

It should be noted, however, that not all rule-based theories of abstract linguistic structure make an explicit commitment to innate linguistic knowledge: in constraint-based approaches (see, e.g., Dressler 1985; Prince and Smolensky 2008), constraints can be argued to have functional motivations (see, e.g., Boersma 1998; Boersma and Hayes 2001). In phonology, for instance, voiceless realizations might be dispreferred due to voiced segments, as voiced segments require more articulatory effort, and hence more energy, than voiceless segments. In syntax, constraints might also be functionally grounded. For the dative alternation, for instance, a functional rationale motivating the observed preferences for particular constituent orders would be to provide a consistent and predictable flow of information, with given referents preceding non-given referents, pronouns preceding non-pronouns, definites preceding indefinites, and shorter constituents preceding longer constituents (Bresnan et al. 2007). However, even for constraints with reasonably plausible functional motivations, it is unclear how these constraints are learned. The problem here is that what is a hard constraint in one language, can be a soft constraint in another, and not a constraint at all in yet a third language. Skeptics of functional explanations will argue that functionally motivated constraints are unhelpful because it is not clear under what circumstances they are more, or less, in force.

Would it be possible to induce rules without invoking innate principles or presumed functional constraints? At least one proposal – the minimum generalization learning algorithm of Albright and Hayes (2003) – seeks to do exactly this in the domain of morphology. The algorithm gradually learns more abstract rules by iteratively comparing pairs of forms. Each comparison identifies what a pair of forms have in common, and wherever possible creates a more abstract rule on the basis of shared features.

For instance, transposed to syntax, given the utterances *you want milk* and *you want juice*, the minimum generalization learning algorithm would derive the structure

OFFER(MOTHER, CHILD, Z)
ASK(MOTHER, CHILD, IS-TRUE(DESIRE(CHILD,Z))
Z [type: thing;
properties: concrete, inanimate, imageable, fluid, ...;
function: to be consumed by drinking]

by deletion of the feature-value pairs [source:cow] and [source:fruit] in the respective semantic structures of the individual sentences.

For the pair of utterances *you want to play* and *you want to eat*, the shared abstract structure would be

OFFER(MOTHER, CHILD, Z)
ASK(MOTHER, CHILD, IS-TRUE(DESIRE(CHILD, Z)))
Z [type: event;
properties: volitional agent, social activity, ...;
agent: the child].

When in turn these structures are compared for further abstraction, all that remains is

OFFER(MOTHER, CHILD, Z)
ASK(MOTHER, CHILD, IS-TRUE(DESIRE(CHILD, Z)))

In turn, when the utterances are used with different interlocutors, this will undergo a further abstraction to

OFFER(X, Y, Z)
ASK(X, Y, IS-TRUE((DESIRE, Y, Z)))

A salient property of abstractionist theories is that although the rules and constructions are deduced from a systematic and comprehensive scan of any and all of the utterances in a language, the utterances themselves are discarded once the rules and constructions have been properly inferred. From the perspective of language processing, this raises several questions: First, if the original utterances are required for rule deduction, and hence have to be available in memory, why would they be discarded once the rules have been discovered?

Second, rule deduction requires a comprehensive set of utterances, but in real life, utterances become available one by one over time. We must thus assume that at some point in late childhood, after rule deduction is complete and the language has been learned, that the traces of past experience with the language can therefore be erased from a learner's memory. Yet this kind of fundamental discontinuity in the learning process seems at odds with recent evidence that language learning is a process that continues throughout one's lifetime (see, e.g., Ramscar et al. 2014, 2013d).

Third, the number of utterances that need to be stored in memory for rule deduction may be prohibitively large. Corpus surveys have revealed that there are hundreds of millions of sequences of just four words in English. Yet while some studies have reported frequency effects for sequences of words (Bannard and Matthews 2008; Arnon and Snider 2010; Tremblay and Baayen 2010), which have been argued to support the existence of representations of multi-word sequences in the mental lexicon (or mental construction), Shaoul et al. (2013) observed that knowledge about word sequences appears to be restricted to sequences no longer than four, perhaps five, words. Accordingly, it is unlikely that syntactic rules, especially those for complex sentences with main and subordinate clauses, could arise by a process of abstraction from a large set of stored full sentences, as the evidence suggests that the brain doesn't retain a rich set of memory traces for long complex sentences, but only for shorter sequences of words.

Abstractionist approaches presuppose that language is best understood as a formal calculus. A strength this provides is that it puts at their disposal all of the technology developed over many decades in computer science, and it is worth noting that most computationally implemented theories of various different aspects of linguistic cognition, whatever the very different schools of thought they come from, make use of abstractionist decompositional frameworks, as do most formal linguistic theories. Although the lexical conceptual structures of Jackendoff (1990) and Lieber (2004) look very different from the schemata of Langacker (1987) and Dąbrowska (2004a), these differences concern the aspects of human experience that the different theories seeks to formalize, and the particular flavor of formalization adopted; all of these approaches share the conviction that abstraction is at the heart of the language engine. Thus, for example, if we consider conceptual blending (for details, see the chapter by Turner in this volume), and the production of metaphorical expressions such as *Elephants were the tanks of Hannibal's army*, Veale et al. (2000) propose a computationally implemented model that generates conceptual blends from knowledge structures for elephants, tanks, classical and modern warfare, Hannibal, etc., in conjunction with an abstract rule that searches for n-tuples of knowledge structures across domains (e.g., Roman warfare and Modern warfare). On the basis of their features, n-tuples of knowledge structures in one domain can be matched to another. Given matching features (such as elephants being the strongest and most dangerous units in ancient warfare, and tanks being the strongest and most dangerous units in modern warfare), the algorithm can blend *elephants were the strongest units of Hannibal's army* with *tanks are the strongest units of a modern army* to create *elephants were the tanks of Hannibal's army*. In doing so, the algorithm abstracts away from the specific details of examples, and searches for correspondences across knowledge domains.

The tools of computer science provide the language engineer with valuable control over how a given computational operationalization will function. A further advantage they provide is that, in principle, computational implementations can be evaluated precisely against empirical data. However, this technology also has its share of disadvantages. First, the representations and rules employed by these formalisms typically require extensive, labor-intensive handcrafting.

Second, and more importantly, it would appear that language itself is fundamentally contextual. A sentence such as *She cut her finger with a knife* typically suggests that the finger was not completely severed from the hand, whereas the sentence *These lumberjacks cut trees for a living* typically means that any trees involved were cut down and severed from their roots. The interpretation of the verb in *Outlines of animals were cut out of paper* is different yet again. Here, the verb indicates creation by means of cutting.

It is important to note here that the contexts in which words such as *cut* are encountered generate expectations that arise surprisingly early in the comprehension processing record (see, e.g., Elman 2009, for a review). Moreover, these expectations arise much earlier than one would expect given theories that assume an initial stage of abstract, purely form-based processing. Thus while it is of course true that within the abstractionist enterprise, one can distinguish between different senses of *cut* (WordNet distinguishes 41; see also Geeraerts volume 2), each with its own semantic structure, with sufficiently narrowly defined features to make a sense fit only in very specific contexts, this still doesn't solve the problem posed by these early expectations, because it appears that they depend on exactly those subjects – she, lumberjacks, and outlines of animals – that these theories seek to abstract away from. Accordingly, while one might consider specifying in the lexical representation for lumberjack that this is a person whose profession it is to cut down trees, it stretches belief that outlines of animals (a lexical entry used by Google as a caption for images of outlines of animals [as of October 20, 2014]) would have an entry in the mental lexicon specifying that these are cutable.

Paradigmatic effects in language processing pose yet further problems for traditional abstractionist theories, because the paradigmatic dimensions of language are difficult to capture in abstractionist frameworks. Consider prepositional phrases in English, such as *with the onion, over the onion, in the onion, ...* When abstraction is taken as the basis of generalization, then a structure such as [$_{PP}$ P [$_{NP}$ the [$_N$ N]]] captures crucial aspects of the abstract knowledge of prepositional phrases, in conjunction with the set of prepositions and the set of nouns in the lexicon. As far as language processing is concerned, all prior experiences with actual prepositional phrases (*with the onion, over the onion, in the onion ...*) are lost from memory. The abstractionist grammar reduces a rich slice of experience to a prepositional symbol, freely replaceable without reference to context by a single instance from the set of prepositions, followed by a definite determiner, in turn is followed by a noun symbol that is again selected without reference to context, from the set of nouns.

However, it would appear that different words make use of different prepositions in very different ways. To judge from both behavioral (Baayen et al. 2011) and electrophysiological (Hendrix and Baayen to appear) evidence, these paradigmatic differences influence, and indeed serve to co-determine lexical processing: Nouns that make use of prepositions in ways that are very different from the way an average noun uses its prepositions show very different characteristic profiles in processing. A measure capturing how well the use of prepositions by a specific noun corresponds to how prepositions are used in general is the Kulback-Leibler divergence, also known as relative entropy:

$$\text{relative entropy}(p, q) = \Sigma_i \, (p_i \log_2 (p_i \,/\, q_i)),$$

where p and q refer to the probability distributions of prepositional use given a specific noun, and the corresponding unconditional probability distribution of prepositions across all nouns. It turns out that when the relative entropy for a noun is large, i.e., when the noun makes atypical use of prepositions, response latencies to the noun, even when presented in isolation in the visual lexical decision task, are longer. Furthermore, in measures of speech production (gauged by a picture naming paradigm) relative entropy turns out to be an effective statistical predictor of the brain's electrophysiological response (Hendrix and Baayen to appear). Crucially, the effect of relative entropy arises irrespective of whether nouns are presented in isolation, or whether nouns are presented in the context of a particular preposition. What matters is how much a noun's use of prepositions differs from prototypical prepositional use in English. This paradigmatic effect poses a fundamental challenge to abstractionist theories, precisely because the point of assuming that learners create an abstract representation of "the" prepositional phrase is because it is assumed that language processing fundamentally relies on abstract representations. It is assumed that, for the purposes of processing, learners may as well have amnesia about how any given noun is actually used. Yet the way that speakers actually use nouns and prepositions indicates that not only do learners acquire and retain contextual information, but also that this contextual information plays a critical role in their processing of language.

3 Analogy

In traditional grammar, analogy was generally used to denote an incidental similarity-based extension of patterns that are not supported by more general rules. In some recent theories, however, analogy is seen as a much more foundational process of which rules are a special, typically more productive, case (see, e.g., Langacker 1987; Pothos 2005).

In morphology, Matthews (1974) and Blevins (2003) developed a framework known as Word and Paradigm Morphology, in which words, rather than morphemes and exponents, are the basic units in the lexicon. The theory posits that proportional analogy (*hand : hands = tree : trees*) drives the production and comprehension of novel forms, and explicit algorithms for capturing the core idea of analogy-driven prediction have been developed within the context of a class of computational approaches commonly referred to as exemplar models (see also Ramscar and Port this volume).

Exemplar models start from the assumption that learners acquire and store an extensive inventory of instances of language use (typically referred to as exemplars) in memory. Instead of seeking to account for the productivity of language through abstract rules operating over hand-tailored representations, exemplar models base their predictions about novel forms on these stored exemplars, in combination with a general, domain a-specific similarity-driven algorithm. One of the earliest linguistic exemplar models was Skousen's (1989) analogical model of language (AML), which grounds the analogical process in probability theory (Skousen 2002, 2000). The AML algorithm searches for sets of exemplars with characteristics that consistently support a particular outcome. An outcome can be a construction, a phonetic feature, etc., such as voicing alternation (Ernestus and Baayen 2003), or the choice between rival affixes (Arndt-Lappe 2014). The output of this search process is a subset of consistent exemplars, the analogical set, in which the different outcomes are ranked by the number of exemplars supporting them, with the best-supported, highest-ranked outcome being considered the most likely outcome.

Skousen's AML model is computationally expensive, which makes the processing of data with many features difficult. Memory based learning (MBL), a framework developed by Daelemans and Van den Bosch (2005) sidesteps this computational problem. As in AML, the algorithm searches for a set of nearest neighbors, from which it selects the exemplar with the best support in the nearest neighbor set as its choice of outcome. In the very simplest set-up, the nearest neighbors are those instances in memory that share most features with a given case for which an appropriate outcome class has to be determined. This simplest set-up is not very useful, however, because in the presence of many irrelevant predictors, classification accuracy can plummet. By weighting features for their relevance for a given choice problem, accuracy can be improved dramatically while keeping computational costs down. By way of example, consider the choice of the plural allomorph in English, which is [ɨz] following sibilants, [s] following voiceless consonants, and [z] elsewhere. Knowledge of a word's final consonant nearly eliminates uncertainty about the appropriate allomorph, whereas knowledge of the initial consonant of the word is completely uninformative. Since manner of articulation and voicing of the final consonant are informative features, they can be assigned large weights, whereas manner and voicing for initial consonants can be assigned low weights. The values of these weights can be estimated straightforwardly from the data, for instance, by considering to what extent knowledge of the value of a feature reduces one's uncertainty about the class outcome. The extent to which uncertainty is reduced then becomes the weight for the importance of that feature.

One important message that has come from the literature on memory based learning is that forgetting is harmful (Daelemans et al. 1999): The larger the set of exemplars MBL is provided with, the better it is able to approximate human performance. This points to a conclusion that is exactly the opposite of that of abstractionist models, which seek to keep the knowledge base as lean as possible. However, in principle at least, these differences are not so large as they would seem. As Keuleers (2008) points out, abstraction, in the form of minimum generalization (MGL) learning, and memory based learning (under certain parameter configurations) are all but indistinguishable mathematically. However, whereas minimum generalization learning first deduces rules, then forgets about exemplars, and uses rules at run-time (greedy learning), memory-based learning simply stores exemplars, and runs its similarity-based algorithm at runtime (lazy learning).

Another similarity between MGL and MBL is that a new model is required for each individual problem set within a domain of inquiry. For instance, when modeling phonological form, one model will handle past tenses, another model the choice between the allomorphy of nominalizations in *-ion*, and yet a third model the allomorphy of the plural suffix. Thus, both approaches work with different rules (or schemas) for different phenomena, and differ only as to how these rules/schemas are implemented under the hood.

Exemplar models such as AML and MBL offer several advantages over abstractionist approaches. First, because analogical rules are executed at runtime, new exemplars in the instance base will automatically lead to an update in prediction performance. In MGL, by contrast, once the rule system has been deduced, it remains fixed and cannot be updated for principled reasons. (Technically, of course, the rules can be recalculated for an updated set of exemplars, but doing so implies that the exemplars are held in reserve, and are not erased from memory.) Another important advantage of AML and MBL is that getting the algorithms to work for a given data set requires very little hand-crafting: the algorithms discover themselves which features are important.

Of course, these models also have disadvantages. First, compared to handcrafted abstractionist systems developed over many years and fine-tuned to all kinds of exceptions, AML and MBL can show a lack of precision. Second, it remains to be seen how plausible it is to assume that each and any exemplar is stored in memory. As we noted above, hundreds of millions of four-word sequences would have to be stored in an English mental lexicon. When it comes to languages with highly productive inflectional systems, millions of forms will have to be stored, just at the word level. Furthermore, the rampant variability in the speech signal makes it highly unlikely that each pronunciation variant of every word ever heard would be stored in memory (indeed, this last point highlights a problem posed by the idea of an exemplar itself, namely that of deciding at which level of abstraction something is to be considered a type or a token of an exemplar; see Ramscar and Port this volume).

4 Hybrid models

Hybrid models hold that schemata (or rules) and exemplars exist side by side. For instance, Langacker (2010: 109) argues for a hybrid approach when he states that, "structure emerges from usage, is immanent in usage, and is influenced by usage on an ongoing basis". The co-existence of rules and exemplars (see also Langacker 1987; Dąbrowska 2004b) implies a system that contains a great deal of redundancy, such that, for instance, in comprehension, an interpretation can be arrived at either by retrieving the appropriate holistic exemplar, or by application of a rule or schema to the relevant exemplars of smaller units. For morphological processing, Baayen et al. (1997) made a similar argument for the existence of whole-word representations for complex words, side by side with a parsing mechanism operating on the morphemic constituents of these words.

The redundancy offered by hybrid models is generally taken to make the processing system more robust. For instance, when one processing route fails to complete, another processing route may still be effective. In horse race models, which make the assumption that processing routes run independently and in parallel, a process of statistical facilitation can take place: If processing time is determined by the first route to win the race, and if the distributions of the completion times of the different routes overlap, then, across many trials, the average processing time of the combined routes will be shorter than the average processing time of the fastest route by itself (Baayen et al. 1997).

It should be noted, however that, in embracing both abstractionist and exemplar based approaches, hybrid models inherit many of the problems of both. Because they incorporate exemplars, hybrid models also posit large, high-entropy exemplar spaces. As we noted above, these pose deep practical and conceptual problems. For example, while it might be argued that not all exemplars are stored, but only large numbers of exemplars, this raises the question of under what circumstances exemplars are, or are not, stored. Positing a frequency threshold for storage runs into logical difficulties, because any new exemplar will start with an initial frequency of 1, far below the threshold, and hence will never be stored.

From abstractionist models, hybrid models inherit the problem of selecting the correct analysis from the multitude of possible analyses (Bod 1998, 2006; Baayen and Schreuder 2000). When schemata are assumed to be in operation at multiple levels of abstraction, how does the system know which level of abstraction is the appropriate one? How is competition between more concrete and more abstract schemata resolved?

5 Discrimination

It is clear that abstractionist approaches, exemplar models and hybrid models offer many insights into language production, comprehension and processing. However, as we noted above, when it comes to explaining how people learn to productively use language, and what they learn in order to do so, each approach has its weak points. Thus while we agree with Langacker's (2010) suggestion that usage shapes the grammar on an ongoing basis (Ramscar and Baayen 2013), we believe that in order to answer questions about the way people learn to use language, or the way that usage shapes the grammars people learn, it is essential to begin with learning theory, and the process(es) of learning itself.

Modern learning theory begins with Ivan Pavlov and his famous observations about bells and dog-food. Pavlov first noticed that his dogs salivated in the presence of the technician who usually fed them. He then devised an experiment in which he rang a bell before he presented the dogs with food. After a few repetitions, the dogs started to salivate in response to the bell, anticipating the food they expected to see (Pavlov 1927). Pavlov's initial results led to a straightforward theory of learning that seems obvious and feels intuitively right: If a cue is present, and an outcome follows, an animal notices the co-occurrence and subsequently learns to associate the two.

It turns out, however, that this simple associative view of learning provides a one-sided and misleading perspective on the actual learning process and its consequences. For example, a dog trained to expect food when a bell is rung, can later be given training in which a light is flashed simultaneously with the bell. After repeated exposure to bell and light, followed by food, only a light is flashed. Will the dog drool? Surprisingly, the answer is no: the dog doesn't drool. Even though the light consistently co-occurred with the food in training, the dog does not learn to associate it with the food, a phenomenon known as blocking.

The problem for, e.g., memory-based learning is that this theory would pick out the light as an informative cue for food. After all, whenever the light is present, food is present. Since there is no uncertainty about the food given the light, the model predicts that the light should be an excellent cue, and that this cue should build strong expectations for food, contrary to fact.

The learning equations that Rescorla developed together with Wagner (Rescorla and Wagner 1972), however, perfectly capture this finding. The reason that the light never becomes an effective cue for food is that the bell is already a perfectly predictive cue for the food. Because there are no situations in which the light predicts food but the bell does not, the light does not add any new information: it is not predictive of the food over and above the bell. As this and many similar experiments have revealed, associative learning is sensitive to the informativity of co-occurrences, rather than their mere existence.

Learning theory (Rescorla 1988) not only predicts a substantial body of findings in the animal and human behavior (Miller et al. 1995; Siegel and Allan 1996) but it has also recently been found to predict many aspects of first language acquisition as well as implicit linguistic learning in adults (see, e.g., Ramscar and Yarlett 2007; Ramscar and Gitcho 2007; Ramscar et al. 2010, 2013c, 2014). Learning theory specifies how the association weights from the cues in the environment (such as a bell and a flashing light in the case of Pavlov's dog) to an outcome (e.g., food) should be modified over time. The basic insights are, first, that if a cue is not present, association weights from that cue to outcomes are left untouched. For instance, whiskers are visual cues to various animals, such as cats, rabbits, rats, and mice. If there are no whiskers to be seen, then the weights on the links between whiskers and cats, rabbits, rats, and mice, are left unchanged, even though these animals might be present (as when they are observed from the back). When whiskers are seen, and a cat is present but no rabbits, rats, or mice, then the weight from whiskers to cat is increased. At the same time, the weights from whiskers to rabbits, rats, and mice are decreased, even though these animals have whiskers. This is a crucial element of modern theory that sets it apart from its associationist, even behaviorist, predecessors (Rescorla 1988). Learning is sensitive not only to associations forming when cues and outcomes co-occur. Learning is also sensitive to the success and failure of the implicit predictions that prior experiences relating cues to outcomes generate. Whiskers do not only predict cats, but also rabbits and other rodents. When these predictions turn out to be false, the weights that connect whiskers to the animals that were mispredicted to be present will be tuned down. As a result of this, outcomes (cats, rabbits, mice, rats) compete for the cues, while at the same time, cues compete for outcomes.

Baayen et al. (2011) used the Rescorla-Wagner equations to build a computational model for the reading of words, as gauged by the visual lexical decision task. The basic structure of the model is very simple, and is exemplified by Figure 5.1. The bottom layer of the network has nodes representing letter pairs (digraphs). The top layer of the network specifies lexemes, in the sense of Aronoff (1994), that is, as lexical nodes that are the symbols linking to rich form information (such as letter digraphs) on the one hand, and rich world knowledge (not shown in Figure 5.1) on the other hand. A system of lexemes is a set of symbolic focal points that serves to mediate and discriminate both between linguistic forms and our experiences of the world. Lexemes are, in themselves, neither forms nor meanings, but rather they systematically aggregate the form

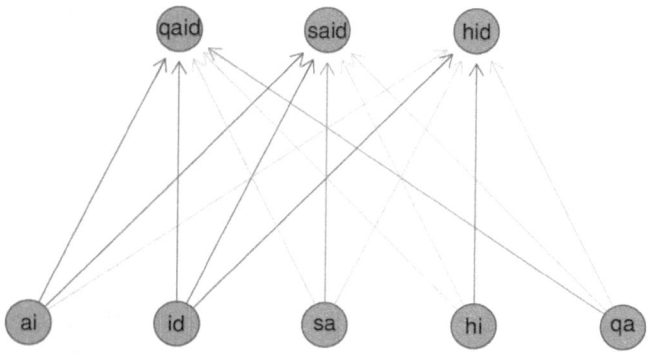

Fig. 5.1: A Rescorla-Wagner network with five digraphs as cues, and three lexemes as outcomes.

and meaning contrasts that a speaker hearer has learned to discriminate, and potentially communicate, at any given time.

Of course, this raises the question how the elements of form (n-graphs, n-phones) and the elements of experience (the lexemes) themselves are learned. Here, we assume that these units are simply available to the learner. Any computational implementation has to work with units that are primitives to that implementation, but which themselves have arisen as the outcome of other learning and classification processes, or the same processes at another level of abstraction. In this latter vein, one process that might give rise to these units is unsupervised category learning (see, e.g., Love et al. 2004, for a computational implementation, and also Ramscar and Port this volume).

The first word in Figure 5.1, the legal scrabble word *qaid* ('tribal chieftain'), has one letter pair, *qa*, that uniquely distinguishes it from the two other lexemes. The Rescorla-Wagner equations predict that this cue is strongly associated with *qaid*, and negatively associated with *said* and *hid*. Conversely, the letter pair *id* occurs in all three words, and as a result it is not very useful for discriminating between the three lexemes. As a consequence, the weights on its connections are all small. The total support that cues in the input provide for a lexeme, its activation, is obtained by summation over the weights on the connections from these cues (for *qaid*, the cues *qa*, *ai*, and *id*) to the outcome (the lexeme of *qaid*). This activation represents the learnability of the lexemes given the cues.

The naive discriminative learner model of Baayen et al. (2011) takes this simple network architecture and applies it rigorously to word triplets in the British National Corpus. For each word triplet, all the letter diphones in the three words were collected. These served as cues. From the same words, all "content" lexemes and "grammatical" lexemes (number, tense, person, etc.)

were collected and served as outcomes. The Rescorla-Wagner equations were then used to adjust the weights from the digraph cues to the lexeme outcomes. For any given word in the corpus, its activation was obtained by summing the weights from its orthographic cues to its lexemes. For words with multiple lexemes, such as a plural or a compound, the activations of its lexemes were summed. (In the actual implementation, a mathematical shortcut, due to Danks [2003], was used for estimating the weights.) It turns out that these activation weights are excellent predictors of lexical decision latencies: words with longer responses are the words with lower activations, i.e., the words that cannot be learned that well given their orthographic properties. The activation weights turn out to mirror a wide range of effects reported in the experimental literature, such as the word frequency effect, orthographic neighborhood effects, morphological family size effects, constituent frequency effects, and paradigmatic entropy effects (including the abovementioned prepositional relative entropy effect). What is especially interesting is that the model covers the full range of morphological effects, without having any representations for words, morphemes, exponents, or allomorphs.

In this approach, both the morphology and the syntax are implicit in the distribution of cues and outcomes, which jointly shape a network that is continuously updated with usage. Since morphology and syntax are implicit in the usage, we also refer to the discriminative approach as implicit morphology and implicit grammar. Interestingly, this approach to language dovetails well with the mathematical theory of communication developed by Shannon (1948).

When a photograph is sent over a cable from a camera to a laptop, it is not the case that the objects in the photograph (say a rose on a table, next to which is a chair), are somehow "encoded" and sent down the wire one by one (first the chair, and than the rose plus table). To the contrary, the picture is transformed into a binary stream that is optimized for the transmission channel as well as protected against data loss by error-correcting code. The laptop is able to reconstruct the picture, not by applying a grammar to "extract" the picture from the signal, but by making use of the same coding scheme that the camera used in order to select the appropriate distribution of pixel colors over the canvas, thereby discriminating the appropriate pattern of pixel colors from the possible distributions of pixel colors that the coding scheme allows for.

To make this more concrete, consider a coding scheme devised to transmit for experiences: the experience of a fountain, the experience of a fountain pen, the experience of an orange, and the experience of orange juice. Assume a code, shared by encoder and decoder, specifying that the four experiences can be signaled using the digit strings 00, 01, 10, and 11 respectively. When seeking to communicate the experience of a fountain pen, the speaker will encode 01, and thanks to the shared code, the listener will decode 01, and select the appropriate experience (a fountain pen) that the code discriminates from her total set of possible experiences. There is no need whatsoever to consider whether the individual ones and zeros compositionally contribute to the experiences transmitted.

Thus we can view language-as-form (ink on paper, pixels on a computer screen, the speech signal, gestures) as a signal that serves to discriminate between complex experiences of the world. The success of the signal hinges on interlocutors sharing the code for encoding and decoding the signal (see also Wieling et al. 2014). The same (or at least, a highly similar) code that allows the speaker to discriminate between past experiences in memory and encode a discriminated experience in the language signal, is then used by the listener to discriminate between her past experiences.

Discrimination is important here, as speakers will seldom share the same experiences. Consider, for example, a speaker mentioning a larch tree. The interlocutor may not know what exactly a larch tree is, because she never realized the differences between larches, spruces, and pine trees. Nevertheless, the communicative event may be relatively successful in the sense that the listener was able to reduce the set of potential past experiences to her experiences of trees. She might request further clarification of what a larch tree is, or, not having any interest in biology, she might just be satisfied that some (to her irrelevant) subspecies of trees is at issue. Thus implicit grammar views the language signal as separating encoded relevant experiences from the larger set of a listener's irrelevant experiences.

Thus far, we have discussed comprehension. What about speech production? The model we are developing (see also Baayen and Blevins 2014), proposes a two-layered knowledge structure, consisting of a directed graph specifying the order between production outcomes on the one hand, and of Recorla-Wagner networks associated with the vertices in the network on the other hand. Figure 5.2 presents such a knowledge structure for the sentences *John passed away*, *John kicked the bucket*, *John died*, *John passed the building*, and *John went away to Scotland*. The left panel presents the directed graph specifying the potential paths defined by these sentences, and the right panel summarizes the connection strengths between lexemic cues (rows) and word outcomes (columns) in tabular form. These connection strengths are obtained with the Rescorla-Wagner equations applied to all sentences containing *John* (for detailed discussion of these equations, see Ramscar et al. 2010 and Baayen et al. 2011).

All sentences in this simple example begin with *John*, hence this is the top node. Given *John*, the possible continuations are *kicked*, *passed*, *died*, and *went*.

Chapter 5: Abstraction, storage and naive discriminative learning — 131

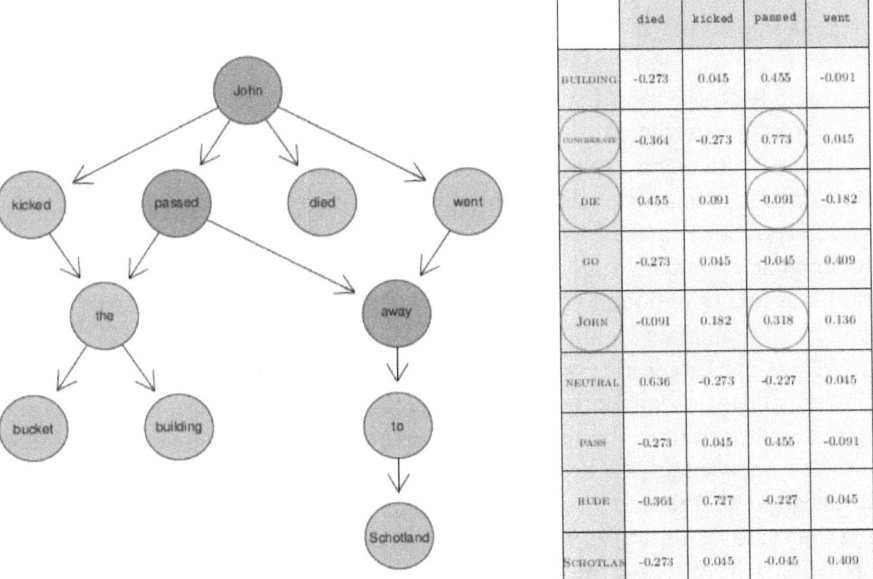

Fig. 5.2: An example of a directed word graph and the Rescorla-Wagner control network at the node John.

When the speaker has the intention of communicating in a considerate way that John died (indicated by the lexemes *John*, *die*, *considerate*, highlighted in the table of weights), then the word *passed* has a total activation of 1 (the sum of the highlighted weights in the passed column), whereas the other continuations have activations of zero. Thus, sentences emerge as paths through the directed graph, where each choice where to go next is governed by the accumulated knowledge discriminating between the different options, guided by past experience of which lexemes predict which word outcomes.

Knowledge structures such as those illustrated in Figure 5.2 can be formulated for sequences of words, but also for sequences of diphones or demi-syllables. It is currently an open question whether separate structures above and below the word are really necessary. What is important is that the digraphs provide a very economical storage format. In a word graph, any word form is represented by a single vertex. In a diphone graph, any diphone is present only once. This is a large step away from standard conceptions of the mental lexicon informed by the dictionary metaphor, in which a letter or diphone pair is represented many times, at least once for each entry. The directed graph also sidesteps the problem of having to assume distinct exemplars for sequences of demi-syllables or sequences of words. In the present example, for instance, an opaque idiom (*kick the bucket*), a semi-transparent idiom (*to pass away*), and a literal expression (*die*) are represented economically with dynamical control from the Rescorla-Wagner networks.

From the discriminative perspective, questions as to how opaque and semi-transparent idioms are "stored" in the mental dictionary, decomposed, or not decomposed, simply do not arise because words are now part of a signal for which traditional questions of compositionality are simply not relevant. Thus, in implicit grammar, rules, schemata, constructions, inheritance hierarchies, multiple entries of homonyms in dictionary lists, and all other constructs based on formal grammars are unnecessary.

These constructs may provide high-level descriptions of aspects of language that may be insightful for the analyst reflecting on language, but in the discriminative approach, they are not taken to imply a corresponding cognitive reality.

The knowledge structures of implicit grammar do not permit redundancy, in the sense that different sets of representations, and different rules for achieving the same result, would co-exist. The theory acknowledges that the linguistic signal is rich, and that the experiences we encode in the signal are richer by many orders of magnitude (see Ramscar et al. 2010 for a discussion of the problems this dimensional mismatch poses to any traditionally combinatorial theory). But redundancy in the sense of having multiple ways in which to achieve exactly the same goal is ruled out. The directed graph and the Rescorla-Wagner networks define one unique most-probable path for the expression of a given message.

Research on child language acquisition (e.g., Bannard and Matthews 2008; Tomasello 2009) has shown that children are conservative learners who stay very close to known exemplars, and initially do not use constructions productively. One explanation holds that initially, children work with large unanalyzed holistic chunks, which they learn, over time, to break down into smaller chunks, with as end product the abstract schemata of the adult speaker (Dąbrowska 2004b; Dąbrowska and Lieven 2005; Borensztajn et al. 2009; Beekhuizen et al. 2014). Implicit grammar offers a very different – and currently still speculative – perspective on the acquisition process (Arnon and Ramscar 2012).

Consider a child inquiring about what activity her interlocutor is engaged in. Typically, an English-speaking child in North America or the U.K. will have ample experience with such questions, which often arise in the context of reading a picture book (*What's the bear doing? It's eating honey!*). However, with very little command over her vocal apparatus, in the initial stage of speech production, the full message (a question about the event an actor is engaged in) has to be expressed by the child in a single word, e.g., *Mommy?*. However, single-word expressions will often not be effective, as *Mommy?* could also be short-hand for what adults would express as *Mommy, where are you?* or *Mommy, I'm hungry*. From a learning perspective, the word uttered (*Mommy*), and the lexemes in the message (question, event, Mommy) constitute the cues in a learning event with the success of the communicative event as outcome. Over the course of learning during the one-word stage, the lexemes question, event, agent will acquire low or even negative weights to communicative success. Only Mommy will acquire substantial positive weights, thanks to the single-word utterances being successful for attracting attention.

By the end of the one-word stage, the child has a production graph with only vertices and no edges. Once the child succeeds in uttering sentences with more than one word (*What's Mommy doing*), thanks to increasing motor control over the articulators, the chances of successful communication rise dramatically. This will prompt the reuse of multi-word sequences, and the construction of edges between the vertices in the graph, together with the Rescorla-Wagner networks that discriminate between where to go next in the graph given the child's communicative intentions. The first path in the graph will be re-used often, consolidating both the edges between the vertices in the directed graph, as well as the associated Rescorla-Wagner control networks, which, in terms of what the child actually produces, will enable the child to demonstrate increasing fluency with multiword productions.

In this approach to learning, the empirical phenomenon of children proceeding in their production from a prefab such as *What's Mommy doing?* to utterances of the form *What's X V-ing?*, analysed in cognitive grammar as schematization, in implicit grammar does not involve any abstraction. What is at stake, instead, is learning to think for speaking (Slobin 1996). During the one-word stage, children gradually learn that many aspects of the experiences they want to express cannot be packed into a single word. Once they have accumulated enough articulatory experience to launch word sequences, they can develop their production graph and the associated control networks. As this graph is expanded, syntactic productivity, which is already nascent in small worlds such as shown in Figure 5.2, will increase exponentially.

It is worth noting that the process of chunking in acquisition, with the child as a miniature linguist trying to find units at varies hierarchical levels in the speech signal, is also is at odds with the ACT-R theory of cognition, according to which chunking evolves in the opposite direction, starting with the small chunks that are all that can be handled initially, and that only with experience over time can be aggregated into the greater chunks representing the automatization of cognitive skills (Anderson 2007).

Theoretical frameworks have developed different notational schemes for describing the semantics of utterances such as you want milk, as illustrated in

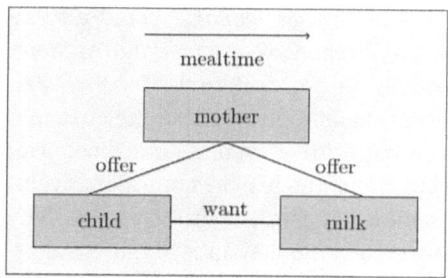

```
OFFER(MOTHER, CHILD, Z)
ASK(MOTHER, CHILD, IS-TRUE(CHILD(DESIRE, Z)))
    ⎡ type:       thing                                    ⎤
  Z ⎢ properties: concrete, inanimate, imageable, fluid, … ⎥
    ⎣ function:   to be consumed by drinking               ⎦
```

Fig. 5.3: Semantic representations in the style of cognitive grammar (after Dąbrowska (2004: 221) and Jackendoff's lexical conceptual structures).

Figure 5.3 for cognitive grammar (top) and lexical conceptual structures (bottom) in the style of Jackendoff (1990). From the perspective of implicit grammar, the knowledge summarized in such representations is valuable and insightful, but too dependent on a multitude of interpretational conventions to be immediately implementable in a discriminative learning model. What needs to be done is to unpack such descriptions into a set of basic descriptors that can function as lexemes in comprehension and production models. For instance, OFFER(MOTHER, CHILD, MILK) has to be unpacked into lexemes not only for *offer*, *mother*, *child*, and *milk*, but also for the mother as the initiator of the offering, the milk as the thing offered, etc. In other words, the insights expressed by the different frameworks can and should be made available to the learning algorithms in the form of lexemic units. How exactly these units conspire within the memory system defined by the directed graph and its control networks is determined by how they are used in the language community and the learning algorithms of the brain.

Implicit grammar is a new computational theory, and it is still under development. We have illustrated that this theory makes it possible to reflect on language and cognition from a very different perspective. Computational simulations for comprehension indicate that the model scales up to corpora with many billions of words. For speech production, simulations of the production of complex words promise low error rates (Baayen and Blevins 2014), but whether the same holds for sentence and discourse production remains to be shown.

Implicit grammar grounds language in discrimination learning. There is, of course, much more to language and cognition than implicit discriminative learning. For discussion of the role of higher-order cognitive processes in resolving processing conflicts and integrating implicit learning with speakers' goals, and also the importance of the late development of these higher-order processes, see Ramscar and Gitcho (2007); Ramscar et al. (2013a, 2013b).

A further complication is that with the advent of the cultural technology of writing, literate speakers bring extensive meta-linguistic skills into the arena of language use and language processing. How exactly the many multimodal experiences of language use at both implicit and conscious levels shape how a given speaker processes language is a serious computational challenge for future research, not only for implicit grammar, but also for abstractionist and exemplar approaches, as well as hybrid models such as cognitive grammar.

6 Concluding remarks

When comparing different algorithms, it is important to keep in mind, irrespective of whether they come from abstractionist, exemplar-based, or discriminative theories, that they tend to perform with similar precision. For instance, Ernestus and Baayen (2003) compared AML, stochastic optimality theory, and two classifiers from the statistical literature, among others, and observed very similar performance. Keuleers (2008) showed equivalent performance for memory-based learning and minimum generalization learning for past-tense formation in English. Baayen et al. (2013) compared two statistical techniques with naive discrimination learning, and again observed similar performance. This state of affairs indicates that the typical data sets that have fuelled debates over rules, schemas, and analogy, tend to have a quantitative structure that can be well-approximated from very different theoretical perspectives. Therefore, the value of different approaches to language, language use, and language processes will have to be evaluated by means of the simplicity of computational implementations, the neuro-biological support for these implementations, and the extent to which the models generate concrete, falsifiable predictions regarding unseen data. That is, the extent to which it is the models themselves that generate insight, rather than models merely embodying the insights of their makers.

7 References

Albright, Adam and Bruce Hayes (2003): Rules vs. analogy in English past tenses: A computational/experimental study. *Cognition* 90: 119–161.

Anderson, John R. (2007): *How Can the Human Mind Occur in the Physical Universe?* Oxford: Oxford University Press.

Arndt-Lappe, Sabine (2014): Analogy in suffix rivalry: The case of English -ity and -ness. *English Language and Linguistics* 18(3), 497–548.

Arnon, Inbal and Michael Ramscar (2012): Granularity and the acquisition of grammatical gender: How order-of-acquisition affects what gets learned. *Cognition* 122(3): 292–305.

Arnon, Inbal and Neal Snider (2010): More than words: Frequency effects for multi-word phrases. *Journal of Memory and Language* 62(1): 67–82.

Aronoff, Mark (1994): *Morphology by Itself: Stems and Inflectional Classes*. Cambridge: MIT Press.

Baayen, R. Harald and James Blevins (2014): Implicit morphology. Manuscript, University of Tuebingen.

Baayen, R. Harald, Ton Dijkstra, and Robert Schreuder (1997): Singulars and plurals in Dutch: Evidence for a parallel dual route model. *Journal of Memory and Language* 36: 94–117.

Baayen, R. Harald, Laura Janda, Tore Nesset, Anna Endresen, and Anastasia Makarova (2013): Making choices in Russian: Pros and cons of statistical methods for rival forms. *Russian Linguistics* 37: 253–291.

Baayen, R. Harald, Petar Milin, Dusica Filipovic Durdevic, Peter Hendrix, and Marco Marelli (2011): An amorphous model for morphological processing in visual comprehension based on naive discriminative learning. *Psychological Review* 118: 438–482.

Baayen, R. Harald and Robert Schreuder (2000): Towards a psycholinguistic computational model for morphological parsing. *Philosophical Transactions of the Royal Society* (Series A: Mathematical, Physical and Engineering Sciences) 358: 1–13.

Bannard, Colin and Danielle Matthews (2008): Stored word sequences in language learning: The effect of familiarity on children's repetition of four-word combinations. *Psychological Science* 19: 241–248.

Beekhuizen, Barend, Rens Bod, Afsaneh Fazly, Suzanne Stevenson, and Arie Verhagen (2014): A usage-based model of early grammatical development. *Proceedings of the 2014 ACL workshop on cognitive modeling and computational linguistics*, 46–54. Baltimore, Maryland USA, June 26th, 2014. Association for Computational Linguistics.

Blevins, James (2003): Stems and paradigms. *Language* 79: 737–767.

Bod, Rens (1998): *Beyond Grammar: An Experience-based Theory of Language*. Stanford: CSLI.

Bod, Rens (2006): Exemplar-based syntax: How to get productivity from examples. *The Linguistic Review* 23(3): 291–320.

Boersma, Paul (1998): *Functional Phonology*. The Hague: Holland Academic Graphics.

Boersma, Paul and Bruce Hayes (2001): Empirical tests of the gradual learning algorithm. *Linguistic Inquiry* 32: 45–86.

Borensztajn, Gideon, Willem Zuidema, and Rens Bod (2009): Children's grammars grow more abstract with age – evidence from an automatic procedure for identifying the productive units of language. *Topics in Cognitive Science* 1(1): 175–188.

Bresnan, Joan, Anna Cueni, Tatiana Nikitina, and R. Harald Baayen (2007): Predicting the dative alternation. In: G. Bouma, I. Kraemer, and J. Zwarts (eds.), *Cognitive Foundations of Interpretation*, 69–94. Amsterdam: Royal Netherlands Academy of Arts and Sciences.

Dąbrowska, Ewa (2004a): *Language, Mind and Brain. Some Psychological and Neurological Constraints on Theories of Grammar*. Edinburgh: Edinburgh University Press.

Dąbrowska, Ewa (2004b): Rules or schemas? Evidence from Polish. *Language and Cognitive Processes* 19: 225–271.

Dąbrowska, Ewa and Elena Lieven (2005): Towards a lexically specific grammar of children's question constructions. *Cognitive Linguistics* 16(3): 437–474.

Daelemans, Walter and Antal van den Bosch (2005): *Memory-based Language Processing*. Cambridge: Cambridge University Press.

Daelemans, Walter, Antal van den Bosch, and Jakub Zavrel (1999): Forgetting exceptions is harmful in language learning. *Machine Learning* 34: 11–41.

Danks, David (2003): Equilibria of the Rescorla-Wagner model. *Journal of Mathematical Psychology* 47(2): 109–121.

Dressler, Wolfgang (1985): On the predictiveness of natural morphology. *Journal of Linguistics* 21: 321–337.

Elman, Jeff (2009): On the meaning of words and dinosaur bones: Lexical knowledge without a lexicon. *Cognitive Science* 33: 1–36.

Ernestus, Mirjam and R. Harald Baayen (2003): Predicting the unpredictable: Interpreting neutralized segments in Dutch. *Language* 79: 5–38.

Hendrix, Peter and R. Harald Baayen (to appear): Distinct ERP signatures of word frequency, phrase frequency, and prototypicality in speech production. *Journal of Experimental Psychology: Learning, Memory and Cognition*.

Jackendoff, Ray (1990): *Semantic Structures*. Cambridge: MIT Press.

Keuleers, Emmanuel (2008): *Memory-based Learning of Inflectional Morphology*. Antwerp: University of Antwerp.

Langacker, Ronald (1987): *Foundations of Cognitive Grammar*. Volume 1: *Theoretical Prerequisites*. Stanford: Stanford University Press.

Langacker, Ronald (2010): How not to disagree: The emergence of structure from usage. In: K. Boye and E. Engberg-Pedersen (eds.), *Language Usage and Language Structure* (Trends in linguistics: studies and monographs 213), 107–143. Berlin/New York: Mouton de Gruyter.

Lieber, Rochelle (2004): *Morphology and Lexical Semantics*. Cambridge: Cambridge University Press.

Love, Bradley, Douglas Medin, and Todd Gureckis (2004): Sustain: a network model of category learning. *Psychological Review* 111(2): 309.

Matthews, Peter (1974): *Morphology. An introduction to the Theory of Word Structure*. Cambridge: Cambridge University Press.

Miller, Ralph, Robert Barnet, and Nicholas Grahame (1995): Assessment of the Rescorla-Wagner model. *Psychological Bulletin* 117(3): 363.

Pavlov, Ivan (1927): *Conditioned Reflexes: An Investigation of the Physiological Activity of the Cerebral Cortex* (trans. G. V. Anrep). Oxford: Oxford University Press.

Pothos, Emmanuel (2005): The rules versus similarity distinction. *Behavioral and Brain Sciences* 28(01): 1–14.

Prince, Alan and Paul Smolensky (2008): *Optimality Theory: Constraint Interaction in Generative Grammar*. Hoboken: John Wiley and Sons.

Ramscar, Michael and R. Harald Baayen (2013): Production, comprehension and synthesis: A communicative perspective on language. *Frontiers in Psychology* 4: 233.

Ramscar, Michael, Melody Dye, Jessica Gustafson, and Joseph Klein (2013a): Dual routes to cognitive flexibility: Learning and response conflict resolution in the dimensional change card sort task. *Child Development* 84(4): 1308–1323.

Ramscar, Michael, Melody Dye, and Joseph Klein (2013b): Children value informativity over logic in word learning. *Psychological Science* 24(6): 1017–1023.

Ramscar, Michael, Melody Dye, and Stewart McCauley (2013c): Error and expectation in language learning: The curious absence of mouses in adult speech. *Language* 89(4): 760–793.

Ramscar, Michael and Nichole Gitcho (2007): Developmental change and the nature of learning in childhood. *Trends in Cognitive Science* 11(7): 274–279.

Ramscar, Michael, Peter Hendrix, Bradley Love, and R. Harald Baayen (2013d): Learning is not decline: The mental lexicon as a window into cognition across the lifespan. *The Mental Lexicon* 8: 450–481.

Ramscar, Michael, Peter Hendrix, Cyrus Shaoul, Petar Milin, and R. Harald Baayen (2014): Nonlinear dynamics of lifelong learning: The myth of cognitive decline. *Topics in Cognitive Science* 6: 5–42.

Ramscar, Michael and Robert Port (this volume): Categorization (without categories). Berlin/Boston: De Gruyter Mouton.

Ramscar, Michael and Daniel Yarlett (2007): Linguistic self-correction in the absence of feedback: A new approach to the logical problem of language acquisition. *Cognitive Science* 31(6): 927–960.

Ramscar, Michael, Daniel Yarlett, Melody Dye, Katie Denny, and Kirsten Thorpe (2010): The effects of feature-label-order and their implications for symbolic learning. *Cognitive Science* 34(6): 909–957.

Rescorla, Robert (1988): Pavlovian conditioning. It's not what you think it is. *American Psychologist* 43(3): 151–160.

Rescorla, Robert and Allan Wagner (1972): A theory of Pavlovian conditioning: Variations in the effectiveness of reinforcement and nonreinforcement. In: A. H. Black and W. F. Prokasy (eds.), *Classical Conditioning* II, 64–99. New York: Appleton-Century-Crofts.

Shannon, Claude (1948): A mathematical theory of communication. *Bell System Technical Journal* 27: 379–423.

Shaoul, Cyrus, Chris Westbury, and R. Harald Baayen (2013): The subjective frequency of word n-grams. *Psihologija* 46(4): 497–537.

Siegel, Shepard and Lorraine Allan (1996): The widespread influence of the Rescorla-Wagner model. *Psychonomic Bulletin and Review* 3(3): 314–321.

Skousen, Royal (1989): *Analogical Modeling of Language*. Dordrecht: Kluwer.

Skousen, Royal (2000): Analogical modeling and quantum computing. Los Alamos National Laboratory.

Skousen, Royal (2002): *Analogical Modeling*. Amsterdam: Benjamins.

Slobin, Dan (1996): From 'thought to language' to 'thinking for speaking'. In: J. Gumperz and S. Levinson (eds.), *Rethinking Linguistic Relativity*, 70–96. Cambridge: Cambridge University Press.

Steels, Luc. and Joachim De Beule (2006): A (very) brief introduction to fluid construction grammar. *Proceedings of the Third Workshop on Scalable Natural Language Understanding*, 73–80. New York, June 8th, 2006. Association for Computational Linguistics.

Tomasello, Michael (2009): *Constructing a Language: A Usage-based Theory of Language Acquisition*. Cambridge: Harvard University Press.

Tremblay, Antoine and R. Harald Baayen (2010): Holistic processing of regular four-word sequences: A behavioral and ERP study of the effects of structure, frequency, and probability on immediate free recall. In: D. Wood (ed.), *Perspectives on Formulaic Language: Acquisition and communication*, 151–173. London: Continuum.

Turner, Mark (this volume): Blending in language and communication. Berlin/Boston: De Gruyter Mouton.

Veale, Tony, Diarmuid O'Donoghue, and Mark Keane (2000): Computation and blending. *Cognitive Linguistics* 11(3/4): 253–282.

Wieling, Martijn, John Nerbonne, Jelke Bloem, Charlotte Gooskens, Wilbert Heeringa, and R. Harald Baayen (2014): A cognitively grounded measure of pronunciation distance. *PloS One* 9(1): e75734.

Ronald W. Langacker
Chapter 6: Construal

1 Nature

Construal is our ability to conceive and portray the same situation in alternate ways. In cognitive linguistics, the term indicates an array of conceptual factors (such as *prominence*) shown to be relevant for lexical and semantic description. It underscores the role of conception in linguistic meaning, something denied even in semantics textbooks of the modern era (e.g., Palmer 1981: §2.2).

An expression's meaning depends on both the conceptual *content* invoked and how that content is construed. Content is roughly comparable to truth conditions, a state of affairs, or the objective situation described; in a conceptualist semantics, it amounts to the neutral apprehension of a situation, conceived in its own terms. But since the world does not just imprint itself on our brains, conception is never really neutral – it consists in mental activity, being shaped by the previous experience, capabilities, and current state of the conceptualizer. Thus every conception and every linguistic expression construes the content invoked in a certain manner.

Content and construal are equally important aspects of the processing activity that constitutes linguistic meaning. They cannot be neatly separated (indeed, the selection of content is itself an aspect of construal). The rationale for distinguishing them is that the apprehension of a situation is more than just a representation of its elements. While content and construal are ultimately indissociable, the distinction draws attention to the flexibility of conception and the variability of expression even in regard to the same objective circumstances.

If cognition resides in neurological activity, it presents itself to us as mental experience. In principle we want to understand how the former gives rise to the latter, and certain dimensions of construal (e.g., *dynamicity*) can hardly be discussed without invoking processing factors. But in practical terms, the usual strategy is to start with conceptual experience as manifested in linguistic meaning and revealed through linguistic analysis. Working along these lines, cognitive linguists have noted that aspects of construal needed for describing language are analogous to basic aspects of visual perception. Talmy (1996) thus coined the term *ception* to cover both *per*ception and *con*ception. In Cognitive Grammar both are referred to as *viewing* (Langacker 1987: §3.3, 1993a, 2008a:

Ronald W. Langacker, San Diego, USA

https://doi.org/10.1515/9783110626476-007

261). Their extensive parallelism reflects the primacy of vision and the grounding of cognition in perceptual and motor interaction. It is not presumed that conception is exclusively visuospatial in origin. In fact, the dimensions of construal all have manifestations in other sensory modalities.

Construal encompasses numerous interrelated factors. While natural groupings can be observed, no one classificatory scheme captures all the relationships or does justice to a single factor. For instance, *immediate scope* – the general locus of attention – can equally well be discussed under the rubric of the *perspective* taken on a scene, the *selection* of conceptual content, or the relative *prominence* of conceived entities. The adoption of any particular classification is thus a matter of expository convenience. Rather than a definitive list or taxonomy, the objective of this chapter is to characterize construal factors with reasonable precision and investigate their linguistic manifestations.

2 Dimensions

The many aspects of construal will be considered under five broad headings: *perspective*, *selection*, *prominence*, *dynamicity*, and *imagination*. Like the factors they subsume, they overlap and all come into play in a given expression.

2.1 Perspective

Fundamental to conception is the asymmetry between its *subject* and its *object*. The subject (S) is the locus of neural activity through which it engages some facet of the world, the object (O). Activity mediated by receptor organs constitutes perceptual experience. The neural control of effective activity (instigation, proprioception, guidance) constitutes motor experience. As we construct our mental world, reaching progressively higher levels of abstraction and complexity, an increasing proportion of our experience is related only indirectly to perceptual and motor activity. But even when the object engaged is mentally constructed, it is still apprehended by a conceptualizing subject.

In an instance of conceptual engagement, the subject is by definition active (the locus of neural activity and experience), while the object (as such) merely functions as the target. Being social creatures, we recognize the existence of other conceptualizers, who engage us as objects just as we engage them. And through our further capacity for simulating another subject's experience, we achieve the intersubjective awareness crucial for cognitive development, language acquisition, and linguistic interaction. Canonical language use involves

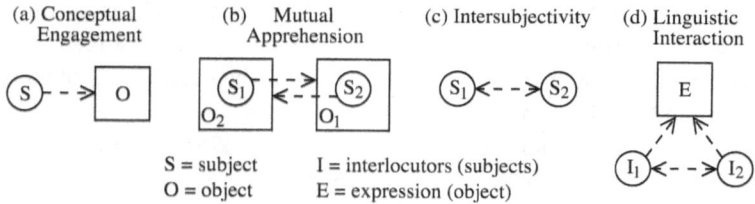

S = subject   I = interlocutors (subjects)
O = object   E = expression (object)

Fig. 6.1: Subject and object of conception.

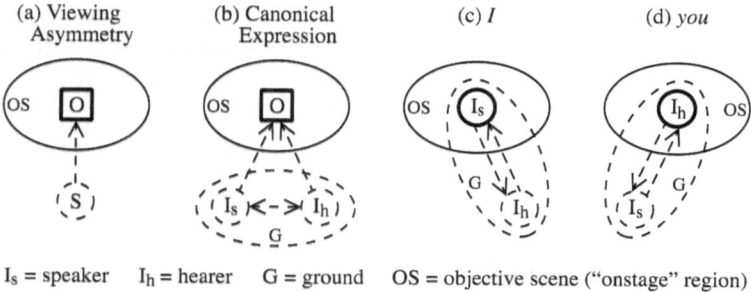

I_s = speaker I_h = hearer   G = ground   OS = objective scene ("onstage" region)

Fig. 6.2: "Onstage" vs. "offstage" elements.

conceptual engagement in each of two dimensions. Along one axis the interlocutors engage one another, intersubjective awareness being one component of their interaction. Contributing to this awareness is their joint apprehension, along the other axis, of the expression's form and meaning.

Whereas the subject is *active*, the object is *salient* in the subject's experience. The subject apprehends the object but – *qua* subject – is not itself apprehended. So in contrast to the bird's-eye view of Figure 6.1(a), where S and O are equally prominent, the subject's actual experience is more akin to Figure 6.2(a), where only O has any salience. Metaphorically, we can speak of S being the offstage viewer and O the onstage entity being viewed. Status in regard to this asymmetry is one facet of an element's construal: S is construed *subjectively*, and O *objectively* (Langacker 2006).

This viewing asymmetry is reflected linguistically in the fact that the interlocutors – the joint subjects of conception – are always implicated in expressions even though they are commonly left implicit. In the canonical ("unmarked") case of third-person statements, e.g., *She bought an iPad*, the interlocutors and their interaction are external to the *objective scene*, i.e., the situation described. These offstage entities are nonetheless essential to the expression's meaning,

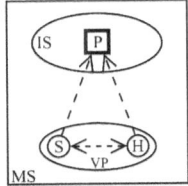

S = speaker
H = hearer
VP = vantage point
MS = maximal scope of conception
IS = immediate scope (onstage region)
P = profile (focus of attention)

Fig. 6.3: Canonical viewing arrangement.

defining the deictic center and providing the basis for person, tense, and illocutionary force. They constitute the *ground*.

The semantic import of the ground is more evident in expressions that depart from the canon, e.g., with speech acts other than simple statement. A very common departure is for the situation described to include some portion of the ground. Most obviously, a pronoun like *I* or *you* makes an interlocutor explicit, in which case it functions not only as a subject of conception but also as the object – both directly (for the other interlocutor) and indirectly (via simulation of the other's experience) (Langacker 2007). Performatives (e.g., *I order you [to stop]*) represent the extreme case of overlap, where the objective scene and the speaker-hearer interaction coincide (Austin 1962; Langacker 2008a: 469–470).

In addition to its salient onstage elements, an expression's meaning includes a *viewing arrangement*. Its canonical form is sketched in Figure 6.3, which introduces two additional perspectival factors: *vantage point* and *scope*. A vantage point is the location from which a situation is apprehended. In the canonical arrangement, the interlocutors are together in space as well as time, viewing the objective scene from the same vantage point offstage. Scope pertains to conceptual content: the extent of the content invoked and degrees of centrality imposed by viewing. The *maximal scope* is all the content that figures in an expression's meaning, even if only peripherally. Within that, the *immediate scope* is the portion being attended to (the onstage region). And within the immediate scope, the expression's *profile* is maximally prominent as the specific *focus* of attention. These notions have counterparts in vision: the maximal field of view is everything visible from a certain vantage point; within that is the region being looked at (the stage); and in that region a particular element stands out as the focus of attention. For language we are mainly concerned with their general conceptual analogs.

Analogs of spatial vantage point can be recognized for time and for other domains, e.g., a kinship network, where one's position determines who to address with terms like *father*, *uncle*, or *grandma*. Expressions differ as to how centrally vantage point figures in their meaning. For some it is peripheral in

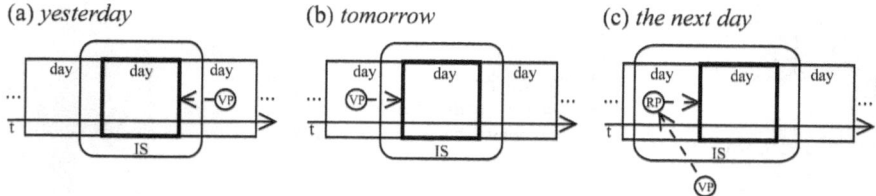

Fig. 6.4: Temporal vantage point and reference point.

that the same description applies from any vantage point: Denver can be described as a *city*, or as being *in Colorado*, from any location. At the other extreme are cases where vantage point is crucial. It is only its relation to a temporal vantage point that distinguishes *yesterday* from any other day. Whether something is *on the left* or *on the right* depends on both vantage point and the related factor of *orientation*. This too has non-spatial analogs. What distinguishes *yesterday* from *tomorrow* is whether the viewer focuses attention on the adjacent day while oriented toward the past or toward the future.

Multiple viewers and vantage points figure in all but the simplest expressions (Langacker 2008a: § 12.3.2). The interlocutors recognize other viewers (including each other) and to some extent simulate their experience. Their actual position in the ground therefore functions not only as the default-case vantage point, but also as point of departure for invoking and simulating others. Expressions vary in the extent to which viewing is invoked and the strength of its association with the ground. For example, *tomorrow* consistently invokes the actual ground (except in special discourse modes). Normally a successor day is specified periphrastically with a non-deictic locution: *She delivered her lecture and left {the next day / *tomorrow}*. As shown in Figure 6.4(c), such locutions invoke an onstage temporal *reference point* (RP) whose relationship to the day in question is apprehended from an external vantage point.

The notions vantage point and reference point are distinct but closely related. By definition, a vantage point is the location from which a situation is apprehended (hence offstage for the viewer in question), whereas a reference point is part of that situation, invoked in order to mentally access an onstage target (Langacker 1993b). In *Bill's father*, for example, Bill functions as reference point for the target *father*, with the interlocutors as viewers. Given the overall objective of relating the target to the viewer, it is natural and efficient for the viewer itself to be invoked as the basis for computing the relationship. There is then no separate or explicit reference point, the offstage viewer assuming its role: to indicate her own male parent, the speaker need only say *father*. Alternatively, the speaker can go onstage, describing the relationship from the standpoint of

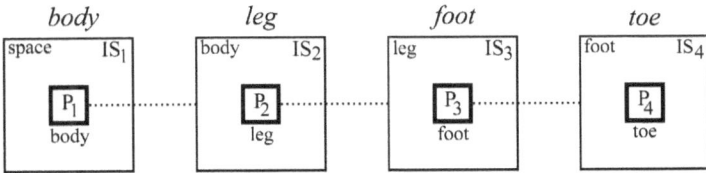

Fig. 6.5: Immediate scope relations.

an external viewer: *my father*. The same options are available for spatial reference points: *She lives across the hall from Bill* (with Bill onstage as RP) vs. *She lives across the hall from me* (with the speaker onstage as RP) vs. *She lives across the hall* (described from the speaker's offstage VP).

As for construal in general, the same perspectival factors are important for both lexicon and grammar. Consider immediate scope: the array of conceptual content attended to as the direct basis for apprehending an expression's profile (focus of attention), hence the immediate context for this purpose. While the boundary may be fuzzy, the immediate scope is limited in extent. For example, a kinship network extends indefinitely, but the lexeme *father* directly invokes just a small portion (what we call the *immediate family*), and *uncle* a slightly larger one. The lexical import of immediate scope is clearly evident in whole-part hierarchies, notably with body-part expressions, e.g., *body > leg > foot > toe*. Although a toe is part of the body, the direct basis for its characterization is the conception of a foot, which in turn is characterized directly in relation to a leg. The lexical meanings are thus related as in Figure 6.5, where the profile of each expression functions as immediate scope for the next. Precisely analogous relationships function grammatically in a general compounding pattern, whereby $N_1 + N_2$ describes an immediate part of N_1. Responsible for a large number of lexicalized expressions (e.g., *fingertip, asshole, windowpane, car seat*), it also sanctions novel combinations (*toetip, nosehole, doorpane, truck seat*).

The progression *body > leg > foot > toe* illustrates another perspectival factor, the distinction (always relative) between a *global view* of a situation and a *local view* subsuming only part of it. This correlates with *scale*: *head, torso, arm*, and *leg* designate large-scale components of the body, evident in a global conception; *thigh, knee, calf, ankle*, and *foot* refer to smaller-scale components, more salient in a local view comprising just the leg.

Additional perspectival factors involve departures from the canonical viewing arrangement. As already noted, it is common for the ground and immediate scope to overlap, some facet of the ground being put onstage as an explicit object of description. Departing more drastically from the canon are cases where the interlocutors are separated in space – as in speaking by phone – or even time. Consider the following message on an answering machine: *I'm not here today. Try calling again tomorrow.* In canonical circumstances, *I'm not here* is contradictory (by definition, *here* is where I am). But the speaker is describing things from the temporal vantage point of an imagined later caller, when she expects to be elsewhere. *Today* and *tomorrow* are likewise relative to the time of calling.

Such examples make the obvious point that the presupposed viewing arrangement determines what it makes sense to say and how to say it. Normally, for instance, it makes no sense for towns to be described as *frequent*. But it is perfectly natural to say *The towns are getting less frequent* when the viewers are moving rather than stationary – another common departure from the canon.

2.2 Selection

Selection stems from the disparity between the vast complexity of our mental world and the severe limits on our processing capacity. It is therefore fundamental: if we had to describe everything, we could never describe anything. It is also ubiquitous, as everything expressed stands out against the backdrop of indefinitely much that is not expressed. Content selected for expression is never autonomous or self-contained, but embedded in an elaborate *conceptual substrate* comprising presupposed and associated knowledge (Langacker 2008a). Linguistic coding serves not to remove it from this substrate, but to activate it and make it accessible.

Every expression omits much more than it explicitly conveys. For the most part omission is not a matter of specific intent but a by-product of attention: since we can attend to only so much at a given moment, everything else is either peripheral to our awareness or outside it altogether. Thus the degrees of centrality in Figure 6.3 – organization into focus of attention, onstage region, and maximal scope of awareness – are not only perspectival but represent the most basic aspect of selection.

When a situation has been chosen for description, additional selective factors come into play. One is the level of *specificity* (or its converse, *schematicity*) at which the onstage content is characterized. It is a matter of "resolution" or "granularity": whether the situation is described in fine-grained detail or only in coarse-grained terms. This aspect of construal is manifested lexically in hierarchies such as *thing > creature > person > female > girl*, where each expression is schematic relative to the one that follows. Of course, specificity can also be achieved periphrastically, through longer descriptions (e.g., *young human female* for *girl*). Degree of specificity is one of the grounds for distinguishing lexicon and grammar (cf. Talmy 1988; Boye and Harder 2012). By and large, elements toward the grammatical end of the spectrum are quite schematic, their main import residing in the construal imposed on lexical content. For instance, progressive *-ing* is perspectival, its meaning residing in the immediate temporal scope imposed on the event designated by a verb stem (excluding its endpoints). A grammatical construction (e.g., V + *-ing*) is schematic vis-à-vis the specific content of instantiating expressions (*working, examining*, etc.); it is simply their reinforced commonality, hence immanent in them.

Another factor is the choice of *profile*, the focus of attention within the immediate scope. Although profiling is a kind of prominence, its selective aspect merits separate discussion. A key point is that meaning comprises considerably more than explicitly coded content, even in regard to the objective scene. Overtly mentioned elements are neither free-standing nor exhaustive of the situation described, but are embedded in a substrate providing the basis for a coherent interpretation. Reference to a single element may then be sufficient to evoke the entire conceptual complex. When multiple elements are capable of doing so, the speaker selects a particular element for explicit mention, so that it functions as point of access to the remainder. We speak of *metonymy* in cases where an entity accessed only secondarily, via this point of reference, is nonetheless pivotal for some evident purpose.

Metonymy reflects the general strategy of focusing entities that are salient or easily accessible, relying on the substrate for essential content left implicit. It thereby achieves both processing ease and coding efficiency. While conversing in a parking lot, *I'm over there* provides a natural, compact alternative to *My car is parked over there*. But it is not just a matter of efficiency, as the former frames the situation in terms of the speaker's experience and projected movement. It represents an alternative construal which has the advantage of conferring linguistic prominence on items of greater intrinsic interest.

Metonymic construal is pervasive in lexicon and grammar (Kövecses and Radden 1998; Panther and Radden 2004; Panther et al. 2009; Barcelona this volume). Non-explicit content is commonly invoked for grammatical composition. The verb *park*, for instance, profiles a telic event of brief duration: *She parked the car in a jiffy*. But since the car is expected to stay there for a while, *park* can also occur with adverbials specifying the duration of a stable situation: *You can park here for two hours*. Through conventionalization, this shift in focus produces a new lexical sense, so that *park* can mean either '**put** (and keep) in place' or '(put and) **keep** in place'. Alternative profiling is a major source of lexical polysemy (Gries Volume 3). In a car you can *roll down the* **window** (the glass pane), and if the door is broken you can *crawl out through the window* (the opening). Relational expressions are commonly polysemic in regard to the choice of focused participant, e.g., *hear a* **car** vs. *hear the* **sound** *of a car*.

Respectively, these view the profiled relationship in terms of the element with greater cognitive salience vs. the one that figures in it more directly (Langacker 1990: ch. 7).

2.3 Prominence

Many kinds of prominence need to be differentiated for linguistic purposes (Tomlin and Myachykov this volume). We can first distinguish between inherent prominence and that conferred by linguistic means. Included in the former are the privileged cognitive statuses of space and vision, as well as salience asymmetries such as concrete vs. abstract, human vs. non-human, whole vs. part. Linguistic prominence has both phonological and semantic components. For phonology, obvious examples are accent and degrees of sonority. Relevant for construal are various types of semantic prominence and their manifestations in lexicon and grammar.

In sorting these out, it is useful to begin with the fundamental asymmetry between the subject and the object of conception. By nature it is a prominence asymmetry: being the onstage focus of attention, the object is highly salient, whereas the subject (when functioning exclusively as such) has no salience whatever, for it is not itself conceived. Attention is not the only source of prominence, however. The focus of attention is salient *within* the conception, as part of the conceptual experience. But we also speak of salience in regard to factors responsible for shaping that experience. Frequent, well-entrenched linguistic units are salient in the sense of being easily activated. Prototypes are prominent within their categories. Conceptual archetypes motivate basic aspects of language structure. Inhering in the subject's cognitive organization, these sorts of prominence are offstage and not per se apprehended, but are matters of *accessibility* and *degree of influence* in the shaping of onstage content.

Both onstage prominence (salience within a conception) and offstage prominence (accessibility/influence in shaping a conception) involve a central element and others that are more peripheral. Characterized as the onstage focus of attention, an expression's profile is central within the conception evoked as its meaning. The profile stands out as salient within the immediate scope (the content directly relevant to its apprehension), which defines the onstage region. But since meanings are never self-contained, the onstage conception recruits or elicits others, which in turn invoke still others, as shown for *toe* in Figure 6.6. The focused element is thus embedded in a substrate that extends indefinitely with diminishing levels of salience.

The offstage region centers on the subject of conception. As the very locus of experience (and the activity constituting it), the subject could not be more

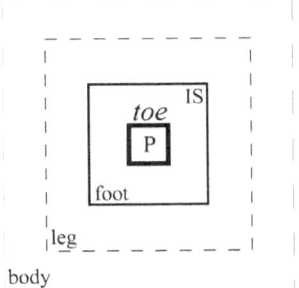

Fig. 6.6: Degrees of onstage prominence.

accessible and influential in shaping the apprehension of onstage content. Organized around it are several other kinds of offstage elements with varying degrees of prominence. Still quite central, in the sense of inhering in the subject, are the mental resources exploited in conception: a vast array of established structures (including linguistic units) whose differential salience consists in their ease and likelihood of activation. More extrinsic to the subject are the ground and the discourse context. Being primarily responsible for constructing an expression, the speaker is central to the ground: her own experience is real and immediate, the hearer's being accessible only via mental simulation. However, both interlocutors function as subjects, and each simulates the other's experience, so jointly they comprise a higher-level subject engaged in intersubjectively apprehending the ground and the wider context. An important facet of the context is the ongoing discourse. Along the discursive axis, the expression currently being processed is onstage by virtue of being attended to. When the next one comes along it is pushed offstage, becoming a shared resource employed by the interlocutors in processing the new one. Its offstage salience depends on recency: the most recent expression is generally the most accessible and has the greatest influence in shaping the new one.

Distinguishing onstage and offstage prominence resolves the conundrum of the speaker and the ground being both non-salient (usually not even mentioned) and highly prominent (in that everything revolves around them): it is just a matter of their onstage salience being minimized, and their offstage salience maximized, in the canonical viewing arrangement. Owing to their offstage salience, an implicit vantage point is normally identified with that of the speaker or the ground, as in *She lives across the hall*. The semantic contrast with *She lives across the hall from me* – less canonical because the speaker is construed objectively – nicely illustrates the distinction between offstage and onstage prominence. Further illustration is provided by discourse topics. When first in-

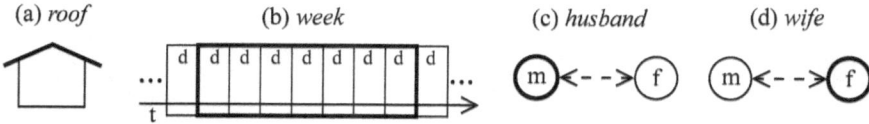

Fig. 6.7: Examples of profiled things.

troduced, a topic is made explicit as a salient onstage element (*She has **a good job** ...*). Once established, a topic is often left implicit but is still invoked, due to its offstage salience, as the basis for interpreting what follows (*... There's no pressure, and the benefits are excellent*).

To be mentioned explicitly is to be *profiled* by some expression. An essential factor in onstage prominence, profiling is the intersubjective focusing of attention induced by symbolization: through the directive force of symbolic expression, the interlocutors momentarily attend to the same entity in the objective scene. An expression's profile is thus its *conceptual referent* – the entity it designates or refers to within the array of content invoked (the *base*).

As described in Cognitive Grammar, expressions can profile either *things* or *relationships* (both abstractly defined). A few examples of the former are sketched in Figure 6.7. (As standard notational conventions, the profile is shown in bold, with circles often used for things, and lines or arrows for relationships.) *Roof* evokes as its base the conception of a house or building, within which it profiles the covering part on top. *Week* designates any sequence of seven consecutive days. *Husband* and *wife* profile the male and female participants in a relationship of marriage. Observe that these latter expressions have the same essential content, referring to different elements within the same conceptual base. Their semantic opposition can only be ascribed to the difference in profiling.

Some examples of profiled relationships are sketched in Figure 6.8. *Tall* situates a thing on a scale of height. *Above* and *below* locate two things in relation to one another along the vertical axis. While they commonly endure, these relationships are fully manifested at a single point in time (hence observable in a photograph). By contrast, other expressions construe the profiled relationship as evolving along the temporal axis, so that a span of time is required for its full manifestation. Thus *fall* tracks through time the changing location of a single thing along the vertical axis.

Profiling is pivotal to a basic proposal of Cognitive Grammar which linguists are strongly inclined to resist (Hudson 1992; cf. Langacker 2013): that basic grammatical categories are susceptible to general conceptual characterization (Langacker 2008a: ch. 4). Very roughly, it is claimed that a noun profiles a

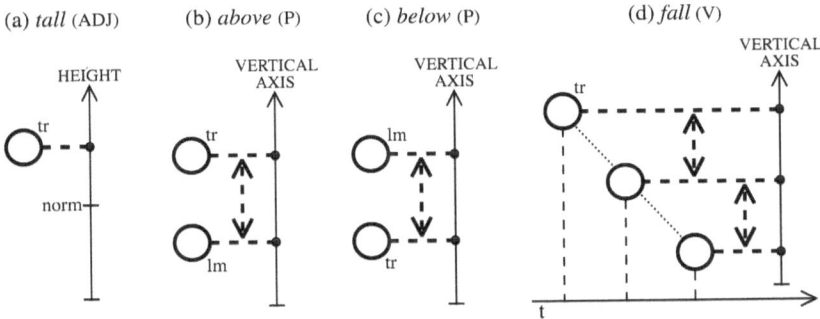

Fig. 6.8: Examples of profiled relationships.

thing, a verb profiles a "process" – a relationship tracked through time – while adjectives, adverbs, and prepositions profile non-processual relationships. The validity of this claim is not at issue here. It is however evident that an expression's category specifically reflects its profile, not its overall (or even its most important) conceptual content. For example, *husband* and *wife* are nouns because they profile things, even though the essential content is a relationship in which they participate.

Profiling is the focusing of attention through symbolic reference. Expressions that profile relationships involve an additional sort of focal prominence pertaining to participants. A relationship is *conceptually dependent* on its participants, i.e., they are inherent in its conception. Within a profiled relationship, a single participant is usually made salient as the one being assessed in regard to location, properties, or activity. This primary focal participant is called the *trajector* (tr). There is often a secondary focal participant, called a *landmark* (lm), with a salient role in assessing the trajector. The relationship profiled by an adjective (like *tall*) or an intransitive verb (*fall*) has just one focused participant, which is thus the trajector, whereas prepositions and transitive verbs have both a trajector and a landmark. As with profiling, trajector/landmark alignment may be solely responsible for a difference in meaning. For example, *above* and *below* have the same content and profile the same spatial relationship; the semantic distinction is just a matter of whether trajector status (as the participant being located) is conferred on the higher or the lower participant.

Like profiling, trajector/landmark alignment is necessary for semantic description but also has an important role in grammar. As proposed in Cognitive Grammar, it figures in the conceptual characterization of basic categories: what distinguishes adjectives and adverbs is whether their trajector is a thing or a relationship; prepositions are neutral in this respect (so prepositional phrases

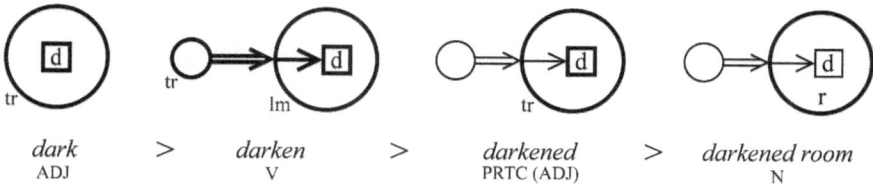

Fig. 6.9: Profiling and focal participants at successive levels of organization.

can function in either capacity) but differ by having a thing as their landmark. It is further proposed that trajector and landmark provide a general conceptual basis for the grammatical notions subject and object (Langacker 2008a: §11.2). While these claims are controversial, it is evident that profiling and trajector/landmark alignment pertain to both lexical and grammatical elements as well as complex expressions. In a full account of meaning and grammar, these (and other construal factors) have to be specified for each component element and the structure obtained at each level of composition.

Shown in Figure 6.9, for example, are the results of composition at several successive levels. The adjective *dark* profiles the relationship of its trajector exhibiting a certain property. From this the verb *darken* derives by suffixation. Semantically, a derivational element is schematic for the category it derives by imposing its profile on the stem. The suffix *-en* is thus a schematic causative verb, and *darken* a specific one: it profiles an event in which its trajector causes (double arrow) the change (single arrow) of its landmark becoming dark. Observe that the same conceived entity is both the adjectival trajector, at the lower level of organization, and the verbal landmark, at the higher level.

From *darken*, *-ed* derives the stative-adjectival participle *darkened*. The profiled relationship is that of the trajector exhibiting a certain property (making it adjectival) by virtue of having undergone a change of state (unprofiled at this level). Thus *dark* and *darkened* profile the same relationship, with the same trajector, but differ in meaning because the latter specifically portrays this as resulting from the process *darken*. Finally, in *darkened room* the adjectival participle combines with a noun, which specifies its schematic trajector and imposes its nominal profile on the composite expression. *Room* is the *head* in the sense of determining the profile – hence the grammatical category – of the whole: *darkened room* functions as a complex noun (not an adjective).

2.4 Dynamicity

Language and conception are things that *happen*. Consisting in patterns of activity, they unfold through *time*, and the specific way in which they do so –

their *time course* – is essential. Despite its inherent seriality, the processing involved does not reduce to a single linear sequence. It runs concurrently in different dimensions, at different levels of organization, and on different time scales (from the coordination of articulatory gestures to global discourse planning). It is organized hierarchically when elements that on one time scale are accessed sequentially, in separate processing windows, function as a single element in a window on a larger time scale. Additional departures from strict linearity are recall, anticipation, backtracking, and the interruption of one processing task by another.

Time has different linguistic roles. A fundamental distinction pertains to the subject vs. the object of conception. *Processing time* (T) inheres in the subject's activity: it is time as the medium of conception, through which processing occurs. Processing of even the smallest element has some duration, however brief. Conception occurs through time regardless of whether time per se figures in its content. To the extent that it does, it assumes the role of *conceived time* (t): time as an object of conception.

A conception unfolds through processing time in a certain manner, even in a non-linguistic task where conceived time is not a factor (e.g., observing the objects in a static array). On a small enough time scale, its elements are activated in some sequence, each with some duration, and need not all be active at any one instant. The *path of access* defined by this ordering is one facet (however minor) of the mental experience. Thus different paths of access to the same conceptual content constitute alternate ways of construing it.

As an aspect of linguistic meaning, sequential access has varied sources and functions. A very general source is symbolization. Because sounds evoke the associated meanings (and conversely), the order of symbolic elements induces the corresponding order of conception as one facet of the overall processing activity. The semantic effect of different orders may be quite minimal (even vacuous) in terms of the situation described. But it is never wholly negligible: the conceptions evoked by *X Y* and *Y X* are less than fully identical if only due to their components being accessed in different sequences.

As a matter of processing efficiency, the order of presentation tends to follow *natural paths* of mental access, such as causal chains, paths of motion, event sequences, established associations, and rankings for salience or other properties. While it need not (and cannot) align with all such paths, one that does mesh with the order of expression is reinforced by this iconicity. A sequence of elements that could represent a natural ordering thus invites the inference that it does: *She went to Denver, Boston, and Miami* suggests that Denver was the first stop, Miami the last. To varying degrees the alignment of expression with a natural path is established as part of the conventional import of particular constructions. For instance, a conventional pattern of English specifies location by "zooming in" to smaller and smaller areas: *It's in the garage, in the cabinet, on the top shelf, behind some paint cans*. Established to a lesser degree is the alternative of "zooming out" to larger and larger areas: *It's behind some paint cans, on the top shelf, in the cabinet, in the garage*. With either construction one follows a natural path of access obtained by successively contracting or expanding the immediate spatial scope. The two paths represent alternate construals of the same situation. The example shows that a natural path aligned with the order of expression need not be based on conceived time. Nor does order of expression have to be used iconically: like segmental content, it can participate in essentially arbitrary symbolic pairings (e.g., to mark grammatical relationships).

Within a symbolized conception, time (t) has a number of different roles with varying degrees of centrality. It may be effectively absent, as in the minimal apprehension of an object (*cup*), property (*blue*), or configuration (*above*). But time is too fundamental to be easily avoided altogether. It enters the picture with the evocation of events, even as part of background knowledge (e.g., the use of a cup for drinking). Its role is less peripheral with a verb or a clause, which profiles a relationship specifically viewed as evolving through time, either a bounded event (*fall*) or a state of indefinite duration (*resemble*). More central is its role as the domain in which a profiled relationship is manifested; for example, time is the domain for *before* and *after* in the same way that space is for *above* and *below*. Finally, time itself – or some instantiation of time – can itself be the profiled entity: *time, period, week* (cf. Evans 2004, Volume 3).

Though essential for a verb or a clause, conceived time is not itself the focus of attention, nor even the most central domain. The focus is the profiled relationship, which is usually spatial or at least non-temporal. Time figures at a higher level of conceptual organization, where the profiled relationship is followed in its temporal evolution. This is shown for *fall* in Figure 6.10: through time (t), the mover occupies a series of successively lower positions along the vertical axis. Their distribution through time is crucial: without it, nothing would distinguish *fall* from *rise*. This inherent dimension of organization constitutes a natural path of mental access. It is thus proposed in Cognitive Grammar that the temporal phases of a verbal process are accessed ("scanned") sequentially as one aspect of its apprehension, so that conceived time correlates with processing time (T). This accords with a general hypothesis that any conception of ordering or directionality resides in sequenced mental activity at some level of processing (Langacker 1990: ch. 5).

When an event is directly observed, its apprehension coincides with its occurrence: its temporal phases are accessed serially, each being fully activated

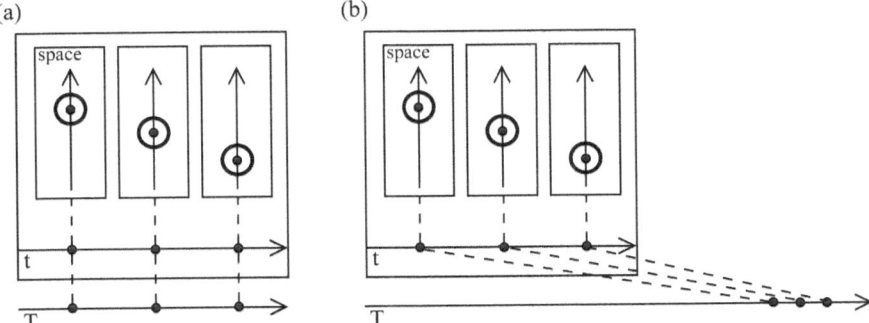

Fig. 6.10: Sequential scanning.

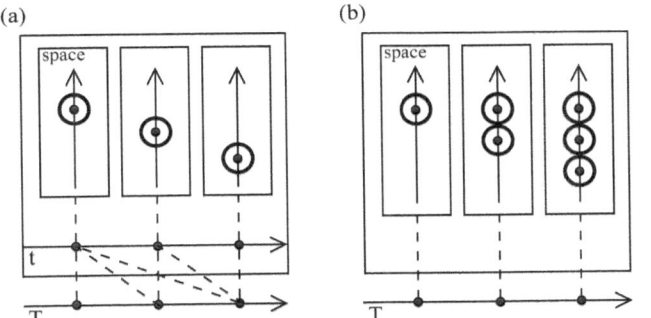

Fig. 6.11: Summation.

just when it is manifested. In this case conceived time and processing time are effectively equivalent, as in Figure 6.10(a). Usually, though, an event's occurrence and its apprehension in describing it linguistically are non-coincident, as shown in (b). In this case conceived and processing time clearly need to be distinguished. Occurrence and conception being independent, they normally differ in duration. There is however a correspondence, as the event's characterization requires that its phases be accessed (through T) in the sequence of their manifestation (through t). This sequential scanning of the event constitutes a mental simulation of its observation (Langacker 2008b).

Importantly, our apprehension of events is not exclusively sequential. We can also view them holistically through *summation*, represented by the additional dashed lines in Figure 6.11(a). These indicate that a temporal phase of the event, once activated at a given point in T, remains active as subsequent phases are processed. The resulting conceptual experience is sketched in Figure

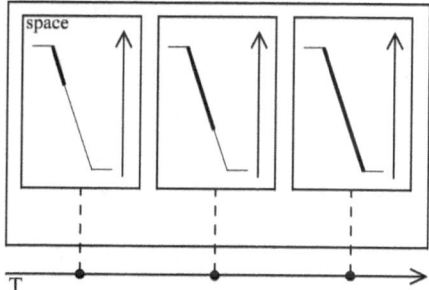

Fig. 6.12: Fictive motion.

6.11(b): each successive configuration is superimposed on those already active, until they are all active simultaneously, as in a multiple-exposure photograph. This increasingly complex configuration is solely a product of conception (in T), not taken to be an objective occurrence, so t is omitted from the diagram. Summation may well coexist with sequential scanning, perhaps emerging as a by-product. In any case, it comes to the fore when a verb's inherent sequentiality is overridden at higher levels of grammatical organization. It is claimed in Cognitive Grammar that holistic construal is one factor in the formation of infinitives (*to fall*), participles (*falling, fallen*), and derived nouns (*[a] fall*), which are therefore non-processual despite their verbal origin (Langacker 1991).

Summation can also be applied to static scenes. The result is *fictive motion* (Langacker 1990: ch. 5; Talmy 1996; Matsumoto 1996; Matlock 2004; Matlock and Bergmann Volume 3), where a motion verb occurs even though, objectively, nothing moves. Such expressions, e.g., *The cliff falls steeply to the valley floor*, describe the shape of entities having sufficient spatial extension to occupy all the points along a path at one time (t). The motion involved is subjective: the conceptualizer scans mentally along this path, building up a more and more elaborate structure, until arriving at a full conception of its shape. As shown in Figure 6.12, the conceptual experience is that of the cliff "growing" downward through processing time (with *rise*, of course, it grows upward instead).

Fictive motion is one of many linguistic phenomena effecting the dynamic construal of static situations. To cite just one more case, certain adverbs whose basic sense pertains to conceived time can instead be interpreted with respect to processing time. For example, *already* normally indicates that something happens earlier than expected: *It's already getting dark.* But it is also used in regard to stable circumstances: *Forget about algebra and calculus – arithmetic is already beyond me.* The import of *already* is quite comparable in this use. The main difference is that the event it concerns – what happens earlier than expected – is not an objective occurrence (in t) but consists in mental processing (through T). The expression invokes a scale on which mathematical subjects are ranked for difficulty. It indicates that, in scanning upward along this scale, a subject too difficult for the speaker is encountered sooner than might be anticipated.

A final point is that sequential access (through T) constitutes the essential semantic import of various grammatical notions. Prime examples are topic, anaphoric, and (at the most schematic level) possessive relationships, which share the essential feature of invoking one conceived entity as a *reference point* affording mental access to another (Langacker 2008a: §14.1). For instance, a topic relation has no objective content – it is not per se a facet of the situation described. Instead it pertains to how the onstage content is accessed and apprehended: by evoking associated knowledge, a topic allows the comment clause to be properly interpreted. Because it represents a natural path of mental access, the progression from topic to comment tends to align with the order of presentation: *Your daughter, she's very talented*. But natural paths do not always co-align, nor does language processing reduce to a single linear sequence. So while it may be less efficient, the non-congruent order is often possible: *She's very talented, your daughter*. In this case apprehension of the topic-comment relationship, instead of coinciding with phonological expression, has to be effected post hoc (a kind of backtracking).

2.5 Imagination

All cognition is imaginative in the sense that the world as we experience it (including what we accept as the "real world") is mentally constructed. Far from being a passive mirror of reality, the mind consists in non-determinate processing activity which inherently imposes some construal on whatever is apprehended. In labeling certain conceptions as "fictive", "virtual", or "imaginative", we presuppose a contrast with others that are not. While this is a relative matter, with no clear line of demarcation, certain kinds of experience – notably the direct observation of physical objects and events – clearly have a privileged status. From this *baseline* we build up our mental world through many levels of conceptual elaboration. It is suggested that baseline and imaginative conceptions rely on the same basic mental capacities: *extensionality, integration, disengagement,* and *abstraction*.

By *extensionality* is meant the capacity for entertaining multiple entities as part of a single experience (in the same "representational space" or "processing window"). They are then subject to mental operations which serve to connect them and thereby effect their conceptual *integration*. In a temporal processing window, for example, a series of syllables is perceived as a word by virtue of prosodic grouping and phonetic integration. Two objects appearing in the visual field are connected by operations (assessments of distance, orientation, etc.) comprising a spatial relationship. And in processing windows of various sizes, simpler symbolic structures are integrated – semantically and phonologically – to form composite expressions. Plausibly analyzed as higher-level analogs of these capacities are some pervasive and fundamental imaginative phenomena: *mental spaces*, *metaphor*, and *blending* (Fauconnier 1985; Lakoff and Johnson 1980; Fauconnier and Turner 2002; Turner this volume).

Mental spaces are separate conceptual "working areas", each hosting a limited array of content which has its own status and function within the global conception that encompasses them. They are largely imaginative, representing myriad departures from baseline reality: fictional worlds; hypothetical situations; abstracted generalizations; projected future occurrences; the thoughts, beliefs, and desires of other conceptualizers; and so on. Spaces are connected through natural paths of access and correspondences between their elements. For example, *If Bill had a watch he would break it* defines an access path leading from the speaker's conception of reality, to the counterfactual situation of Bill having a watch, and then to the imagined event – predictable from this situation – of his breaking it. These spaces are further connected by correspondences. Bill is an element of all three spaces: accepted by the speaker as a real individual, he is also identified as the person who has a watch and who breaks it. The watch is only fictive, being introduced as part of the counterfactual situation, but figures as well in the predicted consequence.

Within each space, elements are connected by correspondences effecting their conceptual integration. In the counterfactual situation, for instance, Bill is identified with *have*'s trajector, and the watch with its landmark. But the same is true at a higher level of organization, where the spaces are connected to form a space configuration. Apprehension of this higher-order structure requires a more inclusive representational space (a processing window on a larger time scale) with sufficient extensionality for connections to be established. For the example in question, the overall space configuration is sketched in Figure 6.13, where boxes delimit mental spaces, and dashed arrows indicate a path of mental access. While conceptual integration is naturally looser at this higher level, the configuration is a coherent structure in its own right: the initial situation and predicted occurrence are subspaces within the overarching counterfactual space, which (despite some overlap) is distinct from the speaker's conception of reality.

Metaphor and blending represent particular kinds of mental space configurations. In metaphor (Gibbs this volume), the *source* and *target domains* are

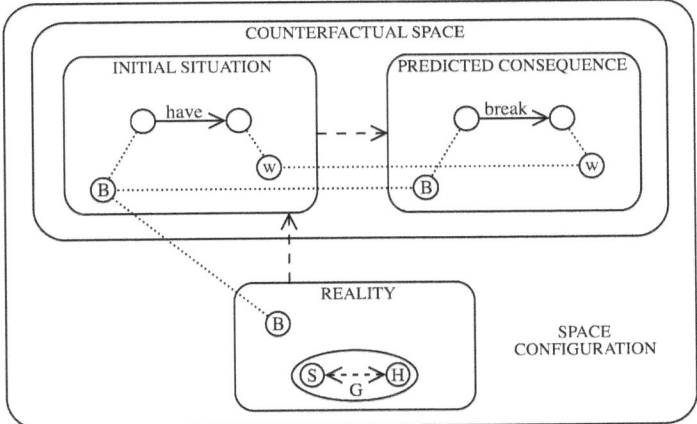

Fig. 6.13: A mental space configuration.

spaces connected by mappings between their elements. As the terms suggest, the space configuration involves a functional asymmetry with inherent directionality: whereas the target is the actual object of description, it is mentally accessed via the source, which offers a structural analogy (perceived or imposed) for its apprehension (Gentner 1983; Lakoff 1990). Co-activation of the source and target produces a new conception with features of both: that of the target as structured by the source. Metaphor can thus be viewed as a case of blending. Defined more broadly, blending consists in selected elements from two *input spaces* being projected as elements of another space (the *blend*) with its own structure and emergent properties. A blend is always imaginative at least in the sense of being distinct from both inputs, e.g., brunch is not quite the same as either breakfast or lunch. Likewise, a corporation construed metaphorically as a person is not equivalent to either one.

The role of these phenomena in constructing our mental world could hardly be exaggerated. Equally important are the related capacities of disengagement and abstraction. We can speak of *disengagement* when processing activity that originates in a certain context is later carried out independently of that context. A prime example is sensory and motor *imagery*, consisting in the partial autonomous occurrence of activity responsible for perception and motor action (Shepard 1978; Kosslyn 1980). This is an important component of lexical meaning (e.g., *bell* invokes an auditory image, *grasp* a motor image). More generally, disengagement manifests as *mental simulation* (Bergen 2012), the presumed basis of numerous essential phenomena. Among these are recall (the simulation of a previous experience), the projection of future events, the ability to adopt a non-actual vantage point, as well as to apprehend the experience of other conceptualizers. Disengagement is also the crucial factor in fictive motion (e.g., *the cliff falls steeply*). In apprehending actual motion, the conceptualizer scans mentally through both space and conceived time. As shown in Figures 6.11 and 6.12, fictive motion results when the spatial scanning is disengaged from the latter, applying instead to the conception of a static shape.

Abstraction refers to the loss of information inherent in the formation of any kind of mental representation. A memory, concept, or semantic structure is necessarily impoverished relative to the full, rich, specific detail of the original experience it is based on. An abstracted structure can be impoverished in regard to either its internal characterization or its place within a more inclusive context. A typical lexeme, e.g., *bird*, is quite limited in both respects. On the one hand, its characterization abstracts away from the specific features distinguishing different kinds of birds. Even terms for particular species and varieties (e.g., *ruby-throated hummingbird*) are schematic vis-à-vis the fine-grained conception of actual instances. On the other hand, a lexeme represents a *type* rather than an *instance* of that type. The type conception symbolized by *bird* abstracts away from the external circumstances allowing instances to be differentiated and identified (e.g., *this bird* vs. *that bird*).

As described in Cognitive Grammar, a type is *instantiated* by being anchored to a distinguishing location in a certain domain – time in the case of verbs, space for typical nouns (Langacker 1991: §2.2.1). Conversely, a type is obtained from instances by abstracting away from their locations and focusing on their common characterization. Types are thus imaginative, being transcendent with respect to baseline experience (the direct observation of objects and events). But instances can also be imaginative, representing various kinds and degrees of departure from the baseline.

In direct observation, a distinguishing location is known and an instance can be identified by pointing: *this [☞] watch*. More commonly, though, an instance is simply imagined as having a distinct location (at a given moment) without the speaker actually knowing where it is. Thus it either remains unidentified (*a watch*) or is identified in some other manner, e.g., being accessed via a reference point (*Bill's watch*). For the interlocutors, who abstract away from any particular location, the instance "floats unattached" within some range. A more drastic departure from the baseline consists in the referent being confined to a special mental space distinct from reality (e.g., *if Bill had a watch*), making it imaginative in the strong sense of being a *virtual* (or *fictive*) instance of the type. Virtual instances are also employed in making generalizations. For example, *Each boy wore a watch* generalizes over a certain range of actual occurrences by invoking and describing a virtual one conceived as being *representative*

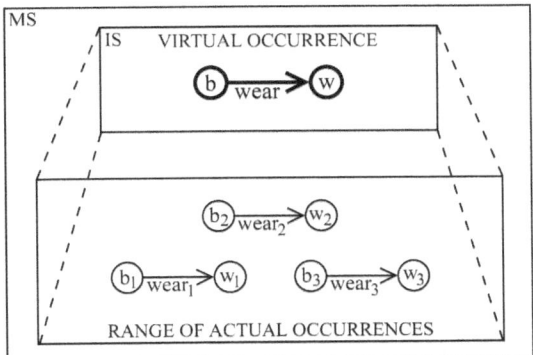

Fig. 6.14: Generalization by means of virtual instances.

of them. The imagined instances of *boy*, *wear*, and *watch* float unattached within that range, as in Figure 6.14, being neither identified with nor distinct from any particular one. With a fully general statement the range is unrestricted (e.g., *A watch is a timepiece*).

Among the virtual entities invoked linguistically are imagined scenarios that remain implicit but are evident from their overt symptoms. There are many traces of fictive speech interactions (Pascual 2006). In speaking of *his can-do spirit*, for instance, we conjure up a scenario in which he always says *can do* when charged with a task. Also common are scenarios involving spatial motion, e.g., *It's pretty through the canyon*, where *through the canyon* invokes an otherwise implicit event of travel, and *it's pretty* describes the view at any moment of this imagined journey. A fictive motion scenario accounts as well for the apparent use of frequency adverbs as nominal quantifiers. On one interpretation, *A lawyer is usually devious* is equivalent to *Most lawyers are devious* in terms of what it says about the world. Yet they construe this circumstance rather differently. *Usually* does not mean *most* – it still pertains to the frequency of events. These events, however, are only fictive, part of an imagined scenario of traveling through the world, encountering lawyers, and ascertaining their properties. In the context of this scenario, it is *usually* the case that the lawyer examined proves to be devious.

3 Validation

An account of construal is based primarily on linguistic analysis and description. The notions proposed are motivated by their role in cogently and explicitly describing varied kinds of expressions (including their meanings). A limited set of descriptive constructs, each required for the characterization of specific phenomena, prove to have broad applicability, both within a language and crosslinguistically. Hence they are not adopted a priori or by appealing to intuition, but have a principled empirical basis (Dodge and Lakoff 2005: 58).

More specifically, a particular descriptive notion is supported by the convergence of three considerations: (i) it is needed for semantic description; (ii) it has psychological plausibility; and (iii) it plays a role in grammar (Langacker 1999: ch. 2). It is worth going through a few examples:

- SPECIFICITY/SCHEMATICITY: (i) This is a well-known dimension of semantic organization (*do* > *look at* > *examine* > *scrutinize*). (ii) It amounts to nothing more than resolution (granularity). (iii) Grammatical elements (*do*, *be*, *-ing*) are more schematic than typical lexemes; constructions are schematizations of instantiating expressions (*be Ving* > *be working*).
- PROFILE: (i) The choice of profile distinguishes the meanings of expressions with the same content (*husband* vs. *wife* [Figure 6.7], *darken* vs. *darkened* [Figure 6.9]). (ii) Profiling is just the focusing of attention through symbolic expression. (iii) An expression's profile determines its grammatical category (despite their relational content, *husband* and *wife* are nouns).
- TRAJECTOR/LANDMARK: (i) These distinguish the meanings of relational expressions with the same content and profiling (*above* vs. *below* [Figure 6.8]). (ii) They are akin to figure/ground organization (Talmy 1978). (iii) They provide the basis for the grammatical notions subject and object.
- IMMEDIATE SCOPE: (i) This is evident in whole-part hierarchies (*body* > *leg* > *foot* > *toe* [Figure 6.5]); imposition of an immediate temporal scope accounts for the "internal perspective" on events characteristic of progressives (*be working*). (ii) This notion reflects the fact that we can attend to only so much at a given moment. (iii) It is needed to describe the $N_1 + N_2$ compounding pattern for partonomies (*fingertip*, *windowpane*, but not **armtip*, **housepane*).

Once proposed and supported on linguistic grounds, such notions are subject to validation and refinement by independent empirical means. Coming up with testable predictions is not an easy matter given the subtlety of the factors involved, the complexity of language processing, and the limitations of available methods. Validation is however possible in principle and increasingly in practice. Certain factors are amenable to corpus investigation. For example, if the dynamic construal induced by order of presentation does indeed tend to co-align with and reinforce a natural path of mental access, the congruent pattern *from X to Y* is expected be more frequent than the non-congruent *to Y from X*.

The non-congruent order should also be harder to process, which can be tested experimentally. Though not intended as such, research by Tomlin (1995) and Forrest (1996) nicely illustrates the potential for experiments aimed at a specific construal factor. They tested whether focusing attention on one participant in a relationship would influence the choice of subject in a sentence describing it. The results were striking: when time constraints did not allow attention to wander, the focused participant was coded as subject with great consistency. This is evidence for the claim that a subject expresses the trajector, characterized as the primary focal participant in a profiled relationship.

Fictive motion has been extensively studied experimentally and shown to be grounded in the conception of actual motion (Matlock 2001, 2004; Matlock et al. 2004; Matlock and Bergmann Volume 3). Metaphor has likewise been the target of experimental work demonstrating its grounding in bodily experience (Gibbs 1990, this volume; Gibbs et al. 2004). More broadly, a large amount of research indicates that the mental simulation of sensory and motor experience has an important role in higher-level cognition. In particular, experimental and neural imaging evidence show that sensorimotor activity and its apprehension via language overlap in terms of processing resources and neural substrates (Bergen et al. 2007; Svensson et al. 2007; Taylor and Zwaan 2009; Bergen 2012, this volume).

Another source of validation is the computational modeling of language processing. While the empirical support this offers is indirect, it is at least suggestive when particular descriptive notions, e.g., trajector and landmark (Petitot 2011; Regier 1996), prove efficacious for modeling purposes. Ultimately, an account of construal should mesh with a comprehensive computational model, encompassing multiple levels of processing (from linguistic to neurological), as envisaged in the Neural Theory of Language and Embodied Construction Grammar (Lakoff and Johnson 1999: Appendix; Feldman 2006; Feldman et al. 2010). The two are mutually constraining. On the one hand, accommodating the many aspects of construal poses a major challenge for the model. On the other hand, construal notions can be validated by showing that they follow from general features of the model. Achieving this synthesis would be a major step toward the fundamental goal of understanding, in specific terms, how neurological activity gives rise to language and experience.

4 References

Austin, John L. (1962): *How to Do Things with Words*. Cambridge: Harvard University Press.
Barcelona, Antonio (this volume): Metonymy. Berlin/Boston: De Gruyter Mouton.
Bergen, Benjamin K. (2012): *Louder Than Words: The New Science of How the Mind Makes Meaning*. New York: Basic Books.
Bergen, Benjamin K. (this volume): Embodiment. Berlin/Boston: De Gruyter Mouton.
Bergen, Benjamin K., Shane Lindsay, Teenie Matlock and Srini Narayanan (2007): Spatial and linguistic aspects of visual imagery in sentence comprehension. *Cognitive Science* 31: 733–764.
Boye, Kasper and Peter Harder (2012): A usage-based theory of grammatical status and grammaticalization. *Language* 88: 1–44.
Dodge, Ellen and George Lakoff (2005): Image schemas: From linguistic analysis to neural grounding. In: B. Hampe (ed.), *From Perception to Meaning: Image Schemas in Cognitive Linguistics*, 57–91. (Cognitive Linguistics Research 29.) Berlin/New York: Mouton de Gruyter.
Evans, Vyvyan (2004): *The Structure of Time: Language, Meaning and Temporal Cognition*. (Human Cognitive Processing 12.) Amsterdam/Philadelphia: John Benjamins.
Evans, Vyvyan (Volume 3): Time. Berlin/Boston: De Gruyter Mouton.
Fauconnier, Gilles (1985): *Mental Spaces: Aspects of Meaning Construction in Natural Language*. Cambridge: MIT Press.
Fauconnier, Gilles and Mark Turner (2002): *The Way We Think: Conceptual Blending and the Mind's Hidden Complexities*. New York: Basic Books.
Feldman, Jerome (2006): *From Molecule to Metaphor: A Neural Theory of Language*. Cambridge: MIT Press.
Feldman, Jerome, Ellen Dodge and John Bryant (2010): Embodied Construction Grammar. In: B. Heine and H. Narrog (eds.), *The Oxford Handbook of Linguistic Analysis*, 111–137. Oxford/New York: Oxford University Press.
Forrest, Linda B. (1996): Discourse goals and attentional processes in sentence production: The dynamic construal of events. In: A. E. Goldberg (ed.), *Conceptual Structure, Discourse and Language*, 149–161. Stanford: CSLI Publications.
Gentner, Dedre (1983): Structure mapping: A theoretical framework for analogy. *Cognitive Science* 7: 155–170.
Gibbs, Raymond W., Jr. (1990): Psycholinguistic studies on the conceptual basis of idiomaticity. *Cognitive Linguistics* 1: 417–451.
Gibbs, Raymond W., Jr. (this volume): Metaphor. Berlin/Boston: De Gruyter Mouton.
Gibbs, Raymond W., Jr., Paula Lenz Costa Lima and Edson Francozo (2004): Metaphor is grounded in embodied experience. *Journal of Pragmatics* 36: 1189–1210.
Gries, Stefan Th. (Volume 2): Polysemy. Berlin/Boston: De Gruyter Mouton.
Hudson, Richard A. (1992): Review of Ronald W. Langacker: Concept, Image and Symbol: The Cognitive Basis of Grammar. *Journal of Linguistics* 28: 506–509.
Kosslyn, Stephen Michael (1980): *Image and Mind*. Cambridge: Harvard University Press.
Kövecses, Zoltán and Günter Radden (1998): Metonymy: Developing a cognitive linguistic view. *Cognitive Linguistics* 9: 37–77.
Lakoff, George (1990): The invariance hypothesis: Is abstract reason based on image-schemas? *Cognitive Linguistics* 1: 39–74.
Lakoff, George and Mark Johnson (1980): *Metaphors We Live By*. Chicago/London: University of Chicago Press.

Lakoff, George and Mark Johnson (1999): *Philosophy in the Flesh: The Embodied Mind and Its Challenge to Western Thought.* New York: Basic Books.
Langacker, Ronald W. (1987): *Foundations of Cognitive Grammar*, Volume 1: *Theoretical Prerequisites.* Stanford: Stanford University Press.
Langacker, Ronald W. (1990): *Concept, Image and Symbol: The Cognitive Basis of Grammar.* (Cognitive Linguistics Research 1.) Berlin/New York: Mouton de Gruyter.
Langacker, Ronald W. (1991): *Foundations of Cognitive Grammar*, Volume 2: *Descriptive Application.* Stanford: Stanford University Press.
Langacker, Ronald W. (1993a): Universals of construal. *Proceedings of the Annual Meeting of the Berkeley Linguistics Society* 19: 447–463.
Langacker, Ronald W. (1993b): Reference-point constructions. *Cognitive Linguistics* 4: 1–38.
Langacker, Ronald W. (1999): *Grammar and Conceptualization.* (Cognitive Linguistics Research 14.) Berlin/New York: Mouton de Gruyter.
Langacker, Ronald W. (2006): Subjectification, grammaticization, and conceptual archetypes. In: A. Athanasiadou, C. Canakis and B. Cornillie (eds.), *Subjectification: Various Paths to Subjectivity*, 17–40. (Cognitive Linguistics Research 31.) Berlin/New York: Mouton de Gruyter.
Langacker, Ronald W. (2007): Constructing the meanings of personal pronouns. In: G. Radden, K. Köpcke, T. Berg and P. Siemund (eds.), *Aspects of Meaning Construction*, 171–187. Amsterdam/Philadelphia: John Benjamins.
Langacker, Ronald W. (2008a): *Cognitive Grammar: A Basic Introduction.* New York: Oxford University Press.
Langacker, Ronald W. (2008b): Sequential and summary scanning: A reply. *Cognitive Linguistics* 19: 571–584.
Langacker, Ronald W. (2013): On grammatical categories. *Foreign Studies* 1(4): 1–23.
Matlock, Teenie (2001): How real is fictive motion? PhD dissertation, University of California, Santa Cruz.
Matlock, Teenie (2004): Fictive motion as cognitive simulation. *Memory and Cognition* 32: 1389–1400.
Matlock, Teenie and Till Bergmann (Volume 3): Fictive motion. Berlin/Boston: De Gruyter Mouton.
Matlock, Teenie, Michael Ramscar, and Lera Boroditsky (2004): The experiential basis of motion language. In: A. Soares da Silva, A. Torres and M. Gonçalves (eds.), *Linguagem, Cultura e Cognição: Estudios de Linguística Cognitiva*, Volume 2, 43–57. Coimbra: Almedina.
Matsumoto, Yo (1996): Subjective motion and English and Japanese verbs. *Cognitive Linguistics* 7: 183–226.
Palmer, Frank R. (1981): *Semantics.* 2nd edition. Cambridge: Cambridge University Press.
Panther, Klaus-Uwe and Günter Radden (eds.) (2004): *Metonymy in Language and Thought.* (Human Cognitive Processing 4.) Amsterdam/Philadelphia: John Benjamins.
Panther, Klaus-Uwe, Linda L. Thornburg, and Antonio Barcelona (eds.) (2009): *Metonymy and Metaphor in Grammar.* (Human Cognitive Processing 25.) Amsterdam/Philadelphia: John Benjamins.
Pascual, Esther (2006): Fictive interaction within the sentence: A communicative type of fictivity in grammar. *Cognitive Linguistics* 17: 245–267.
Petitot, Jean (2011): *Cognitive Morphodynamics: Dynamical Morphological Models of Constituency in Perception and Syntax.* (European Semiotics 11.) Bern: Peter Lang.

Regier, Terry (1996): *The Human Semantic Potential: Spatial Language and Constrained Connectionism*. Cambridge: MIT Press.

Shepard, Roger N. (1978): The mental image. *American Psychologist* 33: 125–137.

Svensson, Henrik, Jessica Lindblom, and Tom Ziemke (2007): Making sense of embodied cognition: Simulation theories of shared neural mechanisms for sensorimotor and cognitive processes. In: T. Ziemke, J. Zlatev and R. M. Frank (eds.), *Body, Language and Mind*, Volume 1, *Embodiment*, 241–269. (Cognitive Linguistics Research 35.1.) Berlin/New York: Mouton de Gruyter.

Talmy, Leonard (1978): Figure and ground in complex sentences. In: J. H. Greenberg (ed.), *Universals of Human Language*, Volume 4, *Syntax*, 625–649. Stanford: Stanford University Press.

Talmy, Leonard (1988): The relation of grammar to cognition. In: B. Rudzka-Ostyn (ed.), *Topics in Cognitive Linguistics*, 165–205. (Current Issues in Linguistic Theory 50.) Amsterdam/Philadelphia: John Benjamins.

Talmy, Leonard (1996): Fictive motion in language and "ception". In: P. Bloom, M. A. Peterson, L. Nadel and M. F. Garrett (eds.), *Language and Space*, 211–276. Cambridge: MIT Press.

Taylor, Lawrence J. and Rolf A. Zwaan (2009): Action in cognition: The case of language. *Language and Cognition* 1: 45–58.

Tomlin, Russell S. (1995): Focal attention, voice, and word order. In: P. Downing and M. Noonan (eds.), *Word Order in Discourse*, 517–554. (Typological Studies in Language 30.) Amsterdam/Philadelphia: John Benjamins.

Tomlin, Russell S. and Andriy Myachykov (this volume): Attention and salience. Berlin/Boston: De Gruyter Mouton.

Turner, Mark (this volume): Blending. Berlin/Boston: De Gruyter Mouton.

Antonio Barcelona
Chapter 7: Metonymy

1 Introduction. The notion of metonymy

To many cognitive linguists, conceptual metonymy is a fundamental cognitive tool in cognition and language. Langacker (this volume) regards it as a type of construal. Lakoff (1987: 113–114, 154, Chapter 5) regarded it as one of the mechanisms involved in the creation of cognitive models, together with conceptual metaphor, our "framing ability" and our image-schematic ability (Lakoff, however, seems to regard metaphor as a more important cognitive phenomenon).

This chapter is organized around four major themes: The *notion of metonymy* (which is the topic of the rest of the present section), the *typology of metonymy* (section 2), the *ubiquity of metonymy*, which the bulk of the chapter (sections 3–8) is devoted to,[1] and *research methods* in the study of metonymy (section 9). The brief final section (10) contains a general comment on the chapter.

Before providing a "technical" definition of conceptual metonymy a few examples should help us introduce the notion informally:

(1) "*That's really his name, Marshall Brain, and he is* a brain *and he has a wonderful way of describing how everything works, how stuff works, everything from a computer to DNA.*" (Spoken)

(2) "*The White House says the travel and tourism industry represented 2.7 percent of gross domestic product and 7.5 million jobs in 2010.*" (Written)

(3) "*A friend of mine has a r1 and he painted his flat* black *and it looks a purplish brown color now.*" (Written)

(Examples (1) and (2) have been taken from the Corpus of Contemporary American English and (3) resulted from a Google search on March 12, 2014.)

---

[1] For a more detailed survey of research on the role of metonymy in cognition, grammar and discourse, see Barcelona (2011b), on which sections 3–9 are based.

Note: I am grateful to Günter Radden and two anonymous reviewers for their insightful comments on an earlier draft of this chapter. Any remaining inaccuracies are my sole responsibility. The present paper has been supported in part with the financial aid granted by the Spanish government to project FFI2012-36523 (see Blanco et al. 2018).

Antonio Barcelona, Córdoba, Spain

https://doi.org/10.1515/9783110626476-008

In (1) the speaker seems to mean that Marshall is an intelligent person. A body part typically associated with intelligence in our encyclopedic knowledge evokes a certain type of person; this type of conceptual shift is known in cognitive linguistics (CL) as a PART FOR WHOLE metonymy (Lakoff and Johnson 1980: 36) and in traditional rhetoric as *synecdoche*. Example (2) means that the U.S. President's staff (or perhaps the President himself) made the statement reported. Here a location is used to evoke one or more entities located in it. Both the location and the "located" are two elements or "parts" of a type of spatial relation (the "locational" relation); therefore the conceptual shift from location to located is seen by some cognitive linguists (e.g., Radden and Kövecses 1999: 41–42) as a PART FOR PART metonymy. Finally, the normal understanding of (3) is not that the man painted the *whole* of his flat (including the floor, the door handles, the taps, washbasins, etc.) but only the ceiling and walls and perhaps another element such as the doors. A whole entity (in this case, a physical entity like a flat) is used to evoke its (normally) most relevant part(s) with respect to the action of painting; this type of conceptual shift is usually known as a WHOLE FOR PART metonymy.[2]

Like metaphor (see Gibbs this volume), metonymy is claimed in CL to be a *conceptual* process (Lakoff and Johnson 1980: 36; Lakoff 1987: Chapter 5, *inter alia*). That is, for CL metonymy is not simply a figure of speech, in the spirit of traditional rhetoric, or a mere "contextual effect", as claimed by certain relevance theorists (Papafragou 1996). CL regards it as an essentially conceptual process, which is reflected in various types of semiotic modes, particularly human language (both oral and sign language), but also gesture, art (music, painting, sculpture), etc.

Despite the universal agreement within CL on the conceptual nature of metonymy, not all the other properties of metonymy suggested by the initial proponents of the cognitive theory of metonymy, namely Lakoff and Johnson (1980: Chapter 8) and Lakoff and Turner (1989: 100–108) have been accepted by all cognitive linguists. Metonymy is characterized by these scholars as a process occurring within the same domain, whereby one conceptual entity, the source, "stands for" and is projected ("mapped"), with a primarily referential purpose, onto another conceptual entity, the target. This is what could be called the "initial cognitive definition of metonymy" (ICD). The ICD includes both uncontroversial and controversial additional properties of metonymy.

---

[2] Examples (1) and (2) are metonymically more complex (e.g. (1) is also due to WHOLE (brain) FOR PART (salient property "(seat of) intelligence")) but I have decided to mention only their more salient metoymy in this initial presentation of the notion.

Among the uncontroversial properties we find these:
- Metonymy involves two conceptual entities which are *closely associated in experience* (Lakoff and Johnson 1980: 35); that is, metonymy is experientially grounded and it involves elements which are experientially (hence conceptually) contiguous (unlike metaphor). In (1)–(3) above the metonymy involves entities which are conceptually contiguous, like people and their body parts, locations and people or institutions located in them, or houses and their relevant parts.
- Metonymy often provides a conceptual perspective on the target, as in *We have some good heads for the project*, where *good heads* is used to refer to a group of people who are conceptualized in terms of their intelligence (Lakoff and Johnson 1980: 74). This property is implicit in the above definition, since the projection of the source (HEAD as the seat of intelligence in the example) imposes a perspective on the target (PEOPLE) (see Barcelona 2011a: 13–14).

All the other properties included in the ICD, which were at first accepted by many cognitive linguists (including myself), are either decidedly controversial or in need of further clarification:
- Referentiality. Some cognitive linguists seem to consider metonymy to be *necessarily* a referential device (the metonymies in (2) and (3) are referential, since they operate in referential noun phrases), while most others also recognize the existence of non-referential metonymies, like that in (1), which operates in a predicational, i.e., non-referential, noun phrase. The pioneers of the cognitive theory of metonymy, Lakoff and Johnson (1980: 74), however, had simply suggested that metonymy had a *primarily* referential function, and in Lakoff's (1987) study of cognitive models, non-referential metonymies are explicitly recognized.
- The nature of the "conceptual entities": Is metonymy a relationship between "entities" or a relationship between "domains"?
- The nature of the so-called "stand-for" relationship and of the "projection" or "mapping": What does the mapping consist of? Is it unidirectional (source to target) or also bidirectional (target to source)?

And the most controversial of all of these properties:
- The "same domain" property as a way of distinguishing metaphor from metonymy, that is, the claim that metonymy operates within the same conceptual domain, whereas metaphor connects two different conceptual domains.

In an attempt to take a stand on these and other problematic issues, some other direct or indirect definitions of metonymy were later provided in CL. One of them is Croft 2002 (1993), who characterized metonymy as the "highlighting" of a domain within a domain matrix, borrowing the latter notion from Langacker (1987: Chapter 4). Another, highly influential definition is Kövecses and Radden's (1998: 39; see also Radden and Kövecses 1999: 21): "Metonymy is a cognitive process in which one conceptual entity, the vehicle, provides mental access to another conceptual entity, the target, within the same domain, or ICM".

These and similar definitions, however, raise a further set of problematic issues, among others:

- What is the difference between "domain highlighting" and "mental access to a conceptual entity"? Do they result in the mental "activation" of the target? What does this activation consist of?
- Is *any* type of "highlighting", "mental access" or "activation" metonymic? In particular, since the notion of "mental access" is borrowed by Kövecses and Radden from Langacker (1993, 1999: 199, 363, 2009), who claims that what he calls a "reference point" provides mental access to a conceptual target, what is the exact difference between metonymy and reference point phenomena? This issue affects, in particular, the activation of certain parts from their corresponding wholes, as in *I read a book*, where the semantic content of the book is activated. Panther and Thornburg (2007: 241–242) have suggested that the connection between metonymic source and target is "contingent" (i.e., not conceptually necessary), which would exclude entailment relations from metonymy like the entailment of a superordinate concept by a hyponymic one; the problem with this view is that it would rule out MEMBER FOR CATEGORY metonymies such as the use of *aspirin* (Panther and Thornburg's example [2007: 241]) to designate any pain-relieving tablet (Kövecses and Radden 1998: 53), and cases like the one in 2.1.2 (d) below.
- Is there any essential difference between metonymy and other phenomena such as active-zone/profile discrepancy (Langacker 1999: 33–35, 67, 2009), "modulation" and "facets" (Cruse 2000; Dirven 2002; Croft and Cruse 2004), or even anaphora (Langacker 1999: 234–245 and Chapter 9), which also involve the "mental access" from one conceptual entity to another conceptual entity?
- Finally, another problematic issue is to determine the set of factors determining the conventionality of linguistic metonymy (Taylor 1995: 122–123; Kövecses and Radden 1998: 62–74; Radden and Kövecses 1999: 44–54).

Given the limitation of space I will not be able to discuss all of these issues in this chapter. The reader is referred to Barcelona (2002a, 2003a and 2011a),

Geeraerts and Peirsman (2011), Panther and Thornburg (2007), Paradis (2004, 2011), Ruiz de Mendoza (2011) and to the other contributions in Benczes et al. (2011), for detailed discussions of these and other problematic issues. I will simply offer my own attempt at a broad unitary definition of metonymy (adapted from Barcelona 2011a). It is not essentially different from other well-known definitions within CL (those by Lakoff and Turner 1989; Kövecses and Radden 1998; or Panther and Thornburg 2003b, 2007), and may well be regarded as a synthesis of them all, with some additional ingredients:

> Metonymy is an asymmetric mapping of a conceptual entity, the source, onto another conceptual entity, the target. Source and target are in the same frame and their roles are linked by a pragmatic function, so that the target is mentally activated.

This definition alone is not sufficient to solve all the problematic issues enunciated above, but it does provide an answer to most of them, especially the distinction between metaphor and metonymy.[3] The other issues (in particular the distinction between metonymy and other phenomena of activation or mental access) involve supplementing a unitary definition like this with a prototype-based approach to the notion of metonymy (section 2).

Let me now briefly discuss the above definition, especially its technical terms (more extensive discussions of the grounds for this definition are presented in Barcelona 2002a, 2003a, and 2011a).

As stated above, metonymy does not only have a referential function, hence the definition does not include referentiality as an essential property.

Let us now discuss the nature of the "mapping" or "conceptual projection" in metonymy. Lakoff and Turner (1989: 103–104) claim that metonymy is a mapping occurring between entities in the same conceptual domain, whereas metaphor is a mapping occurring across two different conceptual domains. Unlike metaphor, which symmetrically and systematically projects part of the conceptual structure of the source onto that of the target (Lakoff 1993), metonymy is "asymmetric". In the metaphor LIFE IS A JOURNEY, the beginning of the journey is mapped onto the beginning of life, the obstacles in the journey onto life's difficulties, etc. Metonymically linked elements do not normally exhibit any degree of structural similarity or equivalence. Wholes do not exhibit a similar abstract structure to that of their parts, and when the mapping relates two parts of the same ICM (e.g., the PRODUCER and the PRODUCT in the PRODUCTION ICM,

---

[3] The issue of the exact distinction from metaphor is more complex, however, as it involves other aspects that cannot be discussed here (Barcelona 2002a, 2011a). A recent proposal sees metonymy and metaphor as the two extremes of a multidimensional continuum (Barnden 2010).

as in *I bought a Stradivarius*), those parts are seldom, if ever, similar, and never equivalent functionally (the PRODUCER in that ICM is not functionally equivalent to the PRODUCT).

"Frame" is preferable to the term "domain", used by Lakoff and Turner (1989: 103) to designate the conceptual structure *within* which metonymic mappings are supposed to occur. The term "frame" designates an entrenched, knowledge-rich model of a recurrent, well-delineated area of experience (Fillmore 1985). That is actually the type of conceptual structure within which metonymy occurs. Frames are equivalent to one of the types of Lakoff's (1987) "Idealized Cognitive Models" (ICMs), namely "propositional ICMs". The terms "domain", "ICM" and "frame" are often used interchangeably but they should probably be distinguished. The reason is that "domain" is ambiguous: It can be used both in a "taxonomic" sense and in a "functional" sense. "Taxonomic domains" represent the classification and sub-classification of broad areas of experience, such as PHYSICAL ENTITIES, which include LIVING BEINGS and INERT PHYSICAL ENTITIES, etc. in our encyclopedic knowledge (Radden and Dirven 2007: 9–12). What I have called "functional domains" elsewhere (Barcelona 2002a, 2003a, 2011a) organize our detailed knowledge about more specific areas of experience; this term is thus synonymous to "frame" and "(propositional) ICM".[4]

The relevant frames in metonymy are those that assign a *role* to source and target. Frames can be fairly specific or relatively generic. In example (1), the relevant frame is the HUMAN BEING frame, which represents speakers' detailed encyclopedic knowledge about human beings (their bodies and body parts, physiology, emotions, interaction, life cycle, etc.). The relevant frame in example (2) seems to be the (SPATIAL) LOCATION frame, which represents encyclopedic knowledge about the spatial location of entities (the basic properties of locations, the types of locations, the types of located entities, the relation between location and located and the constraints on that relation, etc.). And the relevant frame in (3) is the BUILDING frame (more exactly, its FLAT sub-frame); the relevant frame is different from that in (2) because the roles involved in (3) are

---

[4] It must be said, however, that Lakoff and Turner's (1989: 79–80) notion of "conceptual domain" seems to be equivalent to their notion of conceptual "schema" and to Lakoff's notion of "category", both of which are in turn similar to that of a (complex) "frame" or "propositional ICM", since all of them are supposed to be conceptual representations of relatively rich knowledge about a field of experience. The same applies to Langacker's (1987) notion of "domain matrix." The metonymic source and target "conceptual entities" can be argued in turn to constitute relatively complex domains in either sense (for details, see Barcelona 2011a); hence the frequent use of the terms "source domain" and "target domain" in metonymy.

related mainly to speakers' knowledge of the physical structure of buildings, whereas the role of the building in (2) is related exclusively to its locational connection with other entities.[5] An alternative, more specific relevant frame for (2) is the UNITED STATES POLITICAL INSTITUTIONS frame, which anyway assigns the same LOCATION-LOCATED roles to source and target.

The reason why we claim that metonymy operates within frames (see also Radden and Dirven 2007: 12–15; Radden and Kövecses 1999: 19–21) is that if we claimed, along with the initial cognitive definition (ICD), that metonymy occurs within one "domain", given the ambiguity of this term, we might be forced to regard as metonymic many mappings which are normally regarded as metaphorical, like the one operating in

(4) *Marshall is a bulldozer*

(meaning that he is an overbearing person, perhaps a bully), since both inert physical objects and human beings are included in the domain of physical entities (Barcelona 2002a). However, in (4) the knowledge that inert objects and living beings are included in that "taxonomic domain" is not relevant for the metaphorical mapping of BULLDOZER onto OVERBEARING PERSON. What is relevant is the fact that people and bulldozers, though different types of physical entities, are construed as sharing a certain number of properties, particularly the ability to overcome any counterforce, physical (bulldozer) or psychosocial (overbearing person). In other words, although people and machines can be taxonomically included in the same domain, they are not presented in (4) as included in the same frame. Therefore, if metonymy is claimed to operate within one frame/propositional ICM whereas metaphor is claimed to operate across two different frames, the mapping in (4) can be described as metaphorical. And the mapping in (2) can be regarded as metonymic since the projection of an inert physical entity, a building, onto one or more people occurs within the SPATIAL LOCATION frame.

The inclusion of source and target within the same frame is a necessary, but not a sufficient condition for metonymicity. Source and target must, furthermore, be linked by what Fauconnier (1997) called a "pragmatic function". A "pragmatic function" is a privileged conceptual link in our long-term memory

---

5 Of course, one could claim that part of our knowledge of the BUILDING frame is that buildings are at least potentially locations for other physical entities. By the same token, our knowledge of the LOCATION frame includes the types of locations, buildings among them. But these are in principle different frames. As is well known, frames, like all cognitive models, tend to be interrelated.

between the roles of metonymic source and target within the corresponding frame: CAUSE-EFFECT, PRODUCER-PRODUCT, AGENT-ACTION, CONDITION-RESULT, AGENT-INSTRUMENT, THING-REPRESENTATION, etc. (see section 2). This privileged link is an essential condition for the mental activation of target by source. The nose and the mouth are included in the HUMAN PERSON frame, where their roles are not connected by a pragmatic function; therefore neither normally acts as a metonymic source for the other (Kövecses and Radden 1998: 48–49). However, the pragmatic function SALIENT BODY PART-PERSON allows the mouth to act as a metonymic source for the whole person, as in *He only earns four hundred pounds a month and, with five* mouths *to feed, he finds this very hard*. As can be seen the classic "contiguity" criterion for metonymicity is not really reliable.

2 Types of metonymy

To my knowledge, there does not exist in CL a universally accepted typology of general, high-level conceptual metonymies operating in English or in other languages, let alone one of metonymies operating cross-linguistically.[6] Metonymies can be classified on the basis of several criteria. We present below some of those criteria and a sample of the resulting typologies.

2.1 Types in terms of pragmatic function

The most important of these criteria is the type of *pragmatic function* (see section 1) linking source and target within the relevant frame. In fact, most of the typologies in the literature apply this criterion, whether or not their proponents use the term "pragmatic function" to designate it; the other criteria described below (2.2–2.3) depend on this one. Unfortunately, there does not seem to exist a commonly accepted list of pragmatic functions. Below I offer a few common examples of metonymies classified in terms of this criterion and drawn at random, for illustrative purposes only, from those repeatedly mentioned in the literature (see in particular Fass 1997; Kövecses and Radden 1998; and Peirsman

---

[6] I lead a small research project on metonymy funded by the Spanish government (FFI2012-36523) aimed at the creation of a detailed database of metonymy in English (see the chapters by Barcelona, Blanco and Hernandez in Blanco et al. 2018). The present paper has been supported in part with the financial aid granted to that project.

and Geeraerts 2006). They are, at the highest level, roughly grouped into the WHOLE-PART, PART-WHOLE and PART-PART generic types.

2.1.1 WHOLE FOR PART metonymies

a) GEOGRAPHICAL UNIT FOR SALIENT PART, as in *America* used to refer to the United States.
b) ENTITY FOR RELEVANT PART(S), as in example (3), where "flat" activates its relevant parts i.e., its "active zone" (Langacker 1999) with respect to the action of painting.
c) CATEGORY FOR MEMBER, as in *The use of the pill has reduced the birth rate in many countries*, where "pill" activates "contraceptive pill" (Kövecses and Radden 1998: 53). On the corresponding reverse metonymy, see 2.1.2 d.

2.1.2 PART FOR WHOLE metonymies

a) SUB-EVENT FOR COMPLEX EVENT, as in *They stood at the altar*, where a sub-event of a wedding ceremony activates the whole complex event (Kövecses and Radden 1998: 52).
b) SALIENT PROPERTY FOR PERSON CATEGORY, as in *She is a beauty*, where these roles are respectively filled by "beauty" and "beautiful person".
c) SALIENT BODY PART FOR PERSON CATEGORY, as in example (1), where the brain activates "intelligent people".
d) MEMBER FOR CATEGORY, as in *That young man may become a new Aristotle* (said of someone who is a highly talented philosopher), where "Aristotle", an ideal instance of the GREAT PHILOSOPHER category, stands for that category (see section 6).

2.1.3 PART FOR PART metonymies

a) LOCATION FOR LOCATED, as in (2) above, where these roles are respectively filled by the White House and the U.S. President's staff (or perhaps the President himself).
b) PRODUCER FOR PRODUCT, as in *I'll have a Heineken*, where the beer maker stands for the beer itself. A special subtype is AUTHOR FOR WORK, as in *Proust is tough to read* (Croft [1993] 2002), where the novelist activates his literary work.

c) EFFECT FOR CAUSE, as in *You are my joy*, where the emotion of joy activates the person causing it, or as in *The car screeched to a halt* where a certain sound activates the motion causing it (Kövecses and Radden 1998: 56).
d) CONTROLLER FOR CONTROLLED, as *I am parked out there*, where the driver (*I*) activates the vehicle (s)he drives, i.e., controls; and its reverse metonymy, CONTROLLED FOR CONTROLLER, as in *That Mercedes is a bastard*, where the car is used to refer to its driver.
e) CONTAINER FOR CONTENT, as in *He drank a couple of cups*, where the cups activate their liquid content.
f) POSSESSED FOR POSSESSOR, as in *The fur coat left the meeting with a smile*, where the fur coat activates its possessor.
g) INSTRUMENT FOR ACTION, as in *The pen is mightier than the sword*, where pens and swords are instruments for the actions which they respectively evoke, i.e., communication (linguistic action) and reasoning, on the one hand, and violence and war on the other hand. On other metonymies arising within the "Action ICM" (ACTION FOR AGENT, AGENT FOR ACTION, etc.), see Kövecses and Radden (1998: 54–55).

I have followed Kövecses and Radden (1998: 54) in their classification of the metonymies in 2.1.3 as PART FOR PART, because, as they convincingly argue, the source and target roles connected by the corresponding pragmatic functions are conceptual elements within an ICM, i.e., "parts" of it. The relevant ICM is, furthermore an event or in general a relational ICM (action, causation, possession, containment, etc.), which is less clearly delineated than the "things"[7] corresponding to the wholes, including abstract wholes, in WHOLE FOR PART and PART FOR WHOLE metonymies.

As noted by many linguists, a large number of metonymies have their reverse, i.e., a metonymy with source and target reversed. For lack of space only two examples have been presented (in 2.1.1c and 2.1.3d). Reversibility, however, should not be confused with bidirectionality, i.e., the mapping does not take place in both directions simultaneously and is very different in each case (for details, see Barcelona 2011a: 15).

2.2 Types in terms of generality

Most of the metonymy types resulting from the pragmatic function criterion can be arranged into *hierarchies*, at whose top, i.e., its highest level of generality,

---

[7] In Langacker's (1987: 183–213) technical use of this term in Cognitive Grammar.

we find the traditional basic typology WHOLE FOR PART, PART FOR WHOLE and PART FOR PART.[8] The metonymy lists in 2.1.1, 2.1.2, and 2.1.3 constitute partial hierarchies consisting of a *generic* and a subordinate level represented by each of the metonymies in the list. But the hierarchies are more complex. In sentence (1), we can just describe the metonymy at the *generic* level (PART FOR WHOLE), or describe it at increasingly more specific levels, that is, at a *high level* (SALIENT BODY PART FOR PERSON CATEGORY) or at a *low level* (BRAIN FOR INTELLIGENT PERSON). On a detailed discussion of the problems with metonymic hierarchies see Barcelona's chapter in Blanco et al. (2018).

2.3 Types in terms of prototypicality

This is not a traditional classification. However, two recent complementary proposals in CL (Barcelona 2002a, 2003a, 2011a and Peirsman and Geeraerts 2006) suggest the existence of degrees of prototypicality in metonymy; see also Dirven (2002). Therefore, prototypicality can be added as an additional typological criterion. Both proposals are very complex and I can only present an oversimplification here.

Barcelona (2002a, 2003a, 2011a) characterizes "prototypical" metonymies as referential metonymies with an individual entity or a group (not a class or category) of individual entities as target, like those in examples (2) and (3). These are the metonymies usually studied in traditional rhetoric and semantics. A lower degree of prototypicality is exhibited by the metonymies he calls "(simply) typical", which are those whose target is a "secondary domain" (Langacker 1987: 165, 222),[9] within the source of WHOLE (source) FOR PART (target) metonymies or is not included in the source, as in all PART (source) FOR WHOLE (target) and PART (source) FOR PART (target) metonymies; these metonymies, furthermore, are either not referential, as in example (1), or they are used to refer to a type, class or category of entities, as in

(5) *A good student should read extensively,*

where the generic reference of the subject noun phrase is motivated by the metonymy INSTANCE FOR TYPE (Radden, 2009: 207). Finally, the metonymies called

---

[8] Ruiz de Mendoza (2000) and Geeraerts and Peirsman (2011) reduce generic level metonymies to WHOLE FOR PART and PART FOR WHOLE.
[9] A "primary" domain is one which is obligatorily activated when understanding the meaning of a symbolic unit (i.e., a morpheme, a lexeme or any other grammatical construction), e.g.

"purely schematic" are WHOLE FOR PART metonymies whose target is a "minimally primary" or "minimally secondary" subdomain within the source, that is, deeply included in it; an example is *This book is highly instructive* (ENTITY [BOOK] FOR RELEVANT PART [SEMANTIC CONTENT]). These metonymies are very close to literality, as the semantic shift is very subtle and not immediately perceived by speakers, for which reason their status as metonymies is controversial in CL (the various positions on this issue are discussed by Barcelona 2011a; Ruiz de Mendoza 2000; Croft [1993] 2002; Paradis 2004 and 2011; and Geeraerts and Peirsman 2011, among others). The advantage of the broad, unitary definition of metonymy proposed in section 1 is that it stresses the common cognitive properties of a wide variety of phenomena. Its disadvantage is that it can include "purely schematic" metonymies, which given their marginality within the category, are not accepted as metonymic by all cognitive linguists. This is why that definition is supplemented with the above prototype-based set of definitions. Most of the research reported on from section 3 onwards applies only to uncontroversial instances of metonymy (i.e., "typical" and "prototypical" metonymies).

To Peirsman and Geeraerts (2006), the most highly prototypical metonymies are those operating in the spatial and material domains, particularly in cases where two physical entities reach the maximum degree on the two continua of spatial contiguity they propose: "strength of contact" and "boundedness". This degree is reached in their "material whole-part" relationship expressed by examples (1) (person-brain) and (3) (the walls and doors of a flat). Prototypicality is progressively weakened with lower degrees of boundedness of source or target, as in the metonymy (MATERIAL CONSTITUTING AN OBJECT FOR THAT OBJECT) extending the (unbounded) "substance" sense of *glass* to its (bounded) "object" sense; both senses are represented in *A good glass is made of glass*. The degree of prototypicality is also progressively lower as the strength of contact between source and target diminishes in the spatial and material domains, as in metonymies involving CONTAINER and CONTENT (as in *I drank a glass*), LOCATION and LOCATED (example 2 above) or mere "adjacency" (as in the noun *board* designating a group of people meeting at a council-table). On the whole the metonymies operating in these domains exhibit this gradient of prototypicality in terms of strength of contact, from highest to lowest: material and spatial, temporal, actions-events-processes (AGENT FOR ACTION, etc.), and "assemblies and collections" (CATEGORY FOR MEMBER, etc.).

PHYSICAL OBJECT in *book*. We might then say that a "secondary" domain (a term not used by Langacker) is not (or less) obligatorily activated, e.g. LIBRARY in *book*. Both notions are scalar.

3 The ubiquity of metonymy. Metonymy in cognition, especially in metaphor

Most of the sections of the chapter (3–9) are devoted to reporting on important recent CL research illustrating the ubiquity of metonymy in cognition and language (Bierwiaczonek 2013 is a recent survey): Metonymy in cognition (this section), grammar (sections 4–7) and discourse (section 8). Lack of space prevents us from discussing the role of metonymy in phonology (Barcelona 2002b; Radden 2005) and the applications of metonymy research to work on second language acquisition (Littlemore 2009: Ch. 6; Holme 2009: 101–102, 117–120; Barcelona 2010), to computational linguistics (Fass 1997), or to work on multimodal communication (Forceville and Urios Aparisi 2009).

There are three areas in cognition where metonymy has been found to be particularly relevant: Cognitive models (Lakoff 1987: Chapter 5; Feyaerts 1999; Gibbs 1994, 2007a, on relevant psycholinguistic research), blending (Turner this volume; Turner and Fauconnier 2000; Radden 2009), and metaphor. (On the neural embodiment of metonymy, see Bierwiaczonek 2013: Ch. 6.)

I only have space to comment on metonymy in metaphor (Barcelona 2000a, 2000b, 2011a; Goossens [1990] 2002]; Goossens et al. 1995; Radden [2000] 2002; and Taylor 1995: 138–141). A great many metaphors have been argued to be *conceptually* based on metonymy, i.e., to be conceptually possible thanks to it. In my opinion there are two major types of metonymic motivation of metaphor. The first type consists in the *generalization* or *decontextualization* of a metonymy. The metonymy HEIGHT (UP) FOR QUANTITY (MORE) is due to the frequent experiential association of HEIGHT and QUANTITY in POURING or HEAPING frames/scenarios, as in *The water level in the dam is too* high. *We should release some of it*. When HEIGHT is mapped onto QUANTITY in a context where HEIGHT is no longer really involved, the mapping is metaphorical (MORE IS UP), as in *The high cost of living/Skyrocketing prices* (Radden 2000, 2002). In the second type, which can be called *correlation-abstraction* (Barcelona 2000b, 2011a; see also Rudzka-Ostyn 1995), metaphors like DEVIANT COLORS ARE DEVIANT SOUNDS, as in *That's a loud color*, are made conceptually possible by the metonymic mapping of the salient EFFECT of deviant sounds and colors (IRRESISTIBLE ATTRACTION OF ATTENTION), onto its CAUSE (those sensory stimuli themselves), thereby highlighting the abstract similarity between these sounds and colors and motivating the aforesaid metaphor.

4 Metonymy in grammar: The polysemy of derivational morphemes

This is the first of a series of sections (4–7) surveying the role of metonymy in grammatical structure and meaning. That survey is quite selective for lack of space and does not include the role of metonymy in generic NPs (Radden 2005, 2009) and in the tense-aspect-mood system of English verbs (Brdar 2007; Panther and Thornburg 1998; Janda Volume 3). Langacker (1999: 67) says that though "usually regarded as a semantic phenomenon, metonymy turns out to be central and essential to grammar". For a general survey of the role of metonymy in grammar see Brdar (2007), Ruiz de Mendoza and Pérez Hernández (2001), Ruiz de Mendoza and Otal Campo (2002), Panther et al. (2009), and within the latter volume, Langacker (2009).

Most derivational morphemes are polysemous, often due to metaphor and/or metonymy. Some of the relevant research on this issue is Barcelona (2005: 320–1, 2009a, in preparation) on the nominal suffixal morpheme {ful}, as in *a bottleful* or *a cupful*; Panther and Thornburg (2002) on the complex polysemy of the nominal suffixal morpheme {er}; Palmer et al. (2009) on the Tagalog prefix {ka}; and Radden (2005), on the suffixal morpheme {able}.

One example is the metonymic motivation of a non-central sense of {able} (Radden 2005: 18–19). The central sense of the morpheme is illustrated by the phrase *a movable piano*; this central sense can be paraphrased as "can be VERB-ed" and the phrase *A movable piano* can thus be paraphrased as "a piano that can be moved", where "movability" is an inherent property of the piano. But in *drinkable water*, "drinkable" does not simply denote an inherent property of water, i.e., "can be drunk" abstractly, but also its relevance for humans, that is "can be drunk by humans", "safe to drink" (Radden 2005: 18). The semantic extension is motivated by GENERIC FOR SPECIFIC (or CATEGORY FOR MEMBER).

5 Metonymy in lexical meaning

Like morphemes, words are grammatical constructions, i.e., conventional form-meaning pairs (Goldberg 2006). Metonymy has traditionally been claimed to be a lexical phenomenon. Most of the examples of metonymy offered in rhetoric and semantics handbooks are lexical metonymies, many of them polysemy-creating metonymies like those motivating the "manual worker" or "sailor" senses of *hand*, or the "smelling ability" sense of *nose* (as in *this dog has a good nose*). Further examples of lexical polysemy motivated by metonymy were given in 2.1.1 (c), 2.1.2 (b, c), 2.1.3 (c -*joy*-, e, g -*pen, sword*). These metonymies are well-known in historical linguistics, rhetoric and lexical semantics (Geeraerts Volume 2; Hilpert Volume 2). Additional examples of metonymies operating on lexemes are discussed in section 6 and Bierwiaczonek 2013: Ch. 5.

Lexical metonymies are not necessarily restricted to nouns. The metonymy (CONTROLLER FOR CONTROLLED) in *I am parked out over there* (Nunberg 1995) affects the reference of the pronoun *I* (the speaker's car). Lexical metonymies are very often involved in reference. But referential metonymies are not exclusively lexical phenomena (Barcelona 2011b), since they affect the referential value of a noun *phrase* (even though that value often crucially depends on a metonymy-based lexical sense of the phrasal head), as in *the buses* (i.e., the bus drivers) *are on strike* (Lakoff and Johnson 1980: 38), where the underlying metonymy is called by Radden and Kövecses (1999: 40) CONTROLLED FOR CONTROLLER.

The success of referential metonymies in directing attention to the intended referent often requires inference, hence discourse-pragmatic inferencing (section 8) is often involved (Warren 1999: 123).

6 Metonymy in morphosyntactic processes: recategorization, compounding and abbreviation

The shift in lexical sense or in reference effected by metonymy often brings about a change in the morphosyntactic class of the respective lexeme (recategorization). Compounds are intrinsically metonymic, as they code a complex meaning by highlighting some of its facets (see Bierwiaczwonek 2013: Ch. 3) Abbreviation seems to be often motivated by metonymy.

Grammatical recategorization can be relatively transient or permanent (i.e., fully conventionalized). Both types are discussed below.

Stative predicates are often transiently recategorized as dynamic predicates. The metonymy EFFECT FOR CAUSE motivates this shift, as in *He asked her to be his wife* (paraphraseable as "He asked her to act in such a way so as to become his wife"). *Be someone's wife* profiles a *controllable* (Ruiz de Mendoza and Pérez Hernández 2001; Ruiz de Mendoza and Otal 2002), *resultant* (Panther and Thornburg 2000) state, which constitutes a metonymic source for its implicit causal action (i.e., to act in such a way so as to ...). Compare with *non-controllable, non-resultant states*: **He asked her to be tall*.

English proper nouns are often transiently converted into common nouns. One of the many metonymy-motivated examples of this conversion is *John has five authentic Picassos* (AUTHOR FOR (PIECE OF) WORK). Two special cases are paragons and partitive restrictive modification. On the metonymic motivation of "partitive restrictive modification" (Greenbaum and Quirk 1990: 88), as in *The young Joyce already showed signs of the genius that was to be fulfilled in Ulysses*, see Barcelona (2003c, 2003d, 2009b), Brdar (2007) and Brdar and Brdar-Szabó (2007). The use of names as *paragons* (Barcelona 2003c, 2003d, 2004; Brdar 2007; Brdar and Brdar-Szabó 2007; Pang 2006) is motivated in part by the activation of a class of individuals by one of its ideal members (IDEAL MEMBER FOR CLASS), as in *That graduate student is an Aristotle*, *There aren't any real Aristotles today*. This metonymy directly licenses the transient grammatical re-categorization of a proper name as a common count noun (which takes plural, determiners and restrictive modifiers). This recategorization may become permanent: *lolita* (after Nabokov's character), as in *My 13 year old daughter is starting to act like a lolita*.

Permanent grammatical recategorization includes metonymy-motivated instances of conversion (Martsa 2013 for a general survey) and some instances of affixal derivation.

Mass-count noun conversion is analyzed by Brdar (2007), Ruiz de Mendoza and Pérez Hernández (2001), Ruiz de Mendoza and Otal (2002), and Kövecses and Radden (1998). An example of count-mass conversion motivated by MATERIAL FOR OBJECT MADE OF THAT MATERIAL is *We did not always eat turkey for Christmas dinner* (Brdar 2007), and one of mass-count conversion motivated by OBJECT FOR MATERIAL CONSTITUTING THE OBJECT is *To have won one gold medal and two silvers in those Games was historic* (Brdar 2007).

Noun-verb conversion is dealt with by Dirven (1999), Ruiz de Mendoza and Pérez Hernández (2001), and Ruiz de Mendoza and Otal (2002). Dirven (1999: 275–287) identified three metonymies involved in the process: INSTRUMENT FOR ACTION, as in *He was angling* (from noun *angle* 'fishing rod'); GOAL FOR MOTION, as in *The plane was forced to land in Cairo* (see also Kövecses and Radden 1998: 55, 60); CLASS MEMBERSHIP FOR DESCRIPTION (according to Dirven) or AGENT FOR ACTION (according to Barcelona 2002a), as in *Mary nursed the sick soldiers*.

On the metonymic motivation of adjective-noun conversion like the conversion of the adjective *interstate* (as in *interstate freeway*) into the noun *interstate* 'interstate highway' (as in *an/the interstate*), see Barcelona (2009a, in preparation).

On the metonymic motivation of certain instances of *affixal* derivation, see Panther and Thornburg (2002), on certain *-er* nouns; Szawerna (2007); Palmer et al. (2009); and section 4. One of Panther and Thornburg's examples of *-er* nouns is *cliffhanger* 'suspenseful event', in which the metonymy EXPERIENCER FOR EVENT EXPERIENCED, motivates the shift from the agentive to the eventive sense of the {er} morpheme, whereas CAUSE (THE ACTIVITY OF CLIFFHANGING) FOR EFFECT (SUSPENSE),[10] motivates the shift in the meaning of the lexical base.

On compounding, see Radden (2005), Barcelona (2008, 2009a, in preparation), Benczes (2006, 2011), Geeraerts (2002), and Kosecki (2007). Radden (2005: 19–20) observes that endocentric (or hyponymic) compounds are intrinsically metonymic, as they typically activate all the properties of a category from a salient property (SALIENT PROPERTY FOR A BUNDLE OF PROPERTIES). This is particularly clear crosslinguistically: English *hiking boots* (function highlighted) vs. Spanish *botas de montaña* (literally 'boots of mountain'; location highlighted); see also Radden and Panther (2004: 5–8), on *screwdriver* and its crosslinguistic equivalents. Exocentric compounds, like Spanish verb-object compounds (*matamoscas*, lit. 'kills flies', i.e., 'fly spray') and *bahuvrihi* compounds (a special type of exocentric compounds) such as *highbrow* 'intellectual', *blockhead*, or *featherweight* are also based on the metonymy called by Barcelona (2008) CHARACTERISTIC PROPERTY FOR CATEGORY.

Finally, a few words on abbreviation due to formal metonymy. If one assumes that the set of basic forms[11] of a grammatical construction constitutes a conceptual frame, then metonymy can operate in it (Barcelona 2005, 2007a, 2009a, in preparation; Bierwiaczonek 2007, 2013: Ch. 2; Radden 2005: 17). Constructional forms partially motivated by metonymy include certain lexical abbreviations (like *gas* from *gasoline*) and certain types of ellipsis, as in '*Do you walk to work*' '*Yes, [I walk to work] every day*'; the metonymy at work is SALIENT PART OF FORM FOR WHOLE FORM. On factors determining the salience of the parts retained see Barcelona (in preparation).

7 Metonymy in clausal grammar

I can just comment very briefly on some examples of research in this area.

Ziegeler (2007) argues that analyses in terms of "nominal coercion", as in *She had a beer* (Michaelis 2004), "complement coercion" and "subject coercion" (Pustejovsky 1995) should be replaced by analyses in terms of metonymy. Her alternative proposals to Pustejovsky's are very similar to Langacker's work on

---

10 One of the effects of cliffhanging is creating suspense.
11 That is, the uninflected full (i.e., non-abbreviated) form of lexemes and the full (i.e., non-elliptical or non-defective) form of syntactic constructions.

active zones (Langacker 1999, 2009) and to work by Brdar (2007), Ruiz de Mendoza and Pérez Hernández (2001), and Ruiz de Mendoza and Otal (2002). Take *George began the book* (BOOK FOR RELATION [X READ / WRITE / BIND / ILLUSTRATE ... BOOK]) and '*What could we buy for Mary's birthday?*' '*A book would be a great idea*', where *book* activates "buying a book" (BOOK FOR RELATION [X BUY BOOK]).

An example of work on metonymy and *valency extension/reduction* and *transitivity* (Brdar 2007; Ruiz de Mendoza and Pérez Hernández 2001; Ruiz de Mendoza and Otal 2002; Ruiz de Mendoza and Mairal 2007; Barcelona 2009a, Barcelona in preparation) is *This bread cuts easily*, motivated by the metonymic chain PROCESS FOR ACTION FOR RESULT (Ruiz de Mendoza and Mairal 2007: 45–47).

On metonymy and anaphora see Langacker (1999: 234–245 and Chapter 9, 2009) and Ruiz de Mendoza and Díez Velasco (2004). Metonymy is involved in anaphora resolution, especially in "indirect anaphora" (Emmott 1999), which lacks an explicit antecedent, as in *He speaks excellent French even though he's never lived there*, where the antecedent of *there* is the metonymic target of *French* (LOCATED [LANGUAGE] FOR LOCATION [FRANCE]).

CL research on metonymy in clausal grammar also includes modality (see, among others, Ruiz de Mendoza and Pérez Hernández 2001; Pérez Hernández 2007) and epistemic conditional constructions (Barcelona 2006, 2009a, in preparation).

8 Metonymy in discourse

Research on the role of metonymy in pragmatic inferencing and discourse (pioneered among others by Lakoff 1987: 78–79) has explored the role of metonymy in:
- Grammaticalization (Barcelona 2009a, in preparation; Hilpert 2007; Heine et al. 1991; Hopper and Traugott 1993; Traugott and Dasher 2002).
- Indirect speech acts (Brdar-Szabó 2009; Panther and Thornburg 1998, 2003a; Thornburg and Panther 1997; Bierwiaczonek 2013: Ch. 4).
- Implicature and "explicature" (Barcelona 2002b, 2003b, 2005, 2007a, 2007b, 2009a, in preparation; Panther and Thornburg 2003a, 2007: 248–249; Ruiz de Mendoza and Pérez Hernández 2003; Ruiz de Mendoza and Peña 2005b: 274).
- Other areas, such as speakers' attitudes (especially euphemism), art (including film, and drama), literature, iconicity, sign language, aphasia, etc. (Gibbs 1994: 319–358; Barcelona 2013; Ciepiela 2007; Dzeren-Glówacka

2007; Kuzniak 2007; Kwiatkowska 2007; Littlemore 2009: 115–115, 2015; Pluciennik 2007; P. Wilcox 2004; S. Wilcox Volume 3).

On metonymy and anaphora, see section 7.
I can only offer examples of metonymy in *indirect speech acts* and *implicature*.

Thornburg and Panther (1997) assume that speakers operate on the basis of Speech Act Scenarios like the Scenario for Directive Speech Acts (S = Speaker, H = Hearer, A = Action requested):

(i) the BEFORE: (a) H can do A
 (b) S wants H to do A

(ii) the CORE: (a) S puts H under an obligation to do A
 (b) the immediate RESULT: H is under an obligation to do A (H must/should do A)

(iii) the AFTER: H will do A

PART FOR WHOLE metonymies motivate indirect requests, as in "I need your help. *I would like you to send a message to my mom*" (part i-b activates the whole scenario).

An example of the metonymic guidance of *implicature* is this parliamentary anecdote:

Opposition MP, on the Prime Minister (PM): *But what can we expect, after all, of a man who wears silk underpants?*

PM: *Oh, I would have never thought the Right Honorable's wife could be so indiscreet!*

Barcelona (2003b) showed that it is possible to argue that all the implicatures invited by this exchange are guided by metonymy. Among those invited by the PM's repartee are these (with the chained metonymies guiding their derivation):[12] (a) "The MP's wife knows that the PM wears silk underpants because she has seen him undress" (FACT [knowing the underwear he uses] FOR SALIENT CONVENTIONAL EXPLANATION [seeing him undress]; (b) "She is on "intimate terms" with the PM" (FACT [seeing him undress] FOR SALIENT EXPLANATION [being on "intimate terms" with him].

---

[12] This is an oversimplification of a much more complex analysis.

9 Research methods

Most research on metonymy so far has used "traditional" methods, i.e., collecting a number of more or less contextualized examples and studying them on the basis of introspection with occasional consultation of corpora, dictionaries and informants.

Gibbs (2007b) suggests that, even if cognitive linguists do not have to carry out psychological experiments, they should at least present their claims in a manner amenable to empirical testing. As regards metonymy research, one of the ways to do this is to devise explicit methods to identify linguistic metonymies and investigate their functioning in language, as in Barcelona (2002a), Dirven (2002) and the Pragglejazz Group (2007), whose complex Metaphor Identification Procedure (MIP), later refined as MIP-VU (Steen et al. 2010), has been adapted to metonymy identification (e.g., Zhang et al. 2011). Another complementary way is to study the distribution and variation of metonymy in various types of grammatical structures and discourse types by applying corpus analysis techniques (Markert and Nissim 2003; Stefanowitsch and Gries 2008), usually coupled with statistical and other quantitative methods (Glynn and Fischer 2010). An excellent application of these methods is Zhang (2013). These methods are extremely useful to rigorously characterize "visible" conceptual metonymies, i.e., those manifested in linguistic (especially lexical) meaning or form.

But testing the cognitive "reality" of *conceptual* metonymies, both the visible ones and the "invisible" ones, e.g., those underlying metaphors (section 3) and guiding implicatures (section 8), requires psycholinguistic experiments. Unfortunately, there is very little research in this direction, mainly due to the difficulties in designing the corresponding experiments (Gibbs 2007a). However, this research suggests that conceptual metonymy is regularly active in discourse comprehension (Gibbs 1994: 319–358, especially 329–330, 358; Frisson and Pickering 1999).

10 Conclusions

A rich amount of information has been offered on the role of metonymy in grammar and discourse. Metonymy is ubiquitous because it is a *conceptual mechanism* and a *natural inferencing schema* (Panther 2005) and this explains why we regularly find the same types of conceptual metonymies (EFFECT FOR CAUSE, PART FOR WHOLE, RESULT FOR CONDITION, ENTITY FOR SALIENT PROPERTY, etc.)

at different linguistic levels and in very different expressive and communicative modes.

As tasks for future research, the following could be highlighted (see also Panther and Thornburg 2007):
- The compilation of a generally accepted detailed typology of metonymy which would include information for each metonymy on the relevant metonymic hierarchy/ies, the linguistic domains/ranks where it operates, the factors triggering or constraining it, its patterns of chaining and interaction with other metonymies and with metaphor and blending, and a unification of the terminology used to designate the types of metonymy (Blanco et al. 2018).
- More research on the attitudinal uses of metonymy in discourse (Littlemore 2015).
- More research on the main types of metonymy in pragmatic inferencing.
- Developing a standard methodology in data collection and analysis.
- More psycholinguistic research on the psychological reality of metonymy.
- More studies to investigate crosslinguistic differences in the use of metonymy in such areas as advertising, art, second language acquisition, etc.

11 References

Barcelona, Antonio (ed.) (2000a): *Metaphor and Metonymy at the Crossroads. A Cognitive Perspective*. Berlin/New York: Mouton de Gruyter.

Barcelona, Antonio (2000b): On the plausibility of claiming a metonymic motivation for conceptual metaphor. In: A. Barcelona (ed.), *Metaphor and Metonymy at the Crossroads. A Cognitive Perspective*, 31–58. Berlin/New York: Mouton de Gruyter.

Barcelona, Antonio (2002a): Clarifying and applying the notions of metaphor and metonymy within cognitive linguistics: An update. In: R. Dirven and R. Pörings (eds.), *Metaphor and Metonymy in Comparison and Contrast*, 207–277. Berlin: Mouton de Gruyter.

Barcelona, Antonio (2002b): On the ubiquity and multiple-level operation of metonymy. In: B. Lewandowska-Tomaszczyk and K. Turewicz (eds.), *Cognitive Linguistics Today* (Łódź Studies in Language), 207–224. Frankfurt a. M.: Peter Lang.

Barcelona, Antonio (2003a): Metonymy in cognitive linguistics. An analysis and a few modest proposals. In: H. Cuyckens, K.-U. Panther and T. Berg (eds.), *Motivation in Language: Studies in Honor of Günter Radden*, 223–255. Amsterdam: John Benjamins.

Barcelona, Antonio (2003b): The case for a metonymic basis of pragmatic inferencing: Evidence from jokes and funny anecdotes. In: K.-U. Panther and L. Thornburg. *Metonymy and Pragmatic Inferencing*, 81–102. Amsterdam/Philadelphia: John Benjamins.

Barcelona, Antonio (2003c): La gramática de los nombres propios: un viaje con retorno (por buenos motivos). In: M. White, H. Herrera and C. Alonso (eds.), *La Lingüística Cognitiva en España en el cambio de Siglo (II), Metáfora y Metonimia* [Cognitive linguistics in

Spain at the turn of the century (II), Metaphor and metonymy], 7-30. Madrid: Universidad Autónoma de Madrid.

Barcelona, Antonio (2003d): Names: A metonymic return ticket. *Jezikoslovlje* 4(1): 11-41.

Barcelona, Antonio (2004): Metonymy behind grammar: The motivation of the seemingly "irregular" grammatical behavior of English paragon names. In: G. Radden and K.-U. Panther (eds.), *Studies in Linguistics Motivation*, 357-374. Amsterdam: John Benjamins.

Barcelona, Antonio (2005): The multilevel operation of metonymy in grammar and discourse with particular attention to metonymic chains. In: F. J. Ruiz de Mendoza Ibáñez and S. Peña Cervel (eds.), *Cognitive Linguistics: Internal Dynamics and Interdisciplinary Interaction*, 313-352. Berlin/New York: Mouton de Gruyter.

Barcelona, Antonio (2006): On the conceptual motivation of epistemic conditionals: Metonymy or metaphor? In R. Benczes and S. Csabi (eds.), *The Metaphors of Sixty. Papers Presented on the Occasion of the 60th Birthday of Zoltán Kövecses*, 39-47. Budapest: Eötvos Loránd University, Department of American Studies, School of English and American Studies.

Barcelona, Antonio (2007a): The multilevel role of metonymy in grammar and discourse: A case study. In: K. Kosecki (ed.), *Perspectives on Metonymy. Proceedings of the International Conference "Perspectives on Metonymy"*, 103-131. Frankfurt a. M.: Peter Lang.

Barcelona, Antonio (2007b): The role of metonymy in meaning at discourse level: A case study. In: G. Radden, Günter, K.-M. Köpcke, T. Berg and P. Siemund (eds.), *Aspects of Meaning Construction*, 51-75. Amsterdam: John Benjamins.

Barcelona, Antonio (2008): The interaction of metonymy and metaphor in the meaning and form of 'bahuvrihi' compounds. *Annual Review of Cognitive Linguistics* 6: 208-281.

Barcelona, Antonio (2009a): Motivation of construction meaning and form: The roles of metonymy and inference. In: K.-U. Panther, L. Thornburg and A. Barcelona (eds.), *Metonymy and Metaphor in Grammar*, 363-401. Amsterdam/Philadelphia: John Benjamins.

Barcelona, Antonio (2009b): Partitive restrictive modification of names in English: Arguments for their metonymic motivation. *Quaderns de Filologia de la Universitat de València. Estudis Lingüístics* 14: 33-56.

Barcelona, Antonio (2010): Metonymic inferencing and second language acquisition. In: J. Littlemore and C. Juchem-Grundmann (eds.), *Applied Cognitive Linguistics in Second Language Learning and Teaching. AILA Review*, Volume 23, 134-154. Amsterdam: John Benjamins.

Barcelona, Antonio (2011a): Reviewing the properties and prototype structure of metonymy. In: R. Benczes, A. Barcelona and F.-J. Ruiz de Mendoza Ibáñez (eds.), *Defining Metonymy in Cognitive Linguistics. Towards a Consensus View*, 7-57. Amsterdam: John Benjamins.

Barcelona, Antonio (2011b): Metonymy is not just a lexical phenomenon. In: C. Alm-Arvius, N.-L. Johannesson and D. C. Minugh (eds.) Selected Papers from the 2008 Stockholm Metaphor Festival, 3-42 (http://www2.english.su.se/nlj/metfest_08/Barcelona_08.pdf).

Barcelona, Antonio (2013): Metonymy-guided inferences in creative thinking (humour, theology, art). In: R. Monroy Casas (ed.), *Homenaje Francisco Gutiérrez Díez*, 39-58. Murcia: Universidad de Murcia.

Barcelona, Antonio (in preparation): On the pervasive role of metonymy in constructional meaning and structure in discourse comprehension: An empirical study from a cognitive-linguistic perspective (Provisional title).

Barnden, John A. (2010): Metaphor and metonymy: Making their connections more slippery. *Cognitive Linguistics* 21(1): 1–34.

Benczes, Réka (2006): *Creative Compounding in English. The Semantics of Metaphorical and Metonymical Noun-Noun Combinations*. Amsterdam: John Benjamins.

Benczes, Réka (2011): Putting the notion of 'domain' back into metonymy. In: R. Benczes, A. Barcelona and F.-J. Ruiz de Mendoza Ibáñez, *Defining Metonymy in Cognitive Linguistics. Towards a Consensus View*, 197–215. Amsterdam: John Benjamins.

Benczes, Réka, Antonio Barcelona and Francisco-José Ruiz de Mendoza Ibáñez (eds.) (2011): *Defining Metonymy in Cognitive Linguistics. Towards a Consensus View*. Amsterdam: John Benjamins.

Bierwiaczonek, Boguslaw (2007): On formal metonymy. In: K. Kosecki (ed.), *Perspectives on Metonymy. Proceedings of the International Conference "Perspectives on Metonymy"*, 43–67. Frankfurt a. M.: Peter Lang.

Bierwiaczonek, Boguslaw (2013): *Metonymy in Language, Thought and Brain*. Sheffield: Equinox.

Blanco-Carrión, Olga, Antonio Barcelona and Rossella Pannain (eds.) (2018): *Conceptual Metonymy. Methodological, Theoretical and Descriptive Issues*. Amsterdam/Philadelphia: John Benjamins.

Brdar, Mario (2007): *Metonymy in Grammar. Towards Motivating Extensions of Grammatical Categories and Constructions*. Osijek: Faculty of Philosophy, Josip Juraj Strossmayer University.

Brdar-Szabó, Rita (2009): Metonymy in Indirect Directives: Stand-alone Conditionals in English, German, Hungarian, and Croatian. In: K.-U. Panther, L. Thornburg and A. Barcelona (eds.), *Metonymy and Metaphor in Grammar*, 323–336. Amsterdam/Philadelphia: John Benjamins.

Brdar, Mario and Rita Brdar-Szabó (2007): When Zidane is not simply Zidane, and Bill Gates is not just Bill Gates: Some thoughts on the construction of metaphtonymic meanings. In: G. Radden, K.-M. Köpcke, T. Berg and P. Siemund (eds.), *Aspects of Meaning Construction*, 125–142. Amsterdam: John Benjamins.

Ciepiela, Kamila (2007): Metonymy in aphasia. In: K. Kosecki (ed.), *Perspectives on Metonymy. Proceedings of the International Conference "Perspectives on Metonymy"*, 199–208. Frankfurt a. M.: Peter Lang.

Croft, William ([1993] 2002): The role of domains in the interpretation of metaphors and metonymies. *Cognitive Linguistics* 4(4): 335–371.

Croft, William and David Alan Cruse (2004): *Cognitive Linguistics*. New York: Cambridge University Press.

Cruse, David Alan (2000): *Meaning in Language*. Oxford: Oxford University Press.

Dirven, René (1999): Conversion as a conceptual metonymy of event schemata. In: G. Radden and K.-U. Panther (eds.), *Metonymy in Language and Thought*, 275–287. Amsterdam/Philadelphia: John Benjamins.

Dirven, René (2002): Metonymy and metaphor: Different strategies of conceptualisation. In: R. Dirven and R. Pörings (eds.), *Metaphor and Metonymy in Comparison and Contrast*, 75–112. Berlin: Mouton de Gruyter.

Dzeren-Główacka, Silwia (2007): Beating up intelligence. Metonymy In: Terry Pratchett's novels. K. Kosecki (ed.), *Perspectives on Metonymy. Proceedings of the International Conference "Perspectives on Metonymy"*, 335–348. Frankfurt a. M.: Peter Lang.

Emmott, Catherine (1999): Embodied in a constructed world: Narrative processing, knowledge representation, and indirect anaphora. In: K. van Hoek, A. A. Kibrik and L.

Noordman (eds.), *Discourse Studies in Cognitive Linguistics*, 5–27. Amsterdam: John Benjamins.

Fass, Dan C. (1997): *Processing Metonymy and Metaphor* (Contemporary Studies in Cognitive Science and Technology, Vol. 1). Westport: Ablex Publishing.

Fauconnier, Gilles (1997): *Mappings in Thought and Language*. Cambridge: Cambridge University Press.

Feyaerts, Kurt (1999): Metonymic hierarchies. The conceptualization of stupidity in German idiomatic expressions. In: K.-U. Panther and G. Radden (eds.), *Metonymy in Language and Thought*, 309–334. Amsterdam/Philadelphia: John Benjamins.

Fillmore, Charles (1985): Frames and the semantics of understanding. *Quaderni di Semantica* 6(2): 222–254.

Forceville, Charles and Eduardo Urios-Aparisi (eds.) (2009): *Multimodal Metaphor*. Berlin: Mouton de Gruyter.

Frisson, Steven and Martin Pickering (1999): The processing of metonymy: Evidence from eye-movements. *Journal of Experimental Psychology: Learning, Memory and Cognition* 25: 1366–1383.

Geeraerts, Dirk (2002): The interaction of metaphor and metonymy in composite expressions. In: R. Dirven and R. Pörings (eds.), *Metaphor and Metonymy in Comparison and Contrast*, 435–465. Berlin/New York: Mouton de Gruyter.

Geeraerts, Dirk (Volume 2): Lexical semantics. Berlin/Boston: De Gruyter Mouton.

Geeraerts, Dirk and Yves Peirsman (2011): Zones, Facets and Prototype-based Metonymy. In: R. Benczes, A. Barcelona and F.-J. Ruiz de Mendoza Ibáñez (eds.), *Defining Metonymy in Cognitive Linguistics. Towards a Consensus View*, 88–102. Amsterdam: John Benjamins.

Gibbs, Raymond W. Jr. (1994): *The Poetics of Mind. Figurative Thought, Language and Understanding*. Cambridge: Cambridge University Press.

Gibbs, Raymond W. Jr. (2007a): Experimental tests of figurative meaning construction. In: G. Radden, K.-M. Köpcke, T. Berg and P. Siemund (eds.), *Aspects of Meaning Construction*, 19–32. Amsterdam: John Benjamins.

Gibbs, Raymond W. Jr. (2007b): Why cognitive linguists should care more about empirical methods. In: M. González-Márquez, I. Mittelberg, S. Coulson and M. Spivey (eds.), *Methods in Cognitive Linguistics*, 1–16. Amsterdam: John Benjamins.

Gibbs, Raymond W. Jr. (this volume): Metaphor. Berlin/Boston: De Gruyter Mouton.

Glynn, Dylan and Kerstin Fischer (eds.) (2010): *Quantitative Methods in Cognitive Semantics: Corpus-Driven Approaches*. Berlin: Mouton De Gruyter.

Goldberg, Adele (2006): *Constructions at Work. The nature of Generalization in Language*. Oxford: Oxford University Press.

Goossens, Louis ([1990] 2002): Metaphtonymy: The interaction of metaphor and metonymy in expressions for linguistic action. *Cognitive Linguistics* 1(3): 323–340.

Goossens, Louis, Paul Pauwels, Brygida Rudzka-Ostyn, Anne-Marie Simon-Vanderbergen, and Johan Vanparys (1995): *By Word of Mouth. Metaphor, Metonymy and Linguistic Action in a Cognitive Perspective*. Amsterdam/Philadelphia: John Benjamins.

Greenbaum, Sidney and Randolph Quirk (1990): *The Student's Grammar of the English Language*. London: Longman.

Heine, Bernd, Ulrike Claudi and Friederike Hünnemeyer (1991): *Grammaticalization. A Conceptual Framework*. Chicago: University of Chicago Press.

Hilpert, Martin (2007): Chained metonymies in lexicon and grammar: A cross-linguistic perspective on body terms. In: G. Radden, K.-M. Köpcke, T. Berg and P. Siemund (eds.), *Aspects of Meaning Construction*, 77–98. Amsterdam: John Benjamins.

Hilpert, Martin (Volume 2): Historical linguistics. Berlin/Boston: De Gruyter Mouton.
Holme, Randal (2009): *Cognitive Linguistics and Language Teaching*. Basingstoke: Palgrave Macmillan.
Hopper Paul and Elizabeth Closs-Traugott (1993): *Grammaticalization*. Cambridge: Cambridge University Press.
Janda, Laura (Volume 3): Tense, aspect and mood. Berlin/Boston: De Gruyter Mouton.
Kosecki, Krzyscztof (2007): Some remarks on metonymy in compounding. In: K. Kosecki (ed.), *Perspectives on Metonymy. Proceedings of the International Conference "Perspectives on Metonymy"*, 241–251. Frankfurt a. M.: Peter Lang.
Kövecses, Zoltán and Günter Radden (1998): Metonymy: Developing a cognitive linguistic view. *Cognitive Linguistics* 9(1): 37–77.
Kuzniak, Marek (2007): Part-whole relations in the selected epigrams by J. Staudynger. In: K. Kosecki (ed.), *Perspectives on Metonymy. Proceedings of the International Conference "Perspectives on Metonymy"*, 323–333. Frankfurt a. M.: Peter Lang.
Kwiatkowska, Alina (2007): 'Pre-linguistic and non-linguistic metonymy'. In: K. Kosecki (ed.), *Perspectives on Metonymy. Proceedings of the International Conference "Perspectives on Metonymy"*, 297–307. Frankfurt a. M.: Peter Lang.
Lakoff, George (1987): *Women, Fire and Dangerous Things. What Categories Reveal About the Mind*. Chicago: University of Chicago Press.
Lakoff, George (1993): The contemporary theory of metaphor. In: A. Ortony (ed.), *Metaphor and Thought* (2nd edition), 202–251. Cambridge: Cambridge University Press.
Lakoff, George and Mark Johnson (1980): *Metaphors We Live By*. Chicago: University of Chicago Press.
Lakoff, George and Mark Turner (1989): *More than Cool Reason: A Field Guide to Poetic Metaphor*. Chicago: University of Chicago Press.
Langacker, Ronald W. (1987): *Foundations of Cognitive Grammar*. Vol 1: *Theoretical Prerequisites*. Stanford: Stanford University Press.
Langacker, Ronald W. (1993): Reference-point constructions. *Cognitive Linguistics* 4: 1–38.
Langacker, Ronald W. (1999): *Grammar and Conceptualization*. Berlin/New York: Mouton de Gruyter.
Langacker, Ronald W. (this volume): Construal. Berlin/Boston: De Gruyter Mouton.
Langacker, Ronald W. (2009): Metonymic grammar. In: K.-U. Panther, L. Thornburg and A. Barcelona (eds.), *Metonymy and Metaphor in Grammar*, 45–71. Amsterdam/Philadelphia: John Benjamins.
Littlemore, Jeannette (2009): *Applying Cognitive Linguistics to Second Language Learning and Teaching*. Basingstoke: Palgrave Macmillan.
Littlemore, Jeannette (2015): *Metonymy: Hidden Shortcuts in Language, Thought and Communication*. Cambridge: Cambridge University Press.
Markert, Katja and Malvina Nissim (2003): Corpus-based metonymy analysis. *Metaphor and Symbol* 18(3): 175–188.
Martsa, Sándor (2013): *Conversion in English: A Cognitive Semantic Approach*. Newcastle-upon-Tyne: Cambridge Scholars Publishing.
Michaelis, Laura (2004): Type shifting in construction grammar: An integrated approach to aspectual coercion. *Cognitive Linguistics* 15: 1–67.
Nunberg, Geoffrey (1995): Transfers of meaning. *Journal of Semantics* 12: 109–132.
Palmer, Gary, Russell S. Rader, and Art D. Clarito (2009): The metonymic basis of a 'semantic partial': Tagalog lexical constructions with *ka-*. In: K.-U. Panther, L. Thornburg and

A. Barcelona (eds.), *Metonymy and Metaphor in Grammar*, 111–144. Amsterdam/ Philadelphia: John Benjamins.

Pang, Kam-Yiu (2006): A partitioned-narrative model of the self: Its linguistic manifestations, entailments, and ramifications. Ph.D. Dissertation. University of Otago, New Zealand.

Panther, Klaus-Uwe (2005): The role of conceptual metonymy in meaning construction. In: F. J. Ruiz de Mendoza Ibáñez and S. Peña Cervel (eds.), *Cognitive Linguistics: Internal Dynamics and Interdisciplinary Interaction*, 353–386. Berlin/New York: Mouton de Gruyter.

Panther, Klaus-Uwe and Linda Thornburg (1998): A cognitive approach to inferencing in conversation. *Journal of Pragmatics* 30: 755–769.

Panther, Klaus-Uwe and Linda Thornburg (2000): The EFFECT FOR CAUSE metonymy in English grammar. In: A. Barcelona (ed.), *Metaphor and Metonymy at the Crossroads. A Cognitive Perspective*, 215–231. Berlin/New York: Mouton de Gruyter.

Panther, Klaus-Uwe and Linda Thornburg (2002): The roles of metaphor and metonymy in English -er nominal. In: R. Dirven and R. Pörings (eds.), *Metaphor and Metonymy in Comparison and Contrast*, 279–319. Berlin: Mouton de Gruyter.

Panther, Klaus-Uwe and Linda Thornburg (eds.) (2003a): *Metonymy and Pragmatic Inferencing*. Amsterdam/Philadelphia: John Benjamins.

Panther, Klaus-Uwe and Linda Thornburg (2003b): Introduction: On the nature of conceptual metonymy. In: K.-U. Panther and L. Thornburg (eds.), *Metonymy and Pragmatic Inferencing*. 1–20. Amsterdam/Philadelphia: John Benjamins.

Panther, Klaus-Uwe and Linda Thornburg (2007): Metonymy. In: D. Geeraerts and H. Cuyckens (eds.), *Handbook of Cognitive Linguistics*, 236–263. Oxford: Oxford University Press.

Panther, Klaus-Uwe, Linda Thornburg, and Antonio Barcelona (eds.) (2009): *Metonymy and Metaphor in Grammar*. Amsterdam/Philadelphia: John Benjamins.

Papafragou, Anna (1996): On metonymy, *Lingua* 99: 169–195.

Paradis, Carita (2004): Where does metonymy stop? Senses, facets and active zones. *Metaphor and Symbol* 19(4): 245–264.

Paradis, Carita (2011): Metonymization. A key mechanism in semantic change. In: R. Benczes, A. Barcelona and F.-J. Ruiz de Mendoza Ibáñez, *Defining Metonymy in Cognitive Linguistics. Towards a Consensus View*, 62–87. Amsterdam: John Benjamins.

Peirsman, Yves and Dirk Geeraerts (2006): Metonymy as a prototypical category. *Cognitive Linguistics* 17(3): 269–316.

Pérez Hernández, Lorena (2007): High-level metonymies in the understanding of modality. In: K. Kosecki (ed.), *Perspectives on Metonymy. Proceedings of the International Conference "Perspectives on Metonymy"*, 133–146. Frankfurt a. M.: Peter Lang.

Pluciennik, Jaroslaw (2007): Princess Antonomasia, individualism, and the quixotism of culture: A case of 'Tristram Shandy' by Laurence Stern. In: K. Kosecki (ed.), *Perspectives on Metonymy. Proceedings of the International Conference "Perspectives on Metonymy"*, 349–366. Frankfurt a. M.: Peter Lang.

Pragglejaz Group (2007): MIP: A method for identifying metaphorically-used words in discourse. *Metaphor and Symbol* 22: 1–40.

Pustejovsky, James (1995): *The Generative Lexicon*. Cambridge: MIT Press.

Radden, Günter (2002): How metonymic are metaphors? In: R. Dirven and R. Pörings (eds.), *Metaphor and Metonymy in Comparison and Contrast*, 407–434. Berlin: Mouton de Gruyter.

Radden, Günter (2005): The ubiquity of metonymy. In: J. L. Otal Campo, I. Navarro i Ferrando, and B. Bellés Fortuño (eds.), *Cognitive and Discourse Approaches to Metaphor and Metonymy*, 11–28. Castellón: Universitat Jaume I.

Radden, Günter (2009): Generic reference in English: A metonymic and conceptual blending analysis. In: K.-U. Panther, L. Thornburg and A. Barcelona (eds.), *Metonymy and Metaphor in Grammar*, 199–228. Amsterdam/Philadelphia: John Benjamins.

Radden, Günter and René Dirven (2007): *Cognitive English Grammar*. Amsterdam/Philadelphia: John Benjamins.

Radden, Günter and Zoltán Kövecses (1999): Towards a theory of metonymy. In: K.-U. Panther and G. Radden (eds.), *Metonymy in Language and Thought*, 17–59. Amsterdam/Philadelphia: John Benjamins.

Radden, Günter and Klaus-Uwe Panther (2004): Reflections on motivation. In: G. Radden and K.-U. Panther (eds.), *Studies in Linguistic Motivation*, 1–46. Berlin & New York: Mouton de Gruyter.

Rudzka-Ostyn, Brygida (1995): Metaphor, schema, invariance. The case of verbs of answering. In: L. Goossens, P. Pauwels, B. Rudzka-Ostyn, A. Simon-Vanderbergen, and J. Vanparys (eds.) *By Word of Mouth. Metaphor, Metonymy and Linguistic Action in a Cognitive Perspective*, 205–243. Amsterdam/Philadelphia: John Benjamins.

Ruiz de Mendoza Ibáñez, Francisco José (2000): The role of mappings and domains in understanding metonymy. In: A. Barcelona (ed.), *Metaphor and Metonymy at the Crossroads. A Cognitive Perspective*, 109–132. Berlin/New York: Mouton de Gruyter.

Ruiz de Mendoza Ibáñez, Francisco José (2011): Metonymy and cognitive operations. In: R. Benczes, A. Barcelona and F.-J. Ruiz de Mendoza Ibáñez (eds.), *Defining Metonymy in Cognitive Linguistics. Towards a Consensus View*, 103–123. Amsterdam: John Benjamins.

Ruiz de Mendoza, Francisco José and Olga I. Díez Velasco (2004): Metonymic motivation in anaphoric reference. In: G. Radden and K.-U. Panther (eds.), *Studies in Linguistic Motivation*, 293–320. Berlin/New York: Mouton de Gruyter.

Ruiz de Mendoza Ibáñez, Francisco José and Ricardo Mairal Usón (2007): High-level metaphor and metonymy in meaning construction. In: G. Radden, Günter, K.-M. Köpcke, T. Berg and P. Siemund (eds.), *Aspects of Meaning Construction*, 33–49. Amsterdam: John Benjamins.

Ruiz de Mendoza Ibáñez, Francisco José and José Luis Otal Campo (2002): *Metonymy, Grammar and Communication*. Albolote: Comares.

Ruiz de Mendoza Ibáñez, Francisco José and Sandra Peña Cervel (2005): Conceptual interaction, cognitive operations and projection spaces. In: F. J. Ruiz de Mendoza Ibáñez and S. Peña Cervel (eds.), *Cognitive Linguistics: Internal Dynamics and Interdisciplinary Interaction*, 249–280. Berlin/New York: Mouton de Gruyter.

Ruiz de Mendoza Ibáñez, Francisco José and Lorena Pérez Hernández (2001): Metonymy and the grammar: motivation, constraints and interaction. *Language and Communication* 21(4): 321–357.

Ruiz de Mendoza Ibáñez, Francisco José and Lorena Pérez Hernández (2003): Cognitive operations and pragmatic implication. In: K.-U. Panther and L. Thornburg (eds.), *Metonymy and Pragmatic Inferencing*, 23–49. Amsterdam/Philadelphia: John Benjamins.

Steen, Gerard, Aletta G. Dorst, J. Berenike Herrmann, Anna Kaal, Tina Krennmayr, and Trijintje Pasma (2010): *A Method for Linguistic Metaphor Identification*. Amsterdam: John Benjamins.

Stefanowitsch, Anatol, and Stephan Th. Gries (eds.) (2008): *Corpus-Based Approaches to Metaphor and Metonymy*. Berlin: Mouton De Gruyter.

Szawerna, Michal (2007): Deverbal nominalization as a type of metonymic extension from processes to things. In: K. Kosecki (ed.), *Perspectives on Metonymy. Proceedings of the International Conference "Perspectives on Metonymy"*, 147–155. Frankfurt a. M.: Peter Lang.

Taylor, John ([1989] 1995): *Linguistic Categorization. Prototypes in Linguistic Theory*. Oxford: Clarendon.

Thornburg, Linda and Klaus-Uwe Panther (1997): Speech act metonymies. In: W.-A. Liebert, G. Redeker; and L. Waugh (eds.), *Discourse and Perspective in Cognitive Linguistics*, 205–219. Amsterdam/Philadelphia: Benjamins.

Traugott, Elizabeth Closs and Richard B. Dasher (2002): *Regularity in Semantic Change*. Cambridge: Cambridge University Press.

Turner, Mark (this volume): Blending in language and communication. Berlin/Boston: De Gruyter Mouton.

Turner, Mark and Gilles Fauconnier (2000): Metaphor, metonymy and binding. In: A. Barcelona (ed.), *Metaphor and Metonymy at the Crossroads. A Cognitive Perspective*, 133–145. Berlin/New York: Mouton de Gruyter.

Warren, Beatrice (1999): Aspects of referential metonymy. In: K.-U. Panther and G. Radden (eds.), *Metonymy in Language and Thought*, 121–135. Amsterdam/Philadelphia: John Benjamins.

Wilcox, Phyllis P. (2004): A cognitive key: Metonymic and metaphorical mappings in ASL. *Cognitive Linguistics* 15(2): 197–222.

Wilcox, Sherman (Volume 3): Signed languages. Berlin/Boston: De Gruyter Mouton.

Zhang, Weiwei (2013): Variation in metonymy. A Corpus-based cognitive-linguistic approach. Ph. D. Dissertation. University of Leuven.

Zhang, Weiwei, Dirk Speelman and Dirk Geeraerts (2011): Variation in the (non)metonymic capital names in mainland Chinese and Taiwan Chinese. *Metaphor and the Social World* 1(1): 90–112.

Ziegeler, Debra (2007): Arguing the case against coercion. In: G. Radden, Günter, K.-M. Köpcke, T. Berg and P. Siemund (eds.), *Aspects of Meaning Construction*, 99–123. Amsterdam: John Benjamins.

Ackerman, Joshua, Christopher Nocera, and John Bargh (2010): Incidental haptic sensations influence social judgments and decisions. *Science* 328: 1712–1715.

Raymond W. Gibbs
Chapter 8: Metaphor

1 Introduction

Have you ever asked yourself the question, "Can a person who continually struggles with impure thoughts be genuinely saved?" Although this issue does not come to my mind very often, I stumbled across a website that gave a detailed answer to this challenging query. Part of the response included the following (http://questions.org/attq/can-a-person-who-continually-struggles-with-impure-thoughts-be-genuinely-saved/):

> Although in this life we will never be completely freed from the taint of sin and impure thoughts, we can grow in our ability to control our response to them. ... By responding to our evil and impure thoughts with disciplined resistance, we can go a long way towards cleansing ourselves of habitual, willful sin. But we still live in a fallen world and will continue to struggle with our dark side.

We all roughly understand what is meant by the metaphoric phrases *taint of sin, impure thoughts*, as well as the idea that *with disciplined resistance, we can go a long way towards cleansing ourselves of habitual, willful sin*. Each of these refer, in part, to the common beliefs that good thoughts and behaviors are clean, while bad, or evil, thoughts and behaviors are dirty, contaminated, or polluted in some manner. Most historical approaches to metaphor see it as a special rhetorical tool that may reflect creative thinking and unique aesthetic abilities (Beardsley 1962; Ricoeur 1977). But what do metaphors like *impure thoughts* or *cleansing ... ourselves of sin* imply about people's cognitive and linguistic abilities?

Cognitive linguistic research on metaphor has explored how both conventional and novel metaphoric language reveals important insights into people's common metaphoric conceptions of various, mostly abstract, topics. Similar to research on other topics within cognitive linguistics, metaphoric structure and behavior has been studied not as if these are autonomous from ordinary cognition, but as reflections of general conceptual systems, psychological processing mechanisms, and specific patterns of bodily experience (Gibbs 1994; Lakoff and Johnson 1980, 1999). People speak metaphorically for communicative purposes, but metaphoric language emerges from systematic patterns of metaphoric

---

Raymond W. Gibbs, Santa Cruz, USA

https://doi.org/10.1515/9783110626476-009

thoughts known as "conceptual metaphors". Most importantly, perhaps, cognitive linguistic research on metaphor has advanced the idea that many conceptual metaphors emerge from recurring patterns of bodily experience, which offers compelling links between embodiment, metaphoric thought, and metaphoric language and action.

This chapter describes some of the empirical findings on metaphor within cognitive linguistics, and then considers several of the ongoing debates regarding the cognitive theory of metaphor. Cognitive linguistic approaches now dominate in the multi-disciplinary world of metaphor research. Yet cognitive metaphor theory has always evoked considerable controversy regarding its methods, data, and theoretical conclusions about language, minds, and bodies. My aim is to address some of these criticisms and suggest one way of advancing cognitive metaphor theory to better capture the complex realities of how people's metaphoric thought dynamically shapes their use and understanding of verbal metaphor.

2 Cognitive linguistic findings

The original evidence for conceptual metaphors comes from the systematic analysis of conventional expressions in different languages (Lakoff and Johnson 1980, 1999; Kövecses 2002). Consider the following ways that English speakers sometimes talk about their romantic relationships:

We're headed in opposite directions
We're spinning our wheels
Our relationship is at a crossroads
Our marriage was on the rocks

Cognitive linguistic analyses argue that these individual expressions are not clichéd idioms expressing literal meaning, but reflect, and are said to be partially motivated by, different aspects of the enduring conceptual metaphor LOVE RELATIONSHIPS ARE JOURNEYS. There is a tight mapping according to which entities in the domain of love (e.g., the lovers, their common goals, the love relationship) correspond systematically to entities in the domain of journeys (e.g., the traveler, the vehicle, destinations, etc.). Each linguistic expression above refers to a different correspondence that arises from the mapping of familiar, often embodied, understanding of journeys onto the more abstract idea of a love relationship (e.g., difficulties in the relationship are conceived of as obstacles on the physical journey). The hypothesis that some concepts may be metaphorically structured makes it possible to explain what until now has been seen as unrelated conventional expressions or even "dead metaphors".

Consider one other example of how metaphoric concepts may explain the systematicity among conventional phrases used to talk about abstract topics, related to the examples that opened this chapter (Stefanowitsch 2011: 301):

the *stain* of guilt/sin/illegitimacy
impure thoughts/soul/character
a *dirty* mind/look/word/secret
an *unclean* thought/spirit/mind
to *contaminate* a relationship
to *taint* someone's reputation
to *pollute* someone's mind/thoughts

Each of these expressions may be motivated by the conceptual metaphor MORAL CORRUPTION IS UNCLEANLINESS, which is linked to the corresponding metaphor MORAL GOODNESS IS CLEANLINESS (Lizardo 2012). These conceptual metaphors, arising from bodily experiences related to cleanliness and health, give coherence to varying conventional phrases which otherwise might be seen as having arbitrary roots.

Most work within cognitive linguistics examines the systematicity of individual phrases and expressions, sometimes selected from dictionaries, or from specific corpora containing naturalistic discourse. Cognitive linguists typically do not analyze all the metaphoric words or expressions seen in a corpus, but select different examples from which the existence of particular conceptual metaphors may be inferred. The range of abstract conceptual domains motivated by conceptual metaphor is immense, and includes emotions, the self, morality, politics, science concepts, illness, mathematics, interpersonal relations, time, legal concepts, and many cultural ideologies, to name just a few of the many target domains motivated by conceptual metaphors. Conceptual metaphors have been found in virtually every contemporary language, both spoken and signed, as well as throughout history going back to ancient languages. For example, Cicero's speeches in ancient Rome give evidence of many dozens of conceptual metaphors still active in contemporary metaphor talk. Consider this brief comment, "Greek, which I have seized upon as eagerly as if I had been desirous of satisfying a long-continued thirst, with the result that I have acquired first-hand the information which you see me using in this discussion" (Sjoblad 2009: 59). It is partly structured around the conceptual metaphor DESIRE IS HUNGER/THIRST.

Cognitive linguistic research has also demonstrated that some of the meanings of polysemous words are motivated by conceptual metaphoric mappings (for an overview of polysemy, see Gries Volume 2). For example, the meaning of *see* referring to knowing or understanding as in *I can't see the point of your argument*, is motivated by an enduring conceptual metaphor UNDERSTANDING IS SEEING. Many instances of polysemy are historically derived from conceptual metaphors that are still active parts of human conceptual systems (Cuyckens and Zawada 2001; Sweetser 1990). Under this view, the lexical organization of polysemous words is not a repository of random, idiosyncratic information, but is structured by general cognitive principles, like conceptual metaphor, that are systematic and recurrent throughout the lexicon.

Conceptual metaphor has also been shown to play an important role in grammatical form and structure. Similar to characterizing polysemy relations, various approaches to construction grammar note that metaphor provides an essential link in constructional networks (Goldberg 1995; Langacker 1999). Metaphor has also been shown to be critical for explaining how motion verbs can be metaphorized to convey state of change as in *He went red* and *Here comes the beep*, which emerge from the mapping of the grammar of the source domain onto the grammar of the target domain (Lakoff and Johnson 1999; Panther and Thornburg 2009; Radden 1995). One cognitive theory, called the Lexical Constructional Model, gives metaphor, as well as metonymy, a central role in motivating various grammatical phenomena (Ruiz de Mendoza and Diez 2002). For example, high-level conceptual metaphors, such as EXPRIENTIAL ACTION IS EFFECTUAL ACTION, permit the sensible use of different caused motion constructions, like *John laughed Peter out of the office*. In this manner, high-level conceptual metaphors place external constraints on the ways that grammatical constructions may interact with lexical representations.

Another discovery within cognitive linguistics is that many novel metaphorical expressions do not express completely new source-to-target domain mappings, but are creative instantiations of conventional conceptual metaphors. For instance, the assertion, *Our marriage was a slow crawl through a long mud pit* presents a vivid perspective on how one's romantic relationship can be understood as a very specific physical journey (e.g., LOVE RELATIONSHIPS ARE JOURNEYS). Analyses of literary metaphors (Freeman 1995; Goatly 1997; Lakoff and Turner 1989) and novel metaphorical arguments in expository writing (Eubanks 2000; Koller 2004) demonstrate how many so-called "novel" metaphors are grounded in conventional mappings.

Of course, certain metaphors express "one-shot" metaphoric mappings as seen in resemblance or "A is B" expressions such as *Juliet is the sun*, *Man is wolf*, and *My surgeon is a butcher*. One cognitive linguistic approach to how people interpret "A is B" metaphors, "conceptual blending theory", assumes that multiple mental spaces can participate in a mapping, compared to the two-space or two-domain models in conceptual metaphor theory (Fauconnier and Turner 2002; Turner this volume). Metaphor meaning is captured by a blended space that inherits some structure from each of the input spaces. Consider the familiar metaphor *surgeons are butchers* (Grady et al. 1999). The mapping of information from the source domain of butchery to the target domain of surgery by itself does not provide a crucial element of our interpretation of this metaphorical statement, namely that the surgeon is incompetent. After all, butchers can indeed be as skilled at their job as surgeons are at theirs. Under a blending theory account, the target input space for surgery inherits elements from the corresponding frame for surgery such as of a person being operated upon, the identity of the person who is doing the operation, and the place where this all happens. The source domain butchery input space inherits information such as what a butcher does and his relevant activities such as using sharp instruments to slice up meat. Besides inheriting partial structure from each input space, the blend develops emergent content of its own, which arises from the juxtaposition of elements from the inputs. Specifically, the butchery space projects a means-end relationship that is incompatible with the means-end relationship in the surgery space. For instance, the goal of butchery is to kill the animal and sever the flesh from its bones. But surgeons aim to heal their patients. This incongruity of the butcher's means with the surgeon's end leads to an emergent inference that the surgeon is incompetent. Most generally, blending theory extends conceptual metaphor theory by allowing for mappings that are not unidirectional between multiple domains (see Fauconnier and Lakoff 2013; Tendahl 2008 for a discussion of the commonalities and differences existing between the two theories).

The rise of work in both conceptual metaphor theory and conceptual blending theory has led to significant advances in the study of metaphor in spoken and written discourse (Cameron 2011; Charteris-Black 2004; Hart Volume 2; Koller 2004; Mussolff 2004; Naciscione 2010; Oakley and Hougaard 2008; Semino 2009). This work is generally characterized by close attention to the presence and form of metaphorical ideas in discourse and what these reveal about the cognitive and socio-cultural grounding of metaphorical communication. Many of these discussions focus on the limitations of purely cognitive approaches to talk and text, as well as some of the methodological problems associated with clearly identifying specific conceptual metaphors, and different blending patterns, in naturalistic language. But the increased emphasis in examining situated metaphor use has gone far to illustrate how cognitive linguistic research can be applied to a wide range of discourse domains, which uncovers hidden metaphors in the ways people think about a vast range of abstract topics.

Metaphor is also well studied within corpus linguistics research (Deignan 2005; Gries and Stefanowitsch 2006). Although cognitive linguists often claim that their work is "usage-based", especially in comparison to traditional generative linguistics research, most classic cognitive linguistic studies typically examine isolated individual expressions outside of context. But the corpus linguistic research on metaphor enables scholars to examine specific hypotheses about real-world metaphor use by searching various small and large-scale corpora. The results of these studies demonstrate both important confirmation of facets of conceptual metaphor theory, for example, but also indicate cases where there may be far greater variation in the expression of metaphor than originally anticipated.

One reason why conceptual metaphors may be a prominent part of everyday language and thought is that they are often grounded in recurring patterns of bodily experience. For example, journeys frequently appear as source domains in different conceptual metaphors because of the regularity with which people take various journeys (i.e., starting from a source, moving along a path until reaching a goal). Similarly, people frequently describe good behavior in terms of cleanliness given the strong association between things that are clean and things that are good.

In fact, strong correlations in everyday embodied experience enable the creation of "primary metaphors", such as INTIMACY IS CLOSENESS (e.g., *We have a close relationship*), DIFFICULTIES ARE BURDENS (e.g., *She's weighed down by responsibilities*), and ORGANIZATION IS PHYSICAL STRUCTURE (e.g., *How do the pieces of the theory fit together*) (Grady 1997). In each case, the source domain of the metaphor comes from the body's sensorimotor system. A primary metaphor has a metaphorical mapping for which there is an independent and direct experiential basis and independent linguistic evidence. Blending primary metaphors into larger metaphorical wholes, on the other hand, create complex metaphors. For instance, the three primary metaphors PERSISTING IS REMAINING ERECT, STRUCTURE IS PHYSICAL STRUCTURE, and INTERRELATED IS INTERWOVEN can be combined in different ways to give rise to complex metaphors that have traditionally been seen as conceptual metaphors, such as the expression *The theory started to unravel and soon fell apart.*

There is continuing debate in cognitive linguistics over whether primary metaphors really represent metaphorical mappings as opposed to metonymic ones. For instance, "primary metaphors" may be conceptually possible due to either decontextualization of certain conventional metonymies (Radden 2002) or by a metonymic understanding of the domains connected by metaphor that leads to the recognition of a partial abstract similarity between source and target (e.g., *That is a loud color*) (Barcelona 2000, this volume). Kövecses (2013) argues that correlation metaphors, in particular, emerge from frame-like representations through a metonymic stage (e.g., KNOWING IS SEEING emerges from the logically prior metonymy SEEING SOMETHING PHYSICAL STANDS FOR KNOWING THE THING). These alternative accounts of primary metaphors, at the very least, suggest a greater role for metonymy in the development of metaphorical concepts.

Finally, the embodied nature of conceptual metaphors has led to the development of the neural theory of metaphor (Feldman 2006; Lakoff 2008). This perspective aims to characterize metaphoric mappings as being fundamentally grounded in neural activities, which provides the basis for the emergence of metaphoric concepts and how metaphoric language is used and interpreted. The neural theory of metaphor has frankly not, as yet, been widely influential within cognitive linguistics, although certain cognitive neuroscience evidence is consistent with the idea that sensorimotor brain processes are active when various conventional metaphors are understood (Desai et al. 2011).

Cognitive metaphor theory has done much to situate metaphor within central discussions of minds, bodies, and language within cognitive science, and in many people's view, is the dominant theory in the multidisciplinary world of metaphor research. But cognitive linguistic work on metaphor has evoked much criticism as scholars raise various methodological and theoretical questions about the very idea of conceptual metaphors. I now discuss some of these controversies.

3 Finding metaphor in language and thought

3.1 Identifying metaphoric language

A long-standing complaint about cognitive linguistic theories of metaphor is that many conventional expressions viewed as metaphoric by cognitive linguists are not metaphoric at all (Jackendoff and Aron 1991). Critics argue that expressions like *He was depressed* or *I'm off to a good start in graduate school* are entirely literal, and are not motivated by conceptual metaphors such as SAD IS DOWN or LIFE IS A JOURNEY. Some conventional expressions may have once been recognized as metaphoric, but are really seen by contemporary speakers as "literal" speech, instances of "dead" metaphors, or mere instances of polysemy (McGlone 2007; Murphy 1996).

How do we know if cognitive linguists' intuitions about the metaphoricity of conventional expressions in language are correct? A first step toward answering this question tries to determine which words are metaphorically used in discourse. One proposal, the "metaphor identification procedure" (MIP), sug-

gests that an analyst may find metaphorically used words in context through the following process (Pragglejaz Group 2007):
1. Read the entire text (i.e., written text or talk transcript) to establish a general understanding of the discourse.
2. Determine the lexical units in the text.
3. For each lexical unit in the text, check metaphorical use: Establish the meaning of the lexical unit in context (i.e., how it applies to an entity, its relation in the situation evoked by the text [contextual meaning]). You should take into account what words are before and after the lexical unit. Determine if the lexical unit has a more basic current/contemporary meaning in other contexts than the one in the given context. For our purposes, basic meanings tend to be: more concrete; what they evoke is easier to imagine, see, hear, feel, smell and taste; related to bodily action; more precise (as opposed to vague); and historically older. Basic meanings are not necessarily the most frequent meaning of the lexical unit.
4. If the lexical unit has a more basic current/contemporary meaning in other contexts than the given context, decide whether the contextual meaning can be understood by comparison or contrast with the basic meaning. If yes, mark the lexical unit as metaphorical. Repeat steps 1–4 for each lexical unit.

Consider how MIP may be applied to analyze the first sentence of a newspaper story about former Indian Premier Sonia Gandhi. The lexical units in the sentence are marked by slashes as in the following /For/years/SoniaGandhi/has/struggled/to/convince/Indians/that/she/is/fit/to/wear/the/mantle/of/the/political/dynasty/into/which/she/married/, let alone/to/become/premier/

According to MIP, words such as *for*, *years*, *Sonia Gandhi*, and *has* are not metaphoric. However, *struggled* is deemed to be metaphoric because its contextual meaning, indicating effort, difficulty and lack of success in reaching a goal contrasts with its basic meaning referring to using one's physical strength against someone or something (e.g., *She picked up the child, but he struggled and kicked*). More importantly, the contrast between the contextual and basic meanings of *struggled* is based on comparison, such that we understand abstract effort, difficulty and opposition in terms of physical effort, difficulty, and conflict.[1]

Another word in the opening sentence with possible metaphoric meaning is *wear*. Its contextual meaning, given by the idiomatic *phrase wear the mantle*,

---

[1] MIP does not necessarily embrace the classic idea that metaphor is simply a matter of abbreviated comparison.

refers to some person who has a leading role in a family whose members have occupied high political positions. The basic meaning of *wear* is defined as 'to have something on your body as clothing, decoration or protection', which is also historically prior to other meanings of *wear*. The difference between the contextual and basic meanings is understood by comparison such that we interpret the process of following family members in political positions in terms of physically adorning the clothing that symbolizes that process.

The Pragglejaz Group determined that six of the 27 lexical units in the first sentence of the Gandhi story were judged to convey metaphoric meaning. These decisions about metaphoric meaning are, of course, influenced by how the contextual and basic meanings are actually defined, and the possible differences between these meanings being due to comparison as opposed to some other relationship (e.g., contiguity, opposition) (see Barnden 2011 for a discussion of the problematic distinction metaphor and metonymy).

A variant of MIP, called MIP-VU, has been applied to the analysis of large segments of texts in several discourse genres (Steen et al. 2010). Across different genres, prepositions were determined to be most metaphorical (43 %), followed by verbs (29 %), and then adjectives (18 %). More interestingly, different genres indicate varying degrees of metaphoricity. Academic discourse contains the most metaphorically used words (18 %), followed by news stories (15 %), fiction (11 %), and finally conversation (7 %). Many scholars may suspect that fiction should contain the most metaphoric language, but academic discourse coveys the most metaphoricity given the frequent reference to abstract concepts in these writings.

Metaphor identification schemes like MIP and MIP-VU are now widely employed in metaphor research. These schemes, at the very least, enable researchers to state with greater confidence that some word or phrase really expressed metaphoric meaning. Moreover, the conventional phrases identified as metaphor by cognitive linguists are invariably judged to express metaphoric meanings when seen in realistic discourse contexts. Of course, metaphor exists in larger units than individual words, including longer stretches of text and discourse, and it not clear whether MIP or MIP-VU can be extended to identify metaphor beyond the word level.

It is also important to remember that analysts' conscious judgments about the metaphoricity of a word or utterance may not reflect how ordinary people understand the metaphoric meanings of speakers' utterances. Metaphoricity may really be a matter of cognitive activation for specific individuals in particular moments of speaking and listening (Gibbs and Santa Cruz 2012; Müller 2008). For example, people may use so-called dead metaphors, but still give evidence of having vital metaphorical knowledge motivating a word or phrase's use in context. Thus, a speaker may use the term *depressed* to talk of another individual. Some analysts would claim that the connection between *depressed* and being very sad or having negative affect is quite opaque or even dead. But examination of this same speaker's manual gestures during talk shows her moving her hands in a slow, downward motion when saying *depressed*, which reflects her conceptual understanding of SAD IS DOWN even if her speech may be characterized, by some, as expressing, a dead metaphor (Müller 2008). Determining the degree to which any metaphor is dead, sleeping, or alive depends on assessing a person's communicative actions in the moment, involving analysis of the individual's entire repertoire of language, speech sounds, gestures, and other body movements. Most generally, judgments about whether some word or expression is metaphor or dead, or, in some people's view, "literal" cannot be reliably made by just looking at the language on the page alone.

3.2 Are some metaphors deliberate?

Skepticism about the metaphoric nature of many conventional expressions studied by cognitive linguists has most recently led to the proposal that a select few metaphors are special because they have been deliberately composed, and quite consciously employed for their unique, didactic, qualities and sometimes poetic beauty (Steen 2006). When Shakespeare wrote "Juliet is the sun" in *Romeo and Juliet*, for example, he uttered a falsehood as a deliberate invitation for listeners to understand Juliet from an unusual perspective. Conventional metaphors, on the other hand, are mostly produced and understood automatically without people having to draw any cross-domain mappings (i.e., drawing an inference from the domain of journeys to romantic relationships). People may employ certain "signaling" devices to highlight that a certain metaphor was deliberately composed and employed, such as using the words *metaphorically, actually, quite,* and *utterly,* or via phrases such as *one might say, so to speak,* and *as it were* (Goatly 1997).

Interest in the idea of deliberate metaphor stems from the concern that CMT does not pay sufficient attention to the special communicative role verbal metaphors have in discourse. But the idea that some metaphors, and not others, are deliberate in their composition and use suffers from several problems (Gibbs 2011). First, most of the signals and tuning devices discussed in the literature on "deliberate" metaphor are not at all specific to metaphor! Words and phrases such as *almost, just, and sort of* are found throughout spoken discourse and not just with metaphor. This observation implies that the so-called signaling devices used with deliberate metaphors will not really identify which metaphors are deliberate and which are not. Thankfully, Shakespeare was smart enough to resist signaling his metaphors in this way. (e.g., *Juliet is the sun, so to speak*).

A second problem with the deliberate metaphor proposal is that much cognitive linguistic research demonstrates that even conventional language implicitly conveys cross-domain mappings. Psycholinguistic research, discussed later, indicates that people infer underlying conceptual metaphors when using and understanding a range of conventional metaphoric language, including classic idioms, proverbs, and many so-called clichéd expressions, such as *We've come a long way*. Various conventional nonlinguistic actions, including gestures, music, art, and many human actions, are similarly motivated by cross-domain associations, as will be described later. Critics of cognitive linguistic work on metaphor must address the psychological research showing how conventional expressions typically evoke cross-domain mappings, exactly what is supposed to occur only for selective deliberate uses of metaphor.

Finally, psychological research shows that most creative acts are anything but conscious and deliberate (Gibbs 2011). Many cognitive unconscious forces shape the online production and understanding of metaphors, which are simply not accessible to our conscious intuitions, despite our strong beliefs to the contrary. Rather than envisioning Shakespeare, for example, as being highly conscious and deliberate in his choice of words, including his use of "Juliet is the sun", it may be more accurate to conceive of his writing as in the "flow" of experience where words and phrase cascade from his fingertips without significant conscious effort. Shakespeare may have had various aesthetic, communicative intentions in writing his poems and plays. But we should not assume that some special parts of what he wrote were deliberate, with all others being the automatic product of his unconscious mind.

3.3 Inferring conceptual metaphors

One of the most persistent criticisms of cognitive linguistic research on metaphor is that it has not provided a reliable method for inferring the existence of different conceptual metaphors. For example, Lakoff and Johnson (1980) originally stated that the conceptual metaphor ARGUMENT IS WAR motivates the existence of conventional expressions such as *He attacked my argument* and *He defended his position*. Cognitive linguistic research suggests that any expression about argument that did not fit the WAR theme is really evidence for another theme, such as WEIGHING, TESTING, or COMPARING. But this strategy implies that no linguistic statement can be brought forward as evidence against the ARGUMENT IS WAR metaphor, which makes the basic tenet of conceptual metaphor theory impossible to falsify (Vervaeke and Kennedy 1996). Furthermore, traditional cognitive linguistic analyses suggest that we understand arguments in terms of war because the source domain of war, or physical conflict is more directly related to our past and present experience. But the reverse is also true given that our experiences of arguments, which may occur daily, may be more personally salient than are wars or physical conflict (Howe 2008; Ritchie 2006).

The general question is whether cognitive linguistic analyses necessarily prove that certain conceptual metaphors, and not others, motivate the metaphoric meanings of different words and phrases. There has been fierce debate about this question both among cognitive linguists and from scholars in neighboring disciplines. Most obviously, there is no standard method for inferring the possible presence of conceptual metaphors within systematic clusters of conventional expressions, novel metaphors, polysemy, and nonlinguistic actions. Cognitive linguists learn how to do this from examples, but there is often inconsistency in the results obtained from any linguistic analysis given different analysts and different knowledge domains (Semino et al. 2004).

One possibility is that verbal metaphors have multiple, indeterminate roots which make it impossible to definitely link each verbal metaphor with a single underlying conceptual metaphor (Ritchie 2006). For example, conceptual metaphors such as ARGUMENT IS WAR arise from a large, complex, and densely interconnected set of schemes for competition and conflict, ranging from friendly, low ego-involvement games through highly competitive games, shouting matches, fisticuffs, brawls, all the way to full-scale war (Eubanks 2000). Different individuals may interpret the same expression, such as *He defended his argument*, according to varying implicit metaphors and derive different entailments. Conflict metaphors may originate with war, sports and game competitions, childhood rough and tumble play, or some other forms of interpersonal rivalry. But they all carry a set of potential meanings derived from these activities that are potentially useful to all speakers. Of course, speakers may not intend to communicate all of these, and listeners may infer only selected inferences depending on their motivations and the current discourse context. Determining the conceptual roots of any metaphoric word or phrase may ultimately be a psychological issue that is difficult to completely determine from analyzing the language alone.

A related debate in linguistic circles concerns whether conceptual metaphors are necessarily stored as pre-packaged conceptual entities in the private minds of individuals. One proposal along this line, called the "discourse dynamic approach", emphases the functions that metaphor has in "thinking and talking" rather than seeing verbal metaphors as mere linguistic manifestations of underlying conceptual metaphors (Cameron 2011). Cameron (2011) argues that the micro-level shifts and changes in the dynamics of linguistic metaphor in real discourse demonstrate the emergence of metaphor as an inherently social affair. Conventional metaphors do not have similar meanings in different contexts, but are dynamically re-created depending on the specific histories of the participants at the very points in which their talk unfolds, giving rise to in-the-moment "structural metaphors". For this reason, conceptual metaphors may be better characterized as emergent stabilities that become "actualized" as people solve different problems for themselves and coordinate their actions with others (Gibbs 2014).

4 Nonlinguistic evidence on conceptual metaphors

One longstanding complaint from psychologists about CMT is that it really requires nonlinguistic evidence to directly show that conceptual metaphors are part of thought and not just language (McGlone 2007; Murphy 1996). Finding conceptual metaphors in nonlinguistic experience is required to truly show that conceptual metaphors exist independently from language, as claimed by CMT. In fact, one of the most important applications of CMT is the emergence of studies showing the vast nonlinguistic domains that are partly structured by conceptual metaphoric knowledge (Forceville and Urios 2009; Gibbs 2008).

Take, for instance, cognitive linguistic studies on metaphoric gestures (Casasanto and Jasmin 2012; Cienki and Müller 2008). Several analyses of face-to-face conversations illustrate how metaphoric gestures support and extend information beyond that given by a speaker's words. Consider one exchange between Chinese speakers, presented in English translations (Chui 2011: 446):

S1: "If you still had had contact with the guy."
S2: "Right."
S1: "Then, you had seen him again or whatever, that is, it would have been easy for you to be bogged down in a mess."

As S1 said *bogged down* her right hand, which had been held outward at chest level, was moved down to waist level. This going down movement suggests the metaphoric idea of BAD IS DOWN, referring to the girl getting *bogged down* in the complicated love affair.

Some metaphoric gestures express ideas not strictly communicated by speech alone. Consider the following exchange (Chui 2011: 449):

S1: "We called it 'dried tea'."
S2: "Dried tea."
S3: "What?"
S1: "Dried tea. Yesterday ... it was called 'dried tea' ... when the processing was finished at night."

When S1 produced the temporal adverbial *yesterday*, his left hand moved up from the stomach level, pointing back over his shoulder with an open-palm. This movement reveals how the speaker is not specifically talking about a specific point in time, but conceives herself to be moving through time (i.e., the past is behind the ego).

In general, metaphoric gestures "substantiate cross-domain cognitive mappings ... and they evidence the presence and the real-time activation of the source domain in the mind of the speaker" (Chui 2011: 454).

There is, however, another developing literature from experimental social psychology that offers some of the most exciting, and possibly persuasive, evidence on conceptual metaphors in nonlinguistic experience. These studies have explored how metaphoric thoughts shape various social perceptions, judgments, and bodily behaviors.

For example, there is the widespread set of metaphors suggesting that GOOD IS UP and BAD IS DOWN, concepts that arise from good experiences being upward (e.g., being alive and healthy) and bad ones being downward (e.g., sickness and death).[2] Experimental studies show that people evaluate positive words faster if these are presented in a higher vertical position on a computer screen and recognize negative words faster if they appear in the lower part of the screen (Meier and Robinson 2004). Spiritual concepts are also conceived along vertical spatial dimensions. Thus, people judged words related to God faster when these were presented in the top half of the computer screen, with the opposite occurring for Devil related words (Meier et al. 2007). When asked to guess which people, based on their pictures, were more likely to believe in God, participants chose people more often when their pictures were placed along the higher vertical axis on the computer screen. These findings are consistent with the idea that people conceive of good and bad as being spatially located along some vertical dimension.

People's immediate bodily experiences can also affect their metaphorical social judgments. For example, having people make judgments about strangers'

---

[2] Once again, several linguists argue that these primary metaphors may have a metonymic basis (Barcelona 2000; Kövecses 2013; Radden 2002).

behaviors in a dirty work area caused them to rate the behavior as more immoral than when the same judgments were made in a clean work area (Schnall et al. 2008). Asking people to recall an immoral deed, as opposed to an ethical one, made them more likely to choose an antiseptic wipe as a free gift after the experiment (Zhong and Liljenquist 2006). Both these findings are consistent with the conceptual metaphors GOOD IS CLEAN and BAD IS DIRTY. People also judge a fictitious person to be more important, and a better job candidate, when they made their evaluations while holding a heavy clipboard than when holding a lighter one (Ackerman et al. 2010), which surely reflects the common idea that IMPORTANCE IS WEIGHT. People judge others to be more affectionate interpersonally after holding a warm, as opposed to a cold, cup of coffee (Williams and Bargh 2008), an expression of the basic correlation in experience of AFFECTION IS WARMTH. In general, people's immediate physical experiences have direct effects on the salience of different metaphorical, and possibly metonymic, ideas, which in turn influences their social judgments.

These studies reflect only some of the large number of experimental results showing how metaphoric concepts both emerge from correlations in bodily experience and influence people's social reasoning and actions. This line of research presents a powerful refutation to those scholars who claim that conceptual metaphors are only generalizations from language and have little to do with human thought.

5 Verbal metaphor understanding

Cognitive linguistic research on metaphor typically aims to detail the contents and structure of human conceptual systems, rather than on what specific individuals may be thinking on particular occasions. But, once more, many psychologists are skeptical of claims about human thought based solely on the analysis of linguistic patterns. They strongly argue that proposals about conceptual metaphor must be accompanied by evidence showing what people were thinking when they produced or understood verbal metaphors.

In fact, psycholinguistic studies have explored three related concerns: (a) do conceptual metaphors influence verbal problem solving and decision-making, (b) do conceptual metaphors influence people's tacit understandings of why various words and phrases express particular metaphoric meanings, and (c) do conceptual metaphors have an immediate role in people's online use and understanding of verbal metaphors. The experimental research generally suggests positive answers to all three of these questions.

5.1 Conceptual metaphors shape decision-making

Conceptual metaphor can have a significant role in people's verbal problem-solving behavior. In one set of studies, university students read a report about the crime rate in a fictitious city, named Addison (Thibodeau and Boroditsky 2011). Some of the students saw the report in which the crime was early on described as *a beast preying* on Addison, and the other students saw the crime report with a metaphor of *a virus infecting* Addison. Both stories contained identical information, presented after the metaphor, about crime statistics. After reading their respective stories, the students had to propose a solution to the Addison crime problem. The specific metaphor people read influenced their proposed crime solutions. The participants reading the *beast preying* metaphor suggested harsher enforcement always be applied to catching and jailing criminals. But participants who read the *virus infecting* metaphor proposed solutions that focused on finding the root causes of the crime and creating social programs to protect the community. Interestingly, people's problem-solving solutions was covert as students did not mention the metaphors when asked to state what influenced them the most in coming up with their crime solution (i.e., most people focused on the crime statistics). This study showed how simple metaphoric language can activate complex metaphoric knowledge that constrained people's subsequent decision-making abilities.

A different set of studies explored the ways English and Mandarin speakers solve time problems (Boroditsky 2001). Both English and Mandarin use horizontal front/back spatial terms to talk about time. For example, English speakers use expressions such as *We can look forward to the good times ahead* and *We are glad that the difficult times are behind us*, while Mandarin speakers also use vertical metaphors, so that earlier events are said to be *shàng* or 'up', and later events are described as *xià* or 'down'. About one-third of all time expressions in Mandarin use the vertical metaphor. Experimental studies show that when asked to arrange objects on a table in temporal order, one-third of Mandarins did so along vertical dimension, yet English speakers never used the vertical dimension in completing this time task. These results show how people's temporal judgments are influenced by their most salient conceptual metaphors.

5.2 Conceptual metaphors motivate metaphoric meanings

A major finding from cognitive linguistics is that conventional expressions with similar figurative meanings are sometimes motivated by different conceptual metaphors. For instance, the American conventional phrase *blow your top* expresses anger in terms of a pressurized container whose top blows off under high pressure (ANGER IS HEAT IN A PRESSURIZED CONTAINER), while *jump down your throat* reflects the metaphoric mapping ANGRY BEHAVIOR IS AGGRESSIVE ANIMAL BEHAVIOR by expressing anger in terms of an angry animal that attacks by jumping at someone's throat.

Do people tacitly understand that conventional phrases with roughly similar figurative meanings, such as *blow your top* and *jump down one's throat*, can be motivated by different conceptual metaphors? Nayak and Gibbs (1990) examined this question in a series of studies on people's intuitions about idioms and their relations to conceptual metaphors and their context-sensitive interpretations of idioms. Participants in a first study were quite good at linking idioms (e.g., *blow your stack*) with their underlying conceptual metaphors (e.g., ANGER IS HEATED FLUID IN THE BODILY CONTAINER), suggesting that they have tacit beliefs of conceptual metaphors that motivated their understanding of some idioms.

A later study asked people to read short scenarios that were constructed to prime different metaphorical mappings (e.g., ANGER IS HEAT IN A PRESSURIZED CONTAINER or ANGRY BEHAVIOR IS AGGRESSIVE ANIMAL BEHAVIOR). Participants were asked to rate the appropriateness of each idiom for the given scenario. If people access the metaphoric mappings underlying an idiom, they should choose one idiom as more appropriate given their metaphorical understanding of the story context. This is exactly what was found. These findings showed that idioms are not "dead metaphors" as traditionally assumed, because people can use the information about the conceptual metaphors underlying idiomatic phrases to make sense of why conventional metaphoric language conveys specific metaphoric meanings.

5.3 Conceptual metaphor in immediate verbal metaphor comprehension

Several psycholinguistic studies show that conceptual metaphors affect online processing of verbal metaphor. For example, people read euphemistic metaphors (e.g., *She's turning my crank* motivated by SEXUAL DESIRE IS AN ACTIVATED MACHINE) more quickly in contexts that depicted similar conceptual metaphors than in contexts that conveyed different conceptual metaphors (Pfaff et al. 1997). Similarly, novel metaphors were comprehended more quickly when they were read after a story containing conventional expressions motivated by the same conceptual metaphor than when they followed conventional expressions motivated by a different conceptual metaphor (Thibodeau and Durgin 2008). A different line of research showed that people's reading of idiomatic phrases (e.g., *John blew his stack*) primed their subsequent lexical decision judgments for word strings related to the conceptual metaphors motivating the figurative meanings of the idioms (e.g., "HEAT" for ANGER IS HEATED FLUID IN THE BODILY CONTAINER) (Gibbs et al. 1997). All these experimental studies are consistent with the idea that conceptual metaphors are actively recruited during online verbal metaphor comprehension.

One implication of cognitive linguistic analyses is that switching from one conceptual metaphor to another in discourse may require additional cognitive effort over that needed to understand metaphoric expressions motivated by the same conceptual metaphor. There have been several experimental tests of this idea. In one study, people at an airport (Chicago O'Hare) were presented a priming question about time in either the ego-moving form (e.g., *Is Boston ahead or behind in time?*) or the time-moving form (e.g., *Is it earlier or later in Boston than it is here?*) (Gentner et al. 2002). After answering, the participants were asked the target question *So should I turn my watch forward or back?* that was consistent with the ego-moving form. The experimenter measured response times to the target question with a stopwatch disguised as a wristwatch. Once again, response times for consistently primed questions were shorter than for inconsistently primed questions. Switching schemas caused an increase in processing time. These results again suggest that two distinct conceptual schemes are involved in sequencing events in time.

A different set of experiments examined people's understanding of TIME IS MOTION by first asking people to read fictive motion sentences, as in *The tattoo runs along his spine* (Matlock et al. 2005). Participants read each fictive motion statement or a sentence that did not imply fictive motion (e.g., *The tattoo is next to the spine*), and then answered the "move forward" question (e.g., *The meeting originally scheduled for next Wednesday has been moved forward two days.*). People gave significantly more Friday than Monday responses after reading the fictive motion expressions, but not the non-fictive motion statements. These results imply that people inferred TIME IS MOTION conceptual metaphor when reading the fictive motion expressions which primed their interpretation of the ambiguous "move forward" question (also see Matlock et al. 2011; Matlock and Bergmann Volume 3).

5.4 Embodied experience and verbal metaphor understanding

Many psycholinguistic studies have investigated cognitive linguistic ideas on the role of embodied experience in verbal metaphor understanding (Bergen this volume). For instance, in one series of studies on metaphorical talk about time, students waiting in line at a café were given the statement *Next Wednesday's meeting has been moved forward two days* and then asked *What day is the meeting that has been rescheduled?* (Boroditsky and Ramscar 2002). Students who were farther along in the line (i.e., who had thus very recently experienced more forward spatial motion) were more likely to say that the meeting had been moved to Friday, rather than to Monday. Similarly, people riding a train were presented the same ambiguous statement and question about the rescheduled meeting. Passengers who were at the end of their journeys reported that the meeting was moved to Friday significantly more than did people in the middle of their journeys. Although both groups of passengers were experiencing the same physical experience of sitting in a moving train, they thought differently about their journey and consequently responded differently to the rescheduled meeting question. These results suggest how ongoing sensorimotor experience has an influence on people's comprehension of metaphorical statements about time.

The idea that embodied simulations play some role in people's immediate processing of verbal metaphors, and language more generally, has received much attention in recent psycholinguistic research (Bergen 2012, this volume; Gibbs 2006). People may, for instance, be creating partial, but not necessarily complete, embodied simulations of speakers' metaphorical messages that involve moment-by-moment "what must it be like" processes as if they were immersed in the discourse situation. More dramatically, these simulation processes operate even when people encounter language that is abstract, or refers to actions that are physically impossible to perform. For example, Gibbs et al. (2006) demonstrated how people's mental imagery for metaphorical phrases, such as *tear apart the argument*, exhibit significant embodied qualities of the actions referred to by these phrases (e.g., people conceive of the *argument* as a physical object that when torn apart no longer persists). Wilson and Gibbs (2007) showed that people's speeded comprehension of metaphorical phrases like *grasp the concept* are facilitated when they first make, or imagine making, in this case, a grasping movement. These findings indicate that relevant bodily movement does not interfere with people's comprehension of abstract metaphoric meaning, a position advocated by traditional metaphor theorists. Instead, moving in certain ways enhances the embodied simulations people ordinary construct during their interpretation of metaphoric language (also see Johansson-Falck and Gibbs 2012).

My review of psycholinguistic studies suggests that there is much experimental evidence to support aspects of CMT as a psychological theory of verbal metaphor understanding. Of course, as many critics note, CMT is not a complete theory that explains all aspects of how people interpret metaphoric meanings. Much other social and cultural knowledge is relevant to people's context-sensitive understandings of metaphor. Furthermore, metaphor understanding relies on a variety of other linguistic factors, which linguists and psychologists have taken pains to show are very relevant, and yet ignored by CMT (e.g., Giora 2003, Volume 3; Svanlund 2007). There are also a few experimental studies whose findings appear to be contrary to the claims of CMT (Keysar and Bly 1995; Keysar et al. 2000). Some scholars criticize these contrary studies because of methodological and stimuli problems (Thibodeau and Boroditsky 2011). In general, though, the psycholinguistic evidence together presents an overwhelming body of work showing that conceptual metaphors are significant parts, yet not the only factors, in how people use and understand metaphoric language.

6 Conclusion

This chapter has touched on only some of the relevant linguistic and psycholinguistic work related to cognitive linguistic theories of metaphor. This collected body of research offers strong support for the major claim that enduring metaphoric thoughts have a primary role in verbal metaphor use and understanding. But cognitive linguists, and others, should articulate criteria for identifying metaphoric patterns in language and inferring specific conceptual metaphors from discourse. These procedures should be specified with sufficient detail so that other researchers can possibly replicate the analysis and emerge with similar conclusions (see Gibbs 2007). Adopting explicit procedures for metaphor identification in language and thought should help move cognitive linguistics closer to scientific practices within other fields in the cognitive sciences.

Finally, human cognition and language is always situated and influenced by the history of people's experiences up to that moment in time, as well as expectations about what is likely to occur next in human interaction. Consider a brief conversational exchange between two scientists discussing one of their theories in which one person states that, *I can't see the point of your argument. Your theory needs more support* (Gibbs and Santa Cruz, 2012). Figure 8.1 presents a schematic description of how a listener understands these conventional metaphoric expressions, according to a standard analysis within CMT.

Under this model, a listener hears an utterance and then automatically searches for relevant conceptual knowledge to understand what the speaker means. For the first expression, *I can't see the point of your argument*, people search for and then access the enduring metaphorical idea that UNDERSTANDING IS SEEING. Afterward, listeners apply this metaphoric concept to infer that

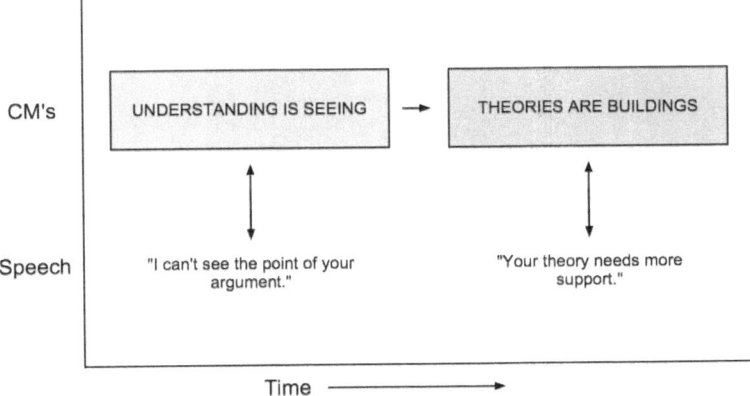

Fig. 8.1: Sequential Activation of Conceptual Metaphors.

the speaker meant he could not understand what his addressee was previously trying to say by his argument. Similarly, listeners next access the relevant metaphoric idea that THEORIES ARE BUILDINGS to interpret the following statement *Your theory needs more support*. In this manner, enduring conceptual metaphors are sequentially retrieved from long-term memory and then applied to create contextually-sensitive interpretations of speakers' metaphorical utterances.

But the complex reality of human interaction suggests that multiple forces simultaneously constrain people's understanding of verbal metaphors. People's interpretation of *Your theory needs more support* may be influenced by conceptual metaphors recruited during understanding of previous verbal metaphors and metaphorical gestures, as well as by conceptual metaphors that are most relevant to the particular utterance currently being processed (i.e., UNDERSTANDING IS SEEING), along with any other presently enacted metaphorical gestures (e.g., imagine the speaker placing a cupped hand outward signifying the foundation for THEORIES ARE BUILDINGS). Figure 8.2 presents a schematic representation of this account.

Under this theoretical model, conceptual metaphors are not necessarily accessed en bloc, with all their possible entailments spelled out, but can contribute partial constraints on people's metaphoric behaviors (i.e., similar to many "constraint satisfaction theories" of human cognition). This dynamical view does not deny that conceptual metaphors are an entrenched part of human cognition, yet sees the conventionalization of metaphoric thought and language as a continually emergent process, serving multiple adaptive purposes in everyday life (see MacWhinney Volume 3).

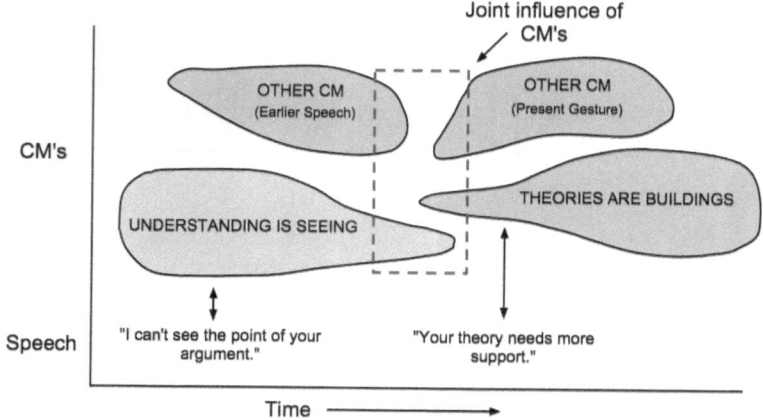

Fig. 8.2: Interacting Subsystem of Constraints.

Cognitive linguists should study more of the complex temporal realities of human interaction to uncover the continuing presence of past conceptual metaphors in their analyses of verbal metaphor understanding. Moreover, we need to explore the ways different metaphoric concepts combine in probabilistic ways to shape any moment of metaphoric experience. The cognitive theory of metaphor has revolutionized the world of metaphor scholarship, but it is time to escape the traditional study of language on the page and see metaphor as something people do rather than something they tacitly know.

7 References

Barnden, John (2011): Metaphor and metonymy: Making their connections more slippery. *Cognitive Linguistics* 21: 1–34.
Barcelona, Antonio (2000): On the plausibility of claiming a metonymic motivation for metaphorical mappings In: A. Barcelona (ed.), *Metaphor and Metonymy at the Crossroads. A Cognitive Perspective*, 31–58. Berlin: Mouton de Gruyter.
Barcelona, Antonio (this volume): Metonymy. Berlin/Boston: De Gruyter Mouton.
Beardsley, Monroe (1962): The metaphorical twist. *Philosophy and Phenomenological Research* 22: 293–307.
Bergen, Benjamin (2012): *Louder than Words: The New Science of How the Mind Makes Meaning*. New York: Basic Books.
Bergen, Benjamin (this volume): Embodiment. Berlin/Boston: De Gruyter Mouton.
Boroditsky, Lera (2001): Does language shape thought? English and Mandarin speakers' conceptions of time. *Cognitive Psychology* 43: 1–22.
Boroditsky, Lera and Michael Ramscar (2002): The roles of body and mind in abstract thought. *Psychological Science* 13: 185–189.

Cameron, Lynne (2011): *Metaphor and Reconciliation: The Discourse Dynamics of Empathy in Post-Conflict Conversations*. London: Routledge.
Casasanto, Daniel and Kyle Jasmin (2012): The hands of time: Temporal gestures in English speakers. *Cognitive Linguistics* 23: 653–674.
Charteris-Black, Jonathan (2004): *Corpus Approaches to Critical Metaphor Analysis*. Basingstoke: Palgrave Macmillan.
Chui, Kawai (2011): Conceptual metaphors in gesture. *Cognitive Linguistics* 22: 437–459.
Cienki, Alan and Cornelia Müller (eds.), (2008): *Metaphor and Gesture*. Amsterdam: Benjamins.
Cuyckens, Hubert and Brigitte Zawada (eds.), (2001): *Polysemy in Cognitive Linguistics*. Amsterdam: Benjamins.
Deignan, Alice (2005): *Metaphor and Corpus Linguistics*. Amsterdam: Benjamins.
Desai, Rutvik, Jeffrey Binder, Lisa Conant, Quintano Mano, and Mark Seidenberg (2011): The neural career of sensory-motor metaphors. *Journal of Cognitive Neuroscience* 23: 2376–2386.
Eubanks, Philip (2000): *A War of Words in the Discourse of Trade: The Rhetorical Constitution of Metaphor*. Carbondale: Southern Illinois University Press.
Fauconnier, Gilles and George Lakoff (2013): On blending and metaphor. *Journal of Cognitive Semiotics* 5: 393–399.
Fauconnier, Gilles and Mark Turner (2002): *The Way We Think: Conceptual Blending and the Mind's Hidden Complexities*. New York: Basic Books.
Feldman, Jerome (2006): *From Molecule to Metaphor: A Neural Theory of Language*. Cambridge: MIT Press.
Forceville, Charles and Eduardo Urios-Aparisi (eds.) (2009): *Multimodal Metaphor*. Berlin: Mouton De Gruyter.
Freeman, Dan (1995): Catch(ing) the nearest way: Macbeth and cognitive metaphor. *Journal of Pragmatics* 24: 689–708.
Gentner, Dedre, Imai, D., and Lera Boroditsky (2002): As time goes by: Understanding time as spatial metaphor. *Language and Cognitive Processes* 17: 537–565.
Gibbs, Raymond (1994): *The Poetics of Mind: Figurative Thought, Language, and Understanding*. New York: Cambridge University Press.
Gibbs, Raymond (2006): *Embodiment and Cognitive Science*. New York: Cambridge University Press.
Gibbs, Raymond (2007): Why cognitive linguists should care about empirical methods? In: M. Gonzalez-Marquez, I. Mittelberg, S. Coulson, and M. Spivey (eds.), *Methods in Cognitive Linguistics*, 2–18. Amsterdam: Benjamins.
Gibbs, Raymond (ed.) (2008): *The Cambridge Handbook of Metaphor and Thought*. New York: Cambridge University Press.
Gibbs, Raymond (2011): Are deliberate metaphors really deliberate? A question of human consciousness and action. *Metaphor and the Social World*. 1: 26–52.
Gibbs, Raymond (2014): Conceptual metaphor in thought and social action. In: M. Landau, M. Robinson, and B. Meier (eds.), *Metaphorical Thought in Social Life*. 17–50. Washington, DC: APA Books.
Gibbs, Raymond, Jody Bogdanovich, Jeffrey Sykes, and Dale Barr (1997): Metaphor in idiom comprehension. *Journal of Memory and Language* 37: 141–154.
Gibbs, Raymond, Jessica Gould, and Michael Andric (2006): Imagining metaphorical actions: Embodied simulations make the impossible plausible. *Imagination, Cognition, and Personality,* 25(3): 215–238.

Gibbs, Raymond and Malaika Santa Cruz (2012): Temporal unfolding of conceptual metaphoric experience. *Metaphor and Symbol* 27: 299–311.

Giora, Rachel (2003): *On our Minds: Salience, Context and Figurative Language*. New York: Oxford University Press.

Giora, Rachel (Volume 3): Default nonliteral interpretations. Berlin/Boston: De Gruyter Mouton.

Goatly, Andrew (1997): *The Language of Metaphors*. New York: Routledge.

Goldberg, Adele (1995): *Constructions: A Construction Grammar Approach to Argument Structure*. Chicago: University of Chicago Press.

Grady, Joseph (1997): Theories are buildings revisited. *Cognitive Linguistics* 8: 267–290.

Grady, Joseph, Todd Oakley, and Seana Coulson (1999): Blending and metaphor. In: R. Gibbs and G. Steen (eds.), *Metaphor in Cognitive Linguistics*, 101–124. Amsterdam: Benjamins.

Gries, Stefan Th. (Volume 3): Polysemy. Berlin/Boston: De Gruyter Mouton.

Gries, Stefan Th. and Anatol Stefanowitsch (eds.) (2006): *Corpus Based Approaches to Metaphor and Metonymy*. Berlin/New York: Mouton de Gruyter.

Howe, James (2008): Argument is argument: An essay on conceptual metaphor and verbal dispute. *Metaphor and Symbol* 23: 1–23.

Jackendoff, Ray and David Aaron (1991): Review of Lakoff and Turner (1989). *Language* 67: 320–328.

Johansson-Falck, Marlene and Raymond Gibbs (2012): Embodied motivations for metaphoric meanings. *Cognitive Linguistics* 23: 251–272.

Keysar, Boaz and Brigitte Bly (1995): Intuitions of the transparency of idioms: Can one keep a secret by spilling the beans? *Journal of Memory and Language* 34: 89–109.

Keysar, Boaz, Yeshahayu Shen, Sam Glucksberg, and William s. Horton (2000): Conventional language: How metaphoric is it? *Journal of Memory and Language* 43: 576–593.

Koller, Veronika (2004): *Metaphor and Gender in Business Media Discourse: A Critical Cognitive Study*. Basingstoke: Palgrave.

Kövecses, Zoltán (2002): *Metaphor: A Practical Introduction*. New York: Oxford University Press.

Kövecses, Zoltán (2013): The metaphor-metonymy relationship: Correlation metaphors are based on metonymy. *Metaphor and Symbol* 28: 75–88.

Lakoff, George (2008): The neural theory of metaphor. In: R. Gibbs (ed.), *Cambridge Handbook of Metaphor and Thought*, 17–38. New York: Cambridge University Press.

Lakoff, George and Mark Johnson (1980): *Metaphors We Live By*. Chicago: University of Chicago Press.

Lakoff, George and Mark Johnson (1999): *Philosophy in the Flesh*. New York: Basic Books.

Lakoff, George and Mark Turner (1989): *More than Cool Reason: A Field Guide to Poetic Metaphor*. Chicago: University of Chicago Press.

Langacker, Ronald W. (1999): *Grammar and Conceptualization*. Berlin: Mouton.

Lizardo, Omar (2012): The conceptual bases of metaphors of dirt and cleanliness in moral and nonmoral reasoning. *Cognitive Linguistics* 23: 367–394.

MacWhinney, Brian (Volume 3): Emergentism. Berlin/Boston: De Gruyter Mouton.

Matlock, Teenie, and Till Bergmann (Volume 3): Fictive motion. Berlin/Boston: De Gruyter Mouton.

Matlock, Teenie, Kevin Holmes, Mahesh Srinivasan, and Michael Ramscar (2011): Even abstract motion influences the understanding of time. *Metaphor and Symbol* 26: 260–271.

Matlock, Teenie, Michael Ramscar, and Lera Boroditsky (2005): On the experiential link between spatial and temporal language. *Cognitive Science* 29: 655–664.

McGlone, Mathew (2007): What is the explanatory value of a conceptual metaphor? *Language and Communication* 27: 109–126.

Meier, Brian and Michael Robinson (2004): Why the sunny side is up. *Psychological Science* 15: 243–247.

Meier, Brian, Michael Robinson, Elizabeth Crawford, and W. Ahlvers (2007): When 'light' and 'dark' thoughts become light and dark responses: Affect biases brightness judgments. *Emotion* 7: 366–376.

Müller, Cornelia (2008): Metaphors Dead and Alive, *Sleeping and Waking: A Dynamic View*. Chicago: University of Chicago Press.

Murphy, Gregory (1996): On metaphoric representations. *Cognition* 60: 173–204.

Mussolff, Andreas (2004): *Metaphor and Political Discourse*. Basingstoke: Palgrave Macmillan.

Naciscione, Anita (2010): *Stylistic Use of Phraseological Units in Discourse*. Amsterdam: Benjamins.

Nayak, Nandini and Raymond Gibbs (1990): Conceptual knowledge in the interpretation of idioms. *Journal of Experimental Psychology: General* 119: 315–330.

Oakley, Todd and Anders Hougaard (eds.) (2008): *Mental Spaces in Discourse and Interaction*. Amsterdam: Benjamins.

Panther, Klaus-Uwe, and LindaThornburg (2009): On figuration in grammar. In: K.-U. Panther, L. Thornburg, and A. Barcelona (eds.), *Metonymy and Metaphor in Grammar*, 1–44. Amsterdam: Benjamins.

Pfaff, Kerry, Raymond Gibbs, and Michael Johnson (1997): Metaphor in using and understanding euphemism and dysphemism. *Applied Psycholinguistics* 18: 59–83.

Pragglejaz Group (2007): MIP: A method for identifying metaphorically-used words in discourse. *Metaphor and Symbol* 22: 1–40.

Radden, Gunther (1995): Motion metaphorized. The case of coming and going. In: E. Casad (ed.), *Cognitive Linguistics in the Redwoods: The Expansion of a New Paradigm in Linguistics*, 423–458. New York: Mouton de Gruyter.

Radden, Gunther (2002): How metonymic are metaphors. In: R. Dirven and R. Pörings (eds.), *Metaphor and Metonymy in Comparison and Contrast*, 407–424. Berlin/New York: Mouton de Gruyter.

Ricoeur, Paul (1977): *The Rule of Metaphor*. Toronto: University of Toronto Press.

Ritchie, David (2006): *Context and Communication in Metaphor*. Basingstoke: Palgrave.

Ruiz de Mendoza, Francisco and Olga Díez (2002): Patterns of conceptual interaction. In: R. Dirven and R. Pörings (eds.), *Metaphor and Metonymy in Comparison and Contrast*, 489–532. Berlin/New York: Mouton de Gruyter.

Schnall, Simone, Jennifer Benton, and Sophie Harvey (2008): With a clean conscience: Cleanliness reduces the severity of moral judgments. *Psychological Science* 19: 1219–122.

Semino, Elena (2009): *Metaphor in Discourse*. New York: Cambridge University Press.

Semino, Elena, John Heywood, and Mick Short (2004): Methodological problems in the analysis of a corpus of conversations about cancer. *Journal of Pragmatics* 36: 1271–1294.

Sjoblad, Aron (2009): *Metaphors Cicero Lived By*. Lund: Center for Languages and Literature, Lund University.

Steen, Gerard (2006): The paradox of metaphor: Why we need a three-dimensional model of metaphor. *Metaphor and Symbol* 23: 213–241.

Steen, Gerard, Dorst, Aletta, Berenike Herrmann, Anna Kaal, Tina Krennmayr, and Trijintje Pasma (2010): *A Method for Linguistic Metaphor Identification*. Amsterdam: Benjamins.

Stefanowitsch, Anatol (2011): Cognitive linguistics as cognitive science. In: M. Callies, W. Keller, and A. Lohofer (eds.), *Bi-directionality in the Cognitive Sciences*, 295–310. Amsterdam: Benjamins.

Svanlund, Jan (2007): Metaphor and convention. *Cognitive Linguistics* 18: 47–89.

Sweetser, Eve (1990): *From Etymology to Pragmatics: Metaphorical and Cultural Aspects of Semantic Structure*. New York: Cambridge University Press.

Tendahl, Markus (2008): *A Hybrid Theory of Metaphor*. Basingstoke: Palgrave.

Thibodeau Paul and Lera Boroditsky (2011): Metaphors we think with: The role of metaphor in reasoning. PLoS ONE, 6 (2): e16782.

Thibodeau, Paul and Frank Durgin (2008): Productive figurative communication: Conventional metaphors facilitate the comprehension of related novel metaphors. *Journal of Memory and Language* 58: 521–540.

Turner, Mark (this volume): Blending in language and communication. Berlin/Boston: De Gruyter Mouton.

Vervaeke, John and John Kennedy (1996): Metaphors in language and thought: Disproof and multiple meanings. *Metaphor and Symbolic Activity* 11: 273–284.

Williams, Lawrence and John Bargh (2008): Experiencing physical warm influences interpersonal warmth. *Science* 322: 606–607.

Wilson, Nicole and Raymond Gibbs (2007): Real and imagined body movement primes metaphor comprehension. *Cognitive Science* 31: 721–731.

Zhong, Chen-Bo and Katie Liljenquist (2006): Washing away your sins: Threatened morality and physical cleansing. *Science* 313: 1451–1452.

Andrews, Mark, Gabriella Vigliocco, and David P. Vinson (2009): Integrating experiential and distributional data to learn semantic representations. *Psychological Review* 116(3): 463–498.

Laura J. Speed, David P. Vinson, and Gabriella Vigliocco
Chapter 9: Representing Meaning

1 Introduction

Understanding the meaning of words is crucial to our ability to communicate. To do so we must reliably map the arbitrary form of a spoken, written or signed word to the corresponding concept whether it is present in the environment, tangible or merely imagined (Meteyard et al. 2012: 2). In this chapter we review two current approaches to understanding word meaning from a psychological perspective: embodied and distributional theories. Embodied theories propose that understanding words' meanings requires mental simulation of entities being referred to (e.g., Barsalou 1999; see also Bergen this volume) using the same modality-specific systems involved in perceiving and acting upon such entities in the world. Distributional theories on the other hand typically describe meaning in terms of language use: something arising from statistical patterns that exist amongst words in a language. Instead of focusing on bodily experience, distributional theories focus upon linguistic data, using statistical techniques to describe words' meanings in terms of distributions across different linguistic contexts (e.g., Landauer and Dumais 1997; Griffiths et al. 2007). These two general approaches are traditionally used in opposition, although this does not need to be the case (Andrews et al. 2009) and in fact by integrating them we may have better semantic models (Vigliocco et al. 2009).

We will highlight some key issues in lexical representation and processing and describe historical predecessors for embodied theories (i.e., featural approaches) and distributional theories (i.e., holistic approaches). We conclude by proposing an integrated model of meaning where embodied and linguistic information are both considered vital to the representation of words' meanings.

2 Key issues in semantic representation

A theory of semantic representation must satisfactorily address two key issues: representation of words from different content domains and the relationship between semantics (word meaning) and conceptual knowledge.

Laura J. Speed, York, UK
David P. Vinson, London, UK
Gabriella Vigliocco, London, UK

https://doi.org/10.1515/9783110626476-010

2.1 Are words from different domains represented in the same way?

The vast majority of research investigating semantic representation has focused on concrete nouns. The past decade has seen increasing research into the representation of action verbs and a beginning of interest in the study of how abstract meaning is represented. A critical question is whether the same overarching principles can be used across these domains, or whether organisational principles must differ.

A fundamental difference between objects and actions is that objects can be thought of in isolation, as discrete entities, but actions are more complex, describing relations among multiple participants (Vigliocco et al. 2011). Connected to this are temporal differences: actions tend to be dynamic events with a particular duration while objects are stable with long-term states.

Because of the stable nature of objects, nouns' meanings tend to be relatively fixed. Verbs' meanings are less constrained and often more polysemous. These differences could underscore different representational principles for object-nouns and action-verbs, but do not preclude a semantic system in which objects and actions are represented in the same manner and differences in organisation arise from differences in representational content. Such an example is described by Vigliocco et al's (2004) FUSS model, in which representations for action and object words are modelled in the same lexico-semantic space, using the same principles and tools. Differences emerge from differences in the featural properties of the two domains rather than different principles of organisation.

When comparing concrete and abstract words, there is a stronger case for assuming different content and different organisational principles. It is well established that processing abstract words takes longer than processing concrete words (the "concreteness effect") for which Paivio's dual-coding theory provides a long-standing account (e.g., Paivio 1986). Under this view two separate systems contribute to word meaning: a word-based system and an image-based system. Whereas concrete words use both systems (with greater reliance on the latter), abstract words rely solely on word-based information. The concreteness effect would occur because concrete words use two systems instead of one, thus having richer and qualitatively different semantic representations than abstract words.

An alternative view, the context availability theory (Schwanenflugel and Shoben 1983), does not require multiple representational systems to account for the concreteness effect. Under this view, advantages for concrete words come from differences in associations between words and previous knowledge (i.e., differences in the number of links, rather than in content/organisation), with abstract concepts being associated with much less context. Here the concreteness effect results from the availability of sufficient context for processing concrete concepts in most language situations, but deficient context for processing abstract words (Schwanenflugel and Shoben 1983).

More recent proposals for the differences between concrete and abstract concepts and words include viewing abstract knowledge as arising out of metaphorical extension (Boroditsky 2000; Lakoff and Johnson 1980; Bergen this volume; Gibbs this volume), or differences in featural properties rather than different principles of organisation for abstract and concrete meaning: sensorimotor information underlying concrete meanings and affective and linguistic information underlying abstract meanings (Kousta et al. 2011).

To summarise, theories of semantic representation make different assumptions about semantic representations for different domains of knowledge, varying from a single, unitary semantic system to a much more fractionated system, where different principles of organisation are specified for different word types. However, there exists no strong evidence for assuming different principles, and following the argument of parsimony, we argue for a unitary system based on the same principles across domains. Instead of different organisational principles, differences across domains come about due to differences in content, namely differences in the extent to which a given type of content is most important for a given domain: sensory-motor information for the concrete domain and emotion and linguistic information for the abstract domain (Vigliocco et al. 2009).

2.2 How is conceptual knowledge linked to word meaning?

The fundamental goal of language is to talk about "stuff" such as objects, events, feelings, situations and imaginary worlds. Thus, there must be a strong mapping between our conceptual knowledge (the knowledge we use to categorise and understand the world) and the language we use. Since we begin life exploring and learning about our world, with language developing later, conceptual knowledge ultimately must develop before language. One important issue then is how words relate to conceptual knowledge. Should we think of word meanings and concepts interchangeably? This relationship has many important implications, for example, the extent of translation equivalency across languages.

One argument for treating words and concepts interchangeably is that many robust phenomena have been found to affect them both. If the same factors affect both and they behave similarly, then they must be closely linked, if not interchangeable. For example, feature type, feature correlations and distinguishing features have been shown to explain category-specific deficits in categorization of concepts (e.g., McRae and Cree 2002) and semantic priming effects for words (McRae and Boisvert 1998). Because characteristics of conceptual features seem to have comparable effects it would be parsimonious to consider conceptual representations the same as word meaning (consistent with Langacker 1982).

There are reasons, however to suggest that there is not a one-to-one mapping between the two. First, we possess far more concepts than words. There are often actions or situations that we know well and understand that are not lexicalized such as "the actions of two people manoeuvring for one armrest in a movie theatre or airplane seat" (Hall 1984 discussed in Murphy 2002). Further, one word can be used to refer to multiple meanings (e.g., polysemy) and so refers to a set of concepts instead of a single concept (see Gries Volume 3). This matter is further complicated when we look at cross-linguistic differences in links between conceptual knowledge and linguistic representations (see Vigliocco and Filipović 2004).

There are many examples of cross-linguistic differences in semantic representations that do not have any obvious explanations. For instance, although both English speakers and Italian speakers use different words to denote *foot* and *leg*, Japanese speakers use the same word *ashi* to describe both. One could hardly argue that conceptually, Japanese speakers do not know the difference between one's foot and one's leg. If linguistic categories are based on one-to-one mappings with conceptual structure, then cross-linguistic differences have clear implications for the assumption of universality of conceptual structure.

With the above issues in mind, below we present the two main perspectives on semantic representation, guided by the ideas that the same organising principles apply across word types and that meaning is distinct from but strongly linked to conceptual knowledge (e.g., Vigliocco and Filipović, 2004).

3 Theoretical perspectives

The main theoretical approaches to word meaning can be clustered into those that consider our sensorimotor experience as the building blocks of semantic representation and those that instead consider statistical patterns in language as the building blocks. This great divide corresponds to disciplinary boundaries between cognitive psychology and neuroscience on one side and computational linguistics and computer science on the other side. Within linguistics, both perspectives are represented as reflecting the distinction between sense and reference since Frege ([1892] 1952).

3.1 Embodiment

Embodied approaches posit that understanding words' meanings involves engagement of the systems used in perception, action and introspection (e.g., Barsalou 1999; Svesson 1999; Evans 2003; Lakoff and Johnson 1999; Bergen this volume). This approach focuses on content of semantic representations rather than relationships among them in semantic memory. Embodied theorists argue against "amodal" models of semantics (Figure 9.1a) because they are missing the vital link between meaning in language and experience in the real world. In other words, it is unclear how the meaning of a word is understood if language is simply made up of arbitrary symbols not linked to referents or experiences in the world (Harnad 1990). Here, to understand a word one simulates its meaning in the brain's sensorimotor systems, similarly to actually experiencing that concept. Instead of transducing information from experience into abstract symbols, the experience itself is, in a way, recreated (Barsalou 1999) (see Figure 9.1b). The distinction between conception and perception is blurred (Lakoff and Johnson 1999).

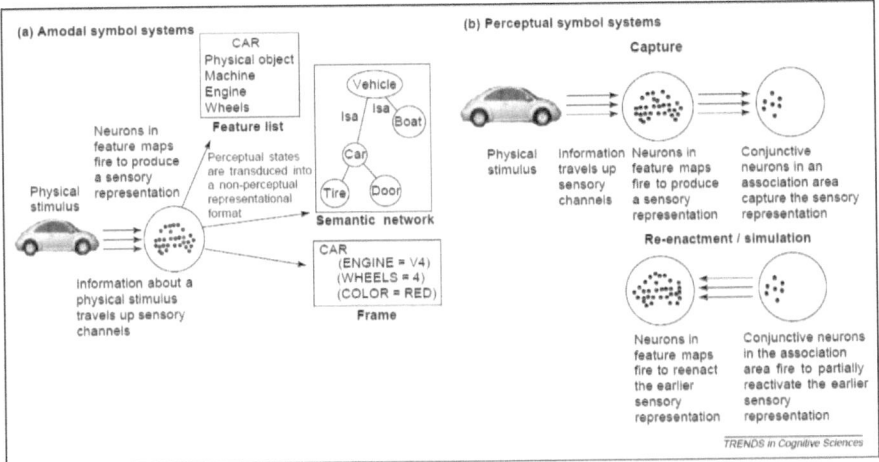

Fig. 9.1: Amodal vs. perceptual symbols. Taken from Barsalou, L. W., Simmons, W. K., Barbey, A., and Wilson, C. D. (2003). Grounding conceptual knowledge in modality-specific systems. *Trends in Cognitive Sciences*, 7, 84–91. (a) In amodal symbol systems neural representations from vision are transduced in an amodal representation such as a frame, semantic network or feature list. These amodal representations are used during word understanding. (b) In perceptual symbol systems neural representations from vision are partially captured by conjunctive neurons, which are later activated during word comprehension to re-enact the earlier state.

3.1.1 Featural theories as precursors to embodiment

Embodiment places emphasis on sensorimotor features as building blocks of meaning. This emphasis is shared with classic featural theories where a word's meaning is decomposable into a set of defining features (e.g., Collins and Quillian 1969; Rosch and Mervis 1975). Sets of conceptual features are bound together to form a lexical representation of the word's meaning. For example, the meaning of *chair* could be defined by features including *has legs*, *made of wood* and *is sat on*.

Featural properties of different word categories have been modeled to explain category-specific deficits in different forms of brain damage and to shed light on the organisation of the semantic system (e.g., Farah and McClelland 1991). By looking at the proportion of perceptual (e.g., *has fur*) and functional (e.g., *cuts food*) features for artifacts and natural kinds, Farah and McClelland (1991) described the topographic organisation of semantic memory in terms of modality rather than category. In their simulations, damage to perceptual features only caused selective deficits for processing of natural kinds, whereas conversely, damage to functional features only caused selective deficits for processing of artifacts. What was once seen as a category-specific deficit therefore emerged as a result of damage to specific feature types, suggesting that semantic memory is organised in terms of sensorimotor features and not categories.

In featural theories, semantic similarity between words can be described in terms of featural correlations and featural overlap. Both measures have been validated as indications of semantic similarity in behavioural tasks such as semantic priming (e.g., McRae and Boisvert 1998). Featural theories have been applied to explain differences between words referring to objects (nouns) and words referring to events (primarily verbs referring to actions) in terms of feature types and associations between features. Nouns' meanings appear to be more differentiated, with dense associations between features and properties (Tyler et al. 2001) across many different sensory domains (Damasio and Tranel 1993). They also have more specific features referring to narrow semantic fields, whereas verbs typically consist of features applying broadly across semantic fields and with less sensory associations (Vinson and Vigliocco 2002). In this sense, verbs could be considered to be more abstract than nouns (Bird et al. 2003). These differences have been invoked to account for patients with selective deficits in retrieving and producing nouns and those who had more problems with verbs (see Vigliocco et al. 2011). It is questionable whether these theories can be extended to account for differences between concrete and abstract words. However, a recently published collection of feature norms found that participants can generate features for abstract words with general agreement across subjects that could not be explained simply by associations (Buchanan et al. 2012).

Featural theories usually focus on concepts, not words (although concepts and words are often implicitly or explicitly assumed as the same). There are theories, however, that assume a separate semantic level where features are bound into a lexico-semantic representation (Vigliocco et al. 2004), and others that hypothesize "convergence zones" in the brain where information from multiple modalities is integrated (Damasio 1989; Simmons and Barsalou 2003; see Vigliocco et al. 2012).

Embodiment theories build upon these earlier accounts, as research that supports featural representations is necessarily compatible with embodied views. For example, semantic priming based on overlapping features (McRae and Boisvert 1998) could be explained by overlap in activation of the same sensorimotor area (e.g., Pecher et al. 2003).

3.1.2 Research supporting embodied theories

A large amount of behavioural evidence demonstrates the use of sensorimotor systems in language processing, typically with interactions between the processing of words' semantic content and sensory information (see Bergen this volume). For example, Meteyard et al. (2007) showed that visual discrimination of moving dots was hindered when processing direction verbs of the same direction (e.g., *dive, rise*). Conversely, lexical decisions to direction verbs were hindered when participants concurrently perceived motion of a matching direction at near-threshold levels (Meteyard et al. 2008). If processing semantic content involves shared sensory-motor systems, then combining word processing and sensory-motor processing should affect performance.

Numerous imaging studies provide support for embodied language processing, showing that areas of the brain involved in perception and action are engaged when processing words with similar content. For example, listening to verbs related to leg, face or arm action such as *kick, lick* and *pick* activates the motor cortex somatotopically (Hauk et al. 2004). This activation reflects action specificity, for example, a region within the bilateral inferior parietal lobule showed differential patterns of activation to words of different levels of specificity e.g., *to clean* versus *to wipe* (van Dam et al. 2010), and moreover is differentially lateralised depending upon participants' handedness indicating that the sensorimotor activation underlying word meaning is body-specific (Willems et al. 2010).

Strong evidence for the role of sensorimotor systems in word comprehension comes from studies in which deficits in motor or sensory processing result in a selective deficit in word processing of the same category. If sensorimotor systems play a critical role in semantic representation, damage to these areas should disrupt semantic processing of those word types. Research of this nature tends to look at patients with impairments in planning and executing actions, e.g., patients with motor neuron disease (e.g., Bak et al. 2001) or Parkinson's disease (e.g., Boulenger et al. 2008). Bak et al. (2001) found comprehension and production of verbs was significantly more impaired than nouns for patients with motor neuron disease but not for healthy controls or patients with Alzheimer's disease who have both semantic and syntactic language impairments. This selective deficit in patients with motor neuron disease suggests that the processes underlying verb representation is strongly related to those of the motor systems (see Vigliocco et al. 2011 for a review). In addition, transcranial magnetic simulation (TMS) over specific brain regions has been shown to influence processing of related word types, such as the motor strip and action verbs (e.g., Pulvermuller et al. 2005).

Critics have argued that embodied results may simply be epiphenomenal: the result of spreading activation from amodal representations to perceptual areas via indirect, associative routes due to the correlation between the two (e.g., Mahon and Caramazza 2008). Mahon and Caramazza (2008) argue that existing evidence can be explained by unembodied theories in which semantic information is independent of sensory-motor information. The observed interactions could come about indirectly; for example, semantic information may engage working memory systems which in turn recruit sensory-motor systems (Meteyard et al. 2012: 3). This argument however seems to fall short of explaining the observed lesion and TMS data. That is, if semantic processing is affected by disruption of the corresponding sensory-motor areas, then the affected areas must be a necessary part of semantic representation, and not epiphenomenal. Mahon and Caramazza's view is not completely disembodied, but rather falls along a continuum, as we will describe in the next section.

3.1.3 Different versions of embodiment

Theories of embodiment vary in terms of how strongly they define the role of the sensorimotor systems in semantic representation. Theories can be considered along a continuum from strongly embodied (full simulation), through weak embodiment and secondary embodiment, and then moving beyond embodiment to fully symbolic, disembodied theories (Meteyard et al. 2012; see Figure 9.2). Distributional approaches could be placed on the extreme, "disembodied" end of the continuum, assigning no role for sensory-motor information. Theories

Label	Unembodied	Secondary embodiment	Weak embodiment	Strong embodiment
Semantic Content	Symbolic/Amodal	Amodal	Cross-modal integration/ Supramodal	Analogue/Multimodal
Neural Architecture	Semantic region(s) have no temporal or spatial overlap with sensory and motor areas	Region for amodal semantic content plus modality specific regions which code experiential attributes	Distributed network of areas which code integrated modal information, proximal to primary sensory and motor regions	Distributed network of areas within primary sensory and motor systems
Relationship to sensory-motor systems	Complete independence	Independent but associated	Partial dependence	Complete dependence
Explanation of interactions	Indirect activation	Secondary activation	Mediation	Modulation
Theories	Collins and Loftus (1975); Landauer and Dumais (1997); Lund, Burgess and Atchley (1995); Griffiths et al. (2007)	Mahon and Caramazza (2008); Patterson et al. (2007); Quillian (1968)	Barsalou (1999); Farah and McClelland (1991); Pulvermuller (1999); Simmons and Barsalou (2003); Vigliocco et al. (2004); Louwerse (2007); Vigliocco et al. (2009)	Glenberg and Gallese (2012); Pecher, Zeelenberg and Barsalou (2003)

Fig. 9.2: A continuum of embodiment. Adapted from Meteyard, L., Cuadrado, S. R., Bahrami, B. and Vigliocco, G. 2012, Coming of age: A review of embodiment and the neuroscience of semantics. *Cortex*, 48(7), 788–804.

supporting secondary embodiment still see semantics as amodal and abstract but propose that semantic representation and sensory-motor information are directly associated, for example, amodal representations derived from sensory-motor input (Patterson et al. 2007). For weak embodiment, semantic representations are partly instantiated by sensory-motor information which does have a representational role, but some degree of abstraction still takes place. Areas adjacent to primary sensory-motor areas are involved in semantic representation and are reciprocally linked to primary areas. From a strong embodiment perspective, semantic processing necessarily activates sensory-motor information and is completely dependent upon it. Here, semantic processing takes place within primary sensory and motor areas and precisely the same systems are used for semantic processing and sensory-motor processing.

A fully symbolic theory is problematic because there is no link between language and world knowledge, which raises the grounding problem and the problem of referentiality: how do we understand what words refer to if they are not linked to the world (Harnad 1990)? Based on the research evidence for sensory-motor activations during semantic processing (Meteyard et al. 2012), it is clear that sensory-motor systems play some role in semantic processing. Strong embodiment also appears to be unsatisfactory: some degree of abstraction must take place in order to extract and combine features into the correct conceptual conjunctions. Based on evidence from TMS and lesion studies, weak embodiment, where sensory-motor information plays an integral, representational role in semantic representation whilst maintaining some degree of abstraction seems the most plausible choice.

3.1.4 Key issues and embodied theories

Since word meanings appear to produce similar activation patterns to their real-world referents, different types of words will necessarily have different patterns of activation. Differences in semantic representations of objects and actions have clearly been demonstrated with neuropsychology (e.g., Damasio and Tranel 1993) and imaging data (e.g., Martin et al. 1995) (for review see Vigliocco et al. 2011). Here, it has generally been found that processing object-nouns involves activation of posterior sensory cortices while processing action-verbs involves activation of fronto-parietal motor areas.

Traditionally it has been argued that embodied theories have problems explaining how abstract concepts are represented. Abstract words pose a special problem to theories of embodied semantics because their content is not strongly perceptual or motoric, and as such, it is often argued that their meaning can only be represented in abstract propositional forms (e.g., Noppeney and Price 2004).

There are now a number of alternative (or complementary) hypotheses on embodiment of abstract concepts. One hypothesis is that the meaning of abstract words is understood through metaphorical mappings (Boroditsky 2000; Lakoff and Johnson 1980; see Gibbs this volume). For example one could conceptualize the mind as a container (Dove 2009) because it holds information. Metaphor allows abstract representations to be based on extensions of more concrete experience-based concepts grounded in perception and action. Boroditsky et al. (2001) showed how the abstract concept of time could be embodied using mental representations of the more concrete domain of space (see Evans Volume 3 for greater discussion on the representation of time). The authors speculated that the link between the two concepts developed via correspondences between space and time in experience: moving in space correlates with time. Language then builds upon these simple correspondences.

Although metaphors highlight similarities between concepts, they do not define the differences (Dove, 2009): although the mind shares similarities with a container insofar as it *contains* information, it is much more than this and this information is not captured in the metaphor. Additionally, one can think of many aspects of abstract knowledge that cannot be accounted for by metaphor (Meteyard et al. 2012), such as scientific technical jargon (but see Glenberg 2011: 15). Although a role for metaphor could be acknowledged, the question is whether metaphorical mappings could really be the foundation of learning and representation of abstract concepts, or if they just provide structure for existing concepts (Barsalou 1999).

The difference between concrete and abstract words may arise because of the number and type of simulations for each word type, similar to differences in context (cf. the context availability theory, Schwananflugel and Shoben 1983). Abstract words' meanings would be based on a wider range of simulations than concrete words, and tend to focus more on social, introspective and affective information than perceptual and motor (Barsalou and Wiemer-Hasting 2005; Kousta et al. 2011; Connell and Lynott 2012). Differences arise between the two word types because the type of information and situations relevant for abstract meaning is more difficult to access.

Kousta et al. (2011) and Vigliocco et al. (2009) described differences between abstract and concrete concepts as arising from the ecological statistical preponderance of sensory-motor features in concrete concepts compared to the statistical preponderance of linguistic and especially affective associations for abstract concepts. They argue that affect may be a critical factor in the learning and representation of abstract knowledge because abstract words tend to have emotional associations, and because emotional development precedes language development in children (Bloom 1998). Abstract words with greater affective associations are acquired earlier with the rate of acquisition rapidly increasing around age three (Bretherton and Beeghly 1982; Wellman et al. 1995), suggesting that affect affects abstract word acquisition. When all other factors are controlled, emotional associations of abstract words facilitate lexical decisions relative to concrete words, reversing the traditional concreteness advantage (Kousta et al. 2009). Unlike dual coding theory (e.g., Paivio 1986) where abstract words are disadvantaged due to their lack of imageability, emotional processing confers further benefits to abstract words (Vigliocco et al. 2013).

At present therefore a growing number of studies are attempting to describe embodiment of abstract concepts. Accounts based on metaphor and the range and nature of simulations successfully explain findings in a number of domains, yet there remain many more abstract and schematic elements of language which are not easily accounted for. For example, it is difficult to imagine how simulation can underlie the representation of abstract and schematic closed-class words such as prepositions and determiners (Meteyard et al. 2012), so a completely embodied semantic system seems unlikely.

Do embodied theories make a distinction between word meaning and conceptual knowledge? In terms of the continuum of embodied theories described above, as one moves further from abstract/symbolic theories to strong versions of embodiment, the content of semantic representation includes gradually more sensory-motor information (Meteyard et al. 2012), blurring the distinction between semantics and conceptual information.

3.1.5 Looking toward the future: Where should embodiment go?

Despite empirical support for embodiment many issues are still outstanding. First, research needs to go beyond simply showing effects of interaction between linguistic and sensory-motor stimuli and focus more on describing the nature of this relationship and the specific mechanisms responsible for these interactions. Simply accumulating evidence for *some* involvement of sensory-motor systems is unsatisfactory. Interaction effects between language and sensory-motor processes have been shown to cause both facilitation and interference effects; the processes underlying these differences need to be explored. For example, Glenberg and Kaschak (2002) found that semantic judgments were faster when direction of a physical response matched the direction described in the language (facilitation) but Kaschak et al. (2006) found slower responses when the direction of motion of an auditory stimulus matched the direction described in language (interference). Such opposing results might be explained by properties of the stimuli and presentation, such as the match in modality of the presented linguistic and perceptual stimuli, or the timing of presentation. To make progress on understanding the specific mechanisms underlying these effects, we need to clarify the influence of these variables.

A commonly raised question about simulation is its necessity. Do we need simulation in order to understand language or is it epiphenomenal (Mahon and Caramazza 2008), with activation in sensorimotor areas simply the result of spreading activation between dissociable systems? Looking carefully at the temporal dynamics of interactions between language and sensorimotor systems could address questions of epiphenomenalism. If language comprehension necessarily recruits sensorimotor systems, such effects should be observed very early in processing (Pavan and Baggio 2013).

Depth of processing is a related issue. It is unclear whether simulation occurs under all circumstances in all language tasks. Simulation may not be necessary for shallow language tasks, where a good-enough representation could be inferred simply from linguistic information alone, using statistical relations between words (Barsalou et al. 2008; Louwerse, 2011). Embodied simulations could instead be reserved for deeper processing.

One aspect of language awaiting future research from this perspective is the learning process. When and how are words linked with sensory systems? There have been some attempts to describe this process, for example via Hebbian learning mechanisms under the combined presence of object naming and the object's sensory affordances (Pulvermuller 1999; Glenberg and Gallese 2012) or by exploiting iconic mappings between linguistic form and meaning (Perniss et al. 2010).

It is clear that to move forward, embodied theories need to delve deeper into the mechanisms that underlie the wealth of empirical data and formulate a clear, precise and testable description of the specific nature of these processes and their temporal properties.

3.2 Distributional theories

Distributional theories, traditionally viewed in sharp contrast with embodied theories, are concerned with statistical patterns found in language itself, such as different types of texts or documents. Here a word's meaning is described by its distribution across the language environment and the mechanisms for learning are clear: words' meanings are inferred from the statistical patterns existent in language (see Gries; Geeraerts; and Divjak and Caldwell-Harris this volume). Distributional approaches have traditionally assigned no role to sensory-motor information, instead using only information present in linguistic data.

Dominant distributional approaches developed within cognitive science are latent semantic analysis (LSA, Landauer and Dumais 1997), hyperspace analogue to language (HAL, Lund et al. 1995) and more recently Griffiths et al.'s topic model (e.g., Griffiths et al. 2007). All these approaches use large samples of text, evaluating properties of the contexts in which a word appears in order to estimate its relationship to other words, but differ in the way contexts are treated and the way relationships among words are assessed (see Riordan and Jones 2010 for a more in-depth review covering a broader range of distributional models). The topic model does consider words in terms of contexts from which they are sampled, but differs to LSA and HAL in its assumptions: contexts have themselves been sampled from a distribution of latent topics, each of which is represented as a probability distribution over words (e.g., Griffiths et al. 2007). The content of a topic is thus represented by those words that it assigned a high probability to, so the semantic representation of each word can be considered to be its distribution over latent topics; and the similarity between two words as similarity in distribution over topics.

These approaches have successfully simulated many aspects of human behaviour with the topic model as the most state-of-the-art as it provides a plausible solution to problems faced by LSA, namely ambiguity, polysemy and homonymy. Words are assigned to topics and can be represented across many topics with different probabilities so each sense or meaning of a word can be differentiated. Figure 9.3 shows how the different meanings of *bank* occur within two different topics. Words that share a high probability under the same topics tend

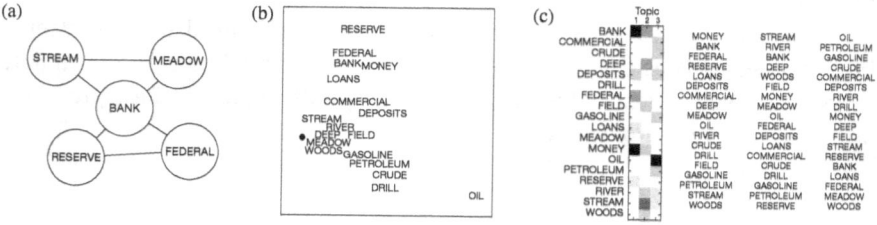

Fig. 9.3: Approaches to semantic representation. (a) In a semantic network, words are represented as nodes, and edges indicate semantic relationships. (b) In a semantic space, words are represented as points, and proximity indicates semantic association. These are the first two dimensions of a solution produced by latent semantic analysis (Landauer and Dumais, 1997). The black dot is the origin. (c) In the topic model, words are represented as belonging to a set of probabilistic topics. The matrix shown on the left indicates the probability of each word under each of three topics. The three columns on the right show the words that appear in those topics, ordered from highest to lowest probability.
Taken from Griffiths, Steyvers and Tenenbaum (2007). Topics in semantic representation. *Psychological Review*, 114(2), 211–244.

to be similar and predictive of each other. A further benefit is that shared components of meaning are made explicit by providing a precise characterization of what "topics" are in terms of probability distributions. In comparison, for models like LSA or HAL it is presumed that words in similar contexts have related meanings but it is not specified how these may be defined or described.

While none of these models themselves are developmental in nature (i.e., modeling language acquisition), as they all compute representations based on a stable input corpus, they nonetheless can be explicitly applied to developmental processes simply by comparing the representations given different types of language corpora (e.g., comparing statistical patterns in corpora taken from children versus adults). Furthermore the probabilistic nature of topic models permits the possibility that distributions of topics, words and contexts may all change over time. As a result distributional models can be applied directly, and make predictions relevant to language development in a way that is not obvious for embodied theories.

3.2.1 Holistic theories

Distributional theories developed primarily from computational linguistics. Within psychology, however, these theories have as predecessors holistic theories, and within linguistics, theories of sense relations: concerned with the organisation, or structure of semantic representations rather than their content, and thus assume concepts are represented in a unitary fashion.

Holistic theories take a non-decompositional, relational view: the meaning of words should be evaluated as a whole, in terms of relations between words, rather than being decomposed into smaller components (such as features). Words take their meaning from relationships with other words, for example by associative links. In early theories of this type, meaning was described by semantic networks (e.g., Quillian 1968; Collins and Loftus 1975) where a word was denoted by a single node in a network and its meaning by connections to other nodes. The full meaning of a concept arises from the whole network, beginning from the concept node which alone is meaningless.

In holistic approaches, semantic similarity effects are explained in terms of spreading activation from an activated node (such as a prime or distractor word) to other concepts by connections between nodes (e.g., Quillian 1967). Response times in experimental tasks would be driven by the time it takes a semantically similar node to reach an activation threshold. As words that are semantically related will be closer together in the semantic space than semantically unrelated words, activation spreads more quickly from a related prime to the target word.

In some holistic models, differences between object-nouns and action-verbs have been modelled in terms of different relational links (e.g., Graesser et al. 1987; Huttenlocher and Lui 1979). In Wordnet (Miller and Fellbaum 1991) this is represented on a large scale with four distinct networks representing nouns, verbs, adjectives and adverbs. The representation of abstract words in Wordnet is no different to more concrete words of the same grammatical class, although abstract words tend to occur in shallower hierarchies.

Regarding the relationship between words and concepts, a strict one-to-one mapping is proposed. Each lexical concept is equal to a single, abstract representation in the conceptual system. This means that conceptual systems must contain representations of all concepts that are lexicalized in all languages. Any lexical differences that appear cross-linguistically must be due to conceptual differences. In order to defend the universality of conceptual structure, one must assume that not all concepts are lexicalized in each language (see Vigliocco and Filipović 2004).

3.2.2 Research supporting distributional theories

LSA (Landauer and Dumais 1997), topic model (Griffiths et al. 2007) and HAL (Lund et al. 1995) have successfully simulated a number of semantic effects including semantic similarity in semantic priming tasks. Using the word association norms of Nelson et al. (1998), the topic model successfully predicted associations between words greater than performance at chance level and outperformed LSA in this as well as a range of other semantic tasks.

LSA has successfully simulated a number of human cognitive behaviours. For example, simulated scores on a standard vocabulary test have been shown to overlap with human scores and simulations can mimic human word sorting behaviour (Landauer et al. 1998). If these theories can successfully approximate human language comprehension then they should be considered valid models of human language processing, reflecting processes to some extent analogous to human language processing (Landauer and Dumais 1997).

Attempts have been made to directly test distributional models and their power to predict neural activations. For example, Mitchell et al. (2008) found that voxel-level, item specific fMRI activations for concrete nouns could be predicted on the basis of distributional statistics based on a large text corpus, and similar data have been obtained using EEG data (Murphy et al. 2009). Such findings suggest that there is a close relationship between statistical co-occurrences of words in texts and neural activity related to understanding those words, further supporting the viability of distributional theories.

3.2.3 Key issues and distributional theories

In comparison to earlier relational approaches, relations between different word types here are not pre-specified; instead the same principles are used for all word types. Differences between word types such as noun-verb differences and concrete-abstract differences are captured in the relationships that result from these statistical models, patterns that exist in the source texts. Thus, distributional models have no problem defining all domains, as long as they are represented in the source texts.

The relationship between word meaning and conceptual knowledge is not explicitly discussed by these theories, and they are therefore implicitly assumed to be the same. The lack of connection between words and sensory-motor experience is a strong limitation of distributional models, as discussed below.

3.2.4 Looking toward the future: Where should distributional theories go?

Despite the power of distributional models in simulating human behaviour, some have argued that the statistical patterns that exist in language co-occurrences are merely epiphenomenal and play no role in semantic representation (Glenberg and Robertson 2000). That language-based models do not take into account information from other sources of meaning, such as perception and introspection, as embodied theories do, is a fundamental criticism that these approaches need to address. In addition the models cannot account for existing behavioural and neuroscientific evidence linking language to the brain's sensory-motor systems. One can use the famous "Chinese room" example (Searle 1980) to highlight the importance of this argument: how can meaning be inferred simply from the relationships that exist between amodal symbols that are themselves void of meaning?

Recently, distributional approaches have been developing in order to solve the "grounding" problem (Harnad 1990) by including experiential information as another type of distributional data, bringing together embodied and distributional ideas that have typically been considered independently. In the next section we will discuss this further.

4 An integrated proposal: Combining language-based and experiential information

Despite the apparent divide between embodied, experiential theories and amodal, distributional theories, these two types of information can be integrated to form a more general model of semantic representation. While maintaining a role for sensorimotor information in learning, linguistic information also plays a role. We have all used dictionaries to learn a word's meaning as well as inferring a new word's meaning from its linguistic context alone. The environment contains a rich source of both embodied and linguistic data: we experience words both in a physical environment and a language environment rather than one or the other. As Louwerse (2007) notes, the question should not be whether semantics is embodied or symbolic, but rather, to what extent is language comprehension embodied *and* symbolic?

Meaning in language could be both embodied and language-based, with the contribution of each system dependent on the language task at hand. Dove (2009) describes the conceptual system as divided into both modal and amodal representations with each responsible for different aspects of meaning. For example, it seems impossible that aspects of cognition such as logical reasoning or mathematics do not depend at all upon amodal symbols (Louwerse 2007).

The symbol interdependency theory (Louwerse 2007) describes meaning as composed of symbols that are dependent on other symbols and symbols that are dependent on embodied experiences. Here symbols are built upon embodied representations, but although they are grounded, language comprehension can proceed simply via interrelations amongst other symbols. Using linguistic representations allows for a more "quick and dirty" response, whereas embodied simulations develop more slowly, accessing a wide variety of detailed experiential information. Here, two predictions emerge. First, for shallow language tasks, involvement of linguistic representations should dominate over embodied representations. Second, for tasks that involve a deeper level of processing, embodied representations should dominate over linguistic. Barsalou et al. (2008) describe similar ideas with lexical processing incorporating two processes: an early activation of linguistic representations taking place in language areas of the brain and a later, situated simulation involving modal systems.

Vigliocco et al. (2009) describe language as another vital source of information, along with experiential information, from which semantic representations can be learnt. Statistical distributions of words within texts provide important information about meaning that can be integrated with sensory-motor experience. For example, a child could learn the meaning of the word *dog* via experience with dogs' perceptual features: having four legs, barking etc., as well as language experience of hearing "dog": it tends to occur with words such as *pet* and *animals*. Combining both distributions of information allows linguistic information to "hook up" to the world, thus grounding it.

Modern computational work is also beginning to model semantic meaning by integrating experiential and linguistic distributional data. It has been shown that models that combine both types of distributional data perform better in simulating semantic effects than either distributions alone (Andrews et al. 2009). The underlying principles employed in distributional models can also be applied to other domains of experience, not simply linguistic data. Johns and Jones (2012) proposed a model integrating both perceptual information (in the form of feature norms) and statistical information from language. Here, a word's full meaning is denoted by the concatenation of perceptual and linguistic vectors. Using a model of global lexical similarity with a simple associative mechanism, perceptual representations for words for which the model had no perceptual information could be inferred based on lexical similarity and the limited perceptual information of other words already existing in the model. Importantly, the inference can also go the other way, with the likely linguistic structure of a word estimated based on its perceptual information. Thus the model is able to infer the missing representation of a word based on either perceptual or linguistic information.

There are some potential shortcomings to current "integrated" models. Since concrete feature norms are generated by speakers verbally and via introspection, using them as "embodied information" means there are possible perceptual, sensorimotor and affective aspects of experiential information that may not be included, suggesting that we cannot generalize the findings to all word types. However, other methods for appropriately modelling experiential information are being explored. Recent methods are beginning to combine information from computer vision with text in distributional models; models including visual information outperform distributional models based on text only, at least when vision is relevant to words' meanings (Bruni et al. 2012a, 2012b). Future work will need to make use of more sophisticated types of perceptual information, as well as incorporating other aspects of bodily experience such as action and emotion.

5 Conclusion

The state of the art in cognitive science proposes that the learning and representation of word meanings involves the statistical combination of experiential information: sensorimotor and affective information gleaned from experience in the world (extralinguistic), and distributional linguistic information: statistical patterns occurring within a language itself (intralinguistic). Research suggests that sensory-motor and affective systems provide a central role in grounding word meaning in our worldly experiences. This grounding is thought crucial for the language system to learn word meanings from existent embodied word meanings. The associations between linguistic units allow learners to more quickly infer word meaning and locate the corresponding experiential information in the absence of any direct experience of the referent. By learning about word meaning from both distributions in parallel, ultimately a richer form of semantic information is gained.

6 References

Bak Thomas H., Dominic G. O'Donovan, John J. Xuereb, Simon Boniface, and John R. Hodges (2001): Selective impairment of verb processing associated with pathological changes in Brodmann areas 44 and 45 in the motor neuron disease-dementia-aphasia syndrome. *Brain* 124: 103–120.

Barsalou, Lawrence W. (1999): Perceptual symbol systems. *Brain and Behavioural Sciences* 22: 577–660.

Barsalou, Lawrence W., Ava Santos, W. Kyle Simmons, and Christine D. Wilson (2008): Language and simulation in conceptual processing. In: M. de Vega, A. M. Glenberg, and A. C. Graesser (eds.), *Symbols, Embodiment and Meaning*, 245–283. Oxford: Oxford University Press.

Barsalou, Lawrence W. and Katja Wiemer-Hastings (2005): Situating abstract concepts. In: D. Pecher and R. A. Zwaan (eds.), *Grounding Cognition: The Role of Perception and Action in Memory, Language, and Thought*, 129–163. New York: Cambridge University Press.

Bergen, Benjamin (this volume): Embodiment. Berlin/Boston: De Gruyter Mouton.

Bird, Helen, David Howard and Sue Franklin (2003): Verbs and nouns: The importance of being imageable. *Journal of Neurolinguistics* 16(2): 113–149.

Bloom, Lois (1998): Language acquisition in its developmental context. In: D. Kuhn and R. S. Siegler (eds.), *Handbook of Child Psychology* 2, 309–370. New York: Wiley.

Boroditsky, Lera (2000): Metaphoric structuring: Understanding time through spatial metaphors. *Cognition* 75(1): 1–28.

Boroditsky, Lera, Michael Ramscar, and Michael Frank (2001): The roles of body and mind in abstract thought. *Proceedings of the 23rd Annual Conference of the Cognitive Science Society*. University of Edinburgh.

Boulenger, Véronique, Laura Mechtouff, Stéphane Thobis, Emmaneul Broussolle, Marc Jeannerod, and Tatjana A. Nazir (2008): Word processing in Parkinson's disease is impaired for action verbs but not for concrete noun. *Neuropsychologia* 46: 743–756.

Bretherton, Inge and Marjorie Beeghly (1982): Talking about internal states: The acquisition of an explicit theory of mind. *Developmental Psychology* 18: 906–921.

Bruni, Elia, Marco Baroni, Jasper Uijlings, and Nicu Sebe (2012a): Distributional semantics with eyes: Using image analysis to improve computational representations of word meaning. *Proceedings of the 2th ACM International Conference on Multimedia*, 1219–1228.

Bruni, Elia, Gemma Boleda, Marco Baroni, and Nam-Khanh Tran (2012b): Distributional semantics in Technicolor. *Proceedings of the 50th Annual Meeting of the Association for Computational Linguistics*, 136–145.

Buchanan, Erin M., Jessica L. Holmes, Marilee L. Teasley, and Keith A. Hutchinson (2012): English semantic word-pair norms and a searchable Web portal for experimental stimulus creation. *Behavior Research Methods* 44(4): 746–757.
Collins, Allan M. and Elizabeth F. Loftus (1975): A spreading-activation theory of semantic processing. *Psychological Review* 82: 407–428.
Collins, Allan M. and M. Ross Quillian (1969): Retrieval time from semantic memory. *Journal of Verbal Learning and Verbal Behavior* 12: 240–247.
Connell, Louise and Dermot Lynott (2012): Strength of perceptual experience predicts word processing performance better than concreteness or imageability. *Cognition* 125(3): 452–465.
Damasio, Antonio R. (1989): Time-locked multiregional retroactivation: A systems-level proposal for the neural substrates of recall and recognition. *Cognition* 33: 25–62.
Damasio, Antonio R. and Daniel Tranel (1993): Nouns and verbs are retrieved with differently distributed neural systems. *Proceedings of the National Academy of Sciences Unites States of America*, 90: 4957–4960.
Divjak, Dagmar and Catherine Caldwell-Harris (this volume): Frequency and entrenchment. Berlin/Boston: De Gruyter Mouton.
Dove, Guy (2009): Beyond conceptual symbols. A call for representational pluralism. *Cognition* 110: 412–431.
Evans, Vyvyan (2003): *The Structure of Time. Language, Meaning and Temporal Cognition.* Amsterdam: Benjamins.
Farah, Martha J. and James L. McClelland (1991): A computational model of semantic memory impairment: Modality-specificity and emergent category specificity. *Journal of Experimental Psychology: General* 120: 339–357.
Frege, Gottlob ([1892] 1952): On sense and reference. In: P. T. Geach and M. Black (eds. and Trans.), *Philosophical Writings of Gottlob Frege*. Oxford: Basil Blackwell.
Geeraerts, Dirk (Volume 2): Lexical semantics. Berlin/Boston: De Gruyter Mouton.
Glenberg, Arthur M. (2011): How reading comprehension is embodied and why that matters. *International Electronic Journal of Elementary Education* 4(1): 5–18.
Glenberg, Arthur M. and Vittorio Gallese (2012): Action-based language: a theory of language acquisition, comprehension and production. *Cortex* 48(7): 905–922.
Glenberg, Arthur M. and Michael P. Kaschak (2002): Grounding language in action. *Psychonomic Bulletin and Review* 9: 558–565.
Glenberg, Arthur M. and David A. Robertson (2000): Symbol grounding and meaning: A comparison of high-dimensional and embodied theories of meaning. *Journal of Memory and Language* 43: 379–401.
Gibbs, Raymond W. Jr. (this volume): Metaphor. Berlin/Boston: De Gruyter Mouton.
Graesser, Arthur C., Patricia L. Hopkinson and Cheryl Schmid (1987): Differences in interconcept organization between nouns and verbs. *Journal of Memory and Language* 26: 242–253.
Gries, Stefan Th. (Volume 3): Polysemy. Berlin/Boston: De Gruyter Mouton.
Griffiths, Thomas L., Mark Steyvers and Joshua B. Tenenbaum (2007): Topics in semantic representation. *Psychological Review* 114(2): 211–244.
Hall, Richard (1984): *Sniglets (snig'lit): Any Word That Doesn't Appear in the Dictionary, But Should.* Collier Books.
Harnad, Stevan (1990): The symbol grounding problem. *Physica* 42: 335.
Hauk, Olaf, Ingrid Johnsrude, and Friedemann Pulvermuller (2004): Somatotopic representation of action words in human motor and premotor cortex. *Neuron* 41(2): 301–307.

Huttenlocher, Janellen and Felicia Lui (1979): The semantic organization of some simple nouns and verbs. *Journal of Verbal Learning and Verbal Behavior* 18: 141–179.

Johns, Brendan T. and Michael N. Jones (2012): Perceptual inference through global lexical similarity. *Topics in Cognitive Science* 4:103–120.

Kaschak, Michael P., Rolf A. Zwaan, Mark Aveyard, and Richard H. Yaxley (2006): Perception of auditory motion affects language processing. *Cognitive Science* 30: 733–744.

Kousta, Stavroula-Thaleia, Gabriella Vigliocco, David P. Vinson, Mark Andrews, and Elena Del Campo (2011): The representation of abstract words: why emotion matters. *Journal of Experimental Psychology General* 140: 14–34.

Kousta, Stavroula-Thaleia, David P. Vinson, and Gabriella Vigliocco (2009): Emotion words, regardless of polarity, have a processing advantage over neutral words. *Cognition* 112(3): 473–481.

Lakoff, George and Mark Johnson (1980): *Metaphors We Live By*. Chicago: University of Chicago Press.

Lakoff, George and Mark Johnson (1999): *Philosophy in the Flesh: The Embodied Mind and its Challenge to Western Thought*. New York: Basic Books.

Landauer, Thomas K. and Susan T. Dumais (1997): A solution to Plato's problem: The Latent Semantic Analysis theory of the acquisition, induction, and representation of knowledge. *Psychological Review* 104: 211–140.

Landauer, Thomas K., Peter W. Foltz, and Darrell Laham (1998): Introduction to Latent Semantic Analysis. *Discourse Processes* 25: 259–284.

Langacker, R. W. (1982): *Foundations of Cognitive Grammar*, Volume 1, *Theoretical Prerequisites*. Stanford: Stanford University Press.

Louwerse, Max M. (2007): Symbolic or embodied representations: A case for symbol interdependency. In: T. Landauer, D. McNamara, S. Dennis, and W. Kintsch (eds.), *Handbook of Latent Semantic Analysis*, 107–120. Mahwah: Erlbaum.

Louwerse, Max M. (2011): Stormy seas and cloudy skies: conceptual processing is (still) linguistic and perceptual. *Frontiers in Psychology* 2(105): 1–4.

Lund, Kevin, Curt Burgess, and Ruth A. Atchley (1995): Semantic and associative priming in high-dimensional semantic space. In: J. D. Moore and J. F. Lehman (eds.), *Proceedings of the 17th Annual Meeting of the Cognitive Science Society*, 17: 660–665.

Mahon, Bradford Z. and Alfonso Caramazza (2008): A critical look at the Embodied Cognition Hypothesis and a new proposal for grounding conceptual content. *Journal of Physiology – Paris* 102: 59–70.

Martin, Alex, James V. Haxby, Francoise M. Lalonde, Cheri L. Wiggs, and Leslie G. Ungerleider (1995): Discrete cortical regions associated with knowledge of color and knowledge of action. *Science* 270(5233): 102–105.

McRae, Ken and Stephen Boisvert (1998): Automatic semantic similarity priming. *Journal of Experimental Psychology: Learning, Memory and Cognition* 24: 558–572a.

McRae, K., and George S. Cree (2002): Factors underlying category-specific semantic deficits. In: E. M. E. Forde and G. W. Humphreys (eds.), *Category-Specificity in Brain and Mind*, 211–250. East Sussex, UK: Psychology Press.

Meteyard, Lotte, Bahador Bahrami, and Gabriella Vigliocco (2007): Motion detection and motion verbs. *Psychological Science* 18(11): 1007–1013.

Meteyard, Lotte, Sara. R. Rodriguez Cuadrado, Bahador Bahrami, and Gabriella Vigliocco (2012): Coming of age: A review of embodiment and the neuroscience of semantics. *Cortex* 48(7): 788–804.

Meteyard, Lotte, Nahid Zokaei, Bahador Bahrami, and Gabriella Vigliocco (2008): Visual motion interferes with lexical decision on motion words. *Current Biology* 18(17): 732–733.

Miller, George A. and Christiane Fellbaum (1991): Semantic networks of English. *Cognition* 41: 197–229.

Mitchell, Tom M., Svletlana V. Shinkareva, Andrew Carlson, Kai-Min Chang, Vicente L. Malave, Robert A. Mason, and Marcel A. Just (2008): Predicting human brain activity associated with the meanings of nouns. *Science* 320: 1191.

Murphy, Gregory L. (2002): *The Big Book of Concepts*. Cambridge: MIT Press.

Murphy, Brian, Marco Baroni, and Massimo Poesio (2009): EEG responds to conceptual stimuli and corpus semantics. *Proceedings of the Conference on Empirical Methods in Natural Language Processing (EMNLP 2009)*, 619–627. East Stroudsburg: ACL.

Nelson, Douglas L., Cathy L. McEvory, and Thomas A. Schreiber (1998): The University of South Florida word association, rhyme, and word fragment norms. http://www.usf.edu/FreeAssociation/

Noppeney, Uta and Cathy J. Price (2004): Retrieval of abstract semantics. *Neuroimage* 22: 164–170.

Paivio, Allan (1986): *Mental Representations: A Dual-Coding Approach*. Oxford: Oxford University Press.

Patterson, Karalyn, Peter J. Nestor, and Timothy T. Rogers (2007): Where do you know what you know? The representation of semantic knowledge in the human brain. *Nature Reviews Neuroscience* 8: 976–987.

Pavan, Andrea and Giosuè Baggio (2013): Linguistic representations of motion do not depend on the visual motion system. *Psychological Science* 24: 181–188.

Pecher, Diane, René Zeelenberg, and Lawrence W. Barsalou (2003): Verifying different-modality properties for concepts produces switching costs. *Psychological Science* 14(2): 119–124.

Perniss, Pamela, Robin L. Thompson, and Gabriella Vigliocco (2010): Iconicity as a general property of language: Evidence from spoken and signed languages. *Frontiers in Psychology* 1: 227.

Pulvermuller, Friedemann (1999): Words in the brain's language. *Behavioral and Brain Sciences* 22: 253–336.

Pulvermuller, Friedemann, Olaf Hauk, Vadim V. Nikulin, and Risto J. Ilmoniemi (2005): Functional links between motor and language systems, European Journal of Neuroscience 21(3): 793–797.

Quillian, M. Ross (1967): Word concepts: A theory and simulation of some basic semantic capabilities. *Behavioural Science* 12: 410–430.

Quillian, M. Ross (1968): Semantic memory. In: M. Minsky (ed.), *Semantic Information Processing*, 227–270. Cambridge: MIT Press.

Riordan, B. and M. N. Jones (2010): Redundancy in linguistic and perceptual experience: Comparing distributional and feature-based models of semantic representation. *Topics in Cognitive Science* 3(2): 303–345.

Rosch, Eleanor and Carolyn B. Mervis (1975): Family resemblance: Studies in the internal structure of categories. *Cognitive Psychology* 7: 573–605.

Santos, Ava, Sergio E. Chaigneau, W. Kyle Simmons, and Lawrence W. Barsalou (2011): Property generation reflects word association and situated simulation. *Language and Cognition* 3: 83–119.

Schwanenflugel, Paula J. and Edward J. Shoben (1983): Differential context effects in the comprehension of abstract and concrete verbal materials. *Journal of Experimental Psychology: Learning, Memory, and Cognition* 9(1): 82–102.

Searle, John (1980): Minds, brains and programs. *Behavioral and Brain Sciences* 3(3): 417–457.

Simmons, W. Kyle and Lawrence W. Barsalou (2003): The similarity-in-topography principle: Reconciling theories of conceptual deficits. *Cognitive Neuropsychology* 20: 451–486.

Svensson, Patrik (1999): *Number and Countability in English Nouns. An Embodied Model.* Uppsala: Swedish Science Press.

Tyler, Lorraine K., Richard Russell, Jalal Fadili, and Helen E. Moss (2001): The neural representation of nouns and verbs: PET studies. *Brain* 124: 1619–1634.

van Dam, Wessel O., Shirley-Ann Rueschemeyer, and Harold Bekkering (2010): How specifically are action verbs represented in the neural motor system: an fMRI study. *Neuroimage* 53: 1318–1325.

Vigliocco, Gabriella and Luna Filipović (2004): From mind in the mouth to language in the mind. *Trends in Cognitive Sciences* 8: 5–7.

Vigliocco, Gabriella, Stavroula-Thaleia Kousta, David P. Vinson, Mark Andrews, and Elena Del Campo (2013): The representation of abstract words: What matters? A reply to Paivio. *Journal of Experimental Psychology: General* 142: 288–291.

Vigliocco, Gabriella, Lotte Meteyard, Mark Andrews, and Stavroula-Thaleia Kousta (2009): Toward a theory of semantic representation. *Language and Cognition* 1: 215–244.

Vigliocco, Gabriella, Daniel Tranel, and Judit Druks (2012): Language production: patient and imaging research. In: M. Spivey, K. McRae and M. Joanisse (eds.), *Cambridge Handbook of Psycholinguistics*, 443–464. Cambridge: Cambridge University Press.

Vigliocco, Gabriella, David Vinson, Judit Druks, Horacio Barber, and Stefano F. Cappa (2011): Nouns and verbs in the brain: A review of behavioural, electrophysiological, neuropsychological and imaging studies. *Neuroscience and Biobehavioural Reviews* 35: 407–426.

Vigliocco, Gabriella, David P. Vinson, William Lewis, and Merrill F. Garrett (2004): Representing the meaning of object and action words: The featural and unitary semantic space hypothesis. *Cognition* 48: 422–488.

Vinson, David P. and Gabriella Vigliocco (2002): A semantic analysis of noun-verb dissociations in aphasia. *Journal of Neurolinguistics* 15: 317–351.

Wellman, Henry M., Paul L. Harris, Mita Banerjee, and Anna Sinclair (1995): Early understanding of emotion: Evidence from natural language. *Cognition and Emotion* 9: 117–149.

Willems, Roel M., Peter Hagoort, and Daniel Casasanto (2010): Body-specific representations of action verbs: Neural evidence from right- and left-handers. *Psychological Science* 21(1): 67–74.

Bolinger, Dwight (1979): To Catch a Metaphor: *You* As Norm. *American Speech* 54: 194–209.

Mark Turner
Chapter 10: Blending in language and communication

1 Elements of blending

Cognitive linguistics analyzes how language derives from and interacts with basic mental operations not exclusive to language. Blending is a basic mental operation, interacting with other basic mental operations such as conceptual mapping, framing, and image-schematic structuring. It plays a pervasive role in language and communication. (See blending.stanford.edu and Turner 2014 for surveys of research).

Blending theory uses a number of new and old terms, presented below.

Mental frame: A frame (Fillmore 1976, 1982) is a small bundle of ideas, stereotypical for a community. We activate parts of frames mentally, often prompted by expressions. Think of a *stockbroker*. We have a mental frame for buying and selling, and a mental frame for the special case of buying and selling securities, particularly stocks and bonds. In it, there are roles for the buyer, the seller, what is sold, and the broker who arranges the transaction. When someone says, *I have to call my stockbroker*, everyone can activate the right mental *frame*.

Mental space: Following Gilles Fauconnier (1985), we use the term "mental space" to mean a small, bundled array of related mental elements that a person activates simultaneously. *Luke is a stockbroker* prompts us to activate a mental space with one element that we take to be a man (presumably) named "Luke", and another element, *stockbroker*, and a relation between them. The relation between them is obvious: Luke is a stockbroker, which is to say, we have a *role-value* relation, with *stockbroker* as the role and *Luke* as its value. If the next sentence is *He is my brother-in-law*, then we activate not just the mental space for *Luke is a stockbroker* but also another mental space, which contains *I*, the speaker. The relations between these mental spaces, and between elements within them, are complicated. For each of these two mental spaces, we need to draw on the kinship frame and its relation *brother-in-law*, which connects two people. In the *Luke* mental space, he is now a brother-in-law to the element *speaker* in the other mental space, so there is a relation connecting those two elements in two different mental spaces. In the *speaker* mental space, the speaker now has a brother-in-law, so there is a relation connecting that role *brother-in-law* in the *speaker* mental space to its value *Luke* in the *Luke* mental space. A network of such mental spaces might be called a *mental web*.

Mental web: A mental web is a set of mental spaces that are activated and connected as one is thinking about a topic. For example, *My brother-in-law, the stockbroker, and his family will travel from San Francisco to Cleveland for Thanksgiving, and we need to learn the time of their arrival so that I can drive down to pick them up* will prompt for many mental spaces, such as a mental space in which I drive my car through complicated holiday traffic, another in which I stop at the appropriate gate at the arrival deck of Cleveland Hopkins International Airport, and on and on. Typically, one cannot hold all these spaces equally active simultaneously in the mind. As we think, we focus on one or another mental space in the mental web. Recently activated mental spaces remain latent and are easier to activate.

Vital Relations: The mental web will have many conceptual connections. The most frequent and important mental connections are the "Vital Relations": *Time, Space, Identity, Change, Cause-Effect, Part-Whole, Analogy, Disanalogy, Representation, Property, Similarity, Category, Intentionality,* and *Uniqueness*. For example, in the mental web about my picking up my brother-in-law and family at the airport, there will be an element in several of those mental spaces corresponding to *I*, and all of those elements in all of those mental spaces will be connected by *Identity* relations. The pickup at the airport is connected by a *Time* connector to the Thanksgiving feast so that the pickup is suitably prior in time to the mental space in which we all have the feast. But the pickup is also connected by a *Time* connector to the mental space for the speaker in the moment of speaking, so that the pickup is suitably later in time than the moment of speaking. The mental space for that pickup at the airport is connected by a *Space* connector to the home where the feast is held, so that we understand that the airport is at a spatial remove from the home. And so on.

Blend. A *blend* is a mental space that results from *blending* mental spaces in a mental web. The blend is not an abstraction, or an analogy, or anything else already named and recognized in common sense, although blending is the basis of the cognitively modern human mind. A *blend* is a new mental space that contains some elements from different mental spaces in a mental web but that develops new meaning of its own that is not drawn from those spaces. This new meaning emerges in the blend. For example, suppose I say, *My brother-in-law, the stockbroker, lives in San Francisco. The stock market opens on the East Coast at 9:30 am, but at that moment, it is 6:30 am on the West Coast. So my brother-in-law must awaken every day at about 5 in the morning if he is going to* *be awake enough to start serious and risky work at 6:30 am. If I were my brother-in-law, I would be miserable.* This passage asks us to build a mental space that contains the brother-in-law and a mental space for me, and to connect many mental spaces, many small ideas. One of the spaces it asks us to build mentally is a mental space in which there is one man (*I*) who is imbued with some of what we think about the speaker and some of what we think about the brother-in-law, but only some in each case. This person in the blend has new ideas attached to it. In the blend, I am my brother-in-law, in a way: there is an element in the blend that has the personal identity of the speaker, but no longer has the speaker's job. It has the emotions of the speaker, but the competence and labor of the brother-in-law. This element is not available from any other space in the mental web. It is unique to the blend. There is a new idea here, one that emerges only in the blend. I-am-my-brother-in-law is a new idea, and a very complicated one.

The blend has many elements and properties that are not available from other spaces in the mental web. In the mental spaces that have the brother-in-law (living in San Francisco, arising at 5am, etc.), he is not miserable. In the mental space that has me, I am not miserable. But in the blend, there is a person who is miserable. This person emerges in the blend.

When a mental web contains a blended space, it is often called a "conceptual integration network", a "blending network", or a "blending web".

Projection. The elements and relations that come into the blend from the mental spaces that are blended are called *projections*. These projections to a blend are always *partial* or rather *selective*. For example, for *If I were my brother-in-law, I would be miserable*, we project to the blend the speaker but only a small part of what we know about the speaker. We do not project the speaker's current employment, for example, because then the speaker could not be a stockbroker. We do not project the speaker's currently living in Cleveland. We project from the mental space with the stockbroker brother-in-law the role *stockbroker* and perhaps even *living in San Francisco and accordingly rising every weekday at 5 am*, but not of course the physical appearance of the brother-in-law, or his family relations, and so on. (Otherwise, in the blend, I might have to be my own brother-in-law, which is taboo.)

Emergent structure in the blend and in the mental web: In the blend, there is a person who is a stockbroker and is miserable. In no other space is it true that anyone is miserable. The misery is *emergent* in the blend. Crucially, there is also new emergent structure in the mental web outside of the blend. Once we have constructed the mental blend, we realize that the speaker in his own actual reality has an aversion to rising early. This is new structure we build for the speaker. There is also emergent structure in the connection between the speaker in his input mental space and the stockbroker in his input mental space, namely a *disanalogy* connection between them having to do with disposition.

Human-scale: Some bundles of thought are tractable and manageable by the human mind. We call them *human-scale*. Other bundles of thought are not tractable, because we cannot grasp them mentally, or they go beyond our mental limits. Political cartoons specialize in providing such human-scale compressions of vast mental webs, as in a cartoon that shows the President of the United States, in a suit, snatching the rice bowl away from a starving child, and we use this human-scale compression to help us grasp the situation in which a presidential veto of legislation in the United States might affect food supply in far distant lands. Most mental webs laying out what we want to think about would be utterly intractable for us except that we can make a human-scale blend drawing on different mental spaces in the web. The blend then gives us a handy, tractable thing to think about. It helps us access, organize, manipulate, and adjust the mental web in which it now sits. For example, in the vast mental web of thinking about life and possibilities, I can have a compact blend in which I actually am a stockbroker – a simulation that arises through blending, going through the motions, and being miserable. The blend in this case is a human-scale mental simulation. I can now do my best to avoid it or anything like it.

Compression and Expansion: A blend is not a small abstraction of the mental spaces it blends and is not a partial cut-and-paste assembly, either, because it contains emergent ideas. It is a tight *compression*. It contains much less information than the full mental web it serves. From it, we can reach up to manage and work on the rest of the vast mental web in which it sits.

We use compressed, tight, tractable blends to help us think about larger mental webs. We might say that we carry small, compressed blends with us mentally, and *unpack* or *expand* them as needed to connect up to what we need to think about. For example, the pithy, compressed little blend with the miserable stockbroker can be used to help the speaker think about any job in a time zone other than the Eastern time zone (GMT −5) and lead him to be vigilant for downsides. He might now make specific inquiry to learn what demands any new job might impose upon him that arise because of events that take place in other time zones where people have sleep schedules that do not match his in universal time (UTC).

2 A Classic example of blending

Fauconnier and Turner (2002) give a quick illustration of these ideas – mental space, mental web, connectors between spaces, emergent structure, projection, compression, expansion, human-scale, blend:

> A Buddhist monk arrives at the foot of a mountain path a little while before dawn. At dawn, he begins walking up the mountain path, reaches the top at sunset, and meditates at the top overnight until, at dawn, he begins to walk back to the foot of the mountain, which he reaches at sunset. Make no assumptions about his starting or stopping or about his pace during the trips. Riddle: is there a place on the path that the monk occupies at the same hour of the day on the two separate journeys?

One way to solve this riddle is to blend the monk's ascent with the monk's descent, so that in the blend, at dawn, there are two monks, one at the foot of the mountain, the other at the top. They then take their journeys, each arriving at the opposite end of the path at sunset. They must meet somewhere, and where they meet is the spot on the path that they occupy at the same hour of the day on the two separate journeys. Again, this is a simulation constructed by blending.

The connected set of ideas for solving this riddle is a mental web. It contains at least three mental spaces. There are connectors between mental spaces, such as identity connectors between the path in the mental space for the ascent and the path in the mental space for the descent. Some but not all the information from those two mental spaces is projected to a blended mental space. We do not, for example, project the date of the ascent and the date of the descent, or the weather on those days, or the fact that the monk is aware of what is around him and would surely be shocked to find himself approaching himself on the path. We do not project the fact that a person cannot be in two places (foot and summit) at the same time. The blend is a compression of parts of its mental web, and it is at human-scale because it is a little vignette about two people approaching each other on a path; this is a simple and familiar scene of human walking. But this compressed blend also has emergent structure. It has two monks, and a meeting. We can use the compressed blend to think about and work on the mental web. We can expand or unpack the blend and connect it back up to elements in the larger mental web. Some of the emergent structure in the blend, namely, the fact that there is a meeting, leads us to project back to create new structure in the mental web itself: now, for example, there is an identity connection between some spot on the path in the ascent mental space and a spot on the path in the descent mental space such that the monk is located at that spot in his travel at the same time of day on the two separate days.

3 Challenges to blending theory

Challenge 1: Isn't blending just epiphenomenal, a kind of linear sum over many other processes (counterfactual thinking, metonymy, categorization, metaphor, other "rhetorical" forms of thought, etc.) that already have names? Why lump them together? Answer: Scientific generalization consists of locating substantive and systematic patterns that run across many apparently different products and effects. Words like "metonymy" and "counterfactual" are only labels, not siloed categories of thought, much less autonomous mental processes. Where there is commonality of mental process across activities, we should model it; where we find distinctions of process, we should model them. This is standard procedure in science: although there are many important differences between the apple's falling from the tree and the moon's orbiting the earth, there is a general pattern – gravitational attraction – governing the disparate events. Blending theory hypothesizes that blending is not epiphenomenal, although it operates at a fairly high level of organization; that there are fundamental patterns of process and intricate mechanics and patterns of compression that run over many different kinds of products. Blending interacts with the vast complexity of grammatical and conceptual operations; it does not replace them. It plays a surprisingly important role in human creative activity, but analyzing its mechanisms and power does not diminish the diversity of activities over which it operates or the differences between those activities. Indeed, blending research uncovers many generalizations about the way in which such diversity emerges (cf. Fauconnier and Turner 2008).

Challenge 2: Everyone has known about blending – the mental combination of old things to get new things – for a long time. So what is new? Answer: If we agree on the power of blending and the need to study it, then, united, we can plant the flag and turn to the minor parts of the challenge. Gilles Fauconnier and I have surveyed the work of invaluable thinkers dating from classical antiquity, including Aristotle, who analyzed particular products of blending quite insightfully, and who sometimes even commented on the general mental power of combining ideas. Yet, these excellent forerunners typically thought of blending as an exotic, exceptional, cognitively-expensive event, used exclusively in rare moments of high creativity, rather than as a basic mental operation, noncostly, constantly deployed in everyday cognition by every cognitively modern human being. Additionally, modern blending theory has proposed that there are overarching systematic principles of blending, generic integration templates, intricate mechanisms, and constraints that run across swaths of mental work whose products look quite different.

Challenge 3: If blending exists, shouldn't we be able to program it algorithmically? Isn't that how we specify a mental process in science? Answer: I have been lucky to participate in projects dedicated to exploring the ways in which blending theory might serve the valuable field of computational creativity and inference. Computational modeling has much to teach us. Yet, the mental process itself does not appear to me to be algorithmic. It is an important part of the flexibility of blending that outputs are not determined algorithmically from inputs, or, at a minimum, computer science, artificial intelligence, and psychology have not been able so far to characterize "inputs" to blending in such a way as to make computational models of blending more than suggestive and illustrative.

Challenge 4: Where are the quick psychological tests to show us how blending works? Why don't you put people into the fMRI machine so we can see where and when blending happens and how it works? Answer: The broad empirical evidence for blending comes from the classic scientific method of making generalizations over in-sample data (grammatical patterns, for example) and then testing those hypotheses against out-of-sample data to determine whether they in fact apply. Blending theory in this way predicts findings rather than effects, a scientific method used, e.g., throughout archeology, from the archeology of early hominins to the archeology of classical antiquity. Turner (2010) surveys possibilities for experiments directed at causal inference (treatment, control, validity) and the great obstacles to designing such experiments for advanced human cognition as opposed to, e.g., pharmaceuticals or visual physiology. McCubbins and Turner (2013) discusses a set of experiments we designed and ran to begin to locate which patterns of blending are more or less tractable for subjects. Turner (2014, Appendix, "The Academic Workbench") reviews possibilities for future experiments and tests, but cautions against hopes for simple models that assume simple consistency or simple linearity. Blending is often thought to have neural correlates. In Gilles Fauconnier's phrase, this is "hardly a surprising assumption. But the correlation is complex: blending creates networks of connected mental spaces, a 'higher level' of organization, if you like. It is presumably not itself a primitive neural process. It is however a capacity of some brains, and perhaps an exclusively human capacity in its double-scope form" (Coulson 2011: 414). As Fauconnier sums it up, "Neuroscience has made awesome progress in recent years, but does not provide direct observation of conceptual operations like mental space mapping" (Coulson 2011: 413).

Challenge 5: But we have no awareness except in rare moments that we are doing any blending, so what is the evidence that it is so? Answer: Awareness is immaterial. We have no awareness during vision that our brains are doing fabulous work and that 50 % of neocortex is implicated in this work. In awareness, we just open our eyes and the visual field comes flooding in. In fact, of course, vision requires spectacular work, and the only moment in which we are likely to notice that anything is going on is when it fails, as when we have motion sickness and the visual field starts to "do" utterly inexplicable things. This makes the job of physiologists of vision quite difficult, since we cannot ask human beings to report their awareness of vision, much less rely on the answer if we could. It's just so with blending: the blending scientist must look far beyond what human beings are aware of for evidence of what is going on.

Challenge 6: But then, how do you know when a mental space, a network of mental spaces, or an integration (blending) network is active? For example, you say that to solve the riddle of the Buddhist Monk, we activate a mental space that selectively blends elements of the monk's ascent and descent. How do we know? Can we read minds? Answer: this is a fundamental question that goes to the heart of any research into human conceptualization. There are no methods for reading minds directly. Every method for detecting human conceptualization is indirect and inferential. Accordingly, cognitive science attempts to bring to bear as many methods as are suitable, and derives greater confidence according as more and more of them point to the same conclusion, the same inferences. One fundamental method, which has been in place at least as long as recorded history, and presumably further, is to check whether someone's behavior is consistent with the meaning we propose that they have constructed. We say, "Please pass the salt", and they pass the salt, or, if they do not, we have cause to seek some reason for their noncompliance. The reason might be physical inability, a disposition to the contrary, or, perhaps, a failure to have constructed the meaning we intended for them to construct. If we say, "Pass the salt", and they respond, "Say *please*", and we respond, "Please", and then they pass the salt, we derive some confidence that our idea of the meanings they have constructed is not fundamentally inaccurate. Looking for behavior consistent with the meaning we think they have constructed can mean looking for linguistic behavior. If we say something to them, and ask them to paraphrase what we have said, and they do, we check whether our understanding of the requirements and constraints of the grammatical constructions they have used in the paraphrase are consistent with our idea of the meaning they constructed. Asking for a paraphrase is an everyday kind of quiz, and science has developed many kinds of quiz to check on the meaning constructed. It quite commonly happens that people do not construct quite the meaning we intended. Consider the riddle of the Buddhist monk. If we ask the riddle, we may find that the addressees constructed none of the meaning we intended because they do not speak the language we used. The construction of meaning moreover depends upon learning many cultural frames and generic integration templates, and people from different cultures and subcultures often do not share the same frames and templates, so it is quite normal in these circumstances that an addressee does not construct the meaning we intended. But suppose we pose the riddle to two people who speak our language close to the way we do and share the same culture. It may easily turn out that one of them activates the blend and the other does not. Many people cannot solve the riddle, which we take as evidence that they have not activated a blended space containing the meeting of the ascending monk and the descending monk. But if they respond, "Yes, there must be a spot on the path that the monk occupies at the same hour of the day on the two successive days: it is the spot where the monk *meets himself*", then we take their use of the verb *meet* in this form and the reflexive personal pronoun as evidence for their having constructed a space in which there are indeed two agents, each corresponding to the monk, and that must be a blend, because in all the mental spaces for the journey, there is only one monk, and no meeting. We can quiz them further to check that they do not think this blended mental space refers to a mental space that is supposed to be actual for the journey. Often, blending researchers find that linguistic behavior leaves unexpressed some important part of the construction of meaning. For example, if we ask subjects to draw a cartoon corresponding to the sentence, "This surgeon is a butcher", we routinely find that the drawing represents the surgeon-butcher with slovenly, dirty, unkempt appearance, and often with an expression associated with some kind of mental deficiency. The drawing in this case is evidence of some covert mental space that is being used for constructing the identity of the surgeon-butcher, which we might otherwise not have detected. Similarly, linguistic paraphrases of "This surgeon is a butcher" frequently do not specify the scene in which the surgeon-butcher is working. But the cultural expectations of drawing usually lead the subject to be more specific about the scene: the surgeon-butcher is almost always drawn as working in an operating room rather than a butcher shop. When we say that someone has activated such-and-such mental spaces and such-and-such mappings, we of course mean that the reading we attribute to them requires such activations, and we may use every device known to science to check whether they have achieved that reading. Even then, attribution can be difficult, as when two different integration networks would both legitimate a particular expression. There is never a sure way to read another mind, and the researcher must always be open to the possibility that there are other constructions of meaning consistent with the subject's behavior and biological activity.

Challenge 7: Isn't blending theory incomplete? Answer: Absolutely. In fact, "blending theory" is more a framework for a research program on conceptual integration, compression, mapping, and so on than it is a theory. Many new insights have been generated inside this framework since its proposal. Its original architects look forward to future developments, which are sure to be considerable.

4 Words and morphemes

Perhaps the most natural beginning for a discussion of blending in language starts with lexical semantics. There are many lexical prompts for blending. *Safe*, for example, said of some situation, prompts us to activate a mental web corresponding to that situation, blend parts of it with the frame of *harm*, understand that the blend is counterfactual with respect to the original situation, and now blend the original situation and the counterfactual blend so that the counterfactual relation between them is compressed to *absence of harm* as emergent structure in the new blend. This compression involves conceiving of *absence of harm* as a property that can be signaled by the adjective *safe*. Other single words prompting for particular blending templates include *danger, lucky, accident, mistake, gap, dent, missing, detour*, and many others. A single sentence can contain many such words, calling for many such compressions, as in the National Public Radio warning a few days before Halloween, October 2000, "A halloween *costume* that *limits* sight or movement is an *accident lurking* in *disguise*."

The morphemes *over* and *under* in *overfish* and *undernourish* obviously call for blending networks. Turner (2007) analyzes the range of blending compressions involved in "We are eating the food off our children's plates. When we overfish, we eat not only today's fish but tomorrow's fish, too". Nili Mandelblit analyzes the use of morphological inflection of a main verb to prompt for blends of the frame of an action with the frame of causation (Mandelblit 2000, reviewed in Fauconnier and Turner 2002).

Fauconnier and Turner (2003) analyze polysemy as a consequence of blending. Through selective projection, expressions applied to an input can be projected to apply to counterparts in the blend. In this way, blends harness existing words in order to express the new meanings that arise in the blend. An example is the use of *here* in network news to mean roughly *present and active in the shared communicative scene of blended joint attention*. Combinations of expressions from the inputs may be appropriate for picking out structure in the blend even though those combinations are inappropriate for the inputs. In consequence, grammatical but meaningless phrases can become grammatical and meaningful for the blend. As an example, consider the news anchor's saying *Let me show you, here on my left,* as she points to her left, even though in the studio there is in fact nothing on her left to which she wishes to direct attention. Rather, the production crew has signaled to her that it will be insetting a clip into a window in the broadcast. The linguistic combination is fully grammatical for the blend but not for any of the individual input spaces. Similarly, one can say for the blend of same-sex marriage, *The brides married each other at noon*, even though this combination would have been infelicitous for a mental web of inputs that included only heterosexual marriage. Other examples include *computer virus* and *the square root of negative one*. Terminology that naturally applies to the blended space serves, through connections in the integration network, to pick out meaning that it could not have been used to pick out if the blend had not been built. As an example, consider the interactive, animated diagrams in (Kirk 2012), in which Olympians in an event over centuries "compete" against each other, in the sense that stick figures in compressed diagrams "race" against each other. All of the language for the frame of competition in an Olympic event applies naturally to the blend and picks out relationships across the mental spaces of the mental web containing all those individual Olympic events, even though one could not say that *Usain Bolt utterly defeated Thomas Burke* [the 1896 winner] of that mental web absent its blend. In all these ways, blending provides a continuum for polysemy effects. Polysemy is an inevitable and routine outcome of blending, but it is only rarely noticed. Some of the products of such blending strike hearers as "metaphoric" for reasons analyzed in Turner (1998).

"Change predicates" arise systematically through blending. For example, Fauconnier and Turner (2002) analyze a generic integration template according to which vital relations of analogy and disanalogy across mental spaces in a mental web are compressed in the blend to provide a human-scale concept. The analogical connections between input spaces are compressed to an identity or unity in the blend, and the disanalogical connections are compressed to change for that element in the blend. Grammar for expressing change can thereby be used of the blend. For example, we can say that "dinosaurs turned into birds" and rely on the hearer to expand from the structure in the blend and hence to recognize that we do not mean that any particular dinosaur changed at all or turned into a bird. In the blend, there is an identity, a group identity, consisting of *dinosaurs*, and this identity "changes" into a different group identity, *birds*. Such change predicates have been widely analyzed in the literature. Examples include *His girlfriend gets younger every year*, *My tax bill gets bigger every year*, and *Make this envelope disappear* [written on the back of an envelope, inviting the customer to sign up for electronic delivery of bills] (all from Fauconnier, personal communication); *The cars get three feet bigger when you enter Pacific Heights*, *The fences get taller as you move westward across the United States* (both from Sweetser 1997); *Your French has disappeared, You need to recover your tennis serve*, and *Kick the habit*. (See Tobin 2010 for a review of change predicates and blending.)

5 Syntax

Blends frequently have new emergent structure. Because linguistic constructions attached to the input spaces in the mental web can be projected down to be used of the blend to express that emergent structure, it is rare that new linguistic constructions are needed in order to express new meaning. But blending also provides a mechanism for creating emergent structure for the form part of a form-meaning pair.

Fillmore and Atkins (1992) presented the classic analysis of the verb *risk*, and the syntax of the verb *risk*, and its meaning. Fillmore and Atkins analyze the frame for *risk* as – in my words – not theirs, a blend of the frames for *chance* and *harm*. The frames for *chance* and *harm* are independent. If I say *There is a chance that it will be 30 degrees Celsius tomorrow and a chance that it will be 31 degrees Celsius tomorrow, but either one is fine*, it means that there is a possibility of one or the other, but no question of harm. Similarly, if harm is inevitable, then chance and possibility are not at issue. Accordingly, harm and chance are independent frames. But when we integrate the frames for *chance* and *harm*, we create one of the basic frames for *risk*, in particular, *running a risk*. Fillmore and Atkins offer the diagram I recreate here:

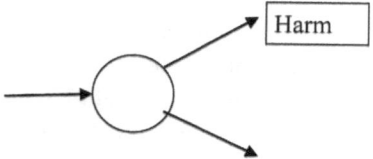

Fig. 10.1: Risk-running.

In this diagram, a circle means *chance*. There is a chance of harm. There is also a chance of something else. This is the structure of the basic frame of running a risk. But Fillmore and Atkins point out that there is yet another blend, one that blends in an additional frame, namely the frame of *choice*. We can *choose* to place ourselves in a position where there is a *chance* of *harm*. Perhaps we are betting on a horse, for example, or we like the thrill of driving fast. Here is the diagram:

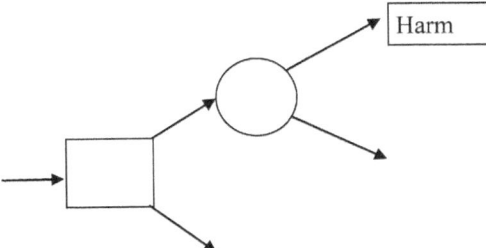

Fig. 10.2: Risk-taking.

In this diagram, a circle means *chance*, and a square means *choice*.

In effect, Fillmore and Atkins have analyzed the lexical meaning of *risk* as a set of frame blends. Importantly, blending is selective: we do not take everything from the frame of *chance* and everything from the frame of *harm* and everything from the frame of *choice* and blend them compositionally. For example, the *harm* frame automatically brings in an evaluator. If there is harm, there must be harm to someone who evaluates it in that way. Think, for example, of a diamond and an owner. If the owner wants the diamond cut, then the cutting does not count as harm. But if the owner did not want the diamond cut, then the same cutting counts as harm. Of course, we might say that a connoisseur of fine diamonds, who is not the owner, might be caused aesthetic pain by the incompetent cutting of the diamond, even if the ignorant owner did not mind. In that case, the connoisseur is the evaluator who feels the harm.

Fillmore and Atkins talk about what they call "derivative syntax", which might instead be called "blended syntax". The syntax in such cases derives from the blending of conceptual frames. For example, Fillmore and Atkins consider the verb *smear*: when you smear something on a surface in such a way that the surface is covered by what you have smeared, then the verb *smear* acquires the syntax of *cover*, as in *I smeared the wall with mud*. In that case, the verb *smear* can be placed where *cover* would go. Similarly, when loading hay onto a truck results in the filling of the truck, then *load* can take on the syntax of *fill*, as in *I loaded the truck with hay*. We can always say that we *filled the truck with hay*, but when the loading results in filling, we can then say *I loaded the truck with hay*. Selective projection in the blending of these frames includes projection of some linguistic elements attached to those frames. Accordingly, blended syntax can result from frame blending.

Fillmore and Atkins observe that when *risk* means *expose to*, then *risk* can take on the syntax of *expose to*, as in "we must reinforce the boat before risking it to the waves". Similarly, "risk" can acquire through blending the syntax for *investing in* something, as in *Roosevelt risked more than $ 50,000 of his patri-*

mony in ranch lands in Dakota Territory. Emergent syntax for "risk" arises as part of the emergent structure of the blend.

Fauconnier and Turner (2002) present a common pattern of blending according to which a concept that is blended with other meaning projects to the blend its category; this is usually called "category extension". An example can be seen from the history of the concept of "number", which has taken on dramatically more complex structure as it has been blended with other structure to produce emergent structure in successive blends for fractions, zero, negative numbers, irrational numbers, real numbers, transcendental real numbers, and complex numbers, but the category *number* has been projected to each of these blends. This pattern in syntax results in nominal compounds, where one noun is taken from each of two blended spaces, and the blend is expressed by a syntactic structure, Noun + Noun, which still counts as something that can combine in the usual ways with constructions that call for a noun. Just as the category *number* was projected from one input to the new structure in the blend, so the category *Noun* is projected from the inputs to the new structure in the blend, except that we are more likely to call it a noun phrase.

Nominal compounds can themselves be composed into new syntactic forms. Consider the nominal compound *girl scout*. The Girl Scouts are an organization. Girl Scouts learn how to hike and camp and so on. *Girl* is a noun, *scout* is a noun, *Girl Scout* is a noun, in the sense that *Girl Scout* can go into the spots in the language that nouns can go. Now take *ballet school*. *School* is a noun and *ballet* is a noun. It prompts for a frame-compatible blend. People learn things in schools and ballet can be one of the things they learn, so the *ballet* frame is subordinated and nests in this case inside the *school* frame. Now take *lace curtain*. Those are two nouns and they produce a nominal compound. It may seem strange to say, *She is a lace curtain ballet school girl scout*. But it is intelligible, and we understand what the grammar is prompting us to do. We see formal composition in the fact that *ballet school girl scout* is a nominal compound composed of two nominal compounds, and this can be again compounded with another nominal compound, *lace curtain*. What we might mean by *Oh, she is a lace curtain ballet school girl scout* could be that she receives a certain education (*ballet*) stereotypical for a certain demographic that is picked out by a style of decoration (*lace curtain*) and, as is stereotypical of these people in this social demographic, she belongs to a certain organization for children. We might even recognize this as a social stereotype if we live in certain parts of the United States.

Fauconnier and Turner (1996, 2002) analyze French double-verb causatives as an example of emergent syntax under blending. Part of the syntactic form comes from each of two input spaces, and part develops specifically for the blend. The blend has emergent syntax relative to the inputs. These causatives blend *faire* ("do") with a verb for the caused action, as in *Pierre fait manger Paul* 'Pierre makes eat Paul', *Pierre fait envoyer le paquet* 'Pierre makes send the package', and *Pierre fait mange la soupe à Paul* 'Pierre makes eat the soup to Paul'. These double-verb forms provide French speakers with ways to evoke a blending network that delivers a compressed, human-scale scene which integrates into one event at least two agents (Pierre and Paul), a causal action, a causal link, and a caused action (eat). The blend takes much of its clausal syntax from a compressed input that can be expressed via one of three single-verb forms (transitive, transfer, and optional transfer), but which does not quite serve the purpose for the causative meaning. French accordingly offers three complex blends for the compressed scene of causation and action. Each has as one input one of three compressed basic single-verb clausal constructions, and as the other input the diffuse chain of causal events with intermediate agents that we want to compress. The blend takes an additional verb from this chain of causal events, and the syntax in the blend thereby acquires two verbs.

6 Phrases, clauses, and sentences

Consider adjectives, such as those in *guilty pleasures, likely candidate,* and *red ball*. Notice that *likely candidate* (Eve Sweetser's example, personal communication) is usually used to refer to someone who is not (yet) a candidate. In that case, we are not composing the meaning of *candidate* and the meaning of *likely*. On the contrary, we are taking *candidate* from one mental space and *likely* from a mental space that includes a particular kind of frame. *Likely candidate* can be taken as prompting us to construct a blended frame in which there is someone who is likely *to become* a candidate. In *Allow yourself this guilty pleasure* and *Chocolate is a guilty pleasure*, it is not the pleasure itself that is guilty. Rather, it is the person who has the pleasure who feels guilty. In this case, there is a cause-effect vital relation between the input spaces – having the pleasure in one space causes the guilt in the other. But now, that outer-space cause-effect relationship is compressed in the blend into a feature of the pleasure. There are many similar examples, such as "grateful memories". The memories are not grateful. The person who has the memories is grateful for the events to which the memories refer. But in the blend that intentional relationship between the person and the person's memories and the events to which they refer is compressed into a feature of the memories.

Linguistic expressions for building "possibility" mental spaces (Fauconnier 1985) – e.g., *If I were a stockbroker, like my brother-in-law* – are routinely used to prompt for blending networks, as analyzed at length in Fauconnier and Turner (2002) and Dancygier and Sweetser (2005). "If-then" conditional constructions are one of the most obvious aspects of grammar used to prompt for blending, but there are many others, e.g. *I could be a stockbroker*.

Fauconnier and Turner (1996) build on Goldberg (1995) to analyze the ways in which basic clausal constructions like Caused-Motion, Resultative, and Ditransitive prompt for blending basic and familiar human-scale frames with sometimes large mental webs in order to produce compressed blends that can be expressed with the clausal form projected to the blend. The result is expressions that use verbs suited to other mental spaces in the web but not necessarily to caused-motion, resultative, or ditransitive frames. Goldberg presented Caused-Motion examples like *He sneezed the napkin under the table* and *She drank him under the table*. Others include *The officer waved the tanks into the compound, Junior sped the car around the Christmas tree* (where the verb comes from the manner of the caused motion), *I read him to sleep, I muscled the box into place*, and *Hunk choked the life out of him*. We can even say, *We blocked him from the door*, despite the fact that *block* is a verb for indicating the stopping of motion rather than the causing of motion. The frame of caused motion and the frame of blocked motion conflict directly, but through blending, we make a blend in which what is caused is absence of continued motion: an agent performs an action on an object that stops the motion of the object in a direction.

The case is similar for the Resultative construction. I can say, *No zucchini, tonight, honey. I boiled the pan dry*. The long causal chain that leads to a dry pan is compressed in the blend into a single action by the agent, although we do not actually know what that action was. Just as in the caused-motion construction, we achieve compressions in the blend. Consider *Roman imperialism made Latin universal*. *Latin* is not a thing and *universal* is not a feature. But in the blend, *Latin* becomes a thing and *universal* becomes a feature. Roman imperialism is not an agent, but in the blend Roman imperialism becomes an agent that works on an object, namely Latin, with the result that Latin becomes universal. This is the same general resultative network we see in *Catherine painted the wall white*. But now it runs over centuries, and hundreds of thousands of people, and vast causal connections: *Roman imperialism made Latin universal*.

The ditransitive construction uses as one of its input mental spaces transfer of an object from one person to another. When we blend that frame of transfer with a perhaps diffuse mental web not actually involving a hand-over, the ditransitive construction can be projected to the blend to express it, and various lexical items can come from the other input spaces, as in examples such as Goldberg provides: *She gave him that premise, She allowed him that privilege,*

She won him a prize, She showed him the view. Consider *She gave him a headache*. She can give him a headache even though she does not have one. In the ditransitive scene, if I give her the eraser, it is because I have one. But now selective projection can create a blend in which the idea of giving has emergent structure. We might project to the blend only the reception, and the causal capacity to effect the result, not the initial possession.

We can use the ditransitive clause with a verb like *denied* or *refused*, which indicates stoppage. The ditransitive clause involves transfer and reception. We create a double-scope blend of two frames that conflict fundamentally, just as we did for *We blocked him from the door*. For *She denied him the job*, "she" did something that had a causal effect on the transfer of something to "him" and what she did was stop it. In the blend, now, the transfer is not completed. Blending is selective. In what Fauconnier and Turner (1996) call the "elaborate ditransitive", the benefit of the action on the object but not the object itself is "transferred" to the recipient, as in Goldberg's *Slay me a dragon*, or James Taylor's *Slide me a bass trombone* (in the song *Steamroller*). *Slide* comes in as the event action that the agent performs; what the speaker receives is not the bass trombone but the benefit of the sliding.

One of the most thoroughly analyzed clausal constructions whose meaning is an elaborate prompt for blending is the XYZ construction (e.g., *Paul is the father of Sally, These fire retardants are the asbestos of our time*). Turner's (1987) analysis of conceptual mappings used as its data kinship terms in patterns like "Death is the mother of beauty", an example of the "X is the Y of Z" construction (xyz). This xyz construction has routine everyday use, as in "Paul is the father of Sally". It has been analyzed by (Turner 1991, 1998; Fauconnier and Turner 2002). xyz contains the "y-of" construction. A "Y of" construction prompts us to perform an elaborate number of conceptual operations and can be composed repeatedly: "The doctor of the sister of the boss of Hieronymous Bosch". Such a composition of forms asks us to construct meanings, but the meanings are not compositions of the meanings in the various component expressions.

We understand an xyz construction as prompting us to find an unmentioned w in the mental space containing y, and to blend the x-z mental space with the y-w mental space. For example, an unmentioned w for "Death (x) is the mother (y) of beauty (z)" might be *daughter*. As (Steen and Turner 2014) discuss, there are two standard patterns for y, as follows: (1) y belongs to a standard frame commonly applied to the x-z scene; y is a role connecting at least two things in that frame; and x is the value of one of those roles and z is the value of the other. Examples are *archbishop* and *aunt*. (2) y is the anchor of an entrenched generic integration template used to blend together two conflicting frames. Examples are ancestor, anchor, architect, author, backbone, bane, birthplace, blood, blueprint, bottleneck, capital, cradle, ... as in phrases like "He is the architect of our business plan and that business plan is the backbone of our operation". But, impressively, one also easily finds very many data (Steen and Turner 2014) calling for blends of strongly conflicting frames where there is no already-entrenched y-based blending template. Examples are "The head of the C.D.C. told Congress MRSA is the cockroach of bacteria", "Bakersfield is the Alaska of California", and "These flame retardants are the asbestos of our time".

There are various constructions related to X is the Y of Z, as explained in (Turner 1991), such as the $xy_{adjective}z$ form. When the y in an xyz conceptual pattern is a commonplace transformation of one thing into another, its form may be $xy_{adjective}z$, so "Language is the fossil of poetry" may be expressed as "Language is fossil poetry". When the y-w conceptual relation is a part-whole frame relation, the form may be $xz_{adjective}y$, so "Las Vegas is the Monte Carlo of America" may be expressed as "Las Vegas is the American Monte Carlo." There are many other relations that permit the z-item to be expressed through a modifier for the y-item. The full form of the xyz figure has a corollary z-y compound noun form: "disc jockey", "road hog", "budget ceiling", "mall rat", "land yacht", "jail bait", "Westerns are back in the TV saddle", and "She is gymnastics royalty".

Eve Sweetser (personal communication) found an interesting example in a *New York Times* headline: "Now 80, George Washington will soon undergo the bridge equivalent of hip replacement" (*NYT* article headline, December 8, 2011, p A-22). This construction is z-equivalent-of-y. But as Gilles Fauconnier observes (personal communication), not all y-of-z constructions convert into z-equivalent-of-y. Although the sky is the daily bread of the eyes, we do not call the sky "the eyes-equivalent of daily bread". Although Paul is the father of Sally, we do not call him "the Sally-equivalent of father". It seems that the use of the z noun in the z-equivalent construction is easiest if z is already established as a common modifier in nominal compounds, e.g. "bridge repair", "bridge replacement", "bridge construction", "bridge span", "bridge jump".

7 Ground and viewpoint

The ground is a general conceptual frame (Fillmore 1976, 1982) for organizing specific communicative situations. It includes "the speech event, its setting, and its participants" (Langacker 1985: 113). Roles in this frame – such as the time and location of the communication – take on values in specific situations. Traditions of rhetoric, philology, semiotics, linguistics, and information theory have in one way or another considered the idea of the ground, and it has been treated by a range of cognitive linguists (Fillmore 1971; Rubba 1996; Talmy 1986).

The ground derives from a basic human frame, *joint attention*. Joint attention occurs in a human-scale scene in which people are attending to something and know they are all attending to it and know also that they are engaged with each other in attending to it (Tomasello 1995; Tobin 2008). In "communicative joint attention", these people are not only jointly attending but also communicating with each other about the focus of their attention. I use "classic joint attention" to refer to perhaps the most fundamental scene of communicative joint attention, in which two (or a few) people face-to-face are not only attending to something that is directly perceptible but are moreover communicating about it, e.g., *That blackbird in the hedge has red stripes on its wings*. The frame of *the ground* is tied to this idea of classic joint attention.

Inevitably, many constructions are specialized for classic joint attention. Deictics and, more broadly, indexicals – such as "I", "you", "here", and "now" – are form-meaning pairs tied to elements in the conceptual frame of *the ground*. Their utility depends on our ability for what Fauconnier and Turner (2002) call "simplex blending". In a simplex blending network, one input mental space is an established conceptual frame and the other input spaces contain elements of just the sort to which the conceptual frame is expected to apply. For example, if one mental space has the kinship frame *father-child*, and another mental space has two people, *Paul* and *Mary*, then the blended space can blend *Paul* with *father* and *Mary* with *child*, and we can prompt for this blend by saying *Paul is Mary's father*. In fact, given our idea that "Mary" is a female name, we are likely to infer that Mary is not just a *child* but a *daughter*.

Now I can help you look for something here in this uses the deictics "Now", "I", "you", "here" and "this" to invite the hearer to make a simplex blend in which the *ground* is activated and elements in it are blended with the particular speaker, hearer, time, and location. These deictics can prompt for meanings far from *the ground*. For example, Bolinger (1979) and Lansing (1989) discuss *impersonal you*, as in *Back in the pre-Cambrian, you couldn't see the sun because of all the steam*. "You" here cannot refer to the addressee, nor indeed to any generic *you* since there were no people in the pre-Cambrian. In the blend, there is a "focalizer", but the focalizer has no referent, individual or generic. The focalizer is a blended quasi-agent who has experience but no existence.

More familiarly, consider the way in which broadcast news anchors routinely use deictics, as in these attested examples:

1. Joining me now, [images of person 1 and person 2, both in studios far removed from the studio in which the anchor is being filmed, appear inset in rectangles on the screen]. All right, guys, thank you both so much for being here.

2. [The anchor looks at the camera] You've heard the news ...
3. This is the view from news-chopper 2. You saw this story unfolding live as breaking news on our CBS news between 5 and 7 am.
4. Welcome back. A quick update for you.
5. Hope to see you at 11 o'clock tonight. Until then, have a great evening.
6. And now you know the news of this Thursday, March the twentieth, 2008. Thanks for having us in.

One input to the broadcast news blend is *classic joint attention*, which provides tight, familiar, human-scale conceptual structure and linguistic constructions to the broadcast news scene of blended joint attention. There are many other potential inputs to the blend: the news reporting team in various places; recorded footage; "B-roll" stock footage; the broadcast studio; remote studios; reporters with a camera crew in the field; the studio production team; the corporation owning the network; a scene in which a particular viewer is viewing the news clip; computer browsers on which the clip can be played; YouTube and other archives of audiovisual clips; people on the street being interviewed, etc.

In the blend, there are roles for speaker, viewer, viewer's time and place, and so on, but those roles need not have any determinate value. That is, we need have no specific mental space with a specific viewer as an input to the blend. In the blended joint attention scene of network news, the roles are interacting even if there are no values for the roles. In this blend, "now" can signal the moment of viewing; "here" can signal the locus of the "object" of joint attention, which can be the blended scene of viewing. In particular, "you" can signal the role of the viewer, who usually is given certain features: the viewer is interested and present and loyal (not switching from channel to channel). Of course, the anchor can refer to any spaces in the mental web: *If you missed our broadcast last night, If you are just joining us*, etc. The anchor can say *Here comes a special report for you now* even when the show is recorded and the anchor cannot possibly know the actual location or moment of the viewing (given that the recording might be played many times by many people in many places) and need not even know the subject of the special report, which will be chosen by the production crew at a later time. The great variety of ways in which the roles in the scene of broadcast news blended joint attention can be filled can all be managed given the usual deictics from the input of classic joint attention, which are projected to the blend.

Such projection of deictic and indexical linguistic elements to serve a blend of joint attention that provides a very tight compression for a vast mental web is familiar from posters, such as "the face" of "Uncle Sam" "looking out" of the recruiting poster, and pointing his finger, saying "I want you for U.S. Army".

We know that in the mental web that this blend serves, there is no single Uncle Sam, no particular "I", no particular "you", no utterance to a particular "you", and so on. We are not deluded, but blending provides us with a compressed, tractable mental conception and also provides us with the linguistic constructions for expressing that blend. Similarly, a U.S. World War II poster shows a man driving a convertible car with a chalk-sketch of Hitler in the passenger's seat. Its text reads, "When you ride alone, you ride with Hitler. Join a Car-Sharing Club Today!". The blend does not actually refer to a specific scene in the world; it is a compressed familiar scene of blended classic joint attention that receives all the language it needs from the inputs. We are not deluded: Hitler is not actually in our car. The person who reads the poster understands that the "you" applies to a role, an implied *you*, with certain features, which the person reading the poster might not possess: the viewer of these posters might be ineligible for recruitment to the army, might lack a driver's license or car, and so on. Scholars of literary and film representation routinely analyze the great complexities in the mental web for the implied roles in the blend, as when the character Huck Finn speaks in the first person to a reader referred to as "you", except that the reader knows that in the mental web there is an author, Mark Twain, and that Mark Twain's implied reader is rather different from Huck Finn's implied reader, or as when the voice of Jonathan Swift's *A Modest Proposal* constructs an implied speaker and an implied reader, who agree with the proposal for all its sound reasons, but Jonathan Swift also has an implied reader, one very different from the speaker's implied reader. *The 1001 Nights* is famously adept at keeping tight communicative blends for vast and cascading levels of mental webs of interacting stories (Turner 1996).

All of these *ground* phenomena are matters of *viewpoint*. Viewpoint arises inevitably from embodiment: participants in any scene of communicative joint attention are embodied, and blending projects selectively from viewpoint in the input mental spaces to the blend (see Sweetser 2012 for a review). Linguistic constructions suited to the expression of viewpoint in scenes of communicative joint attention are routinely projected to express new viewpoint phenomena that arise in blends based on joint attention.

Recanati (1995) analyzes the way in which what he calls "the epistolary present" expresses a blended temporal viewpoint belonging to the blended joint attention that arises for personal correspondence. In the blend, writer and reader are present in the moment and jointly attending, although they know that outside the blend in the mental web organized by the blend they are in different times and conditions. Recanati's attested examples include *J'ai devant moi ta lettre, et tu as devant toi ma reponse* 'I have before me your letter and you have before you my response.' The blend provides a human-scale compression. Of course, the writer is not prevented from expressing structure in mental spaces outside the blend. A letter containing a sentence like *I am so happy and know you are happy to hear it* can conclude with *By the time you receive this letter, I will already be on my way.*

Turner (1996) analyzes other temporal viewpoint blends, as when the wife, headed to the shower, says to her husband (who has asked how a certain task will be accomplished), *My husband took care of that while I was in the shower.* In the blend, the wife certainly has very much of her embodied viewpoint at the moment of utterance. But her blended viewpoint receives projections from the viewpoint of the wife (and husband) in a different, future mental space, after the shower. The wife's viewpoint from that future mental space focuses on a mental space in which the task is accomplished, and that mental space of accomplishment lies in the past, and the accomplishment accordingly has the certainty of the past. The blend provides a human-scale compression. The past tense from the viewpoint of the future space (where it is grammatical) is projected to the blend in order to prompt for new meaning in the blend, namely, that the accomplishment (by the husband) is certain. Projecting from this new structure in the blend back up to the mental space of his present communication, the husband creates not the factual existence of the accomplishment but rather the wife's absolute expectation of its impending accomplishment by him as she heads to the shower. The past tense construction demands a rationale; the husband achieves the rationale by taking the utterance as a prompt to build a mental web that includes this blended viewpoint; the wife used the past tense construction exactly to prompt the husband to build that mental network and to take it that the wife intended him to do so as the result of her using the past tense. The expression calls for a viewpoint blend, drawing on projections from both the viewpoint of the present and the viewpoint of the future.

Nikiforidou (2010, 2012) analyzes the role of blending in a construction she calls "Past tense + proximal deictic", with emphasis on the cases where the proximal deictic is "now". The preferred patterns are "was/were + now", as in *It was now possible ...* and, for a non-copula verb, "now + past tense", as in *He now saw that ...* Nikiforidou provides "a detailed blueprint of the blending mappings cued by the [past + proximal deictic] pattern" (2012). Essentially, the pattern calls for a blend of viewpoints, in which our overall understanding is stage-managed from the point of view of a narrator but some self or consciousness located in a previous time is contextually available and prominent, and the events experienced in that previous time are to be construed "from the point of view of that consciousness, as that character's thoughts, speech or perceptions" (2010). The blended viewpoint takes on elements of different perspectives and compresses a time relation. The mental space of the narrator's condition is still the mental space from which the narrated space is accessed and built up, but the experiential perspective comes from inside the narrated events. There is considerable emergent structure in the blend. In the blend, it is possible to have not only knowledge that is available only at a distance but also to have the experience, perception, and realization available only up close. In a study of the British National Corpus, Nikiforidou shows that this is a highly productive construction, even outside of literary genres.

Presciently, Nikiforidou writes that the grammatical pattern has the "effect of zooming in on the events" (Nikiforidou 2012). Steen and Turner (2014) report that a search in the Red Hen archive (http://redhenlab.org) reveals that documentaries often use the camera (and the blended joint attention scene in which the viewfinder of the camera is blended with the eye of the viewer) to "zoom in" on the "past consciousness" indicated by the *past* + *now* construction. The audiovisual zoom is a multimodal construction that supports *past* + *now*. There is a hitch in providing this *past* + *now* visual zoom, because the narrator speaks *at one time* about a consciousness *at a previous time*. That is a mismatch. The consciousness and its experiences are not available in the narrator's immediate environment, or indeed in any of the mental spaces we have for considering the production and broadcast of the narration. The news production team must provide some suitable prompt for that consciousness in the past. There are several ways to resolve the mismatch. The three most common appear to be (1) have the person who is coreferential with the consciousness we are narrating re-enact the events, with the appropriate setting and staging and so on, and film that scene; (2) find archival still photos of that person at the time and present them, perhaps, e.g., with a Kens Burns effect, as the narrator uses the *past* + *now* construction; (3) find historical film footage containing the person and run that footage as the narrator uses the *past* + *now* construction. One of the most interesting such cases arises when the narrator and the past consciousness are connected by an Identity relation, as in a PBS documentary on the Pentagon Papers, in which Daniel Ellsberg, who leaked the Pentagon Papers, is narrating in advanced age his exploits in the period 1967–1971. There is extraordinary emergent structure in this blend, including Ellsberg's ability to speak for his young self in a way that probably would not have been available to him at the time, and of course an enduring, manufactured, compressed character for "Ellsberg" the man: young Ellsberg and old Ellsberg are of course extremely different things, but the analogies between them, including analogies of viewpoint, can be compressed to a characterological unity in the blend.

Nikiforidou (2012: 179) writes of the linguistic construction, "In blending terms, ... resolution of (apparent) conflict is often achieved through the mechanism of compression, whereby elements that are conceptually separate in the input spaces are construed as one in the blended space. The construction at hand, I suggest, cues a particular kind of compression, namely compression of a time relation. The dynamic, continuously updated character of such blending networks renders them particularly suitable for representing meaning in a narrative, where formal clues may often give conflicting instructions even within the same sentence (as is the case with FIS [Free Indirect Style]).".

Sweetser (2012: 9–10) analyzes deictic displacement as a viewpoint blend:

> [A] clear example is that in English, the correct response to the invitation *Can you come to my party?* is *Sure, I'd love to come*, not *Sure, I'd love to go*. The invitation accepter might later say to a third party, *I'm going to Sandy's party on Friday.* and would be unlikely to say *come* in this context. The acceptance utterance thus participated in the inviter's deictic structure, displacing the accepter's deictic center to the inviter's …
>
> Note that the Speaker of *Can I come to your party?* has not completely recentered her deictic field on the Addressee – *I* still refers to the Speaker, and *you* to the Addressee … But the spatial deictic coordinate space, which is most canonically centered on Ego (hence on the Speaker), in this blend is mapped onto the Addressee as center.
>
> The crucial point here is that our everyday construal of personal viewpoint is a blend. It is a blend that is so common that it is hard to notice it. We normally experience our own bodies simultaneously as loci of our conscious Selves or Egos, agents of our speech and action, spatial sources of our fields of perceptual access and manual reach, interfaces of social interaction, and more. But as stated above, we also naturally create such models for other individuals around us – aided, very possibly, by our mirror neurons, which respond to other humans' grasping actions (for example), as well as to our own. Once that is accomplished, a speaker can naturally describe motion away from herself with *come*, if she is profiling the deictic field structure relative to another participant (and leaving out mention of her own deictic field).

8 Conclusion

Blending is a mental operation constantly and widely deployed in human cognition, almost entirely below the horizon of observation. Far from costly or special, it is central and indispensable to language and multimodal human communication. Over time, groups of people establish generic integration templates, which other members of the group can learn, and which come to count as part of a group's abilities and even its identity. The form-meaning pairs of grammar often have as part of their meaning a set of hints and constraints on integration mapping. Communicative forms do not mean; instead, they prompt human beings to construct meaning. This chapter has been a topical introduction to some of the ways in which form-meaning patterns prompt for patterns of conceptual integration.

9 References

Coulson, Seana (2011): Constructing meaning: An interview with Gilles Fauconnier. *Review of Cognitive Linguistics* 9(2): 413–417.
Dancygier, Barbara and Eve Sweetser (2005): *Mental Spaces in Grammar: Conditional Constructions*. Cambridge: Cambridge University Press.
Fauconnier, Gilles (1985): *Mental Spaces: Aspects of Meaning Construction in Natural Language*. Cambridge: MIT Press.
Fauconnier, Gilles and Mark Turner (1996): Blending as a Central Process of Grammar. In: A. Goldberg (ed.), *Conceptual Structure, Discourse, and Language*, 113–130. Stanford: Center for the Study of Language and Information. [Expanded web version 1998, available at http://markturner.org.]
Fauconnier, Gilles and Mark Turner (2002): *The Way We Think: Conceptual Blending and the Mind's Hidden Complexities*. New York: Basic Books.
Fauconnier, Gilles and Mark Turner (2003): Polysemy and Conceptual Blending. In: B. Nerlich, V. Herman, Z. Todd and D. Clarke (eds.), *Polysemy: Flexible Patterns of Meaning in Mind and Language*, 79–94. Berlin/New York: Mouton de Gruyter.
Fauconnier, Gilles and Mark Turner (2008): Rethinking Metaphor. In: R. Gibbs (ed.), Cambridge Handbook of Metaphor and Thought, 53–66. New York: Cambridge University Press.
Fillmore, Charles (1971): *Santa Cruz Lectures on Deixis*. Bloomington: Indiana University Linguistics Club.
Fillmore, Charles (1976): Frame Semantics and the Nature of Language. *Annals of the New York Academy of Sciences* 280: 20–32. doi: 10.1111/j.1749-6632.1976.tb25467.x
Fillmore, Charles (1982): Frame Semantics. In: Linguistic Society of Korea (ed.), *Linguistics in the Morning Calm*, 111–137. Seoul: Hanshin Publishing Company.
Fillmore, Charles J. and Beryl T. Atkins (1992): Towards a frame-based organization of the lexicon: the semantics of RISK and its neighbors. In: A. Lehrer and E. Kittay (eds.), *Frames, Fields and Contrast: New Essays in Semantics and Lexical Organization*, 75–102. Hillsdale: Erlbaum.
Goldberg, Adele E. (1995): *Constructions: A Construction Grammar Approach to Argument Structure Constructions*. Chicago: University of Chicago Press.
Kirk, Chris (2012): How Badly Would Usain Bolt Destroy the Best Sprinter of 1896? *Slate* 26 July 2012.
Langacker, Ronald W. (1985): Observations and speculations on subjectivity. In: J. Haiman (ed.), *Iconicity in Syntax*, 109–150. Amsterdam/Philadelphia: John Benjamins.
Lansing, Jeff (1989): Impersonal you. Unpublished manuscript.
Mandelblit, Nili (2000): The grammatical marking of conceptual integration: From syntax to morphology. *Cognitive Linguistics* 11(3/4): 197–252.
McCubbins, Mathew D. and Mark Turner (2013): Concepts of Law. *Southern California Law Review* 86(3): 517–572.
Nikiforidou, Kiki (2012): The constructional underpinnings of viewpoint blends: The *Past + now* in language and literature. In: B. Dancygier and E. Sweetser (eds.), *Viewpoint in Language: A Multimodal Perspective*, 177–197. Cambridge: Cambridge University Press.
Nikiforidou, Kiki (2010): Viewpoint and construction grammar: The case of *past + now*. *Language and Literature* 19(2): 265–284.
Recanati, François (1995): Le présent épistolaire: Une perspective cognitive. *L'Information Grammaticale* 66: 38–44.

Rubba, Jo (1996): Alternate grounds in the interpretation of deictic expressions. In: G. Fauconnier and E. Sweetser (eds.), *Spaces, Worlds, and Grammar*, 227–261. Chicago: University of Chicago Press.

Steen, Francis and Mark Turner (2014): Multimodal Construction Grammar. In: M. Borkent, B. Dancygier and J. Hinnell (eds.), *Language and the Creative Mind*, 255–274. Stanford: CSLI Publications.

Sweetser, Eve (1997): Role and individual readings of change predicates. In: J. Nuyts and E. Pederson (eds.), *Language and Conceptualization*, 116–136. Oxford: Oxford University Press.

Sweetser, Eve (2012): Introduction: Viewpoint and perspective in language and gesture from the Ground down. In: B. Dancygier and E. Sweetser (eds.), *Viewpoint in Language: A Multimodal Perspective*, 1–22. Cambridge: Cambridge University Press.

Talmy, Leonard (1986): Decoupling in the semantics of attention and perspective. Presentation at the 12th Annual Meeting of the Berkeley Linguistics Society, University of California at Berkeley.

Tobin, Vera (2008): Literary Joint Attention: Social Cognition and the Puzzles of Modernism. PhD dissertation, University of Maryland.

Tobin, Vera (2010): Grammatical and rhetorical consequences of entrenchment in conceptual blending: Compressions involving change. In: F. Parrill, V. Tobin and M. Turner (eds.), *Meaning, Form, and Body*, 329–347. Stanford: Center for the Study of Language and Information.

Tomasello, Michael (1995): Joint Attention as Social Cognition. In: C. Moore and P. Dunham (eds.), *Joint Attention: Its Origins and Role in Development*, 103–130. Mahwah: Lawrence Erlbaum Associates.

Turner, Mark (1987): *Death is the Mother of Beauty: Mind, Metaphor, Criticism*. Chicago: University of Chicago Press.

Turner, Mark (1991): *Reading Minds: The Study of English in the Age of Cognitive Science*. Princeton: Princeton University Press.

Turner, Mark (1996): *The Literary Mind: The Origins of Thought and Language*. New York: Oxford University Press.

Turner, Mark (1998): Figure. In: C. Cacciari, R. Gibbs, Jr., A. Katz and M. Turner (eds.), *Figurative Language and Thought*, 44–87. New York: Oxford University Press.

Turner, Mark (2007): The way we imagine. In: I. Roth (ed.), *Imaginative Minds*, 213–236. London: Oxford University Press and The British Academy.

Turner, Mark (2010): Blending Box Experiments, Build 1.0. [http://ssrn.com/author=1058129].

Turner, Mark (2014): *The Origin of Ideas: Blending, Creativity, and the Human Spark*. New York: Oxford University Press.

Anscombre, Jean-Claude and Oswald Ducrot (1983): *L'argumentation dans la langue*. Liège/Bruxelles: Mardaga.

Arie Verhagen
Chapter 11: Grammar and cooperative communication

1 Meaning in animal and in human communication: managing versus sharing

Compared to animal communication, human language use appears to exhibit an exceptionally high degree of information sharing. Starting with Dawkins and Krebs (1978), behavioural biologists have come to the conclusion that animal signalling is best seen as an instrument for manipulation (both of conspecifics and members of other species), not for sharing information. Owings and Morton (1998) introduce the complementary notions of "management" (for the signaller's side) and "assessment" (for the interpreter's side) to characterize the nature of vocal communication among non-human animals as directly linked to the fundamental biological process of maximizing an organism's fitness; they contrast this with "exchanging information", which they associate with human communication. As they state at the very beginning of their book:

> This book provides a discussion of animal vocal communication that [...] links communication to fundamental biological processes. [...]. Animals use signals in self-interested efforts to manage the behavior of other individuals, and they do so by exploiting the active assessment processes of other individuals. [...] Communication reflects the fundamental processes of regulating and assessing the behavior of others, not of exchanging information. (Owings and Morton 1998: i)

Human communication, linguistic and otherwise, is the exception; as Tomasello (2008:5) remarks about a simple human pointing gesture to indicate something of interest to one's company: "Communicating information helpfully in this way is extremely rare in the animal kingdom, even in our closest primate relatives". Information is a potentially precious resource and sharing it does not obviously enhance fitness. Information sharing thus requires rather special conditions to be biologically adaptive, for example genetic relatedness ("kin-selection"). But

---

Note: I would like to thank the editors, Barend Beekhuizen, Ronny Boogaart, Max van Duijn and an anonymous reviewer for insightful comments on a first draft of this chapter.

Arie Verhagen, Leiden, NL

https://doi.org/10.1515/9783110626476-012

humans also readily share information with non-kin. In the case of humans, the biological conditions consist in the special character of human sociality as exhibiting a level of cooperation that is unique in the animal kingdom (Enfield and Levinson 2006; Tomasello 2009, 2014), which is itself part of our adaptation to life in cultural environments: groups of collaborating individuals sharing a set of cultural practices and competing with other groups (Boyd and Richerson 2006; Richerson and Boyd 2005).

Another hallmark of human languages is that they are fundamentally conventional. A regular association between sound and meaning consists in a process of repeated use that is crucially based on – and at the same time (re)produces – mutually shared knowledge and expectations in a community, i.e., a convention. It is typical for a convention that it contains an element of arbitrariness, in the sense that another behavioural pattern could in principle work equally well. For example, I drive on the left side of the road in Great Britain just because I know that, in this community, everyone else does and that everyone expects everyone else (including me) to do so; I definitely switch to driving on the right when I find out, e.g., upon entering a country on the European continent, that is what everybody in that community does. In the same way, I use the sound *horse* for the concept HORSE just because I know that, in this community, everyone else uses it that way and everyone expects every other member of the community to use it that way. I would readily change my use of this sound if I were to find out that the members of the relevant community were using it in another way (which would amount to my finding out that I was wrong about the meaning of *horse* in this language). So conventionality is predicated on the basic willingness to cooperate in solving coordination problems (Lewis 1969). Thus, some "design features" (Hockett 1960) of language – referentiality, arbitrariness – are directly linked to distinctive characteristics of the human species. The same basic willingness to cooperate also underlies the universal property of language use that in actual utterances more is communicated than what is encoded in the conventional meanings of the signals used (first formulated in philosophy by Grice 1975, now more and more an empirical science, cf. Noveck and Sperber 2004), which in turn makes linguistic systems constantly subject to change (e.g., Keller 1998).

In this chapter, we will explore the connections between the overall structure of human cooperative communication and its cognitive "infrastructure" (Tomasello 2008; this work covers a wealth of empirical evidence concerning both) on the one hand, and distinct types of linguistic meaning on the other. The argument will be that a number of basic conceptual domains that are commonly encoded in the grammars of human languages – deixis ("grounding"), "descriptive" categorization ("frames"), "logical" operations like negation – pertain to particular features of human cooperative communication.

2 Argumentative language use

From the point of view of modern linguistic pragmatics, there is a certain irony in the emphasis on sharing information as a dominant feature of human communication in evolutionary approaches. Especially speech act theory started with the recognition that an important part of ordinary language use consists of all kinds of acts that *cannot* be properly characterized as descriptive statements about the world, i.e., as sharing information (Austin 1962; see Senft 2014, ch.1, for a concise overview). Undertaking commitments (*I promise*), transferring ownership (*It's yours*), issuing requests (*Please stay off the grass*) are ways of *doing* things in the (social) world, not of describing it. Specifically, issuing commands and asking questions – in general: directive speech acts – are attempts to influence the behaviour and mental states of addressees, and thus fit the biological processes of regulating and assessing that Owings and Morton identify as characteristic for animal communication. Indeed, connectives draw this parallel themselves:

> [...] signals are not most usefully thought of as statements of fact that can be judged true or false; signals are more like human [...] speech acts [...] – outputs that serve to achieve some effect on targets. [...] According to this approach, signals are not statements of fact, that can be judged to be true or false, but are efforts to produce certain effects. (Owings and Morton 1998: 211)

Focussing on the *effects* of using certain words and constructions, all kinds of language use that can be described as "argumentative" or "rhetorical" may be seen as serving basic and general biological functions of communicative behaviour. Clear cases are provided by situations in which the choice of words itself becomes an issue of controversy. For example, immediately after the attacks of September 11, 2001 on the New York World Trade Center and other prominent buildings in the USA, several commentators were searching for terminology to talk about the events; these events were felt to be unique, never experienced before, and thus lacking obvious words to describe them. Many people hit upon the notion of "crime" (usually accompanied by adjectives such as *horrendous* to indicate its extreme nature), while some (also) soon started to use the terminology of "war" ("This is an act of war", "America is at war", etc.). While the two terms are not incompatible (and were in fact sometimes used side by side), several commentaries clearly tended more to the use of one term rather than the other, and this became an issue of debate. The Dutch prime minister's initial reaction was in terms of "war", but he soon withdrew this term and apologized for having used it, after several members of parliament had criticized him for it. A few of the critics argued that the events lacked too many characteristics of "ordinary" acts of war (there was no conflict between states, the perpetrators were not an army, etc.), but the absolutely general point of the criticisms was that this terminology might easily lead to a kind of response that was bad or at least undesirable: retaliating with military force, possibly against people who had nothing to do with the terrorists.

So what was at stake was not so much whether the descriptive value of the terms *crime* or *war* fitted the situation better. Those who criticized the use of the term *war* certainly agreed that it was not an ordinary "crime" either. What was at stake was whether the situation at hand justified the *consequences* associated with the terms used: *crime* invites one to think that some kind of *police* force should be deployed, and that the *culprits* should be brought to *trial*, so that *justice* may be done, etc.; *war* on the other hand, invites one to think that the use of *military* force is called for, in order to *defeat* the *enemy*, in a large scale operation that will inevitably also affect others than the perpetrators themselves (*collateral damage*). That is to say, they differ systematically in the kind of *inferences* they invite, and in that sense they are clearly oriented towards specific effects on addressees.

These are phenomena known in cognitive linguistics under such labels as "frames", "(idealized) cognitive models", or "cultural models" (I will return to reasons for preferring the latter term later). Such concepts comprise both criteria for their application ("What features make a situation suitable to be labelled with this term?"), as well as a basis for inviting inferences (see Holleman and Pander Maat 2009; Thibodeau and Boroditsky 2011, for discussion and experimental evidence). It is interesting to notice that controversy easily arises over the applicability of the terms to a situation (what we may call "backward oriented meaning"), but hardly over the invited inferences ("forward oriented meaning"); precisely because of *agreement* over the inferences invited by the terms *crime* and *war*, people *dis*agree whether the 9/11 events are best called one or the other. Thus, we may say that knowing the meaning of category denoting terms like *war* and *crime* includes knowing culturally accepted inferences associated with them, i.e., their argumentative values.

A recent example from (Dutch) political language concerns the terms *religion* and *ideology*. The right-wing politician Geert Wilders, leader of the "Party for Freedom", claims that Islam is not a religion but an ideology, whereas other parties, including the Christian-Democrats, continue to call Islam a religion. In this case, it is especially clear that it would be hard, if not impossible, to specify objective criteria distinguishing a religion from an ideology, but nobody has the feeling that this implies that the meaning of the words is unclear or vague. On the contrary, everybody understands these meanings perfectly well, viz. as suggesting that the strict guarantees for the freedom of religion in The Netherlands, laid down in the country's constitution, should not apply to Islam according to Wilders, while they should according to others; by the same token, Wilders' opponents accuse him of undermining the constitutional state (as he proposes to withhold certain constitutional rights from the adherents of a religion), while Wilders himself uses his opinion[1] to refute this accusation – again: all clearly a matter of inferences being invited by the words, in a way that competent users of the language agree on.

These cases demonstrate the need for taking argumentation into account as a component of the meaning of at least *some* linguistic expressions. Usually, analysts characterize a discourse as argumentative only if many of the utterances in it are presented and understood as reasons for and/or justifications of *another* explicitly stated opinion of which the addressee is to be persuaded, so if they appear in a context of a (real or virtual) dispute. This is the domain of (classical) rhetoric and (modern) argumentation theory (cf. Van Eemeren et al. 2014), as an approach to a presumably special type of language use. However, in a linguistic perspective, there are good reasons to adopt the position that the very same mechanisms operate in language use *in general*; the point is that both words and grammatical constructions work in the same way in "overt" argumentation in disputes and in everyday language use.

It was a profound insight of Ducrot (see Anscombre and Ducrot 1983; Ducrot 1996) that argumentativity does not constitute a special case of language use, but rather a common component of linguistic meaning. Ducrot's example (cf. Verhagen 2005: 11) involves a consideration of the seemingly purely informative statement *There are seats in this room*. He observes that this sentence can be felicitously followed by something like *But they are uncomfortable*, with a contrastive connective, but not by *And moreover, they are uncomfortable*, with an additive one. The use of the term *seats* is in itself sufficient to evoke a certain conclusion about the degree of comfort in the room: expectations about it are raised. But inferences cannot be licensed by a single proposition, so there must be another one functioning as the second premise in an implicit syllogism. This consists in the fact that for members of our culture, knowing what seats are (knowing the concept SEAT, denoted by *seat*) *includes* knowing that as a rule,

---

[1] In the context of negotiations about a coalition government in 2010, the 'Party for Freedom' and two other parties had declared that they 'agree to disagree' in their views of the categorial status of Islam (religion or ideology), clearly recognizing that the use of the terms is not a matter of facts. By the same token, though, this declaration makes it appear as if the use of terms then is a matter of choice (a kind of Humpty-Dumpty view of meaning), not recognizing the conventional, thus supra-individual and normative character of linguistic meaning (cf. Tomasello 2008: 290–292).

they contribute positively to comfort (the "frame", or "cultural cognitive model"). As a consequence, mentioning the presence of seats intrinsically provides justification, an argument, for thinking that the room will provide more than a minimum of comfort. It is this invited inference that is countered by the subsequent assertion that the seats are uncomfortable; and it is this contrast that is marked by *But*, and that is incompatible with the use of *And moreover*. Schematically:

Tab. 11.1: Utterances as arguments: utterances provide specific premises which, together with an associated model providing a general premise, evoke inferences.

Utterances	"There are seats in this room"	"But they are uncomfortable"
Cultural cognitive model	↓ ← NORMALLY, SEATS CONTRIBUTE POSITIVELY TO COMFORT → ↓	
Inferences	a) Raise expectations about degree of room-comfort	b) Cancel a) (i.e., lower the expectations again)

The felicity or infelicity of discourse connectives (in particular *but*) in combination with relevant continuations can thus be used as diagnostics for the argumentative value of the first utterance; *but* does not mark a contrast at the level of objective information (in fact, this seems inherent in the notion of contrast: uncomfortable seats are perfectly possible as part of reality; cf. Sweetser 1990: 103–4). Indeed, connectives function in exactly the same way in apparently innocent claims about seats (*There are seats in this room, but they are uncomfortable*) as in emotionally or politically charged claims about Islam (*There are adherents of Islam in this country, but they do not enjoy freedom of religion*). It may be harder to disagree about the applicability of some terms (like *seat*) than others (like *religion*), but this is not a difference in the structure and working of the semantic machinery: knowing a conceptual category denoted by a linguistic item involves knowing one or more cultural cognitive models that license conclusions of certain kinds. Linguistically, less and more controversial terms do not represent different types of meanings (say, descriptive versus argumentative); they are just less or more controversial.

The power of argumentativity as a systematic property of language was already demonstrated experimentally by Lundquist and Jarvella (1994), and is also highlighted by the fact that it turns out to be the unifying factor underlying the similarity in grammatical behaviour of a number of lexical items and grammatical patterns. The content of argumentation in the examples above comes from the lexical items, but the connective *but* has the very schematic role of countering the rhetorical force of the first conjunct, whatever its content: *The house is very nice but expensive* differs from *The house is expensive but very nice* precisely because the second conjunct rhetorically "wins" in both cases. Similarly, the feature that unifies the grammatical behaviour of different negation operators and perspectival predicates in a language is their effect on the argumentative character of the relevant utterances. The similarity in co-occurrence of *not* and *barely* with respect to the *let alone* construction, for example, reduces to the similarity of their roles as argumentative operators, and the same holds for the grammatical similarities of verbs of communication (*say, promise*) and cognition (*think, know*) with respect to complementation constructions across different person and tense markings and with respect to discourse connectives (cf. Verhagen 2005, 2008a; Fausey and Boroditsky 2010 and Fausey and Matlock 2010 are experimental studies of the argumentative force of different grammatical constructions).

So we now have both reasons to characterize language use as crucially different from animal communication (information sharing being normal) and as similar to it (efforts to produce effects being normal as well). The way to resolve this paradox is to undertake both a more thorough analysis of the types of meaning of the different linguistic expressions involved, and of the structure of communicative events.

3 Cooperative communication and joint cognition

Human cooperative communication involves a large amount of joint knowledge. Much of this functions as "common ground" (Clark 1996), and is a necessary condition for communication to succeed; at the same time, joint knowledge is also updated and expanded as communication proceeds. In section 4, we will look at the first dimension and its linguistic reflexes; section 5 will be concerned with the second dimension. As a basis for both, this section provides a conceptual analysis of what is involved in joint knowledge, in terms of a group of people acting as a cognitive unit.

The role of common ground comes out clearly in the case of the – for humans – simple act of pointing. "Outside of any shared context, pointing means nothing. But if we are in the midst of a collaborative activity (say, gathering nuts), the pointing gesture is most often immediately and unambiguously meaningful ('there's a nut')" (Tomasello 2009: 73). It is because we both *know* that we are engaged in a joint activity – and moreover know that each of us knows – that establishing joint attention through a pointing gesture can provide the basis for a rich and specific inference, as well as the belief that this was precisely what

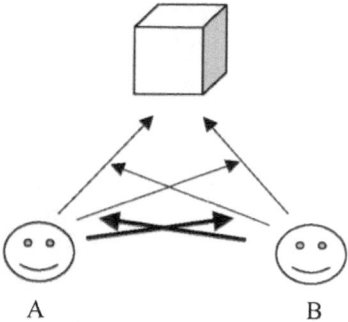

Fig. 11.1: Mutually shared attention.

the pointer intended. The point is that it must be obvious, transparent to all of us that we are engaged in a joint activity and what it consists in.

One way of thinking about this is in terms of the mental states of each participant about the mental states of others. According to Zlatev (2008: 227), joint attention, i.e., *mutually* shared attention rather than just shared attention, comprises an embedding of three levels of attention. Consider figure 11.1.

The idea is that both A and B (1) attend to the same object, (2) know that the other does, and (3) know that the other knows. Without the third level, they can be said to share their attention for some object, but not to *mutually* share it. However, what this way of thinking does not capture, is the insight that A and B form a *group*, are organized into a higher level entity that constrains and co-determines the roles and the mental states of the participants (figure 11.1 does not distinguish between competitive and cooperative situations). Humans have what philosophers call intentionality – ideas, goals, desires, etc.: mental states directed at objects and other individuals. They share this with other animals, certainly other primates. However, humans not only entertain such mental states as individual subjects, but also jointly, i.e., *inter*subjectively. They exhibit what Searle (1995) calls "*we*-intentionality". When two individuals are coordinating their activities in a collaborating group, they are not just two individuals engaged in their own projects (possibly including attention to others), but a "team" that is collectively engaged in a single project, part of which is joint attention for some entity. Recognizing this group-level is crucial for the proper characterization of certain forms of cognition. This becomes especially apparent in the light of tasks that are distributed over members of a group in such a way that coordination allows the group to produce results that no individual could produce on its own; from extensive empirical research into ship navigation (Hutchins 1995), Hutchins (2006: 377) concludes: "social groups can

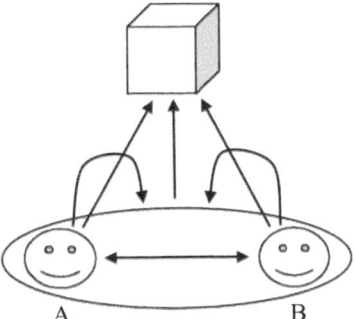

Fig. 11.2: Coordinated group cognition.

have cognitive properties that are distinct from the cognitive properties of the individuals who compose the group" (Hull 1988 provides a lot of empirical evidence that the same holds for scientific research teams). So let us consider a "group-level" conception of joint cognition as represented in figure 11.2, the ellipse indicating the group of (in this case) two individuals that jointly attend to an object.

In this figure, the upward pointing arrows point to the object of attention, the horizontal bi-directional arrow represents the relationship of coordination, and the two bent arrows point from an individual to what the group is jointly attending to rather than to what each single other individual is attending to as in figure 11.1. The group of coordinating individuals is a cognitive unit, an information processing entity the boundaries of which happen not to coincide with a skull; the group is defined by a set of concepts and assumptions – common ground – which all members believe each other to have access to, allowing them to coordinate, which captures the idea of the "transparency" of mutual knowledge in the group. Indeed, this characterization not only applies to joint attention, but also to other joint mental states, like beliefs and goals. In particular, it also applies to the knowledge of conventions, including linguistic ones (Lewis 1969), and thus is in fact a general characterization of "joint cognition".

First of all, this idea provides an intuitively more direct representation of joint ("we", "you and I together") as opposed to shared ("you as well as I") attention, in a way that fits well with insights into conversation and other "joint projects" (Clark 1996, 2006 – below, I will return to Clark's proposals about the *structure* of joint projects), as well as with recently developed insights into specifically human forms of cooperation (Tomasello 2009, 2014).

Secondly, this way of conceptualizing joint cognition has interesting consequences when we realize that figure 11.2 represents an "outside" view. For a

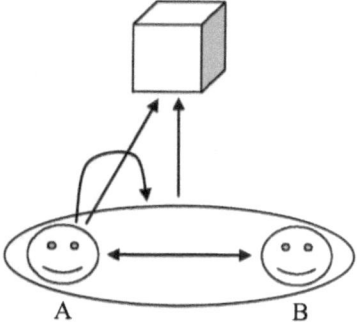

Fig. 11.3: Joint cognition, from individual point of view.

single member *inside* a group involved in joint cognition, it primarily looks as in figure 11.3.

Coordination comprises assigning to others the same mental capacities one has oneself (what Tomasello and Rakoczy 2003 eloquently call "self-other equivalence"); we can therefore allow projection from the group to individual members ("downward percolation"), i.e., deriving inferences about what an individual attends to, knows, believes, etc., from the assumption that s/he is a member of a group involved in attending to object X. Most elementary, it follows that B is attending to the same object and to the group, i.e., the "outside" view depicted in figure 11.2. It also follows that A may assume that B assumes that A is attending to X, and vice versa, i.e., configurations like the one depicted in figure 11.1, or ones with even more levels of embedding, applying the percolation rule over and over again. The same is true for meta-cognitive awareness: A may apply the rule to any group member, so also to ones involving A (e.g., "I know I am looking at X", "I believe that I understand why John thinks we have a problem"). Indeed, the ideas of "self" and subjectivity only make sense in the context of some awareness of *others* and their intentional stances – realizing that one can be the object of another's attention, and that there are different points of view, one of which is one's own (cf. Tomasello 1994). But processes of "recursive mind-reading", to use Tomasello's (2014) term, do not as such enter into the characterization of mutual knowledge, and since this is cognitively unrealistic (as recognized since Lewis 1969; cf. Campbell 2005), the group-level view of *we*-intentionality provides a better characterization than the multiple individuals view.

4 Three types of common ground and three types of meaning

A primary example of linguistic elements that can only be understood against the background of common ground, is constituted by so-called deictic elements. These are elements whose interpretation systematically and crucially is to be computed with knowledge of the communicative situation and its participants, what Langacker calls the "Ground" of an utterance (Langacker 1990, and various other publications). The reference of *I* and *you* is determined in terms of the roles defined by the communicative event: the producer of the utterance (more precisely: who is to be considered responsible for it; think of quotes, but also of a secretary typing a letter for the boss, the message box saying *I accept the conditions* that is to be clicked before installing software, etc.), and the addressee. The interpretation of third person pronouns cannot be determined positively in terms of elements of the common ground, but their semantics still makes crucial reference to it; they indicate that the referent is uniquely identifiable on the basis of joint knowledge of the ongoing communicative event. So it is for good reasons that Tomasello (2008: 5) invokes pronouns to illustrate his point about the special character of human communication:

> The ability to create common conceptual ground [...] is an absolutely critical dimension of all human communication, including linguistic communication with all of its *he*'s, *she*'s, and *it*'s.

Deictic meanings occur in all kinds of linguistic items. The present tense and expressions like *now* or *at this point in time* (due to the element *this*) denote situations that are co-extensive in time with some (first) person's speech act. Here too, we find "negative" deixis as in third person pronouns; although the time of a situation presented in a past tense clause cannot be positively determined, its semantics still makes crucial reference to the Ground: "a non-actual (e.g., remembered or imagined) situation, one that does not directly impinge on present issues". The exact characterization of different elements (in different languages) will differ, but the general point is that their conventional meaning makes essential reference to the Ground.

The consequence is that deictic elements can only be felicitously used when the relevant knowledge of the Ground (and its elements) is in fact mutually shared (at the very least: *made* shared by an additional communicative act, such as a pointing gesture); they *presuppose* sharedness. Suppose I say something like *Please hand me that screwdriver*. My use of the demonstrative *that* – a deictic element – indicates that you and I mutually agree on the same, single, specific exemplar of the category SCREWDRIVER in our present common environment that is the object of my request. This may be for a host of reasons: you may be holding one in your hand, there may be only one screwdriver in our common visual field, or only one that I used most recently (as you know), or there may be only one (mutually obvious to you and me) that is suited for the job I have to do, or whatever. But if the one you hand me turns out not to be the one I want, then something has gone wrong; we have to conclude (with hindsight) that the things co-present to us in the speech situation did not in fact make the same object uniquely salient to both of us – I may have mistakenly thought that you had one in your hand, for example, and then you hand me the one I had just been using myself. In general terms: When a deictic element is used and the relevant knowledge is in fact not mutually shared, communication fails.

Notice that this failure happens at a different level than that of conventional meanings. The problem is not that we do not share knowledge of the conventional function of the element *that*. Such situations occur too, e.g., in conversations between native and non-native speakers of English, such as speakers of Slavic languages, which do not have a system of definite and indefinite determiners like Western European languages. The latter kind of miscommunication is of the same type as when you say *Please hand me the pliers* and I hand you the pincers, resulting from us not sharing knowledge of the conventional rules for using the sound *pliers*. Here, the cause of the misunderstanding does exist at the level of conventional meaning, viz. the meaning of the sound *pliers*. The kind of misunderstanding described above (resulting from lack of joint knowledge of the speech event) cannot occur with a non-deictic term like *pliers*, as its meaning does not refer to, thus does not invoke, shared knowledge of the *present*, specific communicative situation.

This important distinction between levels is not always made fully explicit. For example, Tomasello and Rakoczy (2003: 128), discussing the emergence of a shared symbol when a child imitates an adult's use of some signal, write:

> [...] the child uses the new symbol to direct another person's attention precisely as they have used it to direct her attention (the role reversal comes out especially clearly in deictic terms such a[s] *I* and *you*, *here* and *there*). [...]. We may think of this bi-directionality or intersubjectivity of linguistic symbols as simply the quality of being socially "shared".

While this is not incorrect, it may suggest that deixis is just an extreme case of role reversal, as if this were a continuum on which linguistic items may take different positions. But that masks the categorical difference between these *types* of meanings:
a) all linguistic signals, consisting of (combinations of) conventional pairings of form and function, are understood on the basis of mutually shared knowl-

edge, in a way that can in general be described in terms of role-reversal (I utter the form X to achieve the same effect in you as you achieve in me when you utter X);

b) *on top of that*, for *some* linguistic items, the very *content* of the effect being achieved by a form X is (partly) defined in terms of mutually shared mental states with respect to the specific communicative situation at hand, and may involve role reversal in that specific situation; for example: B utters the sound *I* to make A attend to B, which is the same effect – but only with role reversal – as when A uses the sound *I* to make B attend to A.

In other words: all linguistic items are being understood "intersubjectively" in the sense of being based on mutually shared knowledge of the connection between sound and meaning, but for only *some* of them, the meaning itself refers to mutually shared knowledge of the situation of use.[2] The latter are deictic terms, or more generally, in Langacker's terminology: "grounding predicates" (not all deictic terms have to involve true role reversal; recall the remarks on the past tense and third person pronouns above). The notion "intersubjectivity" is thus applied at different levels of linguistic analysis: generally ("All linguistic communication is based on mutually shared knowledge") and more specifically ("The meaning of some linguistic elements invokes mutually shared knowledge of the communicative situation"). We will see later that there is at least yet one more way to apply "intersubjectivity" in semantics.

Clark and Marshall (1981) relate the distinction between deictic elements and content elements, as well as their common basis in shared intentionality, to different types of *sources of evidence* for mutual knowledge. Based on their discussion, we can distinguish three major types. First, the most immediate source of evidence for mutual knowledge of participants in a communicative event is, of course, that event itself (Langacker's Ground). It is this source of evidence that is tapped by deictic elements.

The second type of evidence consists of the common personal history of interlocutors. In terms of linguistic categories, this is especially what allows the use of proper names to succeed in picking out unique referents. There may be many people by the name of *Andrew*, but if I use this name in a conversation with my wife, I can rely on her picking out a unique individual (not necessarily

---

[2] This difference corresponds to the two types of signals in the evolutionary story of Tomasello (2008). On the one hand pointing, which may be seen as a precursor of linguistic deixis as it basically involves the same cognitive infrastructure not shared by apes; on the other hand pantomiming, i.e., iconic gesturing, which *is* shared with great apes, and can be seen as a precursor of descriptive terms.

present in the speech situation) who is mutually the most salient one for us in our shared history (e.g., our son). And I can use exactly the same name to successfully refer to *another* individual in a conversation with *another* interlocutor, invoking the same mechanism of mutual knowledge of common personal history.

Finally, a third source of evidence for mutual knowledge is membership of the same community: a shared culture. Even before I start a conversation, even with someone I have never met before, I can and will assume all kinds of information to be mutually known to me and my interlocutor on the basis of the assumption that s/he is also Dutch, a linguist, an employee of the same company, etc. Shared knowledge of a language, i.e., of conventions for using certain vocal or visual signals, is another kind of community based mutual knowledge. For example, on the basis of some evidence that my interlocutor is a linguist, I will assume mutual knowledge of a specific meaning of the terms *subject* and *paradigm*. On the basis of evidence that he is Dutch, I assume mutual knowledge about a huge variety of things, such as the system of parliamentary elections in The Netherlands, the name of the Dutch king, the location (roughly) of the airport named *Schiphol*, the fact that the country's capital is not the seat of its government, and also such lexical items as *betekenis* (roughly: 'conventional meaning', as in *This word meant something totally different 200 years ago*) and *bedoeling* (roughly: 'intended meaning', as in *He meant something totally different than what you were thinking*), a conceptual distinction not conventionally associated with formally distinct lexical signals in English, for example. On the basis of evidence that my interlocutor is American, I will not be justified in assuming these pieces of information to be mutually known, but I will be in assigning some others that status, including the lexical items *commitment* and *obligation*, a conceptual distinction not conventionally associated with formally distinct lexical signals in Dutch.

So we have now established a distinction between three major types of meaning based on three major types of evidence for mutual knowledge: deictics invoke the most immediate evidence available to interlocutors, the speech event itself; proper names invoke a wider source of evidence: shared personal history; common nouns and verbs invoke the widest source: a shared culture.[3] The latter two types correspond to the episodic and semantic long term memory, respectively, while the first type corresponds to short term memory.

---

[3] Definite descriptions – the main topic of Clark and Marshall (1981) – do not invoke a specific source of evidence. The construction [*the* X] only indicates identifiability within *some* part of the common ground, be it the speech event (*Hand me the screwdriver*), shared personal history (*I went to see the doctor this morning*), or shared culture (*The king is coming to visit next week*).

It is the third kind of meanings, conveyed by descriptive items denoting conceptual categories, which also provide access to knowledge about the kind of inferences conventionally licensed by the concepts involved. It is because of their basis in the shared culture of a community that the term "cultural models" is especially appropriate for knowledge of this kind. Deictic elements do not activate specific conceptual *content* licensing certain inferences. Proper names activate shared experience with the referents involved. This might in specific cases evoke certain inferences (the effect of uttering *Andrew gave me a pill for this problem* when Andrew is known to be a medical doctor may be different from when he is known to be an electronics engineer), but they do not do so conventionally, while common nouns do.[4] It is these culturally shared concepts that provide the implicit second premises underlying the *general* argumentative impact of "statements of fact" (cf. section 2).

5 Hierarchy in joint projects: the niche for argumentation

We have now seen how human communication in general is based on common ground, and how specific types of linguistic meaning are in turn grounded in different sources of evidence. Now how does argumentation relate to cooperative communication? The answer has to take into account that human activities exhibit a hierarchical structure, and that this has some special consequences when the project is a joint one (Clark 1996, 2006). Hierarchical structure is an elementary property of any goal-directed project. To use Clark's (2006) example, if I plan to construct the do-it-yourself TV-stand that I bought at the furniture store, that constitutes my main project; I then have to decide how to divide the job into subparts – What shall I build first: the top part or the lower part? And again, for the top part: which panels to attach first? And so on. Similarly, when Ann and Burton agree to construct the TV-stand *together*, they divide this entire project into smaller subprojects, each of which is split into smaller ones again, and so on.

With each step partitioning a project into subprojects, one is committed to the higher level project – the subproject is executed in order to achieve the goal

---

[4] This also explains, at least partly, the referentially redundant use of descriptive lexical noun phrases in discourse, such as the use of *the president* where *he* would have been referentially sufficient in *Obama reformed the health insurance system; the president considered it his most important achievement* (cf. Maes 1990).

of the project one-level higher in the hierarchy, and the latter is thus necessarily "on the agenda", presupposed. However, when this is a *joint* project, such commitments are much more strongly *binding* than when it is an individual project. In the latter case, it is no problem to drop a particular subproject midway and decide to change the order of execution of certain subprojects. But in the joint case, several serious risks are connected to such a course of action. The reason is that in a joint project, each participant's commitment is conditional upon *both* participants' commitment to the joint project: I commit myself to you to do my part so long as you commit yourself to do yours, and vice versa (Clark 2006: 130). My commitment therefore does not disappear when I conclude that another course of action would be better. If I abandon an ongoing subproject in the same way as I might in the case of an individual project, this is likely to cause serious harm, in the short run both to myself (because you will continue to do your part, and because it threatens the entire project) and to you (because you cannot do your part properly if I don't do mine, and again: because the entire project is put at risk), and also in the long run, because it threatens my relationship with you, and possibly my general reputation.

This provides additional support for the proposal in section 2 to view joint cognition as a group-level phenomenon rather than as just a phenomenon of a collection of individuals entertaining assumptions about the others and *their* individual cognition. But what is important for our purposes here, is the insight that the strongly binding commitments in joint projects, as long as a person is engaged in one, exist at the higher levels of the joint project but not (yet) at the lowest level that the participants are actually engaged in, because this is where a joint commitment for the further course of action has to be *established*.

It is here that argumentation is crucial for cooperation. Participants have to probe each other's conception of the current state of affairs (each other's mental model of the relevant part of the world), identify points of potential difference between them, and communicate ways of resolving such differences – if they are to achieve their joint goal of successfully executing this step, allowing them to go on to the next step. Consider the following partial exchange in one particular instance of a joint TV-stand-building project (Clark 2006: 128):

(1) A: So, you wanna stick the ((screws in)). Or wait is, is, are these these things, or?
 B: That's these things I bet. Because there's no screws.
 A: Yeah, you're right. Yeah, probably. If they'll stay in.
 B: I don't know how they'll stay in ((but))

At the point where A produces the utterance in the first line, the joint goal is to attach two pieces to each other. A starts with checking if her collaborator's plan is to use "the screws" (taken to be mutually salient). But before a response is forthcoming, A notices something else, within the joint field of attention (*these things*), that provide an alternative (*or*); so now there is an issue, a potential difference, which she puts on stage with her utterance.

B's response is a proposal for resolution, by picking one side of the alternatives presented (*these things*) and motivating it. The latter is done with the negative sentence *there's no screws*, so a proposal to A to change her mental model of the situation (THERE ARE SCREWS) and instead adopt B's; in the present context, given mutual knowledge about the joint project and its components, this also constitutes an argument for the proposal to use *these things*; the argument status is marked by the conjunction *because* (it does not mark the cause of *these things* being present).

A's acceptance (*you're right*) of the proposal to change her mental world model thus also constitutes acceptance of the argument status of the second part of B's utterance, and – again, given the joint commitment to the higher level project – of the conclusion as well. This constitutes reaching agreement on the course of action to be taken in the present subproject. Notice that the modal adverb *probably* does not count as a rejection of the conclusion (*We should use these things to attach the pieces*), but at most as a limitation of the personal responsibility of A for the choice of the course of action, and thus as at most an *opportunity* for B to provide more support or to reconsider; this "weakening" of the acceptance is motivated by A in the form of a conditional implying uncertainty about the functionality of *these things*. B expresses agreement with the uncertainty, but indicates that he is still in favour of the same course of action (*but*).

So what we can say is that the argumentative moves (marked by negation, several connectives (*or, because, but*), a modal adverb, conditionals) contribute to establishing coordination within the lowest subproject being executed, against the background of the joint commitments previously established on higher (sub)projects. It is the recognition of hierarchical structure of joint projects, which presupposes that joint commitments are in place at higher levels and at the same time have to be established for the present subproject, that provides us with the "niche" for argumentation *within* the general framework of human cooperative communication.

Argumentation definitely is a subtype of the kind of processes defining animal communication – "regulating" and "assessing" behaviour – but their character is crucially transformed by their being embedded in cooperative practices. In lexical semantic terms: Argumentation is not a synonym for regulating and assessing, it is a hyponym – a subordinate concept, a special case with special properties of its own, not inherited from its hyperonyms. It *is* directed at influencing an addressee, but the way it works is not by manipulating him or evoke the desired behavioural response directly, but by attempting to cause him to adopt a certain mental state: to be convinced himself, by the arguments provided, that a particular course of action is the optimal one in the given circumstances, to allow the present joint project to proceed. The benefits of that highly indirect way of influencing another person in the context of cooperation, are that it guarantees the most reliable execution of each participant's role, and also little loss of reputation or readiness to cooperate with each other in the future in case the course of action turns out not to work well after all, because responsibility is distributed and shared.

This is not to say that any argument is always a *good* argument, nor that manipulation is absent from human communication. People are most easily persuaded by arguments that they already believe, as these are least costly to introduce or to change.[5] Joint commitments, once established, may also be exploited by one participant to get the other to continue playing his part even if the latter would prefer not to (*You agreed that we were going to build this thing now, didn't you? So do your part!*).[6] But that does not alter the fact that argumentation constitutes an attempt to get the addressee to form the opinion, strengthened by the arguments provided, that X is the best thing to do and/or to believe, and to thereby make precisely this opinion – i.e., the addressee's own, not the sender's signalling behaviour – the *immediate* cause of the addressee's behaviour and/or belief.

If the chosen course of action in the present subproject fails, or the attempt to decide on a joint course of action fails, then this may be a reason to return to the higher level – which then by definition becomes the present subproject for which (new) agreement has to established (*Maybe it is a better idea to build the bottom part first, after all*),[7] and argumentation is relevant. But as Clark's analysis demonstrates, the higher the level of a joint project with respect to the one presently being executed (the "deeper" one gets into a joint project), the harder it becomes to renegotiate it. Joint commitments at very high levels may thus appear virtually impossible to (re)negotiate, as the risks of harm being

---

[5] Drawing on a large body of empirical studies on inferential fallacies like confirmation bias, Mercier and Sperber (2011) use precisely this view of argumentation-in-service-of-human-cooperation to argue that it evolutionarily precedes and underlies human reasoning.

[6] This is one important risk of joint commitments that Clark (2006) discusses in connection with the "Milgram experiments" (designed as psychological experiments on obedience), where the experimenter, when refusing to renegotiate higher level joint commitments, may be said to perform such an exploitation.

[7] One of the conventional functions of an expression like *after all* is to mark such a return to a previously established higher subproject.

done are simply too large to be considered (cf. the force of a threat of the type *You don't want to be excluded from the group, do you?*). Indeed, the fact that it is impossible to volitionally "choose" or change the meaning of linguistic expressions is a special case of this phenomenon; it would effectively result in all cooperation with other members of the community breaking down, i.e., abandoning the joint project of one's culture that makes all other, specific joint projects possible.[8]

Returning to the issue of linguistic meanings, the special role of negation (and other argumentative operators) and of connectives within a specific joint subproject, is to modify the argumentative value of an utterance and to relate such values of discourse segments to each other, respectively. In section 4, we established three types of linguistic meaning, all of which are characterizable as understood "intersubjectively", viz. as invoking the shared communicative situation, the shared personal histories, or the shared culture. The signs discussed here are not of one these "sharing" kinds of intersubjectivity, but they relate to intersubjectivity in yet another way: in order to establish cognitive coordination, participants have to explore, negotiate, and ultimately resolve potential differences, and it is this particular function that negation and other argumentative constructions are dedicated to.

But in service of this primary coordinating function, linguistic negation and other argumentative items invoke common ground as well. Marking an utterance as argumentative indicates a (potential) difference in epistemic stance or attitude towards some object of conceptualization; so there are always two distinct "mental spaces" involved. However, these mental spaces have to *share* an implicit background assumption for the argumentation to work. If I say to you *John didn't pass the first course* or *John barely passed the first course*, I can only thereby intentionally communicate to you that you should give up hope of John being successful in college, if the cultural model that passing a test normally strengthens the assumption that one will be successful is in our common

---

[8] Building on Mercier and Sperber (2011), Tomasello (2014: 110–112) develops a notion of "cooperative argumentation" that is conceptually quite similar to the one elaborated here, but he limits its applicability to the second major step in his account of the evolution of human thinking: that of collective on top of joint intentionality. In section 2 above however, I argued, in line with Verhagen (2005, 2008a, 2008b) that from a linguistic point of view, this limitation does not seem motivated. The structure and expression of overtly recognized justifications and implicit ones are the same; the two allegedly distinct domains do not differ in terms of grammatical properties. For instance, negation and contrast markers work in the same way across both domains. Another telling observation in this connection is, in my view, that negation is acquired very early – admittedly not immediately in all of its adult functions, but certainly with its modal force, about what "ought" not to happen (cf. Dimroth 2010).

ground. As we saw at the end of section 4, it is descriptive lexical items (*pass*, *course*) that provide access to such cultural models, and without these being jointly available, negation and other argumentative operators do not work in actual communication.

The projection of a mental space representing a stance different from the speaker's also makes this other stance *relevant* in the common ground; when saying *Mary is not happy*, the speaker presents "Mary is happy" as relevant.[9] As a consequence, utterances with (syntactic) negations may in a subtle way convey judgments about their topic; when someone says about a student *John did not give the right answer*, he presents "John gave the right answer" as relevant, while he does not evoke that idea when saying *John gave a wrong answer*. In a series of experiments, Beukeboom et al. (2010) show that readers of negative sentences of the first type actually get a more positive image of John's qualities as a student than readers of non-negated sentences of the second type; the sentence with negation implicitly conveys the idea that John normally gives correct answers, i.e., is a good student.

In short, two related systematic properties of natural language negation in usage – the necessity of a shared cultural background model and the joint relevance of a mental space representing a different epistemic stance – confirm that argumentative elements are adapted to cooperative communication just like deictic elements are, although their primary functions relate to different levels in the hierarchical structure of a joint project.

6 Conclusion

The fundamentally cooperative nature of human communication and the cognitive infrastructure associated with it underlie a typology of basic semantic dimensions of natural language expressions. First, the hierarchical nature of joint projects underlies the distinction between two types of expressions, each of which may be said to mark and presuppose intersubjectivity, in different ways. One type is exemplified by *deictics*, invoking mutual knowledge of the communication event to pick out objects for joint attention in agreed-upon subprojects. The other type consists of *argumentative* elements (negation, argumentative connectors, and the like) oriented towards coordination: establishing mutual

---

[9] A recognition he is not committed to when using morphological negation (*Mary is unhappy*). Cf. Verhagen (2005: 70–75) for arguments and a discussion of some consequences, especially so-called double negations of the *not un*-Adjective type (*Mary is not unhappy*).

agreement in the present subproject. These items presuppose possible differences (distinct mental spaces), but they also invoke mutual knowledge – of cultural models associated with "content words" – in order to allow such differences to be removed or resolved, and the project to proceed; the shared models provide the implicit premises necessary to allow conclusions to be drawn from the arguments that are presented explicitly. Although specific items of both types may well provide *some* information about the world they may relate to (think of male vs. female pronouns, for example), their distinctive deictic or argumentative character cannot be characterized in terms of features of objects of conceptualization, but has to be understood in terms of the structure of cooperative communication.

Second, mutual knowledge (common ground) is assumed on the basis of a number of systematically different *sources of evidence*, and these constitute another dimension of types of meanings, orthogonal to the first one. Co-presence in the communication event itself is the most direct source of evidence for what is mutually known, and it defines deictics. Shared personal histories constitute a wider source of evidence, and it especially underlies the use of proper names. The widest source of evidence for mutual knowledge is a shared culture; this underlies the argumentative value of, i.a., common nouns and verbs.

Further refinements and divisions may certainly be envisaged, and they are definitely necessary in studying the way this general conceptual space of cooperative communication is structured in different languages. The rich empirical study of items "attracted" or "repelled" by negative operators in Israel (2011), for example, reveals both detailed structure in the rhetoric of scalar argumentation, as well as intricate patterns of conventional associations between several expressions in English. Or take the difference between pronouns of "distance" and "solidarity", or the nature of honorifics in languages that have them; such markers operate in the dimension of intersubjective relations as well, but they pertain to these *without* a link to the object of conceptualization – the use of a second person pronoun of respect ("your$_{[+respect]}$ house") does not affect the construal of a clause's objective content, very much unlike negation, in particular.[10]

Apart from this, the point of this chapter is that generally recognized *major* types of meanings in human languages may insightfully be characterized in

---

[10] We have seen before that the notion of "intersubjectivity" can be applied in semantic analyses in several ways, and this ("managing interpersonal relations totally independently of the object of conceptualization") is another one. This variability has sometimes caused confusion in the use of the term. Two insightful recent attempts to clarify these matters are Ghesquière et al. (2012) and especially Nuyts (2012).

terms of their specific role with respect to the general structure of human cooperative communication. Sharing information and common ground have traditionally been recognized as distinctive characteristics of language use, and they underlie some of these types. When we take the hierarchical nature of joint projects into account as well, we find that the distinction between higher, agreed-upon levels and the current subproject where coordination has to be established, provides the niche where argumentation, and linguistic items structuring argumentation, play a specific role in the coordination process. Cooperation is generally recognized as a necessary condition for human communication, and human meaning, to evolve. The point is strongly reinforced by the close correspondence between major types of meaning and the basic structure of human cooperative communication. Detailed understanding of the structure of cooperation also allows us to see how, alongside sharing information, "managing others" – typical for animal communication – is also a component of human (linguistic) communication, transformed into argumentation for coordination in ongoing joint projects.

7 References

Austin, John L. (1962): *How To Do Things With Words*. Oxford: Oxford University Press.
Beukeboom, Camiel J., Catrin Finkenauer, and Daniël H. J. Wigboldus (2010): The negation bias: When negations signal stereotypic expectancies. *Journal of Personality and Social Psychology* 99: 978–992.
Boyd, Robert and Peter J. Richerson (2006): Culture and the evolution of the human social instincts. In: N. J. Enfield and S. C. Levinson (eds.), *Roots of Human Sociality. Culture, Cognition and Interaction*, 453–477. Oxford/New York: Berg.
Campbell, John (2005): Joint attention and common knowledge. In: N. Eilan and J. Roessler (eds.), *Joint Attention: Communication and Other Minds*, 287–297. Oxford: Oxford University Press.
Clark, Herbert H. (1996): *Using Language*. Cambridge: Cambridge University Press.
Clark, Herbert H. (2006): Social actions, social commitments. In: N. J. Enfield and S. C. Levinson (eds.), *Roots of Human Sociality. Culture, Cognition and Interaction*, 126–150. Oxford/New York: Berg.
Clark, Herbert H. and Catherine R. Marshall (1981): Definite reference and mutual knowledge. In: A. K. Joshi, B. L. Webber and I. A. Sag (eds.), *Elements of Discourse Understanding*, 10–63. Cambridge: Cambridge University Press.
Dawkins, Richard and John R. Krebs (1978): Animal signals: information or manipulation? In: J. R. Krebs and N. B. Davies (eds.), *Behavioural Ecology: An Evolutionary Approach*, 292–309. Oxford: Blackwell.
Dimroth, Christine (2010): The acquisition of negation. In: L. R. Horn (ed.), *The Expression of Negation*, 39–73. Berlin/New York: Mouton de Gruyter.
Ducrot, Oswald (1996): *Slovenian Lectures/Conférences Slovènes. Argumentative Semantics/Sémantique argumentative*. Ljubljana: ISH Inštitut za humanistične študije Ljubljana.

Eemeren, Frans H. van, Bart Garssen, Eric C. W. Krabbe, A. Francisca Snoeck Henkemans, Bart Verheij, and Jean H. M. Wagemans (2014): *Handbook of Argumentation Theory*. Berlin: Springer.
Enfield, Nick J. and Stephen C. Levinson (eds.) (2006): *Roots of Human Sociality. Culture, Cognition, and Interaction*. Oxford/New York: Berg.
Fausey, Caitlin M. and Lera Boroditsky (2010): Subtle linguistic cues influence perceived blame and financial liability. *Psychonomic Bulletin and Review* 17: 644–650.
Fausey, Caitlin M. and Teenie Matlock (2010): Can grammar win elections? *Political Psychology* 32: 563–574.
Ghesquière, Lobke, Lieselotte Brems, and Freek Van de Velde (2012): Intersubjectivity and intersubjectification. *English Text Construction* 5: 128–152.
Grice H. Paul (1975): Logic and conversation. In: P. Cole and J. L. Morgan (eds.), *Syntax and Semantics*, Vol. 3, *Speech Acts*, 41–58. New York: Academic Press.
Hockett, Charles F. (1960): The origin of speech. *Scientific American* 203: 88–111.
Holleman, Bregje C. and Henk L. W. Pander Maat (2009): The pragmatics of profiling: Framing effects in text interpretation and text production. *Journal of Pragmatics* 41: 2204–2221.
Hull, David L. (1988): *Science as a Process. An Evolutionary Account of the Social and Conceptual Development of Science*. Chicago: Chicago University Press.
Hutchins, Edwin (1995): *Cognition in the Wild*. Cambridge: MIT Press.
Hutchins, Edwin (2006): The distributed cognition perspective on human interaction. In: N. J. Enfield and S. C. Levinson (eds.), *Roots of Human Sociality. Culture, Cognition and Interaction*, 375–398. Oxford/New York: Berg.
Israel, Michael (2011): *The Grammar of Polarity. Pragmatics, Sensitivity, and the Logic of Scales*. Cambridge: Cambridge University Press.
Keller, Rudi (1998): *A Theory of Linguistic Signs*. Oxford: Oxford University Press.
Langacker, Ronald W. (1990): Subjectification. *Cognitive Linguistics* 1: 5–38.
Lewis, David (1969): *Convention. A Philosophical Study*. Cambridge: Harvard University Press.
Lundquist, Lita and Robert J. Jarvella (1994): Ups and downs in scalar inferences. *Journal of Semantics* 11: 33–53.
Maes, Alfons A. (1990): The interpretation and representation of coreferential lexical NPs in expository texts. *Journal of Semantics* 7: 143–174.
Mercier, Hugo and Dan Sperber (2011): Why do humans reason? Arguments for an argumentative theory. *Behavioral and Brain Sciences* 34: 57–111.
Noveck, Ira A. and Dan Sperber (eds.) (2004): *Experimental Pragmatics*. New York: Palgrave Macmillan.
Nuyts, Jan (2012): Notions of (inter)subjectivity. *English Text Construction* 5: 53–76.
Owings, Donald H. and Eugene S. Morton (1998): *Animal Vocal Communication. A New Approach*. Cambridge: Cambridge University Press.
Richerson, Peter J. and Robert Boyd (2005): *Not by Genes Alone. How Culture Transformed Human Evolution*. London/Chicago: University of Chicago Press.
Searle, John R. (1995): *The Construction of Social Reality*. New York: Free Press.
Senft, Gunter (2014): *Understanding Pragmatics*. London/New York: Routledge.
Sweetser, Eve E. (1990): *From Etymology to Pragmatics. Metaphorical and Cultural Aspects of Semantic Structure*. Cambridge: Cambridge University Press.
Thibodeau, Paul H. and Lera Boroditsky (2011): Metaphors we think with: The role of Metaphor in Reasoning. *PLoS ONE*: 6 1–11.

Tomasello, Michael (1994): On the interpersonal origins of self-concept. In: U. Neisser (ed.), *The Perceived Self. Ecological and Interpersonal Sources of Self Knowledge*, 174–184. Cambridge: Cambridge University Press.

Tomasello, Michael (2008): *Origins of Human Communication*, Cambridge/London: MIT Press.

Tomasello, Michael (2009): *Why We Cooperate*. Cambridge/London: MIT Press.

Tomasello, Michael (2014): *A Natural History of Human Thinking*. Cambridge/London: Harvard University Press.

Tomasello, Michael and Hannes Rakoczy (2003): What makes human cognition unique? From individual to shared to collective intentionality. *Mind and Language* 18: 121–147.

Verhagen, Arie (2005): *Constructions of Intersubjectivity. Discourse, Syntax, and Cognition.* Oxford: Oxford University Press.

Verhagen, Arie (2008a): Intersubjectivity and the architecture of the language system. In: J. Zlatev, T. P. Racine, C. Sinha and E. Itkonen (eds.), *The Shared Mind: Perspectives on Intersubjectivity*, 307–331. Amsterdam/Philadelphia: John Benjamins Publishing Company.

Verhagen, Arie (2008b): Intersubjectivity and explanation in linguistics – a reply to Hinzen and Van Lambalgen. *Cognitive Linguistics* 19: 125–143.

Zlatev, Jordan (2008): The co-evolution of intersubjectivity and bodily mimesis. In: J. Zlatev, T. P. Racine, C. Sinha and E. Itkonen (eds.), *The Shared Mind: Perspectives on Intersubjectivity*, 215–244. Amsterdam/Philadelphia: John Benjamins Publishing Company.

Zlatev, Jordan (2008): The co-evolution of intersubjectivity and bodily mimesis. In: J. Zlatev, T. P. Racine, C. Sinha and E. Itkonen (eds.), *The Shared Mind: Perspectives on Intersubjectivity*, 215–244. Amsterdam/Philadelphia: John Benjamins Publishing Company.

Index

References such as '178–9' indicate (not necessarily continuous) discussion of a topic across a range of pages. Wherever possible in the case of topics with many references, these have either been divided into sub-topics or only the most significant discussions of the topic are listed. Because the entire work is about 'cognitive linguistics', the use of this term (and certain others which occur constantly throughout the book) as an entry point has been minimised. Information will be found under the corresponding detailed topics.

abstract concepts 22–23, 26–27, 31, 203, 223, 230–32
– embodiment 22, 231–32
abstract ideas 196
abstract meanings 222–23, 231
abstract representations 122, 231, 236
abstract rules 117–18, 120, 122
abstract schemata 125, 132
abstract structures 116–18, 171
abstract thought 22
abstract words 89, 222–23, 226, 230–32, 236
– representation of 236
abstraction 115–22, 124–25, 133, 141, 157, 159–60, 246, 248
– levels of 92, 94, 99, 102–3, 105, 124–25, 128
– process of 115, 119
abstractionist approaches 115, 119, 122–26, 135
accuracy, classification 77, 123
action verbs 222, 228, 230, 236
activation 29, 41–42, 128–29, 170–71, 227–28, 230, 233, 235
– patterns 230
active voice 44–49, 52–54
addressees 215, 252–53, 263, 268, 273–75, 281, 288
Adelman, J. S. 66–67, 75–76
adjectives 151–52, 203, 236, 254, 259, 273
adverbials 36, 41, 147, 208
adverbs 151, 156, 161, 236, 287
affection 22–23, 209
affective information 231–32, 239
affective systems 25, 29, 239
affixal derivation 182
affordances 15, 20, 88, 233

agent-cued trials 45–46, 49
agents 44–46, 49–50, 52–53, 176, 178, 182, 253, 259–61
– volitional 116, 118
agreement 40, 168, 226, 274, 287–88, 291
algorithms 76, 118, 120, 123–24, 135
alternatives, structural 36–37, 53–54
Alzheimer's disease 101, 228
ambiguity 65, 173, 213, 234
AML 123–24, 135
amodal representations 225, 228, 230, 238
amodal symbols 225, 237–38
analogy 3, 122–24, 135, 159, 246, 255
analysis, linguistic 23, 36, 91, 140, 161, 196, 206, 212
anaphora 170, 184–85
ancient Greek 38
anger 210–12
animal communication 271, 273, 277, 287, 292
animals 11, 16, 96, 120–21, 126–27, 199, 271, 278
apprehension 140, 148–49, 154–55, 157–59, 163
argumentation 275–76, 285–89, 292
– cooperative 289
argumentative language use 273–77
argumentative operators 277, 289–90
argumentative values 274, 276, 289, 291
argumentativity 275–76
arguments 12, 16–18, 205–6, 213–15, 223, 276, 287–88, 290–91
– utterances as 276
Aristotle 175, 182, 250
arrows 43–44, 46, 105, 150, 152, 279
– dashed 158
articulation 53, 123

296 — Index

articulators 39, 133
artifacts 13, 87, 226
artificial communication 106–8
artificial concepts 91–92, 95–96
artificially defined concepts 88, 90
assertions 5, 198, 276
assignment 39, 46, 48, 51, 54
– grammatical-role 47–48, 50, 54
– subject 52–53
– subject-role 49
– syntactic roles 51, 53
association weights 127
associations 42, 67–68, 74–75, 80, 102, 104, 222, 226–27
– affective 231–32
associative learning 29, 104, 127
asymmetry 141–42
– functional 159
– fundamental 148
– prominence 148
– salience 148
– viewing 142
Atkins, B. T. 256–57
attention 1, 3–4, 37–47, 49–50, 140–41, 150–51, 162–63, 278–80
– blended joint 254, 264–65, 267
– distribution of 39, 43
– empirical research 41–53
– focus of 44, 143, 145–48, 154
– mutually shared 278
– role of 37–38
– and salience 3, 36–55
– and syntactic choice 43–53
– theoretical considerations 38–41
– visual 43, 53
attentional control 42–43
attentional focus 42, 44, 46–47, 50, 53–54
attentional processes 37–39
attentional resources 38, 41, 101
attributes 65, 92, 253
– lexical 65–66
automatic mappings 36, 45
automaticity 40, 71
automatization 70–71, 133
awareness 142, 146, 251–52, 280
– intersubjective 141–42
– meta-cognitive 280

background knowledge 154
backtracking 153, 157
backward oriented meaning 274
Bahasa Indonesia 41
basic brain mechanisms 63, 69
basic level categories 6–7, 15, 93–94
basic mental operations 245, 250
basic structure 127, 292
behavioral evidence 80, 227
behavioral outcomes 66, 104
behaviors 40, 96–97, 103, 107, 195, 209, 252, 271
– linguistic 43, 79, 252–53
behavioural methods 4
beliefs 16, 71, 109, 121, 158, 277, 279, 288
bidirectionality 79, 105, 169, 176, 282
Bill's father 144–45, 158, 160, 255
biological processes 271, 273
birds 16, 93–94, 97, 160, 226, 255
blended joint attention 254, 264–65, 267
blended space 199, 247, 249, 253, 255, 258, 263, 268
blended viewpoints 265–66
blending 3, 158–59, 179, 187, 200, 245–68
– challenges to blending theory 250–54
– classic example 249
– elements 245–48
– ground and viewpoint 262–68
– networks 247, 254, 259–60, 263, 268
– phrases, clauses an sentences 259–62
– and syntax 256–59
– words and morphemes 254–56
blends 159, 199, 246–49, 253–68
– compressed 248–49, 260
– frame 257–58
– viewpoint 266, 268
Blevins, J. 122, 130, 134
Blumenthal-Drame, A 64, 71, 74, 77–79
Bock, K. 37, 43, 45–46, 51, 53
bodily experience 13, 16, 22, 163, 195–96, 200, 209, 221
bodily movement 14, 24, 213
body
– and mind 11–12
– parts 21, 145, 168–69, 172, 175, 177
boundaries 20, 94, 145, 279
– disciplinary 224
boundedness 178

Index — **297**

brain 12–13, 25–27, 31–32, 72–73, 102–3, 167–68, 227, 237–38
– circuitry 29–30
– damage 29, 65, 226
– regions 101–4, 228
– systems 22, 25–27, 29, 75
broadcast news 255, 263–64, 267
building blocks 224, 226
bundles of thought 248
Bybee, J. 19, 63, 70–71

calculus 119, 156
canon 143, 145–46
canonicality 45, 47, 52, 142–43, 145–46, 149
capacities 88, 141, 152, 157–59, 251
– human 16, 22, 251
– mental 22, 157, 280
Caramazza, A. 28, 228, 233
categories 87–91, 93, 95–99, 101, 103, 105, 175, 177–78
– basic level 6–7, 94
– conceptual 276, 285
– grammatical 71, 150, 152, 162
– linguistic 37–38, 88, 224, 283
– semantic 105
categorization 1, 3, 15, 87–109, 223, 250
– computational models 96–100
– and concept learning 89, 91–93, 99–102, 104
– concepts and labels 88–91
– literature 88, 90
– neural bases 100–3
– one label, two ideas 91
– tasks 100, 103
– temporal 95
– traditions 95–96
category learning 100, 102, 128
category membership 93–94, 96, 98
causal actions 181, 259
causal events 259
causation 176, 254, 259
caused-motion constructions 17–18, 260
CD see *contextual diversity*
centrality 143, 146, 154
chained metonymies 184–85
chance of harm 256
change predicates 255–56

characterization 1, 70–71, 88, 101, 145, 160, 162, 278–80
– conceptual 150–51
– of entrenchment 70–71
children 19, 42–43, 71–72, 94, 117–18, 132–34, 263, 282
choice 46–47, 52–53, 99, 107, 123–24, 131, 147, 163
– frame of 256–57
– of profile 147, 162
– syntactic 43–53
– of words 205, 273
chunk storage 77–78
chunking 41, 70–71, 77, 132–33
CL research 179, 184
classification 91, 99, 172, 176
– accuracy 77, 123
– error 100
– tasks 93, 100–1
clausal grammar, metonymy in 183–84
clauses 154, 157, 259, 291
clichéd expressions 205
cliffhanging 183
clusters 94, 99–100, 206
CMT 204, 207, 213–14
CNP (conjoined noun phrase) 47
co-occurrence 68, 126–27, 236, 277
coding
– schemes 129
– syntactic 40–41, 54
cognition 2, 13–14, 31–32, 133–34, 140–41, 167, 179, 277–78
– joint 277–80, 286
– linguistic 31, 119
cognitive development 24, 141
cognitive functions 11, 25, 29, 32, 103
cognitive grammar 2, 17–18, 133–35, 140, 150–51, 154, 156, 160
cognitive linguistics see also *Introductory Note*
– definition 1
– future 4–8
– history 2
cognitive models 69, 95, 167, 169, 172–73, 179, 274, 276
cognitive operations 15, 25, 31–32
cognitive organization 70, 148
cognitive processes 2–3, 25, 71, 135, 170

cognitive psychology 6–7, 18, 25, 62, 72, 76, 224
– and embodiment 15–16
cognitive science 1, 3, 7, 11–13, 72–73, 77, 80, 234
cognitive unit 277, 279
coherence 20, 197
collateral damage 274
collocations 67–68, 80, 108
commitments, joint 286–88
common ground 277, 279, 281, 284–85, 289–92
common nouns 182, 284–85, 291
communication 103–4, 106, 245, 247, 249, 251, 261–63, 277
– animal 271, 273, 277, 287, 292
– artificial 106–8
– cooperative 271–73, 275, 277, 279, 281, 285, 287, 289–92
– events 130, 133, 277, 281, 283, 290–91
– human 108, 268, 271, 273, 281, 288, 290, 292
– linguistic 107–8, 281, 283
– personal 255, 259, 262
communicative intentions 105, 133, 205
communities 95, 108, 210, 245, 272, 284–85, 289
competition 125, 206, 255
complement clauses 5, 36
complex nouns 152
complex sentences 119
composite expressions 152, 158
composition 71, 152, 204, 261
– formal 258
compounding patterns 145, 162
compounds 181, 183
– nominal 258, 262
comprehenders 17, 26, 28
comprehension 23–24, 26, 28–29, 32, 38, 107–8, 125–26, 134
– language 28, 233, 236, 238
– word 225, 227
compressed blends 248–49, 260
compression 248–50, 253–54, 260, 267–68
– human-scale 248, 259, 263, 265–66
– tight 248, 264
computation and storage 78
computational linguistics 68, 179, 224, 235

computational modeling 3–4, 78, 163, 251
computational models 76–77, 88, 127, 163, 251
– of categorization 96–100
computer screens 130, 208
conceived entities 141, 152, 157
conceived time 153–56, 160
concept learning 89, 91–93, 99–102, 104
– rule-based 91, 101
concept nodes 96, 235
conception 14, 25, 103, 140–42, 145, 148–57, 160, 163
– object of 148, 153
– subject of 143, 148
concepts 11–12, 14, 87–91, 93–99, 103–6, 108–9, 223–25, 235–36
– abstract 22–23, 26–27, 31, 203, 223, 230–32
– artificial 91–92, 95–96
– artificially defined 88, 90
– concrete 223, 231
conceptual categories 276, 285
conceptual characterization 150–51
conceptual domains 169, 171–72, 197, 272
conceptual entities 106, 168–72, 206
conceptual experience 140, 148, 155–56
conceptual frames 183, 257, 262–63
conceptual mappings 245, 261
conceptual metaphors 167, 196–201, 205–12, 214–16
– and decision-making 210
– in immediate verbal metaphor comprehension 211–12
– inferring 205–7
– and metaphoric meanings 210–11
– nonlinguistic evidence 207–9
conceptual structures 100, 117, 120, 134, 171–72, 224, 236, 264
conceptualization 1, 3, 14, 20, 36, 41, 289, 291
– events 37–38
conceptualizers 39, 140–41, 156, 158, 160
concrete nouns 222, 236
concrete words 222, 231–32, 236
conditional constructions 184, 260
conditional probabilities 67, 69, 79
configuration 51, 124, 154, 156, 158, 280
conjoined noun-phrases 47

connectives 273, 276–77, 287, 289
connectors 246, 249, 290
consistency 163, 251
constraints 74, 117–18, 172, 250, 252, 268
– interacting subsystem 216
construal 3, 140–63, 167, 291
– dimensions 141–61
– dynamic 156, 162
– dynamicity 140–41, 152–57
– factors 141, 152, 163
– imagination 141, 157–61
– metonymic 147
– perspective 141–46
– prominence 148–52
– selection 146–48
– validation 161–63
construction grammar 2–3, 17, 25, 163, 198
constructions 64, 68, 72, 79, 106–8, 119, 261–63, 266–68
– conditional 184, 260
– grammatical 1, 147, 177, 180, 183, 198, 275, 277
– linguistic 105, 256, 264–65, 267
– syntactic 17, 63, 75, 183
containers 20–21, 94, 176, 178, 231
– pressurized 210–11
containment 20, 176
content 140, 143, 146–48, 150–51, 162, 222–23, 234–35, 276–77
– conceptual 140–41, 143, 145, 151, 153
– essential 147, 150–51
– non-explicit 147
– objective 157, 291
– onstage 142, 144–46, 148–49, 157
– representational 28, 222
– semantic 170, 178, 227
context 66–67, 75–76, 99–101, 103–6, 115–16, 120–22, 202, 234–35
– discourse 48, 149, 203, 206
– importance 80
– linguistic 94, 221, 238
– sentence 65, 80
context availability theory 222, 231
context sensitivity 95, 211, 214
contextual diversity (CD) 67–68, 76–77
– and frequency effects 66–67
contextual information 69, 80, 115, 122

contextualized frequency measures 67–69
continuations 130–31, 276
control 43, 120, 195, 251
– attentional 42–43
– motor 27, 30, 133
conventional expressions 196–97, 201, 204–6, 210–11
conventional functions 282, 288
conventional metaphoric language 205, 211, 214
conventional phrases 197, 203, 211
conventionality 170, 272
conversation 5, 62, 203, 207, 279, 282–84
cooperation 272, 279, 286, 288–89, 292
cooperative communication 271–72, 277, 285, 287, 290–92
– and joint cognition 277–80
coordinated group cognition 279
coordination 153, 278–80, 287, 290, 292
– cognitive 289
corpora 4–5, 62, 66–68, 129, 134, 197, 200, 235
corpus linguistics 4–5, 67–68, 80, 199
correlation metaphors 200
correlations 40, 104, 200, 209, 228, 251
– afunctional 40
correspondences 38, 120, 155, 158, 196, 231, 292
cortex 30, 42, 100–2, 227
creation 23, 53, 120, 167, 174, 200
crime 210, 273–74
Croft, W. 7, 71, 170, 175, 178
cross-domain mappings 204–5
cross-linguistic differences 187, 224
Cruse, A. 71, 170
cued locations 44, 50
cued referents 46–47, 49–50
cueing effects 45, 47, 52
cueing paradigm 43, 46, 50
cues 43, 45–48, 52–53, 105, 126–29, 133, 268
– informative 105, 126
– and outcomes 127
– visual 45–47, 49–50, 52–53, 107, 127
cultural models 274, 285, 289–91
culture 94, 253, 275, 289
– shared 284–85, 289, 291

Daelemans, W. 73, 75, 77, 123
damage 29–30, 101, 226, 228
– collateral 274
Damasio, A. 27, 30, 226–27, 230
Dancygier, B. 260
Danks, D. 129
data
– distributional 237–39
– empirical 120, 233
– linguistic 4, 40, 221, 233, 238–39
dead metaphors 23, 197, 203–4, 211
death 208, 261
decision-making, and conceptual metaphors 210
declarative memory systems 74
decontextualization 179, 200
decoration 203, 258
deficits 223, 226–27
– selective 226, 228
deictic elements 281–83, 285, 290
deictics 17, 263–64, 266, 284, 290–91
deixis 31, 272, 281–83
demi-syllables 131–32
denotational meaning 25, 28
derivation, affixal 182
derivational morphemes 180
description, semantic 140, 151, 162
determiners 121, 182, 232, 282
dictionaries 1, 88, 186, 197, 238
– mental 132
differences, potential 286–87, 289
digraphs 127–29, 131
diphones 131
direct mappings 50, 53–54
directed graphs 130–34
direction verbs 227
directive speech acts 185, 273
Dirven, R. 2, 170, 172–73, 177, 182, 186
disanalogy 246, 248, 255
discourse 179, 184, 186, 199, 201–4, 212, 214, 275
– context 48, 149, 203, 206
– metonymy in 184–85, 187
– naturalistic 197
discrimination 100, 102, 104–5, 126–35
– learning 115, 134–35
discriminative learning
– models 107, 134
– naive 3, 78, 115–35

discriminative perspective 107, 132
disengagement 157, 159–60
disposition 248, 252
dissociations 29
distance 158, 267, 291
distribution 68, 94, 125, 129, 154, 186, 233–35, 238–40
– probability 121, 234–35
distributional approaches 228, 233–34, 237
distributional data 237–39
distributional models 234, 237, 239
distributional theories 221, 233–37
– future directions 237
– key issues 237
– research supporting 236
ditransitive frames 260–61
domain-general operations 42
domain matrices 170, 172
domains 95, 105–6, 120, 123–24, 154, 168–70, 172–73, 222–23
– conceptual 169, 171–72, 197, 272
– knowledge 120, 206, 223
– secondary 177–78
– source 22, 24, 26–27, 172, 198–200, 206, 208
– target 24, 158, 172, 197–99
drinking 28, 116, 118, 154
dual-path mapping 52
dualism 12, 16
Ducrot, O. 275
duration 44, 147, 153–55, 222
dynamic construal 156, 162
dynamicity 140–41, 152–57

ego 208, 268
Ellsberg, Daniel 267
embodied experience 200, 212
– and verbal metaphor understanding 212–14
embodied representations 238
embodied simulations 25, 28, 213, 233, 238
embodied syntax 16–18
embodied theories 22, 221, 227, 230, 232–33, 235, 237
embodiment 3, 11–32, 196, 225–33, 265
– analytical phase 14–24
– and cognitive psychology 15–16
– in cognitive science 13–14

- embodied syntax 16–18
- featural theories as precursors 226–27
- and functional role 27–30
- future directions 30–32, 232–33
- history 12–14
- image schemas 20–21
- key issues 230–32
- and metaphors 22–24
- online 24, 27–28, 31
- and polysemy 21
- processes 24–27
- research supporting embodied theories 227–28
- strong 230
- usage-based models 18–19
- versions 228–30
- weak 228, 230

embodiment research 11, 14
emergence 3, 201, 207, 282
emergent structure 247, 249, 254, 256, 258, 261, 267
emergent syntax 258–59
emotions 172, 176, 197, 223, 239, 247
empirical data 120, 233
empirical evidence 39, 251, 272, 279
empirical studies 39, 88, 288, 291
empirical support 74, 163, 232
encoding 53, 74, 97, 99, 105, 129–30, 132
- in context 75–77

English speakers 24, 49, 87–90, 196, 210, 224
entailments 170, 206, 215
entities 87, 89, 147, 150, 168–69, 171–73, 177–78, 196
- conceived 141, 152, 157
- conceptual 106, 168–72, 206
- physical 168, 172–73, 178

entrenchment 3, 61–63, 65–67, 69–77, 79–81
- characterizations 70–72
- definition 69–77
- encoding in context 75–77
- and frequency 61–81
- and frequency measures 79
- learning and the brain 72–77
- neurocognitive basis 73
- procedural and declarative memory systems 74–75
- threshold number of occurrences 73–74
- what can be entrenched 77–78

entropy 69, 121–22, 125, 129
environment 13, 31, 43, 61–62, 66, 73, 75–76, 104
- language 233, 238

epiphenomenalism 12, 228, 233, 237, 250
episodic memories 73, 75
epistemic stance 289–90
equivalence 171, 280
Ernestus, M. 123, 135
errors 18, 65, 71, 102, 134
essential content 147, 150–51
events 36–37, 41–43, 132–33, 154–57, 159–62, 259, 266–67, 273–74
- causal 259
- communication 130, 133, 277, 281, 283, 290–91
- conceptualization 37–38
- perceived 37, 39, 46
- speech 262, 282, 284
- transitive 44, 48–50

evidence 23–24, 74, 100–2, 119, 208–9, 251–53, 283–85, 291
- behavioral 80, 227
- empirical 39, 251, 272, 279
- experimental 213, 274
- linguistic 23, 200
- nonlinguistic 207
- sources of 283–85, 291

exemplar models 98–100, 122–24, 126
expectations 78, 107, 120–21, 214, 253, 266, 272, 275–76
experience 103–4, 128–29, 140–41, 148–49, 159–60, 172, 225, 238–39
- actual 66, 142
- conceptual 140, 148, 155–56
- embodied 200, 212
- individual 16, 18, 31
- language 61, 107, 238
- mental 140, 153
- motor 141, 163
- nonlinguistic 207–8
- sensorimotor 213, 224, 237–38

experiential information 237–40
experimental evidence 213, 274
experimental instructions 44, 46
experimental psychology 24, 62, 64, 208

experimental studies 208, 210, 212, 214, 277
experiments 27, 29, 51, 53, 90, 92–93, 126–27, 251
– psychological 186, 288
expertise 66, 93–94
exposures 16, 51, 74–76, 126
expressions 142–44, 146, 149–51, 197–98, 200–1, 204–6, 253–54, 288–91
– clichéd 205
– composite 152, 158
– conventional 196–97, 201, 204–6, 210–11
– fictive motion 212
– linguistic 140, 196, 259, 275, 277, 289
– meaning 140, 142–43
– metaphorical 120, 198, 212
– profile 143, 145, 148, 150, 162
– relational 147, 162
– symbolic 150, 162
extensionality 157–58
extensions 21, 24, 91–92, 122, 156, 180, 231, 258
external world 90
eye gaze 19
eye-movements 44, 46, 54

face-to-face conversations 207
family resemblance, structure 71, 93
fathers 115, 143–45, 261–63
Fauconnier, Gilles 158, 173, 179, 199, 249–51, 254–55, 258–63
featural properties 222–23, 226
feature norms 226, 239
feature space 97–98
feature-value pairs 118
fictional worlds 158
fictive motion 3, 156, 160, 163, 212
– expressions 212
– sentences 95, 212
Fillmore, C. J. 95, 172, 245, 256–57, 262–63
films 62, 68, 184, 267
fingertips 145, 162, 205
Finnish 48–50, 54
fish 46, 96, 101, 254
FishFilm paradigm 46, 49–50
flexible word order 48–50, 54
fluency 70–71, 133
fluidity 70–71, 116, 118

focal participants 151–52, 163
focus 2, 37, 39, 44, 147, 154, 227, 231–32
– attentional 42, 44, 46–47, 50, 53–54
– visual 44
form, linguistic 37, 40–41, 73, 127, 233
form-meaning pairs 180, 256, 263, 268
formalisms 116, 120
forward oriented meaning 274
frame blends 257–58
frame of choice 256–57
frames 95, 105–6, 171–73, 245, 253–57, 259–63, 272, 274
– conceptual 183, 257, 262–63
– ditransitive 260–61
– of harm 254, 257
– mental 245
frequency 3, 19, 21, 40, 61–74, 77–81, 97, 161
– and contextual diversity (CD) 66–67
– contextualized 67–69
– definition 62–69
– and entrenchment 61–81
– expected 68, 79
– high 63–65, 74, 76, 80, 94
– importance for creation of entrenched representations 80–81
– measures for predicting entrenchment 79
– of occurrence 63, 68
– and processing 64–66
– relative 69, 79
– threshold 74, 125
– token 63–64
– type 63–64
– word 64–67, 69, 77, 80, 94, 129
frequency-as-repetition 68
frequencyrep 66–67, 69, 76
functional asymmetry 159
functional role 27–31
functions 13–14, 16–18, 31–32, 40, 98–99, 102, 143–44, 152–53
– conventional 282, 288
– pragmatic 40, 171, 173–74, 176
– primary 25, 290
– referential 169, 171

games 89, 182, 206
Geeraerts, D. 3, 5–7, 171, 175, 177–78, 183, 233

generality 96, 176
- and metonymy 176–77
generalizations 39–40, 74, 115, 121, 179, 209, 250
- abstracted 158
- making 160, 251
- by means of virtual instances 161
- minimum 118, 124, 135
generic integration templates 250, 252, 255, 261, 268
gestures 4, 27, 31, 130, 168, 204–5
- articulatory 153
- bodily 19
- iconic 27, 283
- metaphoric 207–8, 215
- pointing 271, 277, 281
- verbal 105
Gleitman, L. 46–50, 53
Glenberg, A. M. 25–27, 30, 231–33, 237
Goldberg, A. 4–5, 17–18, 72, 180, 198, 260–61
Goldstone, R. 89–90
Grady, J. E. 20, 22–23, 199–200
grammar 1, 3–4, 16, 18, 36, 38–41, 145–48, 179–80
- cognitive 2, 17–18, 133–35, 140, 150–51, 154, 156, 160
- construction 2–3, 17, 25, 163, 198
- and cooperative communication 271–92
- implicit 129–30, 132–35
- metonymy in 180
- probabilistic 61, 78
grammatical categories 71, 150, 152, 162
grammatical constructions 1, 147, 177, 180, 183, 198, 275, 277
grammatical patterns 251, 267, 276
grammatical recategorization 181–82
grammatical representation 39, 54
grammatical-role assignment 47–48, 50, 54
grammatical structures 20, 180, 186
grammaticality, judgments 16
grammaticalization 3, 40, 184
granularity 106, 146, 162
graphs, directed 130–34
Greek 197
Gries, S. T. 3, 5–6, 19, 21, 64, 68, 79, 198–99

ground 19–20, 143–45, 149, 262–63, 281, 290
grounding problem 230, 237
group cognition, coordinated 279

HAL 234–36
Halliday, M. A. K. 39, 48
hand pantomiming 283
harm 256–57, 286, 288
- chance of 256
- frame of 254, 257
hearers 28, 38, 40, 149, 185, 255, 263
heart 47, 97, 104, 107–8, 120, 252
heat 21, 211–12
hierarchical networks 96–97
hierarchical structure 285, 287, 290
hierarchies 96–97, 102, 146, 176–77, 286
- inheritance 116, 132
- whole-part 145, 162
high frequency 63–65, 74, 76, 80, 94
hints 14, 48, 52, 268
history 12, 197, 207, 214, 258
- cognitive linguistics 2
- shared personal 284, 289, 291
holistic approaches 221, 235
holistic theories 235–36
human communication 108, 268, 271, 273, 281, 288, 290, 292
human languages 6–7, 12, 16, 29, 74, 168, 272, 291
human-scale bundles of thought 248
human-scale compression 248, 259, 263, 265–66
husband 151, 162, 266
hybrid models 125–26, 135
hypothesis testing 4–6, 79

ICD (initial cognitive definition) 168–69, 173
ICLA (International Cognitive Linguistics Association) 2
iconic gestures 27, 283
Idealized Cognitive Models (ICMs) 95, 105–6, 170–73, 176
ideas, abstract 196
identity 45, 53, 199, 246, 253, 255, 268
idiomatic phrases 202, 211
idioms 63, 108, 211–12
image schemas 20–21, 43, 95, 105–6

imagination 141, 157–61
imaging, brain 5, 26–27
imaging studies 101, 227
immediate scope 141, 143, 145, 147–48, 154, 162
impairments 228
implicature 184–86
implicit grammar 129–30, 132–35
implicit morphology 129
implied readers 265
implied speakers 265
inclusion 79, 91, 173
indexicals 263–64
indirect speech acts 184–85
infants 42, 61, 69
inferences 28, 72, 91, 100, 153, 251–52, 274–77, 285
– causal 251
inferencing, pragmatic 181, 184, 187
inferential fallacies 288
inferior temporal cortex (ITC) 100–1
information 73–74, 79, 95–100, 199, 231, 237–39, 271, 284
– concept 106–8
– contextual 69, 80, 115, 122
– experiential 237–40
– lexical 51–52
– linguistic 53, 221, 223, 233, 238–39
– perceptual 36, 43, 51–52, 239
– semantic 228, 240
– sensory-motor 223, 228, 230, 232–33, 238
– sharing 271, 273, 292
– theory 106, 262
informative cues 105, 126
inheritance hierarchies 116, 132
initial cognitive definition see *ICD*
initial position 36–37, 45
input spaces 159, 199, 255–56, 258–60, 263, 268
inputs 39, 41, 75–76, 248, 251, 254–55, 258–60, 263–65
– linguistic 38, 61
instructions, experimental 44, 46
integrated models 221, 239
integration 53, 75–76, 157, 252
– networks 253, 255
– templates, generic 250, 252, 255, 261, 268

intelligence 168–69
– artificial 251
intended meanings 24, 107, 284
intentions 8, 16, 19, 44, 107, 131
– communicative 105, 133, 205
interactions 15–16, 40, 46, 52, 142, 214–16, 227, 232–33
– social 8, 268
interdisciplinarity 6–7
interdisciplinary work 1, 3, 7
interlocutors 105, 119, 130, 132, 142–45, 149, 160, 283–84
International Cognitive Linguistics Association (ICLA) 2
interpersonal relations 14, 197, 291
intersubjective awareness 141–42
intersubjectivity 282–83, 289–91
intransitive verb 151
introspection 4, 6, 186, 225, 237, 239
intuition 18, 63, 104, 109, 162
inventories 39–41, 68, 70–71, 88, 91, 108–9, 122
isolation 67, 77, 80, 122, 222
ITC (inferior temporal cortex) 100–1

Jackendoff, R. 43, 117, 120, 134, 201
Johnson, M. 14, 20, 22, 24, 168–69, 195–96, 198, 225
joint activity 277–78
joint attention 8, 263–65, 278–79, 290
– blended 254, 264–65, 267
joint cognition 277–80, 286
joint commitments 286–88
joint projects 279, 285–90, 292
journeys 171, 196, 198, 200–1, 213, 249, 253
– imagined 161
– physical 196, 198
judgments 16, 30, 94–95, 204, 208–9
– grammaticality 16
– social 208–9
– temporal 95, 210
justice 11, 141, 274

Kaschak, M. P. 25–27, 232
Keele, S. 92
Kersten, A. 89–90
Keuleers, E. 124, 135
kinship networks 143, 145

knowing 5, 160, 185, 198, 274–76
knowledge
– associated 146, 157
– background 154
– base 116, 123
– domains 120, 206, 223
– joint 277, 281–82
– linguistic 8, 17–19, 117
– motor 28–29
– mutual 279–80, 283–84, 287, 290–91
– shared 272, 282–84
– structures 120, 130–32
– world 127, 230
Kousta, S.-T. 223, 231–32
Kövecses, Z. 22, 168, 170–71, 173–76, 181–82, 196, 200, 208
Kruschke, J. 97–99, 102

labels 68, 88–91, 94, 98, 100, 104–5, 250, 274
Lakoff, G. 1–2, 14, 21–22, 24–25, 167–69, 171–72, 195–96, 198–99
landmarks 151–52, 158, 163
language acquisition 8, 71, 141, 235
language-as-form 130
language communities 23, 134
language comprehension 28, 233, 236, 238
language development 19, 42–43, 232, 235
language environment 233, 238
language experience 61, 107, 238
language learning 32, 107, 119
language processing 39, 69, 72, 119, 121–22, 162–63, 227, 236
language production 27–28, 36–38, 107, 126
language stimuli 62, 64, 73
language use 15, 18, 24–25, 28–29, 135, 272–73, 275, 277
– everyday 107, 275
language users 16–17, 19, 23–24, 28–29, 66
latencies, response 68, 122
Latin 38, 260
learnability 107, 128
learners 80, 99–100, 102, 105, 107, 117, 122, 128
learning 72, 74–76, 93, 99–105, 107–9, 126–28, 133, 238–40
– associative 29, 104, 127
– category 100, 102, 128
– concept see *concept learning*
– discrimination 115, 134–35
– frequency-sensitive 61, 64, 73
– and meaning 108–9
– memory based see *MBL*
– minimum generalization 124, 135
– processes 42, 93, 101, 104–6, 119, 126, 233
– systems 101, 103
– theory 126–27
letter pairs 76–77, 127–28
letters 41, 76, 78, 92, 131, 265–66, 281
levels of abstraction 92, 94, 99, 102–3, 105, 124–25, 128
Levelt, W. J. M. 39, 53
Levinson, S. 7, 272
Lewis, D. 272, 279–80
lexemes 127–29, 131, 133–34, 160, 177, 181, 183
– typical 160, 162
lexical attributes 65–66
lexical decisions 66–67, 227, 232
lexical information 51–52
lexical items 24, 64, 67, 77, 80, 276, 284, 290
lexical meaning 76, 145, 159, 257
– metonymy in 180–81
lexical polysemy 147, 180
lexical processing 66–67, 121, 238
lexical representation 121, 198, 221, 226
lexical semantics 3, 181, 254, 287
lexical similarity 239
lexical units 66, 202–3
lexicography 4, 67
lexicon 39, 121–22, 145, 147–48, 198
– mental 119, 121, 131
Lieven, E. 7, 61, 72, 132
light 105, 117, 126, 278
Likert scale 62
linear ordering 48–51, 54
linearity 153, 251
linguistic analysis 23, 36, 91, 140, 161, 196, 206, 212
linguistic behavior 43, 79, 252–53
linguistic categories 37–38, 88, 224, 283
linguistic communication 107–8, 281, 283
linguistic constructions 105, 256, 264–65, 267

linguistic contexts 94, 221, 238
linguistic data 4, 40, 221, 233, 238–39
linguistic evidence 23, 200
linguistic expressions 140, 196, 259, 275, 277, 289
linguistic form 37, 40–41, 73, 127, 233
linguistic information 53, 221, 223, 233, 238–39
linguistic knowledge 8, 17–19, 117
linguistic meaning 20, 104, 140, 153, 272, 275, 285, 289
linguistic metonymies 170, 186
linguistic organization 2–3
linguistic patterns 17–18, 70, 77, 209
linguistic prominence 147–48
linguistic representations 37, 224, 238
linguistic signals 27, 107–8, 132, 282
linguistic structures 7, 16, 63, 70, 117, 239
linguistic units 19, 65, 148–49, 240
links 43, 53, 73, 75–76, 196, 222, 224–25, 230–31
listeners 38, 104, 107–8, 130, 204, 206, 214–15
locations 43–47, 49, 143–44, 168–69, 172–73, 175, 183–84, 262–63
– cued 44, 50
long-term memory 74–76, 173, 215, 284
love 92–93, 99, 104, 128, 196, 268
low frequency words 65, 69, 72, 80

MacWhinney, B. 3, 39, 45, 61, 73, 215
Mahon, B. Z. 28, 228, 233
Malagasy 50
managing v sharing 271–72, 292
Mandarin 41, 210
Mandelblit, Nili 254
manipulation 49, 271, 288
– cueing 47, 50
mappings 39–40, 169, 171, 173, 176, 179, 196, 198–99
– automatic 36, 45
– conceptual 245, 261
– conventional 40, 198
– cross-domain 204–5
– direct 50, 53–54
– dual-path 52
– metaphorical 173, 198, 200–1, 211, 231
– metonymic 172, 179

– one-to-one 224
– positional 47, 54
marginality 178
marriage 150, 196, 198, 255
mathematics 197, 238
Matlock, T. 3, 156, 163, 212, 277
matrices, domain 170, 172
Matthews, D. 3, 8, 19, 61, 65, 119, 122, 132
MBL (memory based learning) 75, 77, 123–24, 126, 135
McClelland, J. L. 65–66, 73–75, 226
McDonald, S. A. 66–67, 69
meaning
– in animal and human communication 271–72
– backward oriented 274
– combining language-based and experiential information 237–39
– denotational 25, 28
– forward oriented 274
– intended 24, 107, 284
– and learning 108–9
– lexical 76, 145, 159, 180, 257
– linguistic 20, 104, 140, 153, 272, 275, 285, 289
– metaphoric 202–3, 206, 209–11, 213–14
– representing 221–39
– theoretical perspectives 224–37
– types 281–85
– word 21, 91, 221–24, 226–27, 230, 232–33, 235, 237–40
medial temporal lobe see *MTL*
memory 70, 72–77, 93, 96, 115–16, 119, 121–24, 259
– episodic 73, 75
– long-term 74–76, 173, 215, 284
– semantic 225–26
– short-term 75
– systems 74–75, 100–1, 134, 228
memory based learning see *MBL*
mental access 157–58, 170–71
– natural path of 153–54, 157, 162
mental capacities 22, 157, 280
mental experience 140, 153
mental model 286–87
mental operations 41–42, 157, 268
– basic 245, 250
mental processes 250–51

mental representations 15, 20, 61, 73–74, 77, 80, 87, 89
mental resources 76, 149
mental simulation 149, 155, 159, 163, 221, 248
mental spaces 2, 158, 245–49, 252–53, 255, 259–61, 263–67, 289–91
mental states 273, 278–79, 283, 288
mental tokens 88, 103–4
mental web 246–49, 254–56, 260, 264–66
mental world 141, 146, 157, 159, 287
Mercier, H. 288–89
meta-cognitive awareness 280
metaphor identification procedure 186, 201
Metaphor Identification Procedure see *MIP*
metaphor research 196, 201, 203
metaphor understanding 205, 214
– verbal 196, 209, 212–13, 216
metaphoric gestures 207–8, 215
metaphoric language 23, 26–27, 195–96, 201, 203, 210, 213–14
– conventional 205, 211, 214
– identification 201–4
metaphoric meanings 202–3, 206, 209–11, 213–14
– and conceptual metaphors 210–11
metaphoric thought 196, 215
metaphorical expressions 120, 198, 212
metaphorical mappings 173, 198, 200–1, 211, 231
metaphorical statements 199, 213
metaphors 22–24, 158–59, 168–69, 171, 179–80, 186–87, 195–216, 231–32
– cognitive linguistic findings 195–201, 205, 209
– conceptual 167, 196–201, 205–12, 214–16
– dead 23, 197, 203–4, 211
– deliberate or not 204–5
– and embodiment 22–24
– novel 198, 206, 211
– primary 23, 200–1, 208
– verbal 196, 204, 206, 209, 211–16
Meteyard, L. 221, 227–28, 230–32
metonymic construal 147
metonymic mappings 172, 179
metonymic motivation 179–80, 182
metonymic source 170, 172, 174, 181
metonymic target 184

metonymies, chained 184–85
metonymy 2–3, 21, 23, 147, 167–87, 201, 203, 250
– in clausal grammar 183–84
– in discourse 184–85, 187
– and generality 176–77
– in grammar 180
– in lexical meaning 180–81
– in morphosyntactic processes 181–83
– non-referential 169
– notion 167–74
– and pragmatic function 174–76
– prototypical 177–78
– referential 177, 181
– research methods 186
– role 167, 179–80, 184
– types 174–78
– typology 167, 187
– ubiquity 179
– unitary definition 171, 178
MI (Mutual Information) 68
mind, and body 11–12
minimum generalization 118, 124, 135
MIP (Metaphor Identification Procedure) 186, 201–3
MIP-VU 186, 203
modality 20, 141, 184, 226–27, 233
modeling, computational 3–4, 78, 163, 251
models 25, 77–78, 96–99, 124, 126–27, 135, 239, 250–51
– cognitive 69, 95, 167, 169, 172–73, 179, 274, 276
– computational see *computational models*
– cultural 274, 285, 289–91
– distributional 234, 237, 239
– exemplar 98–100, 122–24, 126
– hybrid 125–26, 135
– integrated 221, 239
– mental 286–87
– NDR 76–77
– prototype 97–99
– SUSTAIN 100
– topic 234–36
monism 12
morpheme sequences 77–78
morphemes 64, 116, 122, 129, 177, 180, 183, 254
– derivational 180
– suffixal 180

morphological processing 76, 125
morphology 118, 122, 129
– implicit 129
morphosyntactic processes, metonymy in 181–83
Morton, E. S. 271, 273
motion 25, 27, 153, 156, 176, 182, 212, 260
– actual 160, 163
– direction of 25, 232
– fictive 3, 156, 160, 163, 212
– spatial 161, 213
– verbs 156, 198
motivation, metonymic 179–80, 182
motor actions 11, 159
motor areas 30, 230
motor control 27, 30, 133
motor experience 141, 163
motor neuron disease 228
motor systems 26–28, 30, 228
MTL (medial temporal lobe) 101–3
Müller, C. 4, 203–4, 207
Müller-Lyer effect 93
multi-word sequences 74, 78, 119, 133
multimodality 4, 135, 179, 267–68
multimorphemic words 71, 77
Mutual Information (MI) 68
mutual knowledge 279–80, 283–84, 287, 290–91
mutually shared attention 278

naive discriminative learning 115–35
names 4, 21, 43, 65, 75, 182, 283–85, 291
naming 43, 65, 67
– object 94, 233
natural path of mental access 153–54, 157–58, 162
natural paths 153–54, 157–58
NDR model 76–77
negation 272, 277, 287, 289–91
negative sentences 287, 290
networks 73, 75, 127, 129–30, 235, 246, 251–52, 264
– blending 247, 254, 259–60, 263, 268
– hierarchical 96
– integration 253, 255
– kinship 143, 145
– neural 73
– Rescorla-Wagner 128, 130, 132–33

neural activity 141, 201, 236
neural networks 73
neural structures 88, 100
neural systems 14, 24, 103
neuroimaging, studies 41, 71
neurological activity 140, 163
neuronal assemblies 100–1
neurons 30, 73, 101, 225, 268
neuroscience 7, 73, 100, 104, 201, 224, 251
Nikiforidou, K. 266–67
nodes 68, 96–97, 127, 234–35
nominal compounds 258, 262
non-congruent order 157, 163
non-explicit content 147
Non-Synonymy Principle 18
nonlinguistic evidence 207
nonlinguistic experience 207–8
nouns 121–22, 151–52, 181–83, 222, 226, 228, 258, 262
– common 182, 284–85, 291
– complex 152
– concrete 222, 236
novel metaphors 198, 206, 211
number 1–2, 26–27, 62–63, 66–68, 70, 105–6, 231–32, 236

object naming 94, 233
object-nouns 222, 230, 236
objective content 157, 291
objective scene 142–43, 147, 150
objects 26–27, 43–44, 141–43, 152–54, 222–23, 260–61, 278–80, 289–91
– physical 157, 173, 178, 213
observations, direct 157, 160, 251
offstage elements 142, 144, 148–49
offstage prominence 148–49
offstage salience 149–50
offstage viewers 142, 144
one-to-one mapping 224
online embodiment 24, 27–28, 31
online production 25, 205
onstage prominence 148–50
onstage region 142–46, 148–49, 157
onstage salience 149
open questions 62, 77, 131
operators, argumentative 277, 289–90
order 25, 38, 130, 132, 143, 153, 157, 162
– non-congruent 157, 163
– word 54, 117

ordering, linear 48–51, 54
organization 22, 43, 146, 152–54, 158, 162, 250–51, 258
– cognitive 70, 148
– linguistic 2–3
orientation 27, 31, 144, 158
orthographic neighborhood density 66, 129
Osgood, C. 37, 45, 51
Otal Campo, J. L. 180–82, 184
outcomes 28, 117, 123, 126–29, 133
– behavioral 66, 104
oversimplification 177, 185
Owings, D. H. 271, 273

pairs 23, 67–68, 107, 118
– feature-value 118
– form-meaning 180, 256, 263, 268
Paivio, A. 222, 232
Panther, K.-U. 147, 170–71, 180–87, 198
paradigmatic effects 121–22
Paradis, C. 171, 178
Parkinson's disease 101, 228
parsing 42, 70–71, 125
participants 44, 46–47, 49–51, 92–93, 151, 210–12, 226–27, 286
– focal 151–52, 163
passive voice 44–46, 49–50, 52
– sentences 45–47, 49, 53
passive voice frame 52–53
passivization 49
past tense 17, 41, 63, 124, 135, 266, 281, 283
paths 131, 153–54, 156, 158, 200, 249, 253
– natural 153–54, 157–58
Patient-cued condition 49, 52
patient-cued trials 45, 47, 49
patients 29–30, 44–46, 49–50, 52–53, 65, 199, 226, 228
patterns 21, 23, 74–75, 93, 95, 250–51, 266, 268
– grammatical 251, 267, 276
– linguistic 17–18, 70, 77, 209
– recurring 20, 196, 200
– statistical 221, 224, 233, 235, 237, 239
Pavlov, I. 126–27
Peirsman, Y. 171, 174, 177–78
perceived events 37, 39, 46

perception 14, 20, 22, 24–29, 225, 227, 231, 266–67
– social 208
– visual 24, 140
perceptual information 36, 43, 51–52, 239
perceptual priming 45–54
perceptual regions 26, 102
perceptual salience 37, 39, 52
perceptual symbols 7, 225
percolation rule 280
Pérez Hernández, L. 180–82, 184
performance 18, 25, 30, 38, 101, 135, 227, 236
personal communication 255, 259, 262
personal pronouns 74, 253, 281, 283, 291
perspective 62, 103, 107–9, 115, 119, 132, 134, 141–46
– discriminative 107, 132
– social 7–8
PFC see *prefrontal cortex*
phenomenological descriptions 95, 106
phonemes 18, 62, 64, 116
phonology 3, 16, 80, 116–17, 148, 179
phrases 62, 66, 73, 90–91, 106, 203–4, 206, 212–13
– idiomatic 202, 211
– noun 47, 169, 181, 258
– prepositional 121–22, 151
physical entities 168, 172–73, 178
physical journeys 196, 198
physical objects 157, 173, 178, 213
physical structure 32, 173, 200
physiology 100, 172
– visual 251
pictures 21, 44–47, 49, 94, 109, 122, 129, 208
pointers 45, 105, 108, 278
pointing gestures 271, 277, 281
political language 274
politics 22, 197
polysemy 3, 6, 21, 23, 180, 198, 206, 254–55
– effects 255
– instances of 198, 201
– lexical 147, 180
positional mappings 47, 54
Posner, M. 41–44, 46, 92
possession 96, 176, 261

power 48, 236–37, 250, 276
Pragglejazz Group 186, 202–3
pragmatic function 40, 171, 173–74, 176
– and metonymy 174–76
pragmatic inferencing 181, 184, 187
pragmatics 40, 273
pre-emption 72
precision 124, 135, 141
precursors 11, 226, 283
predicates, change 255–56
predictions 5, 25, 27, 103–5, 108, 122–23, 235, 238
– testable 5, 162
predictors 64, 79, 115, 122–23, 129
prefrontal cortex 101
prepositional phrases 121–22, 151
prepositions 20, 43, 121–22, 151, 203, 232
pressurized containers 210–11
preverbal message 39
previewed referents 44–45
primary functions 25, 290
primary metaphors 23, 200–1, 208
prime verbs 52
primed referents 44, 51
priming 37, 51–52, 95
– perceptual 45–54
– referential 44–45
– semantic 224, 226–27, 236
– syntactic 51–52
primitives 116–17, 128
probabilistic grammar 61, 78
probabilities 18–19, 46, 69, 73, 78, 99, 234
– conditional 67, 69, 79
probability distributions 121, 234–35
processes 36–37, 71, 103–9, 125–26, 128, 202–3, 232–33, 250
– attentional 37–39
– biological 271, 273
– cognitive 2–3, 25, 71, 135, 170
– embodiment 24–27
– learning 42, 93, 101, 104–6, 119, 126, 233
– mental 250–51
processing 25–27, 71, 77–79, 121–23, 153–54, 221–23, 226–27, 233
– ease 71, 147
– and frequency 64–66
– language 39, 69, 72, 119, 121–22, 162–63, 227, 236

– lexical 66–67, 121, 238
– semantic 228, 230
– sensory-motor 227, 230, 232
– windows 153, 157–58
– word 80, 227–28
processing units 73, 75
production
– online 25, 205
– sentence 37–39, 45, 48–51, 53–54, 79
– speech 122, 130, 132, 134
productivity 63, 122
– linguistic 115
– syntactic 133
profile 145, 147–48, 150–52, 154, 162
– choice of 147, 162
– expressions 143, 145, 148, 150, 162
profiled relationships 148, 150–52, 154, 163
profiling 147, 150–52, 162, 268
projection, selective 254, 257, 261
projections 159, 169, 173, 247, 249, 257, 264, 266
projects, joint 279, 285–90, 292
prominence 5, 23, 140–41, 147–52
– linguistic 147–48
– offstage 148–49
– onstage 148–50
prominence asymmetry 148
pronouns 118, 143, 181, 281, 291
– personal 74, 253, 281, 283, 291
properties 13–15, 93–94, 96–97, 115–16, 118, 151–54, 169, 246–47
– featural 222–23, 226
– inherent 180
– systematic 276, 290
prototype models 97–99
prototypes 6, 91–92, 95, 97–100, 102, 148
prototypical metonymies 177–78
prototypicality 15–16, 92, 97
– and metonymy 177–78
psycholinguistic research 39, 179, 187, 205, 209, 211–13
psycholinguistics 19, 24–25, 41, 62, 69
psychological experiments 186, 288
psychological research 7, 38, 64, 205
psychologists 3, 6, 80, 87, 104, 207, 209, 214
psychology 2, 5–6, 64, 235, 251
– cognitive 6–7, 15, 18, 25, 62, 72, 76, 224
– experimental 24, 62, 64, 208

quantitative methods 5, 186
Quillian, R. 96–97, 226, 235
Quine, W. van Orman 87–88
quizzes 252–53

Radden, G. 147, 167–68, 170–77, 179–83, 198, 200, 208
Rakoczy, H. 280, 282
readers, implied 265
Recanati, F. 265
recategorization, grammatical 181–82
recognition 200, 273, 287, 290
– conscious 73
– growing 8
recurring patterns 20, 196, 200
redundancy 125, 132
reference point (RP) 144–45, 147, 157, 160, 170
referential function 169, 171
referential metonymies 177, 181
referential priming 44–45
referential salience 49, 51, 54
referentiality 169, 171, 230, 272
referents 28, 37, 44–48, 51, 53–54, 118, 281, 285
– cued 46–47, 49–50
– previewed 44–45
– primed 44, 51
– salient 44–47, 49–50, 53–54
– visual 42, 44
regularities 43, 66, 69, 75, 200
rehearsal 75
relations
– Identity 246, 267
– interpersonal 14, 197, 291
– syntactic 39–40
– systematic 21, 108
– time 266, 268
relationships 77–78, 90, 104–5, 144, 150–52, 169, 196–97, 234–37
– profiled 148, 150–52, 154, 163
– romantic 196, 198, 204
– spatial 151, 158
religion 274–76
repetition 63, 68, 80, 126
– suppression 76
representation
– abstract 122, 231, 236

– amodal 225, 228, 230, 238
– embodied 27, 238
– grammatical 39, 54
– lexical 121, 198, 221, 226
– mental 15, 20, 61, 73–74, 77, 80, 87, 89
– semantic 39, 134, 221–24, 228, 230, 234–35, 237–38
– theories 95, 105–6
representational content 28, 222
representational strength 71–73
Rescorla-Wagner equations 127–30
Rescorla-Wagner networks 128, 130, 132–33
research 6–7, 37–38, 62–63, 79–80, 108–9, 163, 183–84, 186–87
– embodiment 11, 14
– empirical 41, 278
– methods 167, 186
– psycholinguistic 39, 179, 187, 205, 209, 211–13
– psychological 7, 38, 64, 205
– supporting distributional theories 236
– supporting embodied theories 227–28
resolution 37, 146, 162, 267, 287
resources
– attentional 38, 41, 101
– mental 76, 149
– representational 104
response latencies 68, 122
rhetoric 180–81, 262, 275, 291
– traditional 168, 177
risk 256–58, 286, 288
risk-running 256
risk-taking 257
roles
– functional 27–31
– syntactic 51, 53
romantic relationships 196, 198, 204
roots 79, 120, 197, 210
Rosch, E. 6–7, 11, 15–16, 93–95, 106, 226
RP see *reference point*
Rudzka-Ostyn, B. 2, 179
Ruiz de Mendoza, F. J. 171, 177–78, 180–82, 184, 198
rules 70–71, 91–93, 99, 115–16, 118–20, 122, 124–25, 132
– abstract 117–18, 120, 122
Russian 48–50, 53–54, 79

salience 36–37, 39, 41, 43, 45, 47, 49, 148
– asymmetry 148
– and attention 3, 36–55
– offstage 149–50
– onstage 149
– perceptual 37, 39, 52
– referential 49, 51, 54
salient referents 44–47, 49–50, 53–54
scanning 157
– sequential 155–56
– spatial 160
scene 25, 28, 42, 54, 253, 261, 264–65, 267
– human-scale 259, 263
– objective 142–43, 147, 150
schemas 70, 124–25, 135, 172
– abstract 77
schemata 120, 125, 132
– abstract 125, 132
schematization 3, 18, 20, 133, 162
Schmid, H.-J. 61, 68, 71, 79
Schwanenflugel, P. J. 222–23, 231
scope 38, 104, 143
– immediate 141, 143, 145, 147–48, 154, 162
– maximal 143, 146
screen 44, 46, 208, 263
Searle, J. R. 237, 278
secondary domains 177–78
selection 37, 43, 140–41, 146–48
selective deficits 226, 228
selective projection 254, 257, 261
semantic categories 105
semantic content 170, 178, 227
semantic description 140, 151, 162
semantic import 143, 157
semantic information 228, 240
semantic networks 96–97, 225, 234–35
semantic priming 224, 226–27, 236
semantic processing 228, 230
semantic representations 39, 134, 221–24, 228, 230, 234–35, 237–38
semantic similarity 226, 235–36
semantic structure 116–17, 121, 160
semantics 39–41, 221, 225, 228, 230, 232, 281, 283–84
– embodied 230
– lexical 3, 181, 254, 287
– structure-independent 39
sensorimotor experience 213, 224, 237–38

sensory-motor information 223, 228, 230, 232–33, 238
sensory-motor processing 227, 230, 232
sensory-motor systems 227–28, 230, 232–33, 237
sentence context 65, 80
sentence production 37–39, 45, 48–51, 53–54, 79
sentences 25–26, 30, 42–45, 47–48, 51–54, 119–20, 130–31, 133–34
– negative 287, 290
sequences 16, 69–70, 119, 131–33, 150, 153, 155
– morpheme 77–78
– single linear 153, 157
sequential access 153, 157
sequential scanning 155–56
seriality, inherent 153
shallow language tasks 233, 238
Shannon, C. 106, 129
Shaoul, C. 78–79, 119
shared culture 284–85, 289, 291
shared knowledge 272, 282–84
shared personal histories 284, 289, 291
sharing 271–72, 292
Shillcock, R. 66–67, 69
Shoben, E. J. 222–23, 231
short term memory 284
sign language 3, 168, 184, 221
signals 40, 105–8, 129–30, 132, 204, 264, 272–73, 282–83
– linguistic 27, 107–8, 132, 282
– speech 98, 124, 130, 133
– visual 284
similarity
– lexical 239
– semantic 226, 235–36
simulations 28, 134, 226, 228, 231–33, 236, 238, 248–49
– embodied 25, 28, 213, 233, 238
– mental 149, 155, 159, 163, 221, 248
single linear sequence 153, 157
situated metaphor use 199
situatedness 31
Skousen, R. 123
skull 30, 279
sleep 117, 260
– schedules 248

social groups 66, 278
social interaction 8, 268
social judgments 208–9
social perspective 7–8
social turn 7–8
source
– code 106–7
– metonymic 170, 172, 174, 181
– and target 159, 171–73, 176, 178, 200
sources of evidence 283–85, 291
spaces
– input 159, 199, 255–56, 258–60, 263, 268
– mental 2, 158, 245–49, 252–53, 255, 259–61, 263–67, 289–91
spatial motion 161, 213
spatial relationship 151, 158
spatial scanning 160
speakers 37–38, 40–41, 47–54, 103–5, 107–8, 129–31, 213–15, 245–48
– implied 265
specificity 96, 106, 146, 162, 227
speech acts 19, 143, 185, 273
– directive 185, 273
– indirect 184–85
speech events 262, 282, 284
speech production 122, 130, 132, 134
speech signals 98, 124, 130, 133
Sperber, D. 272, 288–89
statistical methods 4–5
statistical patterns 221, 224, 233, 235, 237, 239
statistical pre-emption 72
statistical techniques 135, 221
Steen, F. 186, 203–4, 261–62, 267
Stefanowitsch, A. 68, 186, 197, 199
stimuli 25, 30, 43, 62, 66, 74–76, 80, 91
stimulus dimensions 90, 99, 101–2
stockbrokers 89, 245–48, 259–60
storage 70, 77–78, 99, 125
– chunk 77–78
– and computation 78
strength 2, 19, 26, 48, 54, 68, 72–74, 178
– physical 202
– representational 71–73
striatum 101–3
strong embodiment 230
structural alternatives 36–37, 53–54

structures 39–40, 50–51, 70–71, 117–18, 198–200, 254–56, 276–77, 291–92
– abstract 116–18, 171
– basic 127, 292
– conceptual 100, 117, 120, 134, 171–72, 224, 236, 264
– emergent 247, 249, 254, 256, 258, 261, 267
– family resemblance 71, 93
– grammatical 20, 180, 186
– hierarchical 285, 287, 290
– knowledge 120, 130–32
– linguistic 7, 16, 63, 70, 117, 239
– of natural language concepts 93–95
– new 247, 249, 258, 266
– physical 32, 173, 200
– semantic 116–17, 121, 160
– syntactic 17, 40, 43, 48, 116, 258
students 177, 182, 210, 213, 290
studies
– experimental 208, 210, 212, 214, 277
– imaging 101, 227
– neuroimaging 41, 71
studios 255, 263–64
subject assignment 52–53
subject role 48, 50, 53–54
subject-role assignment 49
subordinate clauses 5, 119
subprojects 285–92
substrates 28, 32, 146–48, 163
suffixation 124, 152, 180
summation 128, 155–56
support 49–50, 94, 96, 98, 102, 104–5, 213–15, 286–87
– empirical 74, 163, 232
surgeons 198–99, 253
SUSTAIN model 100
Sweetser, E. 24, 198, 256, 259–60, 262, 265, 268, 276
symbolic expressions 150, 162
symbolization 150, 153
symbols 90, 225, 238, 282
– amodal 225, 237–38
– perceptual 7, 225
synonymy 18
syntactic choice 43–53
syntactic coding 40–41, 54
syntactic constructions 17, 63, 75, 183

syntactic language impairments 228
syntactic priming 51–52
syntactic relations 39–40
syntactic roles 51, 53
syntactic structures 17, 40, 43, 48, 116, 258
syntax 16–18, 31, 42, 51–53, 117–18, 129, 256–57, 259
– and blending 256–59
– clausal 259
– embodied 16–18
– emergent 258–59
synthesis 109, 163, 171
systematic relations 21, 108
systematicity 23, 197
systems models 99–100, 103

Talmy, L. 2, 4, 7, 37–38, 140, 146, 156, 162
target domains 24, 158, 172, 197–99
taxonomy 15, 64, 96, 141, 172–73
temporal categorization 95
temporal judgments 95, 210
temporal phases 154–55
temporal vantage points 144, 146
tense markings 277
tenses 3, 41, 63, 128, 135, 143, 281
Thornburg, L. 170–71, 180–82, 184, 187, 198
thresholds 71, 74, 99, 125, 227, 235
tight compression 248, 264
time 11–12, 23–25, 41, 73–76, 150–54, 212–14, 246, 261–68
– conceived 153–56, 160
– relations 266, 268
– scales 153, 158
TMS (transcranial magnetic stimulation) 30, 228, 230
token frequencies 63–64, 71, 77
tokens 67, 70, 77, 124, 173, 275
– mental 88, 103–4
Tomasello, M. 7, 19, 263, 271–72, 275, 277, 279–83, 289
topic model 234–36
topicalization 48–50, 54
trajectors 151–52, 158, 162–63
Tranel, D. 30, 226, 230
transcranial magnetic stimulation see *TMS*
transitive events 44, 48–50
transitive verbs 151
transparency 6, 279

trees 15, 87–88, 90, 95, 101, 120, 122, 130
Tremblay, A. 78, 119
trials 46, 125, 274
– agent-cued 45–46, 49
– patient-cued 45, 47, 49
typology 3, 41, 174, 177, 290
– of metonymy 167, 187

ubiquity, metonymy 179
uncertainty 11, 30, 104–6, 108, 123, 126, 287
– reduction 104, 108
understanding 21–24, 38–40, 100, 104, 196, 198, 211, 214–15
unidirectionality 79, 105, 169, 199
unitization 70–71
units 23, 70, 74, 78, 116, 125, 128, 133–34
– cognitive 277, 279
– linguistic 19, 65, 148–49, 240
– processing 73, 75
universality 117, 224, 236, 248, 272
usage 1, 18, 70–72, 116, 125, 129, 290
usage-based linguistics 2, 18–19, 65, 71
utterances 115–19, 133, 203, 265–66, 275–76, 281, 286–87, 289–90
– as arguments 276

validation 161–63
validity 151, 251
values, argumentative 274, 276, 289, 291
vantage points 143–44, 160
– temporal 144, 146
variance 67, 77, 101
verb match 51–52
verbal metaphors 196, 204, 206, 209, 211–16
– understanding 209–14
verbs 17, 19, 47–48, 72, 79, 154, 226–28, 259–61
– action 222, 228, 230, 236
– direction 227
– intransitive 151
– motion 156, 198
– prime 52
– transitive 151
vertical axis 21, 150, 154, 208
vertical dimension 208, 210

viewers 144, 146, 264–65, 267
- offstage 142, 144
viewing arrangements 143, 145–46, 149
viewpoints 37, 262, 265–68
- blended 265–66
- embodied 266
visual cues 45–47, 49–50, 52–53, 107, 127
visual field 158, 252, 282
visual perception 24, 140
visual referents 42, 44
vital relations 246, 255
vocabulary 90, 236
voice
- active 44–49, 52–54
- passive see *passive voice*
volitional agents 116, 118

Wagner, A. 104, 107, 126, 131, 133
warmth 22–23, 209
water 87, 92, 115, 179–80
we-intentionality 278, 280
weak embodiment 228, 230
weights 77, 123, 127–29, 131, 209
whole-part hierarchies 145, 162
Wilcox, S. 3, 27, 185

Wittgenstein, L. 87–89, 92
word comprehension 225, 227
word frequency 64–67, 69, 77, 80, 94, 129
word meanings 21, 91, 221–24, 226–27, 230, 232–33, 235, 237–40
word order 54, 117
- flexible 48–50, 54
word processing 80, 227–28
word types 223–24, 228, 231, 237, 239
Wordnet 121, 236
words
- concrete 222, 231–32, 236
- low frequency 65, 69, 72, 80
- and morphemes 254–56
- multimorphemic 71, 77
- single 77, 132–33, 254
working areas 158
world
- external 90
- fictional 158
- mental 141, 146, 157, 159, 287
world knowledge 127, 230

Zwaan, R. A. 25–27, 163

www.ingramcontent.com/pod-product-compliance
Lightning Source LLC
Chambersburg PA
CBHW021118300426
44113CB00006B/202